Readings in Interpretation

Theory and History of Literature
Edited by Wlad Godzich and Jochen Schulte-Sasse

Readings in Interpretation

Hölderlin, Hegel, Heidegger

Andrzej Warminski

Introduction by Rodolphe Gasché

Theory and History of Literature, Volume 26

University of Minnesota Press, Minneapolis

The University of Minnesota Press gratefully
acknowledges the financial support of the
Frederick W. Hilles Publication Fund of Yale University.

Published by the University of Minnesota Press
2037 University Avenue Southeast, Minneapolis, MN 55414.
Published simultaneously in Canada
by Fitzhenry & Whiteside Limited, Markham.
Printed in the United States of America.

Library of Congress Cataloging-in-Publication Data

Warminski, Andrzej.
    Readings in interpretation.

    (Theory and history of literature; v. 26)
    Bibliography: p.
    Includes index.
    1. Hermeneutics—History. 2. Hölderlin, Friedrich, 1770-
1843—Philosophy. 3. Hegel, Georg Wilhelm Friedrich, 1770-1831.
4. Heidegger, Martin, 1889-1976.
I. Title. II. Series.
BD241.W36   1987   121'.68   86-1310
ISBN 0-8166-1239-0
ISBN 0-8166-1240-4 (pbk.)

The following chapters, in revised form, are reproduced with permission of the original publishers: Chapter 2, "Hölderlin in France,"
Studies in Romanticism (Summer 1983): 173-97, reprinted courtesy of
the Graduate School and Trustees of Boston University; chapter 4,
"'Patmos': The Senses of Interpretation," *MLN* 91 (April
1976): 478-500; chapter 5, "Pre-positional By-play" *Glyph* 3
(Baltimore: Johns Hopkins University Press, 1978), pp. 98-117; the
final pages of chapter 6 appeared under the title "Reading Parentheses:
Hegel by Heidegger," *Genre* (Winter 1983): 389-403; chapter 7,
"Reading for Example: 'Sense-certainty' in Hegel's *Phenomenology of
Spirit*," *Diacritics* 11 (Summer 1981): 83-94; and the epilogue, "Dread-
ful Reading: Blanchot on Hegel," *Yale French Studies* 69
(1985): 267-75.

The University of Minnesota
is an equal-opportunity
educator and employer.

Contents

Acknowledgments

Earlier versions of several of the essays previously appeared in periodicals: chapter 2, "Hölderlin in France," in *Studies in Romanticism* (Summer 1983): 173-97; chapter 4, "'Patmos': The Senses of Interpretation," in *MLN* 91 (April 1976): 478-500; chapter 5, "Pre-positional By-play," in *Glyph* 3 (Baltimore: Johns Hopkins University Press, 1978), pp. 98-117; the final pages of chapter 6 as "Reading Parentheses: Hegel by Heidegger," in *Genre* (Winter 1983): 389-403; chapter 7, "Reading for Example: 'Sense-certainty' in Hegel's *Phenomenology of Spirit*," in *Diacritics* 11 (Summer 1981): 83-94; and the epilogue, "Dreadful Reading: Blanchot on Hegel," in *Yale French Studies* 69 (1985): 267-75. Permission to reprint is gratefully acknowledged.

I am indebted to those who read this book, whether in dissertation form or as an expanded book manuscript: J. Hillis Miller, Karsten Harries, Rainer Nägele, Wlad Godzich, Lindsay Waters, Samuel Weber, and Rodolphe Gasché. I am also grateful to Virginia Hans for her careful copy editing. My greatest debt is to my teachers at Yale, in Freiburg, and in Paris, in particular Paul de Man and Jacques Derrida, to whose teaching and example I owe what I have understood about reading (and writing).

Reading Chiasms
An Introduction
Rodolphe Gasché

Coming to a text (or, for that matter, a collection of texts), the reader-critic normally expects that its constellation yields to the unity of a configuration of thought. Yet, if a work deliberately situates itself between figures, themes, or motifs that could, and normally would, authoritatively confer unity, what, then, is its status? Indeed, what sort of unity does an in-between establish, in particular if the work does not occupy the precise middle of that interspace? If, on the contrary, it is at once in-between and to the side? If the figures of thought at the crisscross of which the work places itself are neither identical to one another nor in a relation of otherness, the difficulty of the work increases considerably. This is definitely true when those figures are themselves inquiries into the intricacies of the in-between. The work we are speaking of, then, sides with an irreducibly endless series of interfaces. Lacking a determining negation by the other, not one of these figures of thought can reflect itself into mere identity; rather, the work in question remains suspended betwixt and between, to the side of, by right, only a virtual middle between nonidentical interfaces. It follows that the question of the (literal and figural) unity of such work must take a different turn.

Although *Readings in Interpretation* invites its reader to think about such a turn, this work must also be regarded as a book on Hölderlin, Hegel, and Heidegger. It is, no doubt, a major contribution to the history of German idealism and romanticism, since it is engaged in the task of reassessing the differences between some of its outstanding exponents—the singular place of

Hölderlin in that history, for instance—differences which, in the wake of romanticism, have become nearly imperceptible. *Readings in Interpretation*, however, is far more than the arduous attempt to correct a significant imbalance in the history of philosophy. It is a study concerned with the concept of history itself, the relation between philosophy and literature, hermeneutical and dialectical interpretation, the inscription of the reader in the philosophical text, as well as the status of representation and exemplarity. Yet, within this array of questions, and through the specific nature of his strategies of questioning, Warminski shows that he is primarily concerned with a problematic whose objectivity is thoroughly different from that of the traditional disciplines and their objects of study. Indeed, Warminski has undertaken the difficult exploration of what constitutes that very space of the in-between (of interpretations, figures of thought, opposing motifs and themes), its relational and differential nature, as well as the crossroads and turning points that divide its fragile unity.

Were it not for the fact that the term is used at random—"à tous les biais et à toutes mesures," as Montaigne would have said—we could, in a certain sense, have called this work "deconstructive." Owing to its micrological analyses, its sometimes vertiginous and seemingly abyssal argumentation, or simply because it does not make for easy reading, the reader may have already classified Warminski's work in this manner. If not, he will hardly be able to resist that temptation when encountering a certain number of so-called key terms that are believed to characterize the perverse critical activity labeled "deconstructive." Undoubtedly, one of these terms is the *always-already*. But would the reader's irritation at the repeated use of that expression lessen if he knew what the term stands for and if he were thus in a position to consider its appropriateness within a given context?

Always-already is an expression that may have found its first systematic use in Heidegger's thinking, where it denotes both the temporal mode of the fore-understanding in which the meaning of Being is available to the *Dasein*, and the specific mode of anteriority in which Being claims man. *Always-already* names something prior to, and it thus seems to correspond to the formal determination of the *a priori*. To speak of *always-already* rather than of *a priori* becomes a necessary move, however, when, as in Heidegger, the temporal character of Being itself is at stake. The *a priori*, which in the ontological tradition serves to denote the determinations of Being, contains the idea of a temporal succession in a very pallid way at best. In Heidegger's thinking, therefore, the *always-already* stands for a temporal priority, which, as that of Being, has nothing to do with time as it is known according to its vulgar concept.

Always-already is put to a similar use in Derrida's philosophy, where it designates the temporal mode of a certain accidentality, contingency, and supplementarity shown to be "constitutive" of presence and essence. Presence and essence within the metaphysical tradition, as Husserl has demonstrated, presuppose the fundamental form of idealization that is the "always again" (*immer wieder*). Whereas this structure accords a privileged position to the pro-tentional dimension of intentionality, Derrida's use of the *always-already* focuses on an anteriority that is, rather, of the order of the retentional dimension of intentionality. But if the *always-already* in Derrida stands for a past and a passivity older than presence and essence, this does not mean that Derrida simply privileges retention. In the same manner that Heidegger's *always-already* names a temporality that is radically different from the vulgar concept of time, Derrida's *always-already* points at a radical past, at an absolute past and passivity that can never be fully reactivated and awakened to presence. Yet, if the absolute past of the *always-already* effaces itself and is from the outset in retreat, it nonetheless leaves a mark, a signature that is retraced in the very thing from which it is withdrawn, that the essence or the presence that it constitutes is this past's belated reconstitution. What is *always-already* has never, and can never, be present itself. The very possibility of essence and presence hinges on such a past, according to Derrida.

The *always-already* is thus not mere wordplay or the result of linguistic infatuation. It is an expression that implies an anteriority to essence and presence, that not only would no longer be a determination *of* Being, as is the *a priori*, but that would also take priority *over* Being: if, as Derrida contends, Heidegger's radical temporality of Being is still caught in the vulgar concept of time that it was supposed to displace, the radical past to Being could no longer be altogether of the order of Being. The specific nature of the time of the quiddity of that past hinted at by Derrida understands Being itself from the past (and not only beings, as in the case of Heidegger). Discussing supplementary substitution at one point in *Of Grammatology*, Derrida asks: "How *was it to be* (*était-elle à être*)—for such is the time of its quiddity—what it necessarily is?"[1] Throughout *Of Grammatology*, this temporal structure of *was to be* appears as that of an imperfect tense which makes it possible for that which *ought to have been* (*aura* or *aurait dû être*)—namely, presence and, in the last instance, Being itself—to come into being. Yet since the absolute past in question can never become present, since it is not the trace of an already constituted and bygone present, it is also, as that which withdraws from what it lets come to the fore, that which ultimately makes presence and Being impossible. Contrary to the *a priori*, therefore, the *always-already* is not only a condition of possibility but a condition of impossibility as well.

Having named the time of the quiddity of the *always-already* as the time of what *had to be* in order for something *to be*, it is obvious that the *always-already* is another expression for the concept of essence, or more precisely—and this explains the substitution of *always-already* for essence—for a certain temporality at the origin of essence. The time of the quiddity of the *always-already* is, indeed, the time of quiddity. Let us recall here that *quidditas* is the consecrated translation not of the Greek *ti esti* but of the Aristotelian expression *to ti en einai*. This strange formula—strange, because of its double use of the verb *to be* and the unexpected use of the imperfect tense—answers the question of what a thing's essence and essential attributes are. It states that the essence of a thing is *what it has been*. The Scholastics translated this formula *quod quid erat esse*, and one will certainly remember Hegel's famous coining of the same formula: *Wesen ist was gewesen ist*. Accordingly, what a thing is in and by itself (*kath'auto*) is determined retrospectively. It is revealed as a past, as what it was to be. Now whether one interprets this anteriority of essence in a Scholastic fashion (as what something existent already was before its actualization or realization) or in (probably) a more Greek fashion, as Pierre Aubenque does (as pertaining to the essence of things of the sublunar world only and as a reflection of the fact that here in the sublunar world essential accidents may, *ex post*, have contributed to determining what a thing or a man will, in the end, have turned out to be), in either case this anteriority is still understood in terms of an already constituted time.[2] Yet the past that Heidegger and in particular Derrida refer to with the *always-already*—the time of quiddity, the time of the essence of Being—is a temporalizing passive synthesis that allows the temporal differences of past, present, and future to appear in the first place. *Always-already* before constituted time, this absolute past or passivity, to which no intramundane concept or metaphor corresponds, accounts for the fact that the anteriority of essence, and permanence of its presence, has been dependent not so much on a particular passage of a given time sequence but on a structure of temporal referral in general. It is this very structure of temporal referral that Derrida calls absolute past or absolute passivity, and that he refers to with the expression *always-already*. In short, then, *always-already* is a term that articulates the "quiddity" of quiddity, and that, according to its nature as a past that was never a past-present and that consequently can never become fully present, is at once the condition of possibility and impossibility of essence. The temporality of the *always-already*, although it reveals that which makes essence possible, is at the same time the *a priori* of a counteressence that prevents it from ever coming into its own, from ever being absolutely itself. An irreducible part of chance and probability is, thus, shown to enter into the constitution of an essence, yet such contingency and accidentality are not graspable through the Aristotelian distinction of inessential accidents and essential accidents (*symbebekota kath'auta*), in which the latter forms a constitutive part of what *has been* the essence of a thing or human being. Deconstruction, in a Derridean sense, is the double affirmation of essence and counteressence, and the expression *always-already* is nothing other than this affirmation.

This lengthy (yet, obviously, all too brief) elaboration on the expression *always-already* should not only clarify what is meant by this notion but also give an inkling of the leading hypotheses that organize Warminski's exploration of the relational and differential space of the in-between. His formula *"always-already* and *always not yet"* is a clear echo of Derrida's double affirmation as well as of the latter's search for *a priori* infrastructures or undecidables that function as conditions of possibility that, at the same time, limit what they constitute. In what follows, it remains for us to examine the terms in which Warminski thematizes in-between structures, as well as the manner in which these structures differ from the results yielded by grammatological and, respectively, rhetorical or tropological readings. To understand the sort of linguistic "inauthenticity" Warminski aims at—a linguistic "property" that is said to be perhaps less tangible than the Derridean infrastructures and ostensibly less scandalous than de Man's interruptive tropes but that is nonetheless equally constitutive (undialectically and untranscendentally)—we cannot avoid lingering for a moment on what is called *reading* in *Readings in Interpretation.*.

Warminski's work, as we have already intimated, is an analysis of the reading implied in interpretation, wherein certain techniques of inversion built into the structure of texts produce discrepancies, and through which, as Wolfgang Iser has shown, the integrating achievement of the *Gestalten* of interpretations is constantly disrupted.[3] By transposing such an analysis to the history of philosophy, Warminski not only understands history as "textual history"—that is, as a history in which thinkers are related to one another in a bipolar fashion—but is also in a position to dispute the integrating achievement of the interpretations of one philosopher by another. In his work, Warminski argues that the act of interpretation consists in neither less nor more than the interpreter's systematic reduction—systematic, and not accidental, nor owing to the interpreter's human finitude—of one or several bipolarly organized oppositions of either concepts or images in the text to be interpreted. *Readings in Interpretation* is, thus, concerned with the stress that interpretative reading places on only one of the poles of the oppositions, or on one of two possible readings. Warminski's work exhibits all sorts of "arbitrary, unverifiable decisions" that lead to such one-sided privileging. In chapter 5, "Pre-positional By-play," it becomes evident that it is the interpreter's competence in, and justification of, differentiating between sides that is particularly under investigation. Apart from the possibility of such recognition of difference, Warminski questions the collapsing of sides insofar as the collapsing of two bipolarly opposed elements renders a text's meaning simplified and decidable. Subjecting the art of division, of distinguishing *specific* differences (i.e., the operation of *diairesis*), to a radical doubt is as decisive as questioning the art of synthesis, because it is in this art that the philosophical claim to totality is grounded. Examining the art of distinguishing differences within and with respect to generic forms, Warminski aims here at fundamental presuppositions of the claim to totality, presuppositions that are necessary to the possibility of interpretation as such.

As Warminski's examples reveal, these decisions constitutive of interpretation are motivated by the history of philosophical exegesis, by what has become sedimented as the substrate of acquired and binding knowledge. Because philosophical interpretation obeys a canon of sanctioned philosophical problems, because it yields to the tradition that decides what philosophical discourse can achieve, and what it cannot, interpretation does not *read* what it interprets. It is, according to Warminski, not concerned with the *text*. Interpretation unreads. In contrast, *reading* would presuppose a certain bracketing of the inherited criteria involved in the process of interpretative decisionmaking. Yet, just as the Husserlian *epoche* by no means represents a negation or annihilation of what is put into parentheses, so does *reading* hardly exclude the interpretative achievements of the tradition, as Warminski's impressive and overwhelming references to secondary literature on the authors he deals with demonstrates. For the same reason, *reading* does not imply nostalgia for an unadulterated and uncontaminated *Ur-text* beyond the blemish of interpretation and history. As understood by Warminski, *reading* precludes the very possibility of a text in and for itself. A text is possible only because it has no self of its own.

A more precise understanding of what happens in interpretation is thus inevitably required if we want to get a further hold on *reading*. The interpreter, by determining the difference between possible meaning in terms of philosophically sanctioned pairs of oppositions, or by collapsing different textual elements into one, flattens out the difference and suppresses what Warminski calls the two-way narrative, the history between what is different. Yet, owing to this two-way history between textual facets, all interpretative readings of a text, precisely because they are reductive, are *read* and undone by the text under interpretation. Thus, Warminski will demonstrate that what remains unthought in Heidegger's interpretation of Hegel submits Heidegger's text, in turn, to a reading by Hegel's text. To suppress this two-way history between textual poles, a history that involves all interpretation in a fundamental double bind and that ensures that what it interprets will interpret it in turn, is to suppress the text. If Warminski's theory of reading did not, in the last resort, exclude the idea of an *Ur-text*, one would, inevitably, come to suspect that *reading* is an operation that aspires to total adequation with the text. Yet this faithfulness that seems to characterize *reading* is pushed here to such a point that, paradoxically, it reveals the constitutive lack of all ultimate textual propriety. To suppress the twofold narrative between the bipolar agencies of a text by deciding, say, on either its literal or its figurative meaning is to erase the literary qualification of the text. The *literary reading* that is faithful to the text insofar as it accepts, in Warminski's own words, "the text as it appears, and presents itself to us, that is, as a written text to be read" (p. 113) "independently" of its history of reception and response—without, however, pretending to any immediate access to it—is a reading that focuses on the play of relations constituting the two-way narrative of the interface between dyadic images, concepts, or principles in a text. According to Warminski, such a literary reading is that which "always comes *before* the text of the interpretation (*Auslegung, Erläuterung*) as its condition of possibility but . . . also always goes *after* the text of the interpretation as its condition of impossibility" (p. 150). Indeed, if every movement of thought and its interpretation are vulnerable to being seen, taken, or read literarily, this is because these movements and interpretations can never hope to master or subsume the simulation and mimicry of literary reading. Literary reading, or *reading* in short, is thus that reading which, by being faithful to the play of relations that forms the in-between space of dyadic textual items, demonstrates the impossibility of reading in the sense of interpreting. And the text that is being *read* in this manner appears, then, as a narrative of the impossibility of reading, that is, as the impossibility of mastering except in always limited readings that are being reread (i.e., undone by the text's neglected and opposite possibilities of interpretation). Contrary to interpretation, which represents an operation of decisionmaking in a totalizing perspective, *reading* is the reading of the text's unreadability, that is, of its structural incapacity to lend itself to unequivocal and unproblematic totalizations. By centering on the relational intertwining that characterizes textual bipolar organization, *reading* aims at what Philippe Lacoue-Labarthe once called a certain "active neutrality of that which is in-between the poles."[4] This space of neutrality is not the space of what the New Critics called ambiguity. It lends itself neither to mediating semantic sublation nor to the pathos of undecidability. Sharply distinguishing between ambiguity and undecidability, Warminski conceives of the latter as the space of a truly and *radically* undecidable difference, that is, of an undecidability that undermines all possibility of pathos by putting the reading subject into question.

As should be evident by now, Warminski's interrogation of the integrating achievements of interpretation is not governed by a totalizing perspective. He certainly does not conceive of the double bind of interpretation in either a reflexive or a speculative manner. On the contrary, Warminski's work is deconstructive precisely insofar as it attempts to synthesize the interplay of mutually self-limiting interpretations in a nondialectical way. Given Warminski's conception of the history of interpretation and of the structure of texts as a web of essentially bipolar and dyadic elements, the structure or figure that will account for the set of relations that characterizes the space between poles will be primarily that of chiasmic reversal. It is in the figure of the chiasm that all the threads of Warminski's analyses initially seem to converge.

Although we are cautioned not to take terms of this kind for master-words or slogans, it may well be appropriate to clarify as succinctly as possible what is meant by the term *chiasm* before discussing the manner in which the chiasm may offer a nondialectical "solution" to the problem of the interplay of textual elements and to the relation between text and interpretation. Since both de Man and Derrida have systematically referred to this figure, Warminski's use of the term—at the crossroads between both thinkers—may, indeed, interweave various determinations of *chiasm* from different sources into a unique combination.

Chiasm or *chiasmus* is an anglicization of the Greek *chiasma*, which designates an arrangement of two lines crossed like the letter X (*chi*) and refers in particular to cross-shaped sticks, to a diagonally arranged bandage, or to a cruciform incision. As a grammatical and rhetorical device, the figure of chiasm corresponds, basically, to inverted parallelism. In chiasm, the order of words in one of two balancing clauses or phrases is inverted in the other so as to produce its well-known crisscross effect. It is not without interest to note that this figure has received rather negative valorization from the early scholiasts on to the more recent standard handbooks of rhetoric. It is usually considered deliberately contrived and artificial, no more than a practical device. Such negative judgment still resonates in the *Dictionnaire de poétique et de rhétorique*, where Henri Morier writes: "The chiasm would only be a sort of silly affectation were it not motivated by a superior reason, the desire for variation, the need for euphony and expressive harmony."[5] But chiasm, which occurs in great abundance in ancient writing, especially in Near Eastern literature, but in Greek and Latin literature as well, is a decisive ordering principle employed on all levels of complexity, that is, with respect not only to sounds but to thoughts as well. As John W. Welch notes, it "may give structure to the thought pattern and development of entire literary units, as well as to shorter sections whose composition is more dependent on immediate tones and rhythms."[6] Certainly, where chiasm is predominantly grammatical and rhetorical, its function may be merely ornamental and may amount to an unpretentious play on crossover effects of words and sounds. But in Hebrew and other Oriental literatures, and, as Welch has shown, in the Greek and Latin literary arena as well, chiastic inversion also rises to much more elaborate levels when it assumes the function of a constructive principle, or structural principle of form. When used as an ordering device of thoughts, the chiasmic reversal is also called *hysteron proteron* (i.e., the latter first). The grammarians and rhetoricians think in particular of Homer's fondness for having his characters answer plural questions in a reverse order. Welch remarks that "*hysteron proteron* describes passages which are constructed so that their first thought refers to some latter thought of a preceding passage, and their latter thought, to some preceding passage's former thought."[7] Although the *hysteron proteron* is formally equivalent to the chiasm of formal rhetoric, it is functionally different, insofar as it gives order to ideas, and not merely to words or sounds. As distinct from chiasm—a distinction largely responsible for the relegation of chiasm to a secondary and merely ornamental role—the *hysteron proteron* is said to serve as principle for creating continuity without the use of transitory particles between multitermed and contrasting passages.[8] The careful ligaturing undertaken by the *hysteron proteron* in order to achieve unbroken and continuous succession in a narrative, as Samuel E. Bassett has shown, is basically a psychological device, a function of the relation of the (Homeric) poet to his listener, "which assists the narrator to hold the attention of his listener with a minimum of effort on the part of the latter."[9] But grammatical, rhetorical, or psychological explanations cannot exhaust the role of chiasm. Indeed, when employed in order to draw together and connect juxtaposed and emphasized terms in opposition, this ordering form exceeds rhetoric and psychology, or *lexis*, especially where, as in Heraclitus, it becomes dependent on content. Chiasm, then, is no longer a merely ornamental or psychological device but, rather, reveals itself as an originary form of thought, of *dianoia*. Originarily, as a form, as *the* form of thought, chiasm is what allows oppositions to be bound into unity in the first place. It is a form that makes it possible to determine differences with respect to an underlying totality. The chiasm, so to speak, cross-bandages the crosswise incision by which it divided a whole into its proper differences. Emmanuel Levinas, therefore, may rightly speak of "a pleasure of contact at the heart of the chiasm."[10]

It is in this sense that the chiasm is one of the earliest forms of thought: it allows the drawing apart and bringing together of opposite functions or terms and entwines them within an identity of movements. In Heraclitus, in particular, the chiasm acquires this role of establishing the unity of opposites. Thanks to the form of chiasm, "that which is in opposition is in concert, and from things that differ comes the most beautiful harmony."[11] Nothing opposite is left standing in an isolated manner; rather, through the chiasm, opposites are linked into pairs of parallel and inverted oppositions on the ground of an underlying unity, a *tauto*, which manifests itself through what is separated. Whether this unity is that of the totality of the universe or that of the singular does not concern us here. On the contrary, what concerns us is the idea that chiasmic reversals secure, by the very movement of the inversion of the link that exists between opposite poles (i.e., through a back-stretched connection), the agreement of a thing at variance with itself. Heraclitus's fragment 51 (according to Herman Diels), to which we are referring here, and which Plato paraphrased in the *Symposium* as "the one in conflict with itself is held together" (*En diapheron eauto*), implies that by linking everything to its opposite (i.e., the terms of a relation, as well as the relation itself when turned back upon itself), not only does one reveal a fundamental and pristine unity underlying the terms, which have in this manner acquired the status of differences, but one also yields to the demands of reason as *logos*.[12] By connecting isolated terms and relations into one whole, the chiasm is a true form of thinking. Its movements have been analyzed by Plato and Aristotle in terms of analogy, the importance of which cannot be overestimated as a form of thought in philosophy. In short, then, the chiasm is a form through which differences are installed, preserved, and overcome in one grounding unity of totality. It is in this sense that the chiasm can be viewed as the primitive matrix of dialectics in its Hegelian form. No one recognized this filiation better than Hegel himself, who claimed to have incorporated all of Heraclitus's propositions into his *Science of Logic*.

One must keep in mind the chiasm's initial function as a form or figure of unity of thought if one wishes to evaluate the significance of the recent recourses to that figure by Derrida and de Man. De Man's frequent and quite systematic use of *chiasm*, particularly in his later work, is familiar. Because he defines *chiasm*, in *Allegories of Reading*, as a rhetorical structure based on substitutive reversals, aligning it with metaphor, metonymy, metalepsis, hypallage, and so forth, de Man may seem to have borrowed the term from the discipline of rhetoric.[13] Yet it becomes clear, throughout the book, that chiasm does not function as a mere figure of elocution, but indeed, as a structure of texts as texts. In addition, and even more important, the chiasm is not a figure of closure for de Man. To determine it in this negative manner is already sufficient indication of the philosophical provenance of de Man's notion of chiasm, and of the nature of his debate.

For de Man, the inversion brought about by the cross-shaped figure is not, interestingly enough, simply chiasmic; it is fundamentally asymmetric. Indeed, contrary to the philosophical notion of the chiasm in which unity is achieved through an attunement turned back upon itself (i.e., through an all-inclusive totalization of all oppositions), de Man's notion of chiasm understands the reversal of polarities as a failing attempt to invert a "first" textual displacement. Instead of harmoniously linking parallel clauses or terms to their inverted order and thus creating unity, the chiasm in de Man's work fails to bring about unity because the inversion does not succeed in neutralizing the rhetorical character of the text. Only such neutralization, according to de Man, could restore the literal, the proper, or truth (i.e., that which could truly confer unity). All the chiasm achieves, however, is a substitution of a substitution, by which it prolongs the rhetorical delusions of the text as such. The figure of the chiasm, instead of allowing a final concluding exchange, a final reflection into self of the text, consequently becomes a figure, or rather a nonfigure, for the rhetorical dimension of the text, a dimension that makes it an infinitely self-deferring and self-exceeding totality. It thus appears that the structure of the chiasm as thematized by de Man, although originating in the tradition of rhetoric, is also a debate with the chiasm as a form of thought. In short, the chiasm, as a rhetorical structure, suspends the totalizing functions of the literal and the figural in a text and, as a figure, endlessly defers (temporalizes, historicizes, allegorizes) the closure of a text—by either its content or its form—through the infinite substitutability implied by its asymmetry. Understood in this manner, the figure of chiasm is one among several figures analyzed by de Man in a similar perspective.

In *Positions*, Derrida states that all writing is caught in and practices chiasmic reversals. "The form of the chiasm, of the X, interests me a great deal, not as a symbol of the unknown, but because there is in it. . .a kind of fork. . .that is, moreover, unequal, one of the points extending its range further than the other," he writes.[14] But this asymmetry becomes visible, according to Derrida, only if one no longer understands the chiasm's crossed-connection-making, and the double participation that it implies, as the mixing of previously separate elements into the punctual identity and simplicity of a *coencidentia oppositorum*, but rather as a *referral back* (*renvoi*) "to a *same* that is not the identical, to the common element or medium of any possible dissociation."[15] As Derrida points out in *Archaeology of the Frivolous*, instead of simply folding opposites into one unity, "the chiasm folds itself with a supplementary flexion."[16] This supplementary fold makes the chiasm a structure that refers all mediation of opposites—whether reflexive or speculative, whether by analogy or dialectically—to "the medium in which opposites are opposed, the movement and the play that links them among themselves, reverses them or makes one side cross over into the other."[17] It is the very reference to this reserve that makes the chiasm an unequal fork. Hence, it is neither simply constitutive nor simply disruptive of totality; rather it is the figure by which a totality constitutes itself in such a manner that the reference to the reserve or the medium of dissociation inseparably inscribed into the figure clearly marks the scope and limits of totality. No unity engendered chiasmically includes within itself the play of difference to which it must refer in order to constitute itself.

Derrida has further developed this chiasmic structure in two essays on Maurice Blanchot: "The Law of the Genre" and "Living On: *Border Lines*." This development is intimately linked to a close reading of Blanchot's *La Folie du jour*. In these two essays Derrida ties the chiasmic reversal to a movement of invagination, thus demonstrating his continued concern with the unthought of "totality." Chiasmic invagination is a movement that constitutes and deconstitutes the border, the limit of a closure. As Derrida has pointed out in "The *Retrait* of Metaphor," a border and a limit are understood in metaphysics as a circular limit bordering a homogeneous field. Regarding the representation of metaphysics as *one* metaphysics, he writes that the "representation of a linear and circular closure surrounding a homogeneous space is, precisely. . .an auto-representation of philosophy in its onto-encyclopedic logic."[18] Because of the twisted figure of the chiasmic invagination, the apparently outer edge of an enclosure "makes no sign beyond itself, toward what is utterly *other*, without becoming double or dual, without making itself be 'represented,' refolded, superposed, *re-marked* within the enclosure, at least in what the structure produces as an effect of interiority."[19] In short, it is the structure according to which a border, which is always seemingly the limit of an interiority set off against an exteriority, cannot but re-mark and reapply that reference to the outer within its interiority, between its center and its circumference.

What is an invagination? It is, writes Derrida, "The inward refolding of *la gaine* [sheath, girdle], the inverted reapplication of the outer edge to the inside of a form where the outside opens a pocket."[20] Where such invagination occurs, it is impossible to settle upon the limits of the border. As a result, the edge *of* a form turns out to be a fold *within* the form. Constantly in excess of the form, the part (the border) is then necessarily greater than the form itself. As "Living On" and "The Law of the Genre" have attempted to argue, using the example of Blanchot's *La Folie du jour*, such an invagination of the borders of a form (corpus or any other enclosed totality) is in principle double and chiasmically inverted. In Blanchot's text, this structure of double crisscross invagination is confirmed by the fact that the upper edge of the outer face (the supposed beginning of *La Folie du jour*), which is folded back inside to form a pocket and an inner edge, extends beyond the invagination of the lower edge (the supposed end of *La Folie du jour*), which is equally folded back inside to form a pocket and an outer edge while extending itself to the upper edge. What consequently becomes clear is the following: since a border encloses an interiority only if this border refers to its outer other, and since this reference to the other cannot but be inscribed within the interiority, not only do borders acquire an extremely twisted structure, but the interiority, the very space where the relationship of the form to itself takes place, appears to be at the same time the gathering space of the double invagination that crosses out the identity of the form.[21]

It is important to note that in *"Living On,"* Derrida's analysis of a text's relation to its limits does not broach this problem in general terms. Not only does "Living On" deal with this question solely insofar as the text *as a narrative* is concerned, but its scope is even more restricted to the extent that it is narrowed down to a narrative narrating a demand for a narrative. Double invagination, as a structure of the borders of a text, thus pertains, at first, only to a text determined in such a manner; it does not represent a truth of all texts. It would, therefore, be foolish to look for it in all texts, totalities, envelopes, or enclosures. The borders of texts are not always *de facto* double invaginated. Yet, it is a possibility that *can* come about in any kind of ensemble. Although the structure of double invagination has been developed only with respect to a very determined sort of text, it could potentially affect all texts since texts are made up of traces. Traces are not only referential, but also characterized by iterability. "The chiasma of this *double invagination* is always possible, because of what I have elsewhere called the iterability of the trace," writes Derrida.[22] Indeed, this possibility of iteration is that of duplication, and where one has duplication one also has the possibility of crisscross invagination. Yet, if double chiasmic invagination is the result of the iterability of the trace, it is always possible, and hence a *necessary possibility* that has to be accounted for when determining the nature and the status of an ensemble. If this possibility, however, delimits ensembles, if it makes it structurally impossible to determine their edges, then it points to an essential *unfinishedness* of all ensembles. This unfinishedness "cannot be reduced to an incompleteness or an inadequacy" since the latter are only the negative of completion and adequacy; unfinishedness constitues ensembles into texts.[23] By illimiting ensembles, it *generalizes* the text.

At this point where double invagination appears as an accident that by right *can* befall all texts as ensembles, which, in consequence, must be conceived as *essentially* unfinished, it becomes necessary to distinguish, however briefly, Derrida's discoveries about the chiasm from those of Merleau-Ponty. In *The Visible and the Invisible*, in a famous chapter entitled "The Intertwining—The Chiasm," Merleau-Ponty refers to the figure of the chiasm in order to conceptualize it in terms of "a new type of intelligibility," leading in principle to "a complete reconstruction of philosophy," to the locus where reflection (coincidence) and world, subject and other are not yet distinguishable, instead coexisting all at once, pell-mell.[24] This "general thing" beyond the body and the world, the reflexivity of the subject and the object, the visible and invisible (the ideas), is, for Merleau-Ponty, a "sort of incarnate principle" that he calls "flesh," or the "generality of the Sensible in itself."[25] In other words, it is an opening toward the world, whose generality and transcendentality is a function of what is intertwined, and which is, thus, marked by an essential *finitude*. This general opening—"that is not the shadow of the actual but is its principle, that is not the proper contribution of a 'thought' but is its condition"—is characterized "by a sort of folding back, invagination, or padding."[26] In it the dehiscence of consciousness and object occurs, yet in such a manner that both are mediated through a reversal or chiasm (a double chiasm, in fact), with the result that, in reality, no bifurcation or positing of isolated and opposite entities takes place. It is imperative to realize that, for Merleau-Ponty, this prereflexive and preobjective mediating reversal does not imply a union of contradictories: "it is a reversibility always imminent and never realized in fact."[27] No coincidence between its poles ever takes place. Its chiasmic folding upon itself does not produce a totality. The reason for this impossibility of closure—an impossibility that is not a failure—lies for Merleau-Ponty, with the finitude of the human being, with the limitations specific to his or her experience. And yet, of this reversibility characteristic of prereflexive experience, he states that it is "the ultimate truth," the element, or "the concrete emblem of a general manner of being."[28]

For Merleau-Ponty, then, the chiasmic reversal that constitutes all prereflexive experience warrants an essential finitude of the truth of consciousness's opening toward the world. Although it secures the generality of that opening, it prevents it from being absolute. As such a figure of finitude, Merleau-Ponty's concept of chiasm remains, however, linked to the problematic of consciousness, to man's experience of him- or herself and the world.[29] Derrida's notion of the chiasm as the possibility of an essential *unfinishedness* of totalities must be clearly set apart from those reasons of *finitude* for which Merleau-Ponty holds that the chiasm prevents totalities from ever coinciding with themselves. The unfinishedness in question does not follow from man's limitations as a human and experiencing being. It is, on the contrary, a *structural* possibility affecting in principle all totalities precisely because their borders refer to an outer, to an other, and hence because iterability characterizes them as traces. It is, therefore, not by chance that Derrida does not speak of the finitude of texts, but rather of their generalizing unfinishedness.

The form of the chiasm, according to Derrida, is the outline of a movement that, by taking note of a totality's irreducible reference to other in the very process of its self-constitution, becomes a counterlaw to the same constitution. Since the reference to other, or the totality's outgate, remains re-marked and reapplied within the totality (i.e., in a noninclusive mode), the structure of the chiasm "is itself related so remotely to a dialectical structure that it even inscribes dialectics."[30] Indeed, the chiasm in Derrida is to be understood as the form of that exceedingly strange space within which the philosophical form of chiasm makes its incision, in order to cross-bandage, by analogy and dialectics, the same wound. In other words, the doubly invaginated chiasm is what both makes possible and deconstitutes dialectics. It is an *a priori* counterlaw to the unifying role of the chiasm, a counterchiasm, so to speak, within which the totalizing function of dialectics is rooted. This counterchiasm does not annihilate dialectics; it does not destroy it but "merely" shows it to its "proper" place.

To conclude this exposition of the form of chiasm in Derrida's philosophy, let us emphasize that the chiasm is only *one* of the possible and manifold consequences of the infrastructure of the trace (i.e., iterability or repeatability and structural referral to otherness). In itself, the chiasmic form has no special privilege in Derrida.[31] Nor is it a necessary empirical characteristic of texts, corpuses, ensembles, or wholes of whatever sort. It is, on the contrary, a necessary possibility of such ensembles. The structure of chiasmic and invaginated reversal corresponds, therefore, to an axiom of nonclosure, to a principle establishing a fundamental law of incompletion with regard to all possible totalities.

Having in this manner distinguished de Man's, Merleau-Ponty's, and Derrida's notions of the chiasm with regard to its philosophical determination as a unifying form of thought, let us now consider its function in Warminski's work, where it seems, as we have suggested, to assume a dominant role.[32] The reader of *Readings in Interpretation* will be struck by the virtuosity with which Warminski handles this figure. In view of the extreme audacity with which positions become inverted in sometimes apparently vertiginous ways, he may suspect Warminski not only of being a dialectician of formidable refinement but even of enacting the originary agonistic nature of dialectics. Indeed, considering the specific style of Warminski's argumentation, one might be tempted to compare his procedure to that of the inventor of dialectics—Zeno of Elea—who, according to his prevailing representation in the history of philosophy, used dialectical reasoning to demonstrate that an adverse thesis contains the radical opposite of what it affirms. Used in this way, dialectics becomes a sometimes invincible tool of refutation and destruction, which seems to be at the service of the most extreme nihilism. But it must be remarked that Zeno's polemical use of dialectics is not simply destructive. It is destructive only of adverse theses that oppose plurality and movement to the Parmenidian One. In other words, it is a negativity that presupposes and promotes the idea of unity and Oneness. Yet, can Warminski's theoretical enterprise be thought of in these terms at all? Is the dialectics in which he seems to excel merely negative or secretly positive? Is his masterly manipulation of chiasmic reversals simply agonistic and polemical, or at the service of a hidden harmony? Is the systematic demonstration of the illusionary character of all interpretation he sets forth a function in fact of a certain enigmatic unity of the texts?

Before trying to answer these questions, let us recall that there is reason to believe that dialectics, as a philosophical method of argumentation, is rooted in the sacred games and fierce riddle contests of ancient Greece. All these ritual riddles are said to have been concerned with describing the unfathomable One, and philosophical thought may indeed have surged from such cultic competitions. Defined by Aristotle as an impossible combination of words, as a juxtaposition of irreconcilable terms, as a joining of adverse notions, the riddle appears to be the basic structure of Heraclitus's chiasmic propositions.[33] The solution of these notoriously obscure statements is, according to the same structure, the invisible attunement by which what is separated becomes united. The One that is divided in itself is the answer to the Heraclitean enigmas.

Rather than manipulating dialectical thought for either negative or positive purposes, Warminski wrestles with the *enigmatic character of dialectics*, or, more precisely, with the enigma of its enigma. He is, indeed, concerned with it in a manner profoundly critical of the negative by which dialectics brings about the riddle's positive solution. As we will see, Warminski aims at a sort of negativity that is not dialectically recuperable and that cuts to the very heart of the enigma of the One. *Readings in Interpretation* is about this negativity that does not yield to the traditional opposition of part and whole but goes to the kernel of the chiasmic relations by which parts are bound into one embracing whole.

If the figure of the chiasm seems to take on a predominant role in Warminski's thinking, this is also because "as a simulacrum of the transcendental" it is a direct function of his "rhetorization" of textual schemes, an operation that he borrows from de Man's later work and that serves to "read only what was always already 'there'—but not in a Hegelian (dialectical) sense or a Heideggerian (hermeneutic) sense" (p. 208). The *a priori* made readable by "rhetorization" is, for Warminski, primarily the structure of chiasmic reversal, an *a priori* structure distinct from similar structures in Heidegger and Hegel, in that it is intended to tackle the problem of unity and totality, particularly insofar as they are both the result of dialectical sublation. Thus, the chiasm's rhetorical provenance does not prevent it from interrogating the philosophical problems of the One and of primary division. Warminski's "rhetorization" of the texts represents an attempt at "an other possible (and necessary) rereading of the all-important *hen diapheron eautō*" (p. 55), of the One differentiated in itself. If this differentiation and unification is chiasmic, as we have seen, Warminski's "rhetorization" will consist in bringing another chiasm to bear, in which the differentiation would not be that of an identical One, and in which what is different is not in a relation of determinate negation.

Although this chiasm that will be located within its philosophical counterpart corresponds to de Man's motion of chiasm, as a movement of endlessly repeated failure to neutralize textual displacements, the questioning of the relation of the chiasm's attuned elements in terms of nondeterminate negation pursues Derridean motifs.

Warminski understands dialectics as an operation taking place according to chiasmic reversals. It is important to remark that the essential moments of dialectical conversion are conceived as both symmetrical and asymmetrical. What makes the dialectical chiasm at once symmetrical and asymmetrical is that one of its poles is in a position of determinate negation with respect to the other. Contrary to what Hegel terms abstract negation (i.e., a negation that altogether negates the singularity of a thing), determinate negation is the negation of a determined thing. Since the determination of a thing consists in defining it as the other of a selfsame, determinate negation serves to enrich one of the poles of a dialectical contradiction. Thanks to this fundamental asymmetry, the whole in which the poles are situated is not irrevocably divided against itself, but open to processwise movement and thus ultimately capable of sublation. Dialectical contradiction, therefore, is a tempered and regulated contradiction in which the exchange or passage into the other leads to the production of unity on a higher level. The nondialectical properties of the chiasm that

Warminski attempts to thematize would, on the contrary, be to the side of, or asymmetrical to, the already dialectical asymmetry. To come to grips with this other figure of the chiasm, *Readings in Interpretation* centers on the analysis of what de Man has pointed out as the void or lack in which the rotating motion of the chiasm is grounded.[34] Warminski is interested not only in the turning points of texts but in what makes them truly vertiginous, or, in other words, with a certain opacity in dual relations, in the pivot of the reversal (i.e., in a negativity that renders the chiasm asymmetrical and that differs from recuperable and sublatable determinate negation without simply being of the order of abstract negation). The negativity pursued in Warminski's work—a negativity of un-settling, because unsublatable, asymmetry—is made visible either in mutually exclusive (abstract in Hegel's terms) and one-sided oppositions or else in op-positions in which the terms are contaminated to the point of *indifference.* Warminski shows these oppositions to be situated laterally to the oppositions within which dialectical and hermeneutical interpretation take place. The two sides of such slanting oppositions cannot be reconciled or mediated because they are either not symmetric at all or symmetric to such a degree that they become indistinguishable; therefore, the two sides of such oppositions cannot enter into a relation of negative determination. They cannot be in a relation of otherness to one another, and hence they remain radically undecidable. Like a cleft at the heart, and to the side, of the chiasm, they prohibit all conclusive ex-change. These bipolar agencies become recuperable only after the philosophical art of division, differentiation, and difference establishes a contact, and thus a unity, between them. In themselves, however, they remain in a transversal posi-tion to such chiasmic or dialectical appropriation, irrevocably divided against themselves, or radically indistinguishable.

Contrary to appearances, Warminski's work is thus less concerned with the chiasm *per se* and its effects than with the chasm in the chiasm. Unlike de Man, for whom the figure of the chiasm describes the endless deferral of the closure of the text, and Derrida, for whom the chiasm is a structure of referral that always divides a totality by what it believes to leave at its borders, Warminski seems to consider the chiasm as the fatal figure or structure of interpretative discourse. In this figure, each interpretative discourse, as a discourse of mastery, becomes reversed by its complementary other. For Warminski, it is the figure of the logic of the unreading of each particular interpretation of a text, a logic that ensures it will be itself undone by the text it decides upon. It is also the movement by which one interpreter's thought is turned upside down by his counterpart. The chiasm, then, not only is the form of thought (of inter-pretation and philosophy) that makes totalizations possible, but is also the form that makes these totalizations mutually undo each other—endlessly, or *always again.* As a function of unreading, and of the millenary constraints of interpretation by the frameworks of the tradition, the chiasm is also an operator of idealization, and of the substitution of one ideal construct for another. The gap that, for *reading*, becomes tangible at the heart of the chiasm is both what ultimately makes chiasmic mastery of thought possible as well as what makes it forever a mock mastery. At the core of the chiasm one sees either an absence of contact between infinitely distant terms or terms contaminated by each other to such an extent that all attempt to distinguish between them corresponds to an arbitrary decision or an act of violence. This excessive gap or excessive opacity allows the chiasmic reversals of interpretation to take place, insofar as they provide the space for interpretative (mis)reading. To *read* that gap at the heart of the chiasm is to suspend the appropriating and totalizing act of interpretation. To bring that radical undecidability into view is also to hold the chiasm in suspension, and with it the possibility of dialectical or analogical unification. The other negativity represented by the chasm therefore appears to suspend the formulation of the enigma, not to speak of its answer. As the pivot around which the differentiation and subsequent chiasmic crossings of bipolar terms occur, this other negativity—other than dialectically determined negation—subverts the presupposed, as well as the final, attunement.

Because of this void's opacity, because of this ultimately radical undecidability, all interpretations are, in the last resort, delusive or illusionary. Interpretations are fundamentally accidental and inessential, although not in the terms of what would normally be considered the essence or truth of the text. Interpretations have the status of examples. They are in essence of the order of the particular and are caught in the logic of *Vorstellung*. *Reading*, for Warminski, is therefore necessarily *exemplary reading*. Examples are traditionally understood as representations of particular cases, which render a universal proposition or a universal concept intuitable. Examples are also conceived as particular cases illustrating a practical rule and are supposed to induce imitation. *Exemplary readings*, however, are not exemplary or typical of either a universal or a generic whole or rule. It is thus exemplarity that is at stake in these readings, for if exemplarity is the enigma that attunes the examples, an *exemplary reading* is nothing less than a literal unraveling of that enigma.

Prefatory Postscript
Interpretation and Reading

Man hat, unter Menschen, bei jedem Dinge, vor allem darauf zu
sehen, dass es *etwas* ist, d.h., dass es in dem Mittel (moyen) seiner
Erscheinung erkennbar ist, dass die Art, wie es bedingt ist, bestimmt
und gelehret werden kann.

> —Hölderlin, "Anmerkungen zum Ödipus"

Reading the Center of the Book: "Patmos"

This is a book of readings. As such, it necessarily offers particular resistance to
the exigencies of an introduction or a preface, no matter how perfunctory (or
elaborate) we would pretend to make it, and the questions of subject—what is
it about?—and method—how does it do what it does? how does it treat its subject matter—proper to it. For the book's most direct answer to these questions
would have to be: both the subject and the method are "reading," and yet
"reading" can be neither subject nor method. But such redundancy—reading
reading—and such a double bind—both . . . and/neither . . . nor—are
hardly answers. If what the book does is to "read reading" and if one of its
main points is that reading is neither a subject nor a method, perhaps the questions of the preface need to be re-posed, rewritten, differently: for example, as
the beginnings and ends of a path. A good way to introduce this path (of
reading) and its beginnings and ends is, as always, a detour. In a prefatory note
to his *L'Espace littéraire* Maurice Blanchot writes: "A book, even a fragmentary one, has a center which attracts it: a center which is not fixed but is displaced by the pressure of the book and the circumstances of its composition.
Yet it is also a fixed center which, if it is genuine, displaces itself, while remaining the same and becoming always more central, more hidden, more uncertain
and more imperious. He who writes the book writes it out of desire and ignorance of this center. The feeling of having touched it can very well be only
the illusion of having reached it. In the case of a book of elucidations, there is a

kind of methodological good faith in saying toward what point it seems to be directed: here, toward the pages entitled 'The Gaze of Orpheus' (*Un livre, même fragmentaire, a un centre qui l'attire: centre non pas fixe, mais qui se déplace par la pression du livre et les circonstances de sa composition. Centre fixe aussi, qui se déplace, s'il est véritable, en restant le même et en devenant toujours plus central, plus dérobé, plus incertain et plus impérieux. Celui qui écrit le livre l'écrit par désir, par ignorance de ce centre. Le sentiment de l'avoir touché peut bien n'être que l'illusion de l'avoir atteint; quand il s'agit d'un livre d'éclaircissements, il y a une sorte de loyauté méthodique à dire vers quel point il semble que le livre se dirige: ici, vers les pages intitulées* Le regard d'Orphée).''[1]

Here the center that "methodoligical good faith" would have us indicate is, on the one hand, relatively easy to point out: it is chapter 4, on Hölderlin's "Patmos," entitled " 'Patmos': The Senses of Interpretation," the physical center of the book. The first chapter written, it serves as a point of departure for the chapters on Hegel (and Heidegger as reader of Hegel) that lead away from it as well as the endpoint for the chapters on Hölderlin (and on the Hegelian and Heideggerian readings of Hölderlin) that lead back to it: the book, one could say, begins and ends in the middle. The "Patmos" chapter introduces the themes pursued in the chapters that follow: its own center—an interpretation of Hölderlin's version of the parable of the sower (inspired by Jean Starobinski's interpretation of this New Testament parable as the "parable of parable" itself)—begins to pose the questions about the peculiar self-reflexivity of a text that includes within itself its own "theory" of interpretation and the consequently necessary self-reflection upon his own procedures of the interpreter who would interpret such a (self-interpreting) text. In short, the chapter introduces the questions of textual self-reflexivity and its opacities that remain central (in various textual guises: "parable," "example," "flyleaf," "caesura," "death," "undecidability," etc.) throughout the book. But if the "Patmos" chapter can be taken as the book's point of departure quite literally—chronologically, thematically, and so on—it is the book's end point, on the other hand, only figuratively speaking: that is, it is an end point, the book's *point d'arrivée*, not as it stands but only as what it stands for—not the chapter that is there, but the chapter that is *not* there and should be. It is easy to say what is there, what is not there, and what should be there. In shorthand: the chapter as it stands is still an interpretation and not yet a reading. Using the "Patmos" chapter as a cipher—an entry in a table of contents, a name for the book's center—we can begin to ask the question of the difference between interpretation and reading.

It turns out that the poem's own "theory" of interpretation, the place where the poem would found the difference between literal and figurative senses and tell us how to distinguish them—that is, Hölderlin's rewritten version of the parable of the sower—is precisely the place where it cannot distinguish literal and figurative senses (and therefore cannot interpret itself). But because the chapter still understands this collapse in terms of *sense*, meaning, and its arbitrary imposition, it remains an interpretation that would uncover (and recover) sense, meaning—even if it means only uncovering (and recovering) the impossibility of sense. One of the consequences of this (ultimately dialectical) recovering of sense is the chapter's still understanding the poem's strange (impossible) self-reflexivity in Hegelian terms—that is, in terms of immediacy and mediation, consciousness and self-consciousness—and its reinscription of the breakdown of sense in a very Hegelian story of Hölderlin's coming to (albeit negative) self-consciousness. The chapter, then, is only a place-holder for another, new, rewritten chapter on "Patmos" that, ideally, should be there in its place, one that would be less ignorant of its own center, that could better mark the difference between a Hegelian and a Hölderlinian account of sense and its lack. But, of course, in another sense, the new, not-yet-written chapter is already there: although the chapter may still be an interpretation, it is also (always already and always not yet) a reading. It is a reading not only because it already begins to articulate the peculiar self-reflexivity of the poem "Patmos" in explicitly linguistic terms (e.g., "catachresis")—in contradistinction to Hegelian phenomenological terms—but also because it is in a sense rewritten by the chapters on Hegel that follow it and the chapters on Hölderlin that (in the book) precede it. The chapters on Hegel seek out those places or moments in his text that function like the "parable of parable" in Hölderlin's "Patmos" and come up with "example," *Beispiel*: the example of example, *Beispiel* of *Beispiel*. The long chapter 6, "Parentheses: Hegel by Heidegger," thematizes the difference between interpretation and reading on the example of Heidegger's interpretation of Hegel (and, as it turns out, Hegel's of Heidegger), which is parasitized by Heidegger's *reading* of Hegel (and Hegel's of Heidegger). The chapters on Hölderlin (in particular chapter 1, "Endpapers: Hölderlin's Textual History") re-pose the question of his texts' self-reflexivity and retrace his itinerary in terms of a different—personal, poetic, world-historical—*textual* history that leads back to "Patmos" by way of a now necessary detour through a rereading of his Hegelian (e.g., Szondi) and Heideggerian (e.g., Heidegger himself) interpreters (in chapter 2, "Hölderlin in France," and chapter 3, "Heidegger Reading Hölderlin" respectively). In short, the words of the central "Patmos" chapter (like the words of the poem "Patmos") may remain the same (as those of 1975), but—to risk playing "Pierre Menard, Author of Don Quixote"—their function (in 1986) is different.

From this difference—between the essay's sameness of constitution and its difference of function in (and relation to) its context—a double picture of the book's constitution (and function) emerges: on the one hand, the "Patmos" chapter, as the book's center—its origin and its end, *arkhe* and *telos* (as befits an apocalyptic poem)—would be the book's *subject*—in the fullest sense, *subiectum*—and the chapters that follow a path away from and back to it, a totalizing path from same to same, subject to subject, would be the book's disclosure of a *method*. In this version, it does not make any difference if we call the first "Patmos" chapter, the chapter that is there—as point of departure or origin—an "interpretation," and the "second" "Patmos" chapter, the chapter that is *not* (yet) there—as end point or end—a "reading," for as long as we understand the difference between them in terms of a sense or a meaning that is both there (implicitly, say) and not there (explicitly, say), we still understand it as an interpretation. In short, as long as the negative between the "Patmos" chapter and itself, between the chapter *there* and the chapter *not there*, is understood as a negative recoverable, mediatable, sublatable, by a logic or a rhetoric—whether (Hegelian) "dialectical" or (Heideggerian) "hermeneutic"—of *sense*, the path that leads from "Patmos" to "Patmos" is (a method of) interpretation, and its beginning and end is (a subject of) interpretation. The only difference such a method can make to its subject is quantitative: more or less meaning, more or less interpretation. But this is only half the picture. Corresponding to the path of method that leads from the subject to itself is, on the other hand, a detour: not from same to same but from same to other, from "Patmos" as interpreted to "Patmos" as read. In order to articulate the difference this detour makes—between interpretation and reading, ultimately—it is necessary to formulate the difference—between, for example, the "Patmos" chapter *there* and the "Patmos" chapter *not there*—in terms of a different, other negative. All the chapters in the book attempt to formulate this other difference and its other negative. It is difficult to do so apart from the specific reading of a specific text, but here—in the context of our attempt to read the place of the "Patmos" chapter in the Contents—a way has already suggested itself in the difference between the central chapter's constitution and its function. That is, on the one hand, the "Patmos" chapter constitutes itself as the center of the book (no matter how much it may displace itself, as long as the negative of that self-displacement remains recoverable for a sense-making process). But, on the other hand, after the detour of the book, the "Patmos" chapter only stands in for the center, it is only a place-holder for the center: its constitution, its "meaning," may be the same, but, after its rewriting in the chapters that follow and precede, its function is different.

As center, subject, *interpretation*, the words—of the "Patmos" chapter, for example—are carriers of sense (or its lack); as self-decentering, subjectless, *reading*, the words are place-holders, markers, of the essay *not there* in a radically other sense. In other words, this difference is not a symmetrical opposition of presence and absence—whatever the mechanism of the negative that would restore symmetry—but rather an asymmetrical difference between center or subject and place-holder for center or subject, between the *meaning* and the *order* of words, between, in short, semantics and syntax. As a syntactical marker, then, the "Patmos" chapter would be a truly self-displacing center: if it is *there* as interpretation and *not there* as reading, it is *not* "not there" as the (recoverable) lack, absence, or negation of meaning but rather as the place-holder or marker of something different from, other than, and devoid of meaning, which is nevertheless the condition of possibility of meaning—just as a word, in order to mean anything at all, has always both to be a carrier of meaning and to serve as a place-holder, a syntactical marker, within an *order* of words: it has by definition no meaning without (a minimal) syntax, and yet syntax by definition, the word as mere place-holder, has no meaning. (And, in the case of the book, this asymmetrical self-displacement is not due to the author's competency [or lack of it]—his lack of foresight at the beginning, say, and his excess of hindsight at the end—but to what Blanchot calls "the pressure of the book and the circumstances of its composition": the pressure of a linguistic necessity, what happens when we give a name and a sense to that which [for example, the center of a book] is nameless and senseless.) Although only the "Heidegger Reading Hölderlin" chapter formulates it in terms of the difference between semantics and syntax, this asymmetry—between interpretation and reading, ultimately—is the common project of all the chapters in the book: it is its true (i.e., self-displacing, asymmetricalizing) center, the beginnings and ends of a path of reading. Why this path of reading is not reducible to a method and why its beginnings and ends are not a subject become clearer if, on the basis of the above, we attempt to state, baldly, theoretically, as it were, the difference between interpretation and reading. What difference does reading make?

Reading Theory

To answer this question it would be good to know, finally, "what reading is." But it is impossible to say what reading is if we can conclude from the above that reading neither *is* nor *is not* in the terms of any dialectical logic or ontologic (or rhetoric subsumable under such logic) of Being and Nothing. And yet if reading—whatever it is—is nevertheless bound inextricably to these logics, it may be possible to formulate it, again, in terms of its other difference from what it is not: that is, interpretation. In three easy steps, then: In order to interpret, it is necessary (1) to understand the opacity in the text's (and the interpreter's) self-reflection in terms of a rigorous conception of the negative; here that conception is, in shorthand, either Hegel's "determinate negation" (*bestimmte Negation*) or Heidegger's "Nothing" (*Nichts*). Obviously these are not the only "rigorous conceptions of the negative." Since what we are talking about is, in a minimal sense, a negative that can account for the difference between apparent and nonapparent meaning, the negative of any coherent body of thought would do. It is certain, however, that without at least attempting to formulate such a negative, we have little chance of making any sense of the hyper-reflexive texts of Hölderlin, Hegel, and Heidegger. In order to begin reading, it is necessary (2) to reformulate, rewrite, this negative in the text's relation to itself (and the interpreter's to himself or herself) in linguistic terms: here those terms are trope and inscription, language as rhetoric and language as writing. Since the "philosophical" conception of the negative was itself the suppression or covering over of what we are calling the "linguistic negative"—whether it be in the Hegelian or Heideggerian readings of Hölderlin or in the texts of Hegel and Heidegger themselves—to reformulate the "philosophical negative" in linguistic terms amounts to a certain restitution of its textual "origins": that is, what the (philosophical) text had to forget in order to constitute, re-member, itself, in order to get itself written. The texts of Hölderlin—Heidegger's "poet of the poet" (*Dichter des Dichters*) who "poetizes" (*dichtet*) the essence of poetry—are exemplary in this respect: whether "poetic" or "theoretical," the logic of these texts' self-reflection is not only rigorous enough to withstand the machinations of any dialectical or ontological interpretation and its negative but also *linguistically* "self-reflexive" enough, "aware" enough of its own *textual* conditions, to resist these machinations and give the lie to any interpretation whose negative would reduce Hölderlin's texts to extralinguistic, extratextual, conditions, whether they be called "self-consciousness" or "Being." In short, the "linguistic negative" of Hölderlin's texts—and hence the necessity of reading them—surfaces in whatever the Hegelian and Heideggerian interpretations cannot account for: an other, heterogeneous, asymmetrical excess or lack irreducible to the work of the dialectical or ontological negative. For instance, the first three chapters of the book attempt to demonstrate that neither the Hegelian nor the Heideggerian interpretations—the philosophically most rigorous interpretations of Hölderlin—can account for Hölderlin's radically textual version of history—more allegorical than historical, more Nietzschean than Hegelian or Heideggerian.

But the second step toward reading—the reformulation or rewriting of the "philosophical negative" in linguistic terms—should not be confused with the mere uncovering of a suppressed, covered over, deeper sense, a symmetrical inversion of negatives that restores what we are calling the "linguistic negative" to its proper, authoritative, original place. This confusion—of interpretation with reading, ultimately—is possible only as long as we understand trope and inscription, rhetoric and writing, *language*, in a traditional (i.e., philosophical) sense: all trope in terms of (symmetrical) transfers of sense between literal and figurative; all writing in terms of a (symmetrical) opposition to speech. Philosophical thought—Hegel's and Heidegger's *par excellence*—has no trouble whatsoever dealing with and disposing of such trope and inscription. To say, for instance, that a philosophical system that denounces the wiles of rhetoric must nevertheless itself use figures of speech is not (yet) to *read* that system as *text*: rather it is only to confirm the system's dialectical power, to demonstrate its ability to contain tropological aberration and render language transparent. Philosophical systems use figures of speech only to use them up—by means of the dialectical resources of their rigorous conceptions of the negative. If our second step of reading is not to be the uncovering of a hidden sense (i.e., interpretation), not the symmetrical inversion of "philosophical" and "linguistic" negatives—that is, *not* replacing a philosophical negative with a linguistic negative because that is what was there in the first place—then there must be a radical asymmetry between philosophical and linguistic negative, between (1) its formulation in rigorously philosophical terms and (2) its reformulation or rewriting in linguistic terms. In short, a "third" step is necessary: (3) to understand "language" and "linguistic," trope and inscription, rhetoric and writing, in a radically other sense, not "philosophically" (i.e., extralinguistically) but linguistically, as it were, in terms of a radically open tropological or "grammatological" system: that is, not as system at all but as *text*. Language is a text in need of being read.

In other words, to retrace this itinerary: the (philosophical) text constitutes itself by putting a philosophical negative in the place of a linguistic negative. But because this substitution is a genuine forgetting, an arbitrary imposition like a catachrestic naming of that which has no name or like the substitution of meaning for marking (i.e., semantics for syntax), its inversion—the replacement of a linguistic negative for a philosophical negative—cannot be a symmetrical substitution or the restoration of the "proper" meaning or the "original" inscription. No, this step is subject to the same (radically) linguistic conditions ("third" step); it is as much an arbitrary (re)imposition of meaning or a reinscription as the "first" inversion; it is a "rewriting" rather than a reformulation. And this rewriting or refiguring remains asymmetrical to the "first" inscription or figuration because its laws are incalculable—better, *undecidable*—in the terms of any (dialectical or hermeneutic) calculus that would attempt to recover lost meaning. They are undecidable on account of language's material conditions of possibility. That is, as trope and as inscription, as rhetoric and as writing, language is a text: a tropological "system" that is radically open thanks to the possibility of, for example, catachresis, an arbitrary imposition or "abuse" of trope that, as an always possible abuse, is at the same time necessarily the material condition of possibility of all tropological substitution; a grammatological "system" that is radically open thanks to writing's enabling material conditions of possibility, for example, iterability—its status as a differential marking system, place-holding or syntax—which has nothing to do with constitution, substance, or meaning (and yet is their condition of possibility).

What this means, then, is that our "third" step of reading—understanding "language" and "linguistic" linguistically, as it were, in terms of a radically (i.e., undecidably) open tropological or grammatological "system," in short as *text*—cannot be a "third" step, for it was already there in the passage from step one to step two, from the formulation of the text's negative in philosophical terms to its rewriting in linguistic terms. That is, it is not a third step at all because it is out of sequence, out of order; its exigencies—the exigencies of language as text—are already in play in the substitution of the linguistic negative for the philosophical negative: they are this inversion's pivot or articulation. In short, this third, other step—to language as trope and inscription, as text—is a necessary supplementary step of reinscription without which no reading in the fullest sense is possible and which renders our attempt to say what reading is in a "theory of reading" a story of reading, an allegory of theory. To schematize this path of reading: (1) the formulation of the negative in a text's self-reflection in philosophical terms and (2) its rewriting in linguistic terms is an inversion, a chiasmic reversal, that restores what the text, in order to constitute itself, had to cover up, suppress, or exclude in the first place. But this inversion, chiasmic reversal, is asymmetrical because the "first" inversion or substitution (of philosophical for linguistic negative) was already subject to the exigencies of language understood in a radical sense (as trope and as inscription, as text), that is, was an arbitrary imposition of sense (catachresis, say) or a differential, nonsignifying, syntactical marker put in the place of that which was *not there* in the first place. In the first place nothing *was there*, but the philosophical interpretation, to constitute itself, mistakes—misreads, does not read—this nothing for a negation, a nothing *of something* (e.g., Being) rather than a nothing of language. Hence the asymmetrical inversion of the second step of reading—rewriting the negative in linguistic terms—brings along with it (3) a supplementary reinscription or rewriting of the terms inverted and their relation to one another. As a path of *reading*, then, the entire process is not a step-by-step procedure or method that could be narrated as a history but rather is a viciously (i.e., and yet asymmetrically) circular story: simultaneously same and different with no possibility of mediating the two. If the philosophical interpretation (and all interpretations *as* interpretations are philosophical) constitutes itself by a leap—of misreading or *not* reading—then to repeat that (same and other) leap, backward as it were, is not to deconstitute it (or to reconstitute its origins) but to tell still another story, (re)write still an other (and the same) supplementary text: an allegory of reading (which, because it cannot read itself [except in an other allegory], is also an allegory of unreadability). If reading is such a supplementary, allegorical superposition, it is no wonder that we cannot state a theory of reading without at the same time staging it, performing it, telling its story, as an allegory or supplement of theory. Reading—especially reading reading—is not so much a method as an ironic strategy (provided we understand irony as a linguistic and not a psychological structure).

If this strategy of an inversion and a ("supplementary," "allegorical") reinscription closely resembles the exemplary "procedure" of what is called "deconstruction"—for example, Derrida's account of the supplementary "relation" of speech and writing, or de Man's account of the tropological system and its undoing in "figures of figure," allegories of (the impossibility of) reading—so much the better. All we would stress is the "third," other, supplementary, allegorical "moment" of reinscription. Although necessary, the "moment" of inversion—setting up reading *against* interpretation, say, or the "linguistic" *versus* the "philosophical" negative—is only a first, merely strategic, move. If we do not take still another step to rewrite, reinscribe, the terms of the inversion differently, otherwise, in an other text, we remain in danger of merely confirming the system of binary, hierarchical oppositions, ourselves identifiable as those who are merely opposed, who are merely *contre*, and who are therefore easily recuperable for the dialectical resources of any hegemonic system.[2] The only thing more foolish than thinking that one can be "against" interpretation, meaning, philosophical systems, and all the (Greek) gifts that, say, phallogocentric humanism brings with it is to think that one can do anything to resist it by invoking the immediacy of the "concrete," "history," "politics," and the like without, before, interpreting its texts, never mind reading them. A double game, a double (ironic) strategy is necessary. If the hegemony is that of systematic nonreading—and this is certainly the system that supports the university, its organization into disciplines and departments, and, one might add, its attempt to neutralize and absorb the texts of "deconstruction" by taking them as still another (albeit negative) approach or method among others (e.g., psychoanalytic, Marxian, structuralist, sociological, etc.) available to the consumer who can afford it, pay for it (usually by not reading its texts)[3]—then reading, for example, the systematically unread texts of Hölderlin, Hegel, and Heidegger, is that strategy. Like the answer to the questions concerning the book's subject and method—which, after all, was "reading"—the answer to the question "what is reading?" can only be: "reading is. . .(only) for example." What, for example? For example, a reading of a much-cited (but little read) metaphor in section 9 of Nietzsche's *Birth of Tragedy* that in exemplary fashion gathers the themes and articulates the questions of interpretation, reading, and their radical asymmetry.

Reading for Example: A Metaphor in Nietzsche's *Birth of Tragedy*

> im Grunde war die Kluft nicht überbrückt
> —Nietzsche, *The Birth of Tragedy,* section 2

The opening paragraph of section 9 of *The Birth of Tragedy* in a modified version of Walter Kaufmann's translation reads: "Everything that comes to the surface in the Apollinian part of Greek tragedy, in the dialogue, looks simple, transparent, and beautiful. In this sense, the dialogue is an image of the Hellene whose nature is revealed in the dance because in the dance the greatest strength is only potential but betrays itself in the suppleness and wealth of movement. Thus the language of Sophocles' heroes surprises us by its Apollinian precision and lucidity, so that we immediately have the feeling that we are looking into the innermost ground of their being, with some astonishment that the way to this ground should be so short. But if for once we look away from the character of the hero as it comes to the surface, visibly—which, at bottom, is nothing more than a bright image projected on a dark wall, that is, appearance through and through—if we rather penetrate into the myth, which projects itself in these lucid reflections, then we suddenly experience a phenomenon that has an inverse relationship to a known optical one. When in a forceful attempt to fix the eye on the sun, we turn away blinded, we then have dark-colored spots before our eyes, as a healing agent, as it were: inversely, those bright image projections of the Sophoclean hero, in short the Apollinian [aspect] of the mask, are necessary productions of a look into the innerness and terror of nature, as it were, luminous spots to heal the look wounded by gruesome night. Only in this sense may we believe that we understand correctly the serious and meaningful concept of 'Greek cheerfulness'; whereas we of course encounter the misunderstood concept of this cheerfulness, as a state of unendangered comfort, everywhere today (*Alles, was im apollinischen Teile der griechischen Tragödie, im Dialoge, auf die Oberfläche kommt, sieht einfach, durchsichtig, schön aus. In diesem Sinne ist der Dialog ein Abbild des Hellenen, dessen Natur sich im Tanze offenbart, weil im Tanze die grösste Kraft nur potenziell ist, aber sich in der Geschmeidigkeit und Üppigkeit der Bewegung verrät. So überrascht uns die Sprache der sophokleischen Helden durch ihre apollinische Bestimmtheit und Helligkeit, so dass wir sofort bis in den innersten Grund ihres Wesens zu blicken wähnen, mit einigem Erstaunen, dass der Weg bis zu diesem Grunde so kurz ist. Sehen wir aber einmal von dem auf die Oberfläche kommenden und sichtbar werdenden Charakter des Helden ab—der im Grunde nichts mehr ist als das auf eine dunkle Wand geworfene Lichtbild, d. h. Erscheinung durch und durch—, dringen wir vielmehr in den Mythus ein, der in diesen hellen Spiegelungen sich projiziert, so erleben wir plötzlich ein Phänomen, das ein umgekehrtes Verhältnis zu einem bekannten optischen hat. Wenn wir bei einem kräftigen Versuch, die Sonne ins Auge zu fassen, uns geblendet abwenden, so haben wir dunkle farbige Flecken gleichsam als Heilmittel vor den Augen: umgekehrt sind jene Lichtbildererscheinungen des sophokleischen Helden, kurz das Apollinische der Maske, notwendige Erzeugungen eines Blickes ins Innere und Schreckliche der Natur, gleichsam leuchtende Flecken zur Heilung des von grausiger Nacht versehrten Blickes. Nur in diesem Sinne dürfen wir glauben, den ernsthaften und bedeutenden Begriff der 'griechischen Heiterkeit' richtig zu fassen; während wir allerdings den falsch verstandenen Begriff dieser Heiterkeit im Zustande ungefährdeten Behagens auf allen Wegen und Stegen der Gegenwart antreffen*).''[4]

The passage takes its place in the general context of Nietzsche's well-known reinterpretation of the "concept of Greek cheerfulness": rather than being their essential nature—integrated, unalienated—the Greeks' cheerfulness is the superficial appearance that covers a deeper reality, the Apollinian mask that covers the reality of Dionysian suffering. Today a cliché of intellectual history, this is the correct sense (as emphasized by the last sentence) in which we should understand the concept of Greek cheerfulness. The more specific context of the passage is a discussion of the relationship between the surface Apollinian appearance and the deep Dionysian reality in terms of the relation between the Apollinian part of the Greek tragedy (i.e., the dialogue) and the Dionysian "part." The latter—it is clear from section 8—can be identified, at least to some extent, with the "choral parts" (*Chorpartien*) of the tragedy, a womb which, as it were, gives birth to the dialogue. In other words, the immediate context of the passage's discussion of the relationship between Apollo and Dionysus is an interpretation of the language proper to the Apollinian and the Dionysian parts of tragedy, respectively. Like everything else in these two parts of tragedy, the language proper to each belongs to two "completely separate spheres of expression" (*völling gesonderte Sphären des Ausdrucks*). We know from section 5 how to characterize these spheres: Apollinian art is plastic, visual, objective, theoretical, self-conscious. It is the dialectical art *par excellence*, and the epic poet Homer is its representative: no matter how much he may *identify* with the images he creates, he nevertheless remains at a contemplative distance from them. ("Thus, by this mirror of illusion, he is protected against becoming one and fused with his figures," section 5.) In short, it is an "aesthetic" art—one that can be accounted for by subject-object aesthetics. In comparison, Dionysian art is of course inchoate, musical, unselfconscious, and best represented by the lyrist who becomes one with the primal oneness, pain, and contradiction of the ground of all things. Rather than maintaining a distance on his images, the lyrist fuses with them; they are nothing but his self. In short, the art of the lyrist is fundamentally *un*aesthetic; the subject-object aesthetics of German idealism cannot account for it. This contrast between the lyrist and the epic poet, music and the visual arts (in particular painting)—or, as the text puts it in section 6, between language that imitates music and language that imitates images—manifests itself in the language of the tragedy in the Dionysian lyrics of the chorus and the dialogue of the "Apollinian dream-world of the scene" ("given birth" by the Dionysian lyrics). This is why the last lines of section 8 can say that in the Apollinian part of the tragedy "Dionysus no longer speaks through forces but as an epic hero, almost in the language of Homer (*jetzt redet Dionysus nicht mehr durch Kräfte, sondern als epischer Held, fast mit der Sprache Homers*)." But this "almost" is important. Indeed, one could say that overlooking it is what leads to the misunderstanding of Greek cheerfulness as the unproblematic comfort Nietzsche laments at the end of our passage. Only if we look at the mere surface of the dialogue, where everything looks "simple" (*einfach*), "transparent" (*durchsichtig*), and "beautiful" (*schön*), can we confuse the "precision and lucidity" (*Bestimmtheit und Helligkeit*) of this (Homeric) language with the "innermost ground" (*innersten Grund*) of its and the tragic heroes' essence. In order to penetrate the true ground of the dialogue's essence, it is necessary to take a second look, as it were, or, better, it is necessary always to look with a double look: one at the simple, transparent, beautiful surface; and one at the doubleness, what it means to look away (*sehen. . . ab*) from the surface of the dialogue (the speeches of the hero of the tragedy, say) and penetrate into (*dringen. . . ein*) the depth of the myth "beneath" it. Since this metaphor is itself both simple and double (*einfach* and *zweifach?*), it will also require a double look: one as interpretation, say, and one as reading.

On the surface, the metaphor functions like a classical (i.e., Aristotelian) metaphor by analogy. This is already clear from the "if. . .then" clause that introduces the metaphor: "if for once we look away from the character of the hero as it comes to the surface visibly—which, at bottom, is nothing more than a bright image projected on a dark wall, that is, appearance through and through—if we rather penetrate into the myth, which projects itself in these lucid reflections, then we suddenly experience a phenomenon that has an inverse relationship to a known optical one." That is, a "known optical phenomenon" is going to be used to figure—but only by inversion—what we experience (*erleben*) when we look away from that which is on the surface, visible, a lucid image, mere appearance, in short, the (Apollinian) dialogue of the tragedy, and penetrate that which is below the surface, invisible, the dark wall (behind the bright image), the reality, in short, the (Dionysian) myth that projects itself in the bright reflections. The apparent symmetry of the oppositions spells out the metaphor's task: the metaphor will in a sense (i.e., figuratively speaking) make that which is invisible, spiritual, and unknown visible, sensuous, and known by comparing it to, figuring it by, that which is visible, sensuous, and known: here, a known optical (*bekannten optischen*) phenomenon (albeit in inverted form). The setup of this metaphor by analogy is classically Aristotelian insofar as it is based on the knowledge of entities—how they are constituted, their being—and their exchangeable properties. In order to figure old age as "the evening of life" or, inversely, to figure evening as "the old age of the day," I must know something about the constitution and properties of all four terms in the analogy—evening is to the day as old age is to life—in order to know which they have in common and can therefore exchange. For instance, I may know that old age comes late in life just as evening comes late in the day or that one's sight grows dim in old age and in the evening. So in the case of the relationship between the visibility of the Apollinian light, surface, appearance, dialogue, and the invisibility of the Dionysian darkness, depth, reality, myth, I must know something about the constitution of the terms of these oppositions to be able to figure, if only by inversion, that which is darkness, depth, reality, myth by that which is light, surface, appearance, and dialogue, that which is Dionysian by that which is Apollinian. In other words, I know the Apollinian in the way one can know and experience an "optical phenomenon," whereas I "know" the Dionysian in a different way—not with the vision of the eyes, say, but with a different "vision." In order for me to be able to figure the latter, different "knowledge" by the former, I must discover the "properties" they have in common, if only by analogy, if only by an analogy guaranteed by opposition, inversion, and negation: so that darkness may be figured by light, depth by surface, reality by appearance, myth by dialogue, Dionysian by Apollinian. In short, if the metaphor is to work as a (classical Aristotelian) metaphor by analogy, a great deal of weight is put on the "inverse relationship" (*umgekehrtes Verhältnis*) between the known optical phenomenon and the optically *un*known "phenomenon" it is supposed to figure: the inversion should have all the force of a symmetrical negation in order that it may hold together the metaphor by analogy, indeed make possible the analogy of the metaphor—that is, the exchange of symmetrically opposed properties (light/dark, surface/depth, etc.). And the burden on this inversion by negation is all the greater because this is not just any metaphor but the metaphor that would figure the relationship between the Apollinian and the Dionysian—the very possibility of representing, figuring, the Dionysian by the Apollinian, in short, the very possibility of tragedy: "When in a forceful attempt to fix the eye on the sun, we turn away blinded, we then have dark-colored spots before our eyes, as a healing agent, as it were: inversely, those bright image projections of the Sophoclean hero, in short the Apollinian [aspect] of the mask, are necessary productions of a look into the innerness and terror of nature, as it were, luminous spots to heal the look wounded by gruesome night." A certain shift, a certain asymmetry, between the "if. . .then" clause that introduced the metaphor—"if we look away from the visible surface. . .then we experience a phenomenon that has an inverse relationship to a known optical one"—and the metaphor itself has taken place. That is, the metaphor does not so much figure what we *experience* when we look away from the Apollinian surface of the dialogue and penetrate the Dionysian myth beneath it, as it does the relation between the terms (light/dark, surface/depth), Apollinion/Dionysian, etc.) of that look, between what we look away from and what we penetrate. We will have to consider the reasons for this shift—why the metaphor does not, indeed cannot, tell us directly what we "experience" when we penetrate the gruesome Dionysian night—later, but first let us interpret the metaphor itself.

The metaphor itself functions, on the surface, as a symmetrical chiasmic reversal in which the parallel and the inverted terms, as well as the pivot of their inversion, are well marked. In the first half of the metaphor, the known optical phenomenon, we have a turn from light to darkness, from the luminous "spot" that is the sun to the dark-colored spots, a turn, if not exactly from sight to blindness, then at least from seeing the light to seeing the dark, the blinding of the light compensated for by the blinding of the dark, which acts as, as it were, a healing agent (*gleichsam als Heilmittel*). The turn from one to the other is explicit—"we turn away blinded" (*uns geblendet abwenden*)—and its cause is natural, physiological, that is, the light of the sun and its blinding effect on the eye that tries to look at it directly. The second half of the metaphor, that which the known optical phenomenon of the first half figures, is carefully constructed as the explicit inversion of the first: just as in the first half we have a turn from light to dark, from a light that blinds to dark-colored spots that heal, so here we have a turn from dark to light, from the darkness of the gruesome (Dionysian) night that wounds the look to the luminous spots of the Apollinian images that heal it. The turn from one to the other is again explicit—the luminous spots are "necessary productions" (*notwendige Erzeugungen*) of the look into the gruesome night—and it would seem to be as natural as our blinded turning away in the first part—that is, the luminous spots are "generations" (*Erzeugungen*) turned by necessity (*not-wendige*). The pivot of the inversion between the first half and the second half of the metaphor is also explicit in the word "inversely" (*umgekehrt*). The parallel terms of the chiasmus are light and dark, and the crossed terms are blinding and healing: that is, in the first half of the metaphor, it is light that blinds and the dark that heals; whereas in the second half, the light heals and the dark blinds. Hence the chiasmic reversal can be schematized:

$$\frac{\text{light (blinding)}}{\text{dark (healing)}} \quad \times \quad \frac{\text{light (healing)}}{\text{dark (blinding)}}$$

In short, light and darkness can be exchanged because they have in common a healing property: the light in the first half of the metaphor can be the figure for the darkness of the second half, and the healing dark-colored spots (*dunkle farbige Flecken*) of the first half can be the figure for the healing luminous spots (*leuchtende Flecken*) of the second half. Everything in this carefully constructed figure seems to stress the symmetry of the terms and their inversion. Interpreted thus, the metaphor brings Apollo and Dionysus into relation with one another as symmetrical interlocutors in a dialogue. The metaphorical exchange would itself be a dialogue—*dia-logos*, a speaking between—that allows Apollo and Dionysus to speak to one another. And since what makes this dialogue possible is an inversion by *negation*, the dialogue would be a truly dialectical mediation, a mediation of *logos* and *mythos* (anti-*logos*?) by *logos*. On the basis of our knowledge of the symmetrically opposed terms of Apollinian and Dionysian—their *meaning*—we can mediate them metaphorically and represent Dionysus (albeit negatively) in Apollinian terms, in a dialogue in which Dionysus (almost) speaks the language of Homer.

In a rich interpretation of this passage, Sarah Kofman stresses the (inverse) symmetry of this dialogue and the homeopathic nature of the Apollinian remedy, a (second) blinding by the Apollinian light that cures the blinding by the Dionysian night: "The light of Apollo heals the wounded eye, for it blinds as to the true links which relate (*apparentent*) Apollo and Dionysus. There is no healing without the blinding by the light. In tragedy, the dialogue, it is this reflection of light, the inverted projection of the myth, that heals the look of him who has plunged into the terrifying night. Just as he who looks directly at the sun turns away from it and has before his eyes dark spots, a natural defensive product against the bedazzlement (*l'éblouissement*); in the same way he who has dared to cast his look into the horrible abyss of nature, of the terrifying mother, produces a defense as natural and as necessary as the preceding one, the Apollinian light. The theatrical remedy is therefore the exact inversion (*l'exacte inversion*) of the optical phenomenon: the latter heals in producing dark spots which protect against the bedazzlement and the blinding by the sun; the former heals the blinding by the horrible Night in procuring a blinding light. The veiled Medusa versus a Medusa stripped of all veil; blinding by the light versus blinding by the Night, such are the remedy-poisons of Apollo: it is a case of homeopathic medication of a cathartic type. There is a double blinding, a double bedazzlement according to whether one passes from shadow to light or from light to shadow: it is what the myth of the cave already taught, that other *camera obscura*. What is new here in relation to Plato and the Greek myths in which the light and the sun are saving agents is that for Nietzsche light and sun do not draw their pharmaceutical power from the Truth and the Good of which they would be the images, but from appearance and illusion, from blinding. It is a matter of a completely other 'version of the sun' (*'version du soleil'*)."[5] In the final sentences of Kofman's interpretation we have the logical counterpart of Dionysus's (in the Apollinian, dialectically mediating metaphor) almost speaking the language of Homer: Nietzsche's (almost) speaking the language of Plato. That is, even though Nietzsche here would overturn Plato by attributing the healing power of light and the sun to their status as mere appearance and illusion and not, as in Plato, their status as images of the Truth and the Good, because this overturning is a *mere* inversion, an exact, symmetrical inversion just as the healing theatrical representation is an exact inversion of the optical phenomenon, his ostensibly *anti*-Platonic account of the relation between Apollo and Dionysus still (dialectically) remains Platonic. In other words, the inversion of Plato only inverts the terms of the opposition appearance/reality but does nothing to alter the structure of the opposition itself. This is explicit in Kofman's interpretation of Nietzsche's denunciation of Euripides (at the end of section 10) in terms of copy and original, simulation and reality: "Because here Nietzsche condemns the simulacrum in a completely Platonic fashion, distanced as it is from the truth, from the presence of Dionysus by an infinity of degrees; because he considers necessary the reference to Dionysus, even though Dionysus can never give himself as such (*en propre*), his reading remains metaphysical. And nevertheless the metaphysical point of view is displaced by the introduction of myth and of a language whose nature is completely rhetorical, as the *Book of the Philosopher* shows: if Dionysus speaks, he can speak only improperly (*improprement*), he can give himself only transposed into metaphors, and that in an indefinite way."[6]

Kofman's interpretation deploys a certain familiar strategy (sometimes—wrongly—called "deconstructive"[7]) to deal with *The Birth of Tragedy*: that is, because of the book's apparent metaphysical valuation of Dionysus as father, ground, ultimate reality, the thing-in-itself, and the like, it remains an ultimately metaphysical, indeed Platonic, work that can be inserted in a genetic scheme or dialectical history of Nietzsche's *oeuvre*. In this interpretation *The Birth of Tragedy* would be a mystified, logocentric point of departure that nevertheless points to its own "deconstruction" in Nietzsche's "detour" through rhetoric in the *Philosophenbuch* and the course on rhetoric (which follow directly upon the writing of *The Birth of Tragedy*), and the detour through rhetoric in turn leads to "a break with the metaphysical conception of art, even before Nietzsche posits the hypothesis of the will to power."[8] There is certainly much to support such an interpretation of *The Birth of Tragedy* and its place in Nietzsche's development: both in the text itself—for example, the Schopenhauerian underpinnings of the book, the metaphysical valorization of Dionysus, the apparent valorization of music over language—and in Nietzsche's own later self-critiques, including the remark in *Ecce Homo* that the book "smells offensively Hegelian." Nevertheless, once we begin reading it, there is even more in the text that would put this interpretation into question by showing that this interpretation is the mapping out along a narrative line of what takes place everywhere and always (already) in *The Birth of Tragedy*: the narrativization of a figure, history put in the place of allegory. In other words, this interpretation depends on a dialectical interpretation of the relationship between Apollo and Dionysus. But the possibility of such a dialectical relation between Apollo and Dionysus already begins to be unsettled in Kofman's own account (above) of Nietzsche's still metaphysical reading of Dionysus: that is, if the "reference" to Dionysus can never be as such (*en propre*), if Dionysus speaks only improperly (*improprement*), only transposed into metaphors (*transposé dans des métaphores*) in an "indefinite or undefined fashion" (*de façon indéfinie*), the dialectical interpretation of these transpositions and metaphors can stand only so long as the particles *im-* of *improprement* and *in-* of *indéfinie* are taken as negatives, as determinate negations of that which would be "proper" and "definite." The *dis*placement of the metaphysical point of view "by the introduction of myth and of a language whose nature would be completely rhetorical" would have to be taken as a determinate negation of *place*. And yet this is belied by Kofman's own account: if Dionysus can speak *only improprement* and never *en propre*, if he can give himself *only* in metaphors and never literally, then these improper, indefinite, displacing metaphors cannot be taken as mere transpositions from proper to improper, from literal to metaphorical, because *there is no* proper, literal, original Dionysus in the first place.[9] The Apollinian, dialectizing metaphors for Dionysus are put in the place of Dionysus's "proper," "literal," "original" lack. That this "lack" of Dionysus "in the first place" can be taken as an "absence," as a determinate negation of his presence, is doubtful. Not only is Dionysus's asymmetry to Apollo stressed throughout the book, but also this asymmetry is always presented as radical: that is, as unbridgeable by dialectics and the work of its negative. If Dionysus is opposed to Apollo, if he is his negation, it is only in the sense that music is "opposed" to and the "negation" of images, that is, only in a figurative sense, only figuratively speaking. And because this opposition is *only* figurative, because it is not an opposition at all but two radically different spheres, its bridging can take place only in figure, only in impossible metaphors that have nothing to do with the mediation by negation of symmetrically opposed terms whose properties are already known and can therefore be exchanged—in other words, only in figures that are not metaphors (in the Aristotelian sense) at all but are something else. A good example of such an impossible bridging in an impossible figure is Nietzsche's genealogical account (in section 5) of the origins of lyric poetry. The detour of reading this figure may help us return to our light/dark, Apollo/Dionysus "metaphor."

Since the art of the lyrist lies at the basis of the choral songs that give birth to the Apollinian scene of the tragedy, the articulations of this genealogy are important, for they constitute an account of the birth of tragedy itself, that is, the "reconciliation" of Dionysus and Apollo, lyric and epic poet, music and images, and the like. This genealogy is articulated in terms of a series of "copies," "images," "recasts," "parables," and so on—with words like *Abbild, Wiederholung, Abguss, Gleichnis, Traumbild, Widerschein, Spiegelung, Exempel, Bild* crowding the passage—which are relatively hard to follow (especially in translation). But since the chain begins with (Dionysian) *music*—with the Dionysian artist's producing music as the copy (*Abbild*) of the primal unity (*das Ur-Eine*) with which he has become one—and ends with the images and appearances of the (Apollinian) "dream-scene" (*Traumszene*), the "image sparks" (*Bilderfunken*) of lyric poems, the crucial pivot of this genealogy is the turn from music—"imageless and conceptless" (*bild- und begrifflos*) as it is—to images: in short, how music becomes visible. Needless to say, it can become visible only in a figure: "*jetzt aber wird diese Musik ihm* [the

Dionysian artist] *wieder, wie in einem* gleichnisartigen Trumbilde, *unter der apollinischen Traumeinwirkung sichtbar.*" Kaufmann translates these lines as follows: "Now, however, under the Apollinian dream inspiration, this music reveals itself to him again as a *symbolic dream image.*" An entire ideological misreading of *The Birth of Tragedy* is contained in this (mis)translation's swerving away from the text: its rendering "this music becomes. . .visible" (*wird diese Musik. . .sichtbar*) by the vague "this music reveals itself" is already a symptom as is its translation of *gleichnisartig* ("parablelike," say) as "symbolic" (and bringing with it the ideology of the "symbol"). But more than symptomatic is the translation of "*wie in einem* gleichnisartigen Traumbilde" ("like in a *parablelike dream image*") by "as a *symbolic dream image.*" Since this phrase would tell us *how* music becomes visible—"this music becomes visible. . .like in a parablelike dream image"—it would seem important to get it across. But what the translation manages to do is to cover up this transition from music to images, from what can only be heard to what can be seen, by itself not making the transition (from German to English), and to suggest that music can become visible in *representation*. This suggestion enters in the translation's importing the little word "as" in "*as* a symbolic dream image." Together with the translation of "becomes visible" by "reveals itself" and "parablelike" by "symbolic," this shift from "like [or "as though"] in a parablelike dream image" to "*as* a symbolic dream image" succeeds in closing the gap between music and image, sound and sight, and therefore in making the crossing from Dionysian to Apollinian possible *as* a representation, as though it were representable. Of course, the price of this transition is the translator's missing the intralinguistic passage from German to English, language to language. This is by no means due to an accident of inattentive translation. Rather the translation that would make the passage from music to images (and from German to English) at all costs is a necessity built into, inscribed in, the text. That is, the German text *does not* make the passage, *does not* close the gap, between music and images, by any mimetic or representational (including dialectically representational) means but rather bridges them by an impossible figure that at the same time insists on the impossibility of the bridge. This becomes clear when we retranslate the crucial phrase "like, as though, in a parablelike dream image" (*wie in einem gleichnisartigen Traumbilde*): music becomes visible "like in a parablelike dream image." The phrase is a simile that is made up of words for simile, image, figure. Its self-consuming, nonrepresentational nature becomes visible if we reduce it by substituting the word "image" or "figure" where it belongs: "like ["imaged"] in a parablelike [in an imagelike" or even "in an image-imaged"] dream image"; or "figured by a figurelike dream figure." In short, music becomes visible figured in a figure of figure—which means that it does not become visible at all as something to be seen but rather becomes "visible" as something to be *read*. To think that one can *see* music in the Apollinian dream images is to behave like a spectator of tragedy who remains what Nietzsche calls the "man of culture" (*Kulturmensch*), who sees, say, the Apollinian scene (hero, dialogue, etc.) of the tragedy but does not see its essence, what it is at bottom—that is, the god Dionysus and his suffering. But in order to "see" Dionysus in all the Apollinian manifestations of the tragedy, it is necessary to see no longer as the "man of culture" but to see oneself as a satyr and as a satyr see the god (Dionysus). And to see *as* a satyr is not at all a matter of representation—how *represent* oneself as a monster, as *not* a self at all?—but rather a "transformation" (*Verwandlung*), an impossible, monstrous translation like that "figured by a figure of figure"—more a stutter than a translation. It is no wonder, then, that the translator had to get the text's impossible translation of music into images wrong. He could not make the intralinguistic transition (from German to English) precisely because he insisted on making the transition from music to images where the text itself did not, could not, make it—except as an impossible combination of words, a stutter (figure. . .figure. . . figure. . .), a monstrous translation. Where in the text there was nothing to read, nothing to translate—except an other, purely linguistic nothing of reading, nothing of translation—the translator could not read, could not translate. Rather than translating the nothing *there*, he did not translate; rather than *reading nothing*, he did not read. This nonreading can help us take a second look and to reread the "nothing" of the light/dark, seeing/blinding metaphor.

In order to take this second look, we need to heed the text's instructions and look away (*absehen*) from the mere "surface" of the metaphor—its "visible" symmetrical "dialogue" of exchangeable properties—and penetrate (*eindringen*) its "myth" (*Mythus*). To make Dionysus (dialectically) "visible" by figuring him as the symmetrical inversion of a known optical phenomenon is precisely *not* to "penetrate" the myth but to reduce the myth to dialogue, *mythos* to (*dia*)*logos*. It means to reduce Dionysus to a simple, superficial Apollo when Apollo is two fold: on the one hand, the Apollinian dream image, the scene and dialogue of the tragedy, *represents* (images, the empirical world, etc.); on the other hand, it impossibly signifies, impossibly *figures* (Dionysian music, the pain and contradiction at the bottom of all things, etc.). And the latter Apollo gives the lie to the former; he is his destruction. Paul de Man, in a much unread essay on *The Birth of Tragedy*, puts it succinctly: "The *actual meaning* of the Apollinian *appearance* is not the empirical reality it *represents* but the Dionysian *insight* into the illusory quality of this reality" [my emphasis][10]—a statement in which there is a radical disparity, asymmetry, between the Apollinian "appearance" and its "actual meaning," between "representing" and "meaning," between representation and a radical, "Dionysian" semiosis. Hence to penetrate the "myth" below the surface cannot mean to return to some primal, original stratum of experience or to "reveal" the ontological priority and authority of Dionysus and his music—since, again, Dionysus *was not there in the first place* in the terms of *any* (dialectical or hermeneutic) ontology—but rather to read Apollo differently, the other, "deadly Apollo."[11] In the case of our carefully constructed metaphor, it means to read the self-destructive *a*symmetry built into the chiasmic inversion of light and dark, seeing and blinding, and its other, asymmetrical, nondialectizable negative. An economical way to do so is to take another look at Sarah Kofman's interpretation of the metaphor's workings as a "blinding of blinding": "The theatrical remedy is therefore the exact inversion of the optical phenomenon: the latter heals in producing dark spots which protect against the bedazzlement and the blinding by the sun; the former heals the blinding by the horrible Night in procuring a blinding light." In short, one blinding heals the other; the second blinding (of the Apollinian images) blinds the first blinding (of the Dionysian night). By blinding the Dionysian blinding, the Apollinian blinding makes us see ("luminous spots" [*leuchtende Flecken*], for example)—an exact, symmetrical inversion, and, according to Kofman, "as natural and necessary" as the "natural defensive product" of the dark spots that protect against the bedazzlement in the first half of the metaphor (i.e., the known optical phenomenon). But if the second blinding is to be understood in any sense as a "natural defensive product"—that is, on the model of, as analogous to, the known optical phenomenon—that in some sense restores sight, it is clear that one blinding must be understood as the (symmetrical) negation of the other: the only way one blinding can heal the other is if it negates it, if he who does not see is made to see. Otherwise, the "blinding of blinding" would be the operation of some sort of joking Jesus who goes around blinding the blind—blinding them to the second power, as it were, as though one blinding were not enough already. In other words, this blinding of blinding cannot be understood in any naturalistic sense—for in this sense it makes mere nonsense or a cruel hoax—but rather one blinding must be taken as the symmetrical negative inversion of the other, one blinding must be the figure for the restoration of sight lost in the other. Obviously enough, then, such a blinding of blinding is not to be understood naturalistically but only as a figure—only by analogy to a known optical, natural phenomenon and the oppositions of light and dark, seeing and not seeing, and so forth. The blinding light that blinds the blinding Night can be only a figure and not a "natural defensive product." This is a first obvious step of the reading: that, naturalistically speaking, the figure makes nonsense. But the naturalistic model—the optical phenomenon—would be redeemed by analogy, in (and as) a figure: that is, precisely, *as* a model. Although the figure may make nonsense naturalistically, it makes sense figuratively: that is, in terms of a figural logic of symmetrical inversions and transfers between the terms of very natural oppositions like light and dark, seeing and blinding, and so forth. If the blinding of blinding is not natural, it is at least comparable to and understandable in the figural terms of (empirical) nature. This would seem to be the sense not only of the blinding of blinding but of the entire metaphor—itself only another version of Apollo's figuring Dionysus. But in order for the blinding of blinding to work as a figure, tropologically speaking, in terms of the figural logic that the metaphor has set up, one blinding has to be understood as the symmetrical negative inversion of the other: that is, in terms of the oppositions seeing/blinding, seeing/not seeing. The Apollinian (blinding) light heals by restoring the vision lost in the gruesome (blinding) Dionysian night. But here the text introduces a slight asymmetricalizing shift that undoes the entire metaphor and, ultimately, the very possibility of an Apollinian *metaphor*—that is, as a classical (Aristotelian) metaphor by analogy—for Dionysus. In a word, the text does not say that the gruesome Dionysian night *blinds* the look but rather that it *wounds* the look: "the look *wounded* by gruesome night (*des von grausiger Nacht* versehrten *Blickes*)." The implications of this asymmetry are far-reaching. First of all, it means that the figure cannot work as a symmetrical inversion of seeing and not seeing, light and darkness. If the look is wounded and not blinded, then *seeing* the Apollinian images, the luminous spots, is *not* its symmetrical inversion. It is not a case of seeing versus not seeing but rather the relation of a *seeing* look to a *wounded* look. In short, the wounding by the gruesome Dionysian night falls outside the easily inverted symmetrical oppositions of light and darkness, seeing and not seeing. Hence the metaphor's chiasmic reversal is asymmetrical and better schematized thus:

To use Kofman's formulation, this is not a "blinding of blinding" but rather a "blinding of wounding." In other words, not only does the figure make nonsense naturalistically, but also, more important, it makes nonsense tropologically, that is, in terms of the system of oppositions and substitutions it has set up.[12] Another way to put it: In order for the figure to work tropologically, the wounding of the look by the gruesome Dionysian night must be taken as a negation of sight, as a blinding, as a *not seeing*, and thereby as analogous to the blinding and restoration of sight in the known optical phenomenon. But the gruesome Dionysian night's wounding of the look is radically asymmetrical to this (ultimately perceptual) tropological model because rather than a case of the look's *not seeing*, it is a *seeing nothing*: that is, it is not a privative or a mere negation *of* the look—such a Dionysus would be the mere (reassuring) negation *of* Apollo, Apollo's own dialectical negation. Instead of not seeing, the look into the Dionysian night sees nothing. And the nothing *it sees* is the nothing *of* the Apollinian light and the images it renders visible—not as the absence, deprivation, negation of light but as something else, something as radically unknowable in the terms of oppositions like dark/light, seeing/not seeing as, say, music. The Dionysian night is "opposed" to the Apollinian light only, again, as music can be said to be "opposed" to images. To attempt to figure the Nothing of the Dionysian night by Apollinian images is like attempting to see music, like making music visible. In the Dionysian night, the look knows nothing, sees nothing—this is why it cannot be figured by a *"known, optical phenomenon."* The only way to do so is to cover over, forget, this Nothing by taking it as a negation: putting *not knowing* in the place of *knowing Nothing*, *not seeing* in the place of *seeing Nothing*. (For the traditional misreading of *The Birth of Tragedy*, it means putting a negative, "tragic" Dionysus—a Dionysus mediatable with Apollo [in Apollinian terms]—in the place of a Dionysus radically other, radically not there, better, radically a *Nothing there*, like the radically unknowable, wounding Silenic wisdom or death: the best thing is "not to be born, not to *be*, to be *nothing* [*nicht geboren zu sein, nicht zu* sein, nichts *zu sein*]," the next best—"to die soon.") In Kofman's interpretation, the symptom of this covering over or forgetting is the straightforward substitution of a "blinding" that restores the symmetry of the metaphor's exchange for a "wounding" that undoes it—like Walter Kaufmann's, a substitution, one could say, of *not reading* for *reading Nothing*. The text's own strategy is more devious. It imports a little wounding into the first half of the metaphor and its opposition of blinding/seeing by way of the invisible word *gleichsam* ("so to speak," "as it were"): we have dark-colored spots before our eyes "as a healing agent, as it were" (*gleichsam als Heilmittel*). If it needs to be *healed*, the blinding of the sun was already something of a "wounding." The *gleichsam* in the second half of the metaphor seems to balance the first by importing a little "blinding" into the wounding/healing opposition: after a look into the innerness and terror of nature, we have, "as it were, luminous spots to heal the look wounded by gruesome night (*gleichsam leuchtende Flecken zur Heilung des von grausiger Nacht versehrten Blickes*)." In the first half of the metaphor, the word *gleichsam* marks the figural shift from the light/dark, seeing/not seeing oppositions to the healing/wounding (curing/illness) opposition: the dark spots are, as it were, a healing agent. In the second half of the metaphor, the word marks the figural shift from the healing/wounding opposition to the light/dark, seeing/not seeing oppositions: the bright images, the Apollinian aspect of the mask, are, "as it were, luminous spots to heal." But this restoration of an inverse symmetry is only apparent. It can take place only figuratively speaking, only "as it were" or "so to speak"—only as long as we do not read—for it has nothing to do with the knowledge of entities and the exchange of their properties, nothing to do with an inversion by negation. It is only a word put in the place of this "nothing," a marker for the impossibility of the passage between Dionysian wounding and Apollinian blinding, Dionysian seeing and Apollinian healing. At the same time as it would restore the symmetry of the metaphor, the truly "invisible" word *gleichsam*—invisible because it has nothing to do with seeing and not seeing and everything to do with reading and not reading—is a sign of the metaphor's radical asymmetry. It is, as it were, the wounding of the metaphor. It is a "riddling *x*" (*rätselhaftes x*)[13] put in the place of the crossing of the chiasmus: it makes the crossing possible by crossing out, as it were, the impossibility of the crossing, standing in its place. Like the phrase from section 5—*wie in einem gleichnisartigen Traumbilde*—the word *gleichsam* is an untranslatable *x*. And the metaphor itself is such an *x* for the relation of Apollo and Dionysus. Hence it is no wonder that the metaphor does not, cannot, say what we "experience" (*erleben*) when we look away from the surface dialogue and "penetrate" (*eindringen*) the myth beneath—and instead gives us a figure for what happens when we look away *from* the Dionysian myth and *to* the luminous spots of the Apollinian appearance—for to do so would be to experience *nothing*, the *nothing* of experience. The figure—an impossible figure for the impossibility of figure[14]—is what we put in the place of this nothing: something to *read*, not something to *experience*. In short, the figure is a bit of non-sense, an *x*—a bit of non-sense, however, that is radically asymmetrical to sense. The nature of this non-sense and its radical asymmetry to sense—and its implications for interpretation and reading (Nietzsche, for example)—can be summarized and given a name.

Like Apollo—blinding and healing, wounding and restoring sight—the metaphor is double: it is a metaphor and something other than a metaphor. That is, on the one hand, the metaphor works like a classical Aristotelian metaphor by analogy. It figures the unknown by the known, the spiritual by the sensuous; it carries over and exchanges properties of light and dark, seeing and not seeing, healing and wounding. It is a "homeopathic" remedy for the wounding of the Dionysian night; it is an Apollinian figure for the way the Apollinian (surface, dialogue, light, image, etc.) figures the Dionysian (depth, myth, darkness, music, etc.)—it makes sense of the senseless. But, on the other hand, since according to this metaphor—and the rest of *The Birth of Tragedy*—the way that the Apollinian figures the Dionysian is by putting an impossible figure, a marker, an *x*, in the place of that which is radically unknown and unknowable, that which is outside the dialectically mediatable oppositions of knowledge and nonknowledge, spiritual and sensuous, like the Silenic wisdom (not just *not to be* but to *be nothing*) or death, the metaphor itself cannot be an Apollinian metaphor for the Dionysian "reality" but rather is a mask, a cover-up, a figure put in the place of that which is unfigurable. The metaphor is a "blind metonymy,"[15] as Paul de Man might say—"metonymy" because it is a substitution by contiguity, mere juxtaposition, mere "putting next to"; "blind" because it does not know anything about what it substitutes for, does not even know whether there is anything there to put something next to it. (In the figure's own terms, one could better say that it is a "wounded metonymy"—and a wound*ing* metonymy for it wounds the metaphor.) In short, like the remedies of Apollo, the figure itself is an allopathic remedy; it makes sense of the senseless by covering over the radical Nothing of sense, by figuring the Nothing of sense as the mere (dialectically recoverable) absence, negation, of sense. The Apollinian figure puts itself in the place of the Nothing of figure. All this is relatively familiar, and as long as we understand this Nothing of sense or figure—in a word, the Dionysian—in ontological terms (as ground, thing-in-itself, Being, etc.), that is, as something outside language, we can continue to make the so-called tragic, existentialist interpretation of *The Birth of Tragedy* and its *Artisten-metaphysik* that would formulate its insight into Being by means of aesthetic categories.[16] All kinds of rigorous conceptions of the negative could be applied to the Dionysian Nothing: for instance, Nietzsche's impossible, asymmetrical analogies for the Dionysian could be interpreted on the model of Kant's philosophical, that is, *regulative* (as distinguished from mathematical, that is, *constitutive*), analogies of experience, which yield knowledge only of the *relation* to a fourth [unknown] term, not the term itself.[17] But, on the "third," other hand, the trouble is that the Dionysian Nothing of sense, the Nothing of figure, is not something that comes from outside language to limit or negate its power of tropological substitution and aberration—that is, its power to make not only naturalistic but also tropological non-sense—but rather is essentially linguistic, it comes from, as it were, inside language, it is the Nothing and the non-sense *of* figure, *of* sense. That is, the possibility of putting figures, words, markers, *x*'s, in the place of a lack of meaning, putting something to see and know in the place where there is nothing to see or know—insofar as it is *always* possible, insofar as all figural transfers or substitutions are subject to it—is a non-sense or a Nothing that is the material (i.e., nondialectical, nontranscendental) condition of possibility of all sense and all figure. It is a material fact of language; it makes language what it is: a text, a radically open tropological system that can be "what it is" only by not being a system, by not being anything that could be "what it is" in the terms of *any* ontology.

What this means for the text of our recalcitrant "metaphor" is that the figure itself—to the extent that its substitutions and transfers have nothing to do with perceptual or phenomenological models of seeing and not seeing, knowing and not knowing (no matter how refined or how powerful their conceptions of the negative)—the figure itself, its materiality, is the wounding of the look into the gruesome Dionysian night. The figure wounds the look by making an arbitrary, metonymical leap from that which we do not see or know (radically, like the Silenic wisdom or death) to that which we can see and know (like the "known optical phenomenon"). That is, it empties the look, devalues it, degrades it to the status of a mere place-holder for that which has nothing to do with the look. Precisely in giving us something to see and know, the figure blinds us and deprives us of knowledge: it puts the negation of seeing and knowing in the place where there was nothing to see, nothing to know (because the *nothing there* was only to be *read* and not seen or known). This wounding, then, is not so much by Dionysus—for Dionysus neither is nor is not in the terms of any decidable opposition of Being and Nothing—but by an other Apollo: not he who represents but he who impossibly points to, signifies, figures, the Nothing of representation. In short, the figure undermines the (extralinguistic) primacy and authority of Dionysus only to gain a (linguistic, or, better, "metalinguistic") "Dionysian insight" into Apollo.

The text's own name for this Nothing of Apollo—and hence the Nothing of representation, sense, figure, metaphor, language (language being an intrinsically Apollinian medium according to *The Birth of Tragedy*)—is, of course, music. Apollo may represent images but what his images mean, what he figures (impossibly), is music. Indeed, as section 6 puts it, "we should distinguish two main currents in the history of the language of the Greek people, according to whether language imitated the world of images and phenomena or the world of music (*dürfen wir in der Sprachgeschichte des griechischen Volkes zwei Hauptströmungen unterscheiden, je nachdem die Sprache die Erscheinungs- und Bilderwelt oder die Musikwelt nachahmte*)." But rather than remaining on the surface of this distinction and concluding that Nietzsche is revaluing music at the expense of language—and hence interpreting *The Birth of Tragedy* as voice-centered, logocentric, and so on—we would do better to ask—and, as we have seen, the text repeatedly forces us to ask—what it can possibly mean for language to *imitate* music, what in language is *like* music. Clearly enough, if language is the intrinsically Apollinian medium that "as the organ and symbol of phenomena, can never by any means disclose the innermost heart of music (*daher kann die* Sprache, *als Organ und Symbol der Erscheinungen, nie und nirgends das tiefste Innere der Musik nach aussen kehren*)," then it cannot "imitate" music; it can only figure it in impossible figures (for figure) that would make music visible, that, like Apollo, represent all kinds of things and yet are mere place-holders for music (and thus represent nothing). But these impossible figures—for figure, for the impossibility of imitating music, making music visible—can bring us closer to the sense in which Nietzsche can talk about language's imitating music. That is, just as these figures have nothing to do with perception and the phenomenological models of cognition (ultimately) based on it (and yet are constitutive of language as an open tropological system), so music is not reducible to and should not be confused with what we can hear, its merely phenomenal (i.e., Apollinian) nature, what is apprehensible with the senses. What we hear is not music but noise—just as in the case of language what we hear is not speech but noise and what we see is not writing but black spots upon the page. Just as speech is not a matter of sound, what we hear, but the (inaudible) relations *between* sounds, the joints or articulations—that is, precisely what we do *not* hear—so music is a matter of the order of sounds, their jointing or articulation, a system of differential markings that cannot be perceived (heard or seen). But they can be—and they have to be if we are to be able to distinguish music (or speech) from noise—read: music is what we read, a text, and it is as text—as articulation, as a system of differential markings, as syntax (the ordering of words, words as place-holders, distinguished from words as carriers of sense)—that language can "imitate" music. As pure syntax, music would be purely linguistic; music could as easily be said to "imitate" language. This is the sense in which we can say that there is no Dionysus except as a mask, aspect, condition, function of Apollo: as semantics, Apollinian language carries meaning, represents images, and so on; as syntax, Apollinian language serves as a mere place-holder, means nothing, represents nothing, and yet is the condition of possibility of meaning and representation, their material (nontranscendental) ground.

Such a reading of the relation of music and language in *The Birth of Tragedy* would necessitate a rereading of the entire book: no longer as a genetic narrative or a history of the birth of tragedy, the origins of Apollinian images in primordial Dionysian music, but as a story language tells to itself, as it were, by figuring itself as image (Apollo) and as music (Dionysus), giving ontological (and historical) priority and authority to the latter (as origin, father, thing-in-itself, etc.) in order precisely to tell its story, to have a story to tell. In short, the new story would be that of language's own self-literalization—in order that there be a story to tell—and the interpreters' story would merely mimic this literalization (in order to have a story of their own to tell—for instance, of Nietzsche's logocentric "romanticism" in *The Birth of Tragedy* and his development out of it). Among other things, such a rereading would entail a new conception of what Nietzsche means by "aesthetic." If one reads *The Birth of Tragedy* (e.g., section 5) with any attention at all, it becomes clear that "aesthetic" is not to be understood in terms of idealist subject-object conceptions of art and aesthetics: both in *The Birth of Tragedy* and in the fragments of the *Philosophenbuch* (e.g., "On Truth and Lie in an Extra-moral Sense") Nietzsche quite explicitly rewrites the word "aesthetic" to mean a linguistic, indeed radically rhetorical "phenomenon."[18] Along with the equivalent "metaphor," the word "aesthetic" is one of his main tools to dislodge the unwarranted claims to truth of idealist theories of (including aesthetic) knowledge that make arbitrary metaphorical jumps (from many to one, from thing to word to concept, etc.) between absolutely different spheres and then forget that all their knowledge is based on an *aesthetic* (i.e., radically metaphorical) relation. This "radically rhetorical," nonmetaphysical conception of metaphor is already operative in *The Birth of Tragedy*. In a statement like the following from section 8, "For the genuine poet, metaphor is not a rhetorical figure but a vicarious image that he actually beholds in place of a concept (*Die Metapher ist für den echten Dichter nicht eine rhetorische Figur, sondern ein stellvertretendes Bild, der ihm wirklich, an Stelle eines Begriffes, vorschwebt*)," the stress should be put not so much on the "reality" (*wirklich*) of the image that hovers before the genuine poet's eyes but on its status as "*vicarious* image" (*stellvertretendes Bild*), a substitute, proxy, an image that *stands in* the place of, holds the place for, a concept. If such a metaphor is not a "rhetorical figure," it is precisely because it is not a symmetrical transfer from conceptual to sensuous—that is, it is not a figure to be understood in terms of a rhetoric subject to the logic of philosophy, a rhetoric that would be merely decorative, flowery speech. In short, it is not that the genuine poet is "naive" or that he takes his figures "literally" but rather that he knows his images to be not *representations* of some original (concept or whatever) but rather stand-ins, place-holders, which bear no mimetic relation to anything else. One could say that the entire, asymmetrical, unmediatable relation between Apollo and Dionysus (or, better, between Apollo and the "Dionysian insight" into Apollo), image and music—semantics and syntax, say—is figured in the "definition" of metaphor as *stellvertretendes Bild*: as Apollinian image (*Bild*), the metaphor represents entities in the empirical world, gives us something to see (whether with the eyes or the mind); as place-holder (*stellvertretend*), the metaphor is a syntactical marker for that which is unrepresentable, Dionysian music, pure syntax. But if such a metaphor is not a "rhetorical figure," what is it? Like his use of the word "aesthetic" to name that which cannot be accounted for by conventional aesthetics, Nietzsche's still saying "metaphor" ("carrying over," "transfer") for that which is not a transposition from sense to sense is indicative of the double game (of inversion and reinscription) in play: rewriting "aesthetic" to use it against aesthetics, rewriting "metaphor" to use it against conventionally conceived rhetoric. Our having to introduce into the arena of tropes and figures—which by definition have to do with sense and its transfers and substitutions—the term "syntax"—which by definition has nothing to with meaning (and yet is its condition)—is another indication of the peculiarity of these "figures": metaphors that are also not metaphors but markers, figural substitutions that are also proper names, figures that are not figures (for anything but the impossibility of figure). We are asking about something that would be, as it were, the syntax of tropes. Luckily, the rhetorical handbooks have a name for it: catachresis, or abusive, far-fetched metaphor like "leg of a table" or "face of a mountain"—in the conventional sense at once a "figurative" expression because it is transferred from elsewhere and "literal" because there is no other way to say it, it is the "proper name" of the thing. But having this name should not be taken as a cure for all that ails metaphor. We should beware of taking the name for the thing, especially in a case where naming—for example, "Dionysus" or "x," for that matter—is the question and not the answer. The uncanny status of catachresis as the "syntax of tropes"—and thus as that which keeps the tropological system from being closed off *as* a system—becomes clearer if we consider its fortunes in the rhetorical handbooks and read it with Jacques Derrida's "White Mythology." Reading it should also help us wrap up Nietzsche's metaphor and return (finally) to the parable of the sower whence we began.

The uncannily double status of catachresis in Fontanier's *Les Figures du discours* provides a point of departure for the reading of catachresis. Although Fontanier cannot assign catachresis a place with the other tropes—indeed, he says that it is not a true figure (*non vraie figure*) and discusses it in a "supplement" to his "Théorie des tropes" proper—because rather than a trope in its own right, it is the *abuse* of trope, the abuse (or "forced use") to which every trope is subject, he does considers his "principles" on catachresis to serve as "the foundation of our entire tropological system" (*nos principes sur la* Catachrèse *servent de fondement à tout notre système tropologique*). The reasons for this double strategy of, on the one hand, excluding catachresis from the tropological system and yet, on the other hand, including it as fundamental to that system are clear. As the abuse of all tropes, catachresis threatens to open up the tropological system and keep it from constituting itself, closing itself off, *as* a system. That is, as a nontrope, catachresis is outside the system of tropes, but as an always possible "outside"—there will always be at least as many forced uses or abuses of trope as there are tropes that we can classify—it has nevertheless to be accounted for in terms of that system; it is also "inside" it. To contain the potential damage, Fontanier resorts to a well-worn philosophical operation: inclusion by negation, *as* a determinate negation. In other words, catachresis may be an abuse of trope, but as an abuse *of* trope it remains governable in terms of and recoverable for the system of tropes. The *ab*use is always the abuse *of use*, the *non*trope is always the trope's own negation. Hence even though catachresis cannot be classed with Fontanier's master-tropes—metaphor, metonymy, synecdoche—it can be mastered in terms of them. The abuse of catachresis is always abuse *of*: catachresis is always the catachresis *of* metaphor, *of* metonymy, *of* synecdoche. This is how that which by definition—that is, as abuse—does not obey the laws of tropological transfer and substitution is nevertheless resubjected to those laws. One could say that the place of catachresis in (and outside) the tropological system is itself catachrestic: it is unique, original, namelessly outside the system, different from, other than, metaphor, metonymy, synecdoche, but at the same time it is a "secondary origin," comprehensible in terms of metaphor, metonymy, synecdoche as an abuse opposed to their use. But the trouble is that the relation between the use and the abuse of trope, between the tropological system and catachresis, is not an opposition: rather than a nontrope (or a "nonmetaphor," "nonmetonymy," or "nonsynecdoche"), catachresis is something other than trope and yet something that every trope is subject to. That is, the *ab*use of catachresis is in no way limited to or determined by the proper *use* of the three main tropes and their operations (resemblance, correspondence, connection). How do we decide that an abusive, forced figure is the abuse of metaphor (resemblance) rather than the abuse of metonymy (correspondence, for Fontanier)? How do we decide *which* trope is being more or less abused? We could say that the relation between the use and the abuse of trope is "metonymic" (purely contiguous), but even this would be saying more than we can know. In what sense can we even say that the abuse is "next to" the use? Obviously enough, the only way we can speak of a "catachresis *of* metaphor, metonymy, synecdoche" is *by* catachresis: by imposing a name and a sense (metaphor—"carrying over," metonymy—"change of name," etc.) on a nameless, senseless, relation, one about which we know nothing, indeed *less* than nothing, for it is asymmetrical to the opposition of knowing and not knowing. In short, the abuse of trope by catachresis is not a negation—it is an (improper) abuse asymmetrical to (proper) use—but just its wearing away, wandering, erring: a permanent exile of sense from which there is no return to the transfers of sense in metaphor, metonymy, synecdoche, and the like. In catachresis, metaphor, metonymy, synecdoche begin to wander. Why this wandering *has* to be asymmetrical to, of a different order from, the path of proper tropological transfer or substitution is easy to understand, for the asymmetry is built into catachresis. That is, on the one hand, catachresis is clearly a transfer from one realm (often the human body) to another and thus is definitely a figurative use of language. To give a "face" to a mountain or a "head" to cabbage or lettuce is clearly a figure. On the other hand, since this figurative (ab)use does not take the place of an already existent, established literal use but rather replaces the lack of the literal, the lack of the proper expression, it is not just figurative; it can often become the proper, the only way to say the *x* of a mountain. But it would be a mistake to call it "literal" and thereby relegate the uncanny doubleness of catachresis to a question of sense, of meaning, of semantics. For catachresis is less a matter of the relation between literal and figurative, proper and transferred, senses than it is a question of naming, marking, putting a word and imposing a sense where there is neither word nor sense. In other words, as much as catachresis is a figure (because it is a transfer of sense), it is also—supplementarily—a mere marker, a place-holder; it has nothing to do with sense; it only stands in the place of a lack. As place-holder for a lack of sense, as a "syntactical plug,"[19] as it were, it is neither literal nor figurative; it is outside, asymmetrical to, questions of sense. It is in this sense that we can call catachresis the "syntax of tropes"—the "place" where trope (catachresis as figural transfer) and inscription (catachresis as place-holder, marker, x) cross. Derrida's reading of Aristotle on metaphor by analogy provides a good example of this asymmetrical crossing and catachresis as the supplement of the tropological system (rather than its dialectically recoverable negation).

Aristotle's theory of metaphor is firmly grounded in his ontology: metaphor is based on being, substance, and it is a means of knowing being and substance. If metaphors are good, it is because they add to our knowledge of things. And those that add most to our knowledge are the best metaphors, that is, metaphors by analogy whose transferences depend on a knowledge of entities and their (similar and dissimilar) exchangeable properties. In order to say that "evening is the old age of the day," I must know something about all four terms of the analogy: day, evening, life, old age. Hence it is not surprising that such an ontologically grounded theory of metaphor asserts "the superiority of the substantive"[20] and has a decided "onomastic" bias: it privileges nouns, names, and everything in language that can be turned into nouns and names, everything nominalizable. It is even less surprising, then, that such a theory would want to exclude everything in language that resists being turned into a substantive: parts of speech, words, parts of words, particles, syllables, letters, etc., which are not nouns and cannot be turned into nouns—all the jointings, hinges, articulations of language. "Metaphor would be a transport of categorematic and not of syncategorematic words *as such*."[21] In short, Aristotle's theory of metaphor privileges the semantic pole of language—the order of the *phōnē sēmantikē*—and tries to exclude the syntactic pole—everything classifiable as *phōnē asēmos*, as nonsignifying sound (and hence equivalent to the "animal," i.e., nonhuman, aspect of language). But, as Derrida says, since these two poles of language are not separated by a simple and continuous line, since "human" language is not so easily divided from its "animal" aspect—rather it is truly, undecidably "monstrous"—all that is excluded comes back to divide (differently) human language against itself and parasitize this theory of metaphor. As always, the theory is undone by its own examples. In the course of giving examples of metaphor by analogy, Aristotle, following through the logic of his theory, admits a particular kind of metaphor by analogy—one in which a term is missing: "At times there may be no name in use for some of the terms of the analogy, but we can use this kind of metaphor none the less. For example, to cast seed is to sow, but there is no special word for the casting of rays by the sun; yet this is to the sunlight as sowing is to seed, and therefore it has been said of the sun that it is 'sowing its divine rays.'"[22] The analogy is as clear as day. Whatever the sun does to its rays is to the sunlight as sowing is to seed; or the sun is to x as the sower is to sowing—hence the sun can be said to sow, the sun is a sower. But for all the blinding clarity of the analogy, a question remains, and Derrida asks it: "Where have we ever *seen* that there is the same relation between the sun and its rays as between sowing and the seed? If this analogy imposes itself—and it does—it is because, in language, it passes by a long and not very visible chain whose first link is extremely difficult—and not only for Aristotle—to display. Rather than a metaphor, is it not a case here of an 'enigma,' of a secret narrative (*récit*) made up of several metaphors, of a powerful asyndeton or hidden conjunction, the essential character of which is 'to describe a fact in an impossible combination of words?' "[23]

The consequences of this question are far-reaching, not only for Aristotle's theory of metaphor but for any conception of tropology as a closed system. First of all, since we do not *see* ("literally" with the eyes or "figuratively" with the mind) what the sun does to its rays—and whatever it does is what makes our seeing possible (hence the privileged status of this example)—saying that the sun sows its rays or calling the sun a sower is not a metaphor by analogy but a catachresis. That is, we transfer sowing from a relation we can see, know something about, and have a name for to a relation we cannot see, know nothing about, and have no name for. Saying that the sun "throws" its rays, or "pitches curve balls" with them, or "bowls" them, or "nails" them, or, for that matter, "plays them on a saxophone," would all be equally "appropriate" and "inappropriate," would all be catachreses. The long, secret narrative that imposes itself and imposes the sun as sower on us is hinged or articulated by the powerful asyndeton or hidden conjunction of this lack of knowledge and the impossibility of the analogy. Like this secret narrative, the figure of the sowing sun supplies a lack of seeing and knowledge; it stands in the place of what we do not see or know. We turn away from the nothing of the sun—what we do not see or know or have a name for—and put the figure of the sower in its place. In doing so, we in a sense "humanize" the sun and "nature" but only at the price of blacking out the sun, violently blinding it, and therefore blinding ourselves—not only to the *x* of whatever the sun does to its rays but also to our very ignorance of this *x*; we once again put *not seeing* in the place of *seeing nothing* (and "metaphor by analogy" in the place of "catachresis," seeing in the place of reading, not reading in the place of reading nothing, etc.). In other words, the figure of the sowing sun, the sun as sower, is outside Aristotle's theory of metaphor; its very possibility (and, as *always* a possibility, its *necessity*) disarticulates that theory; it remains as a kind of blind spot in (and outside) the theory (*theoria*). But it is important to articulate—and the difference between interpretation and reading, say, rests on it—this blind spot correctly. For the nonknowledge that the figure covers over and is a figure for—our ignorance of what the sun does to its rays and our ignorance (in figure) of this ignorance—is not a negation of knowledge but rather outside, asymmetrical to, the opposition of knowing/not knowing and the (ultimately) perceptual (presence/absence) models of cognition (e.g., seeing/not seeing) it is based on. This nonknowledge or ignorance or forgetting is "outside" these oppositions only in the same way—and this too is an illegitimate "analogy"—that the *x* of what the sun does to its rays is "outside" them: that is, only as a marker or a place-holder for that which has no existence (and no *non*existence) *except* as a marker or place-holder. In short, the problem is not our not knowing what the sun is up to—for that could provide an endless source for the (optimistic or pessimistic—it makes no difference) pathos of negativity and its (sublime or ridiculous) dialectical recovery—but rather our *marking* (with an "*x*", or "sower" or whatever) of this nonknowledge and thus our divesting ourselves of it (as either knowing or not knowing) forever: for such a marked—articulated, hinged, jointed, and so on—nonknowledge no longer belongs to anybody—a mark is constituted in relation to other marks and not as belonging to a self or a subject—it is anybody's (or anything's) at all (only) to *read*. In other words, our not seeing what the sun does to its rays is only one blinding. We can recover from it by ignoring it, deifying it, doing more research. But once we give this blinding a name, mark it (with a "sower" or an "*x*"), we introduce a second, other blinding asymmetrical to the first: a blinding from which we cannot recover because it is a blinding that—asymmetrically, catachrestically—blinds the first, that is, prevents us from returning to the model of seeing and not seeing as a binary opposition (and forces us to read or not). This is indeed what happens with the figure of the sun as sower. For in calling the sun a sower, not only do we draw it into the (tropological) system of exchange—a system of which the sun, as the condition of possibility of seeing, is the guarantor, the master-, helio-trope toward which all the others would turn, the symbol of the transcendental—but we also make it enter that system as a mere place-holder, a syntactical marker, and not any kind of full presence (of meaning or whatever). Rather than closing off this system or completing it, the figure of the sun as sower—that is, as mere marker, as "bowler," "pitcher," "saxophone player," "father," "mother," "little brother," "Apollo," "*x*," or whatever—"supplements" it in Derrida's sense, opens it up radically, and requires only a short step to "metaphors" like the "wineless cup" for the shield of Ares (the cup is to Dionysus as the shield is to Ares, therefore. . .) or, say, the "seedless sower." "No reference properly being named in such a metaphor, the figure is carried off into the adventure of a long, implicit sentence, a secret narrative which nothing assures us will lead us back to the proper name. The metaphorization of metaphor, its bottomless overdeterminability (*surdéterminabilité sans fond*), seems to be inscribed in the structure of metaphor, but as its negativity."[24] (Note: since this "overdeterminability" is without bottom (*sans fond*), without *term*, say, it should not be confused with a de*term*inate negation.)

As sower (i.e., as syntactical marker), the sun begins to wander. It wanders away from and will not be returned to any proper name or noun, any substantive, like those joints of language, the pieces of words, particles, letters, dismembered (and dismember*ing*) *x*'s of language. The sun turns into a star "invisible or swathed in night"—"its name is inscribed in a system of relations that constitutes it." Much more—indeed, "supplementarily" more—could be said about this figure's making that which is the condition of possibility of visibility radically invisible (i.e., tropologically, in terms of tropology as a closed system of symmetrical exchanges), a bit of (naturalistic and) tropological non-sense, turning the sun into a burned-out star. For our purposes here, it is enough to re-mark the figure's Nietzschean (and "Hölderlinian" and "van Goghian" etc.) doubleness. That is, on the one hand, the figure of the sowing sun gives us something to see. Like the good metaphorician (according to Aristotle), it puts a picture in front of our eyes, it represents images. We can easily "see" the sun as a sower, for instance, in van Gogh's well-known *The Sower in the Field*: "a ploughed field with clods of violet earth climbing towards the horizon; a sower in blue and white; on the horizon a field of short ripe corn; over all a yellow sky with a yellow sun."[25] This would be the narrowly "Apollinian" face of the figure: like the dialogue of tragedy, it can represent anything at all in the empirical world. But, on the other hand, like Apollo and his representations, the figure of the sowing sun also "figures"—impossibly, catachrestically, what should we call it?—and what it figures, that is, is an allegorical sign, marker, stand-in, or place-holder for, is not only our lack of seeing, that which we do not, cannot, see—the *x* of whatever the sun does to its rays—but also the "lack" of the figure itself (and, always by abusive, catachrestic extension,[26] the "lack" of *all* figure, the "lack" of the tropological system, its radical open-endedness, its parasitization by syntax, its monstrous self-division, etc.). Rather than (or precisely in) giving us something to see or putting a picture in front of our eyes, it gives us nothing to see and instead puts out our eyes. It gives us a picture to read. Like the "Dionysian insight" into Apollo—that the music figured (impossibly) by the Apollinian images gives the lie to these images—such reading necessarily entails the blinding, effacement, or mutilation of the picture that is always a self-blinding, self-effacement, or self-mutilation of the reader. In the case of van Gogh's *Sower*, we may well ask if we do not *see* the analogy between the sun's sowing its rays and the sower's sowing his seed: the painter has even used the same pigment for the sun's rays and the sower's seed. And yet, of course, we do not *see* the analogy between whatever the sun does to its rays and the sower's sowing his seed: the *analogy* is something we impose on the picture by performing an abusive, catachrestic yoking. What we *see* is only sun and sower; the analogy is what we *read* when we perform the violent act of calling the sun a sower. Hence we could say that van Gogh's *Sower* is not a picture at all but rather a figure, an allegorical sign, or, if we still insist on calling it a picture, we would have to say that it is a picture of its self-effacement *as* picture, an allegory that figures its unreadability.

In calling the sun a sower (or reading the analogy into and out of van Gogh's picture), we block out the sun, put a sower in its place, and thereby blind our seeing eyes and put a blind, reading eye in their place. This eye is blind (radically, asymmetrically, catachrestically) because all that it can read is the impossibility of reading the text that constituted it *as* (nonrepresentational "as") a reading eye. This self-mutilation—a mutilating of the self that is not the self's own because it is a self-mutilation "proper" to, constitutive of, language, which is not a self or a subject—need not be as spectacular as a blinded and blinding sowing sun, but it is operative in every catachresis (and hence, by extension, in every figure). Catachresis peoples the landscape with monsters and mutants. It generously gives mountains "faces," even "backs" and "feet" ("the foot of the mountain"), but in doing so it not only does *not give* them, say, eyes, nose, or a mouth, necks, torsos, or limbs, but also positively *deprives* them of such, takes them away, defaces and dismembers mountains, turns them into monsters. It generously "humanizes" cabbages and lettuces by giving them "heads" (as in "head of cabbage"), but in doing so it deprives them of a face, body, and limbs: in giving the cabbage a head, it beheads it. This may be all well and good for cabbages (and even for mountains), but it is another matter for us. For if a mountain can have a face, we can certainly be stone cold; if a cabbage can be a head, we can be beheaded. In other words, all these mutilating figures are only figures for our own figural mutilation, for what happens to us as we disfigure the world by means of these figures, that is, they are figures for our mutilation *by* figures, depriving us of our senses (sensuous and spiritual) in order to give us back both the world and ourselves, but only as monstrous mutilations, as texts to be read—mutilations in which there is as much pathos and tragedy as in being beheaded by a cabbage or blinded by ("seeing") the light.[27]

Among other things, this means that the "tragedy" of Nietzsche's figure—both its surface and its depth, its dialogue and its myth—is already inscribed in the first half of the "metaphor": that is, in the "known optical phenomenon" when "in a forceful attempt to fix the eye on the sun, we turn away blinded, we then have dark-colored spots before our eyes, as a healing agent, as it were." The turn away from the blinding sun would be the figure for a turn away from the world of the senses: in all senses, the world of sense perception, the tropological system based on the knowledge of entities and their exchangeable properties, the entire "solar system" and all that it guarantees. And the turn to the healing dark spots would be the figure for the (written) words, letters, markers (*Flecken*), black suns, or burned-out stars that we put in the place of our not seeing and not knowing. We put blind spots, as it were, in the place of our blinding by the sun. And such a reading does not require much forcing of the text. The attempt to fix the eye on the sun (*die Sonne ins Auge zu fassen*) is not just a matter of optics; the German idiom *ins Auge zu fassen* means "to have in view (to do)," "to contemplate (doing)," that is, it means an intentional act, the act of intention itself. To "fix the eye on the sun," then, has at least an idiomatic trace of a (catachrestic) attempt to have the sun "in view" as the object of an intentional act, as though one had turned the word "sun" into a verb—to have in view sunning, as it were. No wonder that the attempt blinds. The fact that the "optical phenomenon" is a *known* or familiar (*bekannt*) phenomenon would support the reading. In short, the undoing of the metaphor and its reinscription as catachresis that takes place in the asymmetry between the first and second halves of the figure are already taking place, have always already taken place, in the first half: the "known optical phenomenon" that represents all kinds of things but that can figure (impossibly) only figure. To invert the inversion, we could say that the healing dark spots of the optical phenomenon that figure (by inversion) the luminous (Apollinian) spots that heal the look wounded by gruesome night are also the figure for the gruesome night; they are the wounding "itself."

I. Reading Hölderlin

Chapter 1
Endpapers
Hölderlin's Textual History

For Martin Heidegger, Hölderlin was the poet's poet, "the poet of the poet" (*der Dichter des Dichters*),[1] and for most interpreters the problem of "Hölderlin—his life and his work—still comes down to the question of self-consciousness, reflection, and returning. The usual answer to the question of Hölderlin's self-consciousness is what could be called a "narrativization" of a reflexive structure: that is, the explanation of his work (in particular the late hymns and translations) as a story (or a history) told in terms of a turning or returning—toward or away from Greece, toward or away from Hesperia—in terms of *abendländische Wendung* or *vaterländische Umkehr*.[2] Facts of Hölderlin's biography, passages from his late hymns and fragments, historico-philosophical speculations from his essays and letters, as well as documentation of his violently deforming translations of Sophocles, have all been pressed into service as evidence for one or the other turning, one or the other return; and sometimes it is difficult to remember whether it is only an individual history, indeed an individual pathology, that is at stake or whether the entire history of the West rests in the balance. What we would do in the following remarks is to reexamine the stakes by reading three specific instances of the explicit turning of self-consciousness in three exemplary texts from different "periods"

See "endpaper" in *Webster's Third New International Dictionary:* "a folded sheet of paper in books being plain or printed and having one leaf that forms a pastedown and another that forms a flyleaf—called also endleaf, endsheet." And "flyleaf": "*1.* a blank leaf at the beginning or end of a book or similar work; *specif.* the free endpaper 2. paper attached to the inner edge of a paper box to cover the contents or for decoration."

3

in Hölderlin's career: (1) the early fragment called "Judgment and Being" (*Urteil und Sein*) (1795), which is, at least in part, about the "I" understood as self-consciousness; (2) the "Manes-scene" from the so-called third version of Hölderlin's drama *The Death of Empedocles* (1798-1800), which is the story of a particular "I's" turning upon itself (very literally indeed) to sacrifice itself—to repossess itself *by* sacrificing itself; and (3) Hölderlin's interpretation of Sophocles in the late notes to Oedipus and notes to Antigone (1804) organized around his notion of the "caesura" as the place where a tragedy turns upon itself, where, in his words, (dramatic) representation itself appears. This "caesura" not only helps us to understand the "Manes-scene" in Hölderlin's tragedy (and, by extension, the understanding of the model of self-consciousness articulated in "Judgment and Being"), but also may allow us to make some preliminary suggestions for a rereading of Hölderlin's philosophy of history and, by implication, the peculiar self-reflexiveness of the language of his late hymns.

Flyleaf: *Urteil und Sein*

The early text "Judgment and Being" is written on the torn-out flyleaf of a book that Friedrich Beissner conjectures to be Fichte's *Science of Knowledge* (*Wissenschaftslehre*). A paragraph that begins with a definition of "Judgment"—"*Judgment* is in the highest and strictest sense the original separation of the subject and the object which are most intimately united in intellectual intuition, the separation [or sundering] through which subject and object are first made possible, the Ur-separation (Urteil *ist im höchsten und strengsten Sinne die ursprüngliche Trennung des in der intellektualen Anschauung innigst vereinigten Objekts und Subjekts, diejenige Trennung, wodurch erst Objekt und Subjekt möglich wird, die Ur-Teilung)*" (4:216)[3]—is written on the recto side of the flyleaf. Some short paragraphs that begin with "Being"—"*Being* expresses the binding [joining, unification] of subject and object (Sein *drückt die Verbindung des Subjekts und Objekts aus)*"—are written on the verso side of the flyleaf. It is fairly certain that the handwriting is Hölderlin's, and on the basis of orthographical and other data the fragment can be dated as written in early 1795. It was first published in 1961 in the fourth volume of Beissner's Stuttgart edition and under his title "Judgment and Being." The fragment did not receive much attention until Dieter Henrich interpreted it as a basic and key text of German idealism: a kind of "missing link" in the transition from Fichte to Hegel.[4] Indeed, if we tear some sentences out of context (from the passages on Being)—ones of particular interest and use to us—we can easily "recognize" the Hegelian themes of their critique of Fichte: "How can I say: I! without self-consciousness? But how is self-consciousness possible? Through this, that I oppose myself to myself, separate myself in that which has been opposed as the same. But to what extent as the same? I can, I must ask in this way; for in another respect it is opposed to itself

(*Wie kann ich sagen: Ich! ohne Selbstbewusstsein? Wie ist aber Selbstbewusst-sein möglich? Dadurch, dass ich mich mir selbst entgegensetze, mich von mir selbst trenne, aber ungeachtet dieser Trennung mich im Entgegengesetzten als dasselbe erkenne. Aber inwieferne als dasselbe? Ich kann, ich muss so fragen; denn in einer andern Rücksicht ist es sich entgegengesetzt*).'' These lines contain what is a relatively explicit critique of Fichte's absolute "I"—and one that can be found in several of Hölderlin's texts, including a letter to Hegel of 26 January 1795.[5]

The essence of the critique could be summarized as follows: since an absolute "I" would have to contain all reality—it is all and outside of it is nothing—there is no object for such an "I"; but an "I", a consciousness, without an object is unthinkable, an "I" *must* have an object, even if it is only I myself who is that object (and therefore limited and therefore not absolute). In short, if it is an "I", it cannot be absolute, and if it is absolute, it cannot be an "I," for to say "I" always means the self-division of the "I" against itself, a self-exteriorization of the "I" in an other in which it may recognize itself. At first sight, what we have here, then, is a familiar and reassuring version of Hegelian self-consciousness: insofar as that other self is always *my* other self, the "I's" other is *its own* other, this self-sundering, no matter how painful and how negative, is ultimately a self-recognition and a self-recuperation. In such a Hegelian reading of the sentences from "Judgment and Being," the word "as" (*als*) in the repeated phrase "as the same" (*als dasselbe*) would have to be in-vested with the entire problematics of what Hegel will call *Vorstellung*—representation, in particular self-representation. That is to say, the "as" (*als*) of (self-)representation is what makes the self-recognition of self-consciousness possible: in the self-representation that I have "opposed" to myself I recognize my self as *the same*, that is, as *my* selfsame self. But accord-ing to these sentences the "as" (*als*) of representation is also that which makes total self-recognition impossible insofar as from another point of view, in another respect, in another "look back" (*in einer andern Rücksicht*), the "I" does not recognize itself as the same but remains opposed to itself. In other words, in the phrase "as the same" (*als dasselbe*) we can put the stress not on the *sameness* (*dasselbe*) of the self that is to be recognized but rather on the otherness of the self it has opposed to itself: that is, on the "as" (*als*) and not on the same, on the *representation* in self-representation and not on the self- in self-representation. Yet this possibility of self-nonrecognition in the self-representation of the "I"—this possibility of too much representation and too little self—is still eminently dialectizable by turning this excess of self-nonrecognition into a *moment* in the history of self-consciousness. In order to recognize itself as the self in its own other, the "I" must in some way forget that it was the "I" who performed the "original" self-sundering, self-op-positing, in the first place. When I recognize myself in the "I" that I have separated from and opposed to myself, I do so without paying attention to, regardless of, this separation (*ungeachtet dieser Trennung*): in other words, I very precisely forget, do not pay attention to, dis-regard, as it were, that other re-gard, that other re-spect, that other look back (*Rücksicht*), for which the "I" remains opposed to itself. In short, for the Hegelian re-spect (*Rücksicht*), the "I" recognizes and recuperates the "I" as long as it looks back the right way: that is, when it recounts the history of its having separated itself from itself (momentarily), having forgotten that separation (momentarily), and having recognized itself in itself as *its own* other. In this history, the otherness of the other look back is disregarded as *only* the other *of* the right look back, the one that recognizes the self because it has remembered not to look back at the self in an other respect. By doubling the "I"—and by doubling the "as" (*als*) of self-representation and the look back, re-spect (*ungeachtet, Rücksicht*), of the "I" at the "I"—and reinscribing it in a narrative history (even if only one as minimal as that between one respect and another), the "I" is able to say a (speculatively, dialectically) self-identical "I".[6]

Nevertheless, in their hurry to assimilate this text's critique of Fichte to Hegel's or to place its (purportedly Hölderlin's) reflection on "Judgment and Being" in historical context (for instance, as a synthesis of positions culled from Plato, Spinoza, and Kant), the interpreters have perhaps not paid enough attention to the radical critique formulated in its question: that is, the possibility, indeed necessity, that the "I" may not, does not, *in an other respect*, another look back, recognize itself as the same (but rather remains opposed to itself). Perhaps another question about the other respect is possible. To pose that question means to compare the way this fragment has been represented with the way it represents itself; it means, as always, to read it *as* a text with a history of readings inscribed within itself, that is, the various decisions that had to be made or, as is more often the case, that had to be *presupposed* (as always already *having been* made) in order to turn this text into a document documenting a stage in the progress of German idealism. The first decision (made or presupposed) is, as always, that of the title; it contains (and is contained by) all the other decisions of the interpreters. Beissner gives it the title "Judgment and Being" on the basis of the first (underlined and defined) words on each side of the flyleaf. He does not call it "Being and Judgment," for example, because he assumes that the recto side of the flyleaf—determined in relation to the edge where the flyleaf was torn out (in other words, the recto side has the torn edge on its left)—was written (and is to be read) first. As is understandable, this arbitrary decision (of which side is up and which down, which is to be read first and which second, etc.) has been questioned. Both Dieter Henrich and H. S. Harris (in his *Hegel's Develpment: Toward the Sunlight, 1770-1801*), for example, assert that the *verso* (i.e., "Being") was written and is to be read first. Harris's reasons for this new sequence (and, by implication, this new title) are instructive insofar as they allow the implicit decisions of the interpreter—whichever side he reads as up and whichever side as down—to turn up: "This piece was written on the flyleaf of a book and subsequently torn out. The section on Judgment was written on the recto of the leaf and the section on Being on the verso. For this reason Beissner—who supplied the title—prints them in that order. But I agree with Henrich that Hölderlin almost certainly began writing on the verso—as one very naturally might when writing one's reflections on the flyleaf of a book one has been studying—and continued on the recto."[7] Even if we disregard (provisionally) Harris's assumptions about the identity of the author, his assumptions about the self-identity of the text remain as arbitrary and as problematic as those of Beissner. Who can say, who can decide, for example, that the "piece" was first written on the flyleaf and "subsequently" torn out? Is it not equally plausible that the writer wrote on an *already torn out* flyleaf? Who can say whether it is more or less "natural" to write on the verso or on the recto of a flyleaf (whether it be still *in* the book or already torn out of it)? And never mind about deciding which side was originally (i.e., when the flyleaf was blank) recto and which verso. The questions reproduce themselves automatically—no doubt the way one turns over a page recto to verso, verso to recto—and they would be very trivial indeed were it not for the stakes: first of all, the self-identity of this text. For what all the decisions amount to is the presupposition that *Urteil und Sein* (or *Sein und Urteil*) is *one* text by one author, that, for instance, it *continues* from Judgment to Being (or from Being to Judgment), that there is an original unity and an original sundering (*Ur-Teilung*), and that they are related to one another as one to an other, as other to a one, and so on. In short, no matter which is taken to be first, no matter how divided or separated or torn against one another and against themselves, Judgment and Being can be inscribed in a history very much like the history of the double look back of the "I"; just as that history allowed the "I" to recognize itself, so this one allows the "I" of the reader to "recognize" the selfsame text, the text itself.

And yet what remains most bothersome about this textual history is not only the fact that all kinds of arbitrary, unverifiable, decisions must be made in order to recount it—not only the fact that each interpreter must posit an original (book)binding in order to explain (away) the torn edge of the flyleaf, indeed must, in a sense, paste the flyleaf back into the book and tear it out and vice versa over and over again—but also the fact that the decisions that make this history possible are predicted by (and themselves predict) and reproduced in (and themselves reproduce) the text. The two looks back (*Rücksichte*) that had to be inscribed in a history so that the "I" could recognize itself are one example; and the two opening definitions of Judgment and Being are another: Judgment as the original separation, the original tearing, of subject and object presupposes (and posits) an even more original unity; and Being as the original joining or binding of subject and object posits (and presupposes) the separation. One is unthinkable without the other, and hence it would seem not to make too much difference which we read first and which we read second as long as we do read one *as* first and the other *as* second. Dieter Henrich summarizes this dialectical process of mutual position and presupposition: "*Why* the original separation (*Urteilung*) takes place at all is not explained by Hölderlin in this fragment: it is just a fact from which we have to start. Once this separation has happened and the mind has originated, the process of the mind will always depend upon its having been generated by that which is undifferentiated. For that reason, the process of the mind is somehow a process of unification, the re-establishment of unity in the separation. Even at the very beginning, the reference to the subject and object has to be interpreted in terms of this unifying process."[8] But just as the story of the two respects, the two looks back, cannot quite dispose of the constant possibility of still another look back—we cannot call it "third" because it is a look back of another order—the one that does not recognize the "I" as the same, that rather than merely opposing turns away from the "right" (recto?) look back, so the story of Judgment and Being contains an unsettling asymmetry in the very definitions of the two concepts. For we are told not what Judgment *is* and what Being *is*, but rather what Judgment *is*—that is, the original separation of subject and object—and what Being *expresses*—"*Being* expresses the binding of subject and object (Sein *drückt die Verbindung des Subjekts und Objekts aus*)." Whereas Judgment is, Being expresses, means, signifies, *names*. That the relation between "being" (*sein*) and "expressing" (*ausdrücken*)—and therefore between Judgment and Being—could ever be understood in terms of an opposition between self and other, subject and object, is doubtful, especially since the section on Being (understood as absolute Being [*Sein schlechthin*]) explicitly removes it from a relation of mere "identity" like that alleged between subject and object in self-consciousness. Whatever that relation may be, or, better, however that relation is expressed, or, again, whatever name we give it, it is clear that Being is not just opposed to Judgment, not just the verso of the recto (or vice versa), and so on. Hence if Being is—but it never is—the impossible condition of possibility of the original separation of subject and object—one could call it a simulacrum of the transcendental—then the relation between Judgment and Being would be more like the relation between the "two" sides of a Möbius band whose surface(s) remain(s) undecidable unless we make an arbitrary decision and posit the cut where one of the ends was turned one hundred eighty degrees and bound to the other end. It is no wonder, then, that reading the "nonorientable surface"[9] of "Judgment and Being"— that is, of cutting (*Trennung, Teilung*) and binding (*Verbindung*)—means endless turning and returning of the flyleaf, endless attempts at restitution of a first cut and a first turn that could never have taken place in the first place.

But if the self-identity of the text is traversed by an undecidable torn edge, a cutting that is not merely the opposite of binding (*Verbindung*), perhaps we could halt the endless turning over of the flyleaf, the endless looking back from recto to verso and verso to recto, by calling upon the identity of the author. In this regard the interpreters of "Judgment and Being" have been even more rigorously consequential than in their decisions about the identity of the text. There are several difficulties with considering Hölderlin the author of "Judgment and Being": the most serious one is the earliness of the text. As Dieter Henrich puts it: "The text presents a self-conscious attack on Fichte's basic thought. How can it have been written by a poet who still moved within the framework of Kant's conceptualization and not very far beyond its explicit doctrine and who had hardly become acquainted with the marvelled-at teachings of Fichte?"[10] Unless one were to put into question the orthographical statistics—whose evidence seems quite compelling—and attempt to redate the fragment, one would almost have to surmise that Hölderlin is not the author, but that the text is, say, a copied-out excerpt from the work of another or perhaps Hölderlin's notes on a discussion with a friend (like Hegel, say). But, as Henrich points out, "in any event we know of no publication from so early a time with even a comparable content." Yet rather than leave the text unfathered (as a dead letter or an undeliverable and unreturnable *carte postale*)[11], and open to unthinkable and yet quite plausible questions—such as, why do we always have to assume that it is *one* text, one fragment? Why could not the recto have been "authored" by Hölderlin and the verso only copied, and vice versa, and so on and so forth?—Henrich has taken a closer look at the flyleaf and found at least one place in the text that can be understood only on the basis of the presupposition that "the hand of him who conceived [the text] was at work (*dass die Hand des Konzipierenden am Werke war*)." Henrich means a correction that Hölderlin made in the question about the "I's" saying "I": Hölderlin had first written "*Darf ich sagen: Ich! ohne Selbstbewusstsein* (May I, could I, say I! without self-consciousness)" but then crossed out the *darf* and wrote above it *Wie kann* so that the question now reads "*Wie kann ich sagen: Ich! ohne Selbstbewusstsein?* (How can I say: I! without self-consciousness?)." Since the correction is made above the line, it is likely that the rest of the text had already been written and therefore that the correction "means a change in the direction of the thought: The question 'May I, could I, say. . .' appears to demand a discussion; the question 'How can I . . .' is unequivocally only rhetorical—it already includes an answer in the negative. From such an answer Hölderlin's following sentence actually proceeds: if the 'I' cannot be thought without self-consciousness, then one has to ask how such self-consciousness is possible in order to find that it comes into existence through opposition."[12] This correction can be understood only with difficulty, continues Henrich, unless one sees at work in it the hand of him who conceived the text, for had Hölderlin only copied the text, he would have probably not even noticed the mistake. In short, we can tell, we can decide, that the hand of the writer was identical to the hand of the author (he who conceived the text) because it was a hand that could tell, that could decide, the difference between a real, literal, question and a feigned, rhetorical, question. We can tell that the writer was author because we can tell that the writer was also someone who could *read* "his own" writing.

Now there are a number of problems with this decision of the author's identity. Not least of all is the fact that the "original" question "May I, could I. . . (*Darf ich* . . .)" can obviously also be read as a rhetorical question. Henrich admits this, but insists that the new question is more clearly rhetorical than the first—which insistence would bring up the (other) question of how one can tell what is more or less rhetorical if the relation between literal and figurative is not a matter of quantity, not a matter of more or less. But we must pose still another question about this decision to identify the one, real, literal author of the text, the one, real, literal "I" that is able to say, better, that is able to write and read "I" because it can decide between the real, authored, literal "I" and the feigned, unauthored (i.e., copied), rhetorical "I." To put it as succinctly as possible: if being able to tell the difference between literal and rhetorical questions, literal and figurative senses, constitutes the subject, the "I," then who or what—or *which* "I"—constitutes the difference between literal and figurative senses? Or, again, if a "rhetorical," "figurative" reading and writing of the "I" is always a possibility in *any* reading and writing of the "I" whatsoever, how can we ever be sure about *who* is reading and writing "I," how can we ever say (read or write) "I" *non*rhetorically (and the relation between literal and figurative is not oppositional and not symmetrical), literally, without unwarranted substitutions of one "I" for another, of a simulacrum of the "I" for the real "I," and so on? But even to ask such a question is to presuppose that it has been already answered (as literal or rhetorical), that we know *who* is asking the question (literally or rhetorically). For how can one ask, we ask, without knowing whether one asks or does not ask?[13] In other words, once the question of self-consciousness—the question of the double look back—has been decided in terms of literal and figurative, a shift, a turn, has taken place—one that threatens to make the question of the author's identity, the question of the "I" of the text, as undecidable as the Möbius band of Judgment and Being, being and expressing, recto and verso, one look back and an other. Again: the (rhetorical) question "How *can* I say: I! without self-consciousness?" can always be taken literally; it always contains its literalization within itself, and it can always be answered for example: I could say "I" on the stage (but, of course, without really saying it); I could read or write "I" as a copyist, scrivener, scribe, or whatever (but, of course, without really reading or writing it). So that to say "I" in another respect—in another look back of the "I" at the "I"—would be less like the look of Narcissus and more like the look back of Orpheus which, looking back, makes the self it wants to recover from death die again (and a double death at that). Or, better, like the look of Narcissus as read by Blanchot—dying of being *and* not being the other—with the look of Orpheus always already inscribed within it.[14] But that's easy for us to say. What does it mean to say "I" without really saying it? To answer this (rhetorical or not?) question one would have to reread Hölderlin's entire history. We begin by reading an exemplary (and parabolic) moment (and its aftermath) in that history in order to ask, again, what it means for the "I" to look back at the "I" in an other respect.

The Deaths of Empedocles

> Viel Täuschet Anfang/und Ende.
> —Hölderlin, "Einst hab' ich die Muse gefragt. . ."

Although Hölderlin never finished writing his drama *The Death of Empedocles*, his Empedocles returns to die over and over again in the readings of critics who would finish his tragedy and be done with the death of Empedocles.[15] Since reading the play entails not only assembling disparate fragments to make up a finished tragedy but also explaining why Hölderlin himself could not finish it, to dispose of Empedocles requires a complicated strategy: usually Empedocles and his (unfinished) death are identified as a turning point, and that turning point is inscribed in a series of narratives. In the case of the character Empedocles, it is a story of increasing insight into the necessity of his death: from the prereflective self-deification of the so-called first version to the self-conscious self-sacrifice of the so-called third version. In the case of Hölderlin's writing of the play's three versions, it is a story of his growing insight into the nature of tragedy and his final realization that he cannot make a tragedy out of Empedocles' suicide. And, finally, in the case of Hölderlin's career as a poet, the attempt to write the tragedy of Empedocles and its necessary failure are seen as an act of self-reflection that marks the transition from Hölderlin's early work to the mature late hymns, the *vaterländische Hymnen*. Although the relations among these three narratives may not be immediately clear, the story is the same: Empedocles, whether he be the name of a character or of an unfinished play in three versions or of a stage in Hölderlin's poetic history, is each time a turning of self-consciousness. This is what would make *The Death of Empedocles* "the tragedy of tragedy" or even, as Philippe Lacoue-Labarthe puts it in a recent essay, "the tragedy of the theory of tragedy: a work wishing to make itself absolute, in the very power it delegates to itself to reflect back upon itself and rise to the level of the Subject."[16] Now we should already be made a little uneasy by these analogies between the poet and his work, the poet and a character in his work, especially in the case of Hölderlin, who in the very essay that is supposed to mark his self-conscious turning upon his Empedocles project (the *Grund zum Empedokles*, supposedly written between the second and third versions of the play) states that "the tragic poet, because he expresses the deepest innerness, carries over his personality, his subjectivity, as well as the object present to him into a foreign personality, into a foreign objectivity."[17] Since the analogical thematic material (*Stoff*) into which the poet carries over his own subject/object relation is, according to the same essay, "a bolder, more foreign parable and example (*ein kühneres, fremderes Gleichnis und Beispiel*)," we should beware of making any hasty analogies before reading the strange parable and example of Hölderlin's Empedocles. Nevertheless, because even the most meticulous critics need to inscribe Empedocles into histories of self-consciousness, we must ask what it is about Empedocles, what it is about the *reading* of Empedocles' turning upon himself, that makes it necessary for us to assign him his place as the turning point in a narrative with a beginning, middle, and an end.

A good place to begin reading Empedocles and to approach the nature of his peculiar self-consciousness is the (purportedly) last (unfinished) scene Hölderlin wrote of the (purportedly) last version. Here the Egyptian seer (*Seher*) and Empedocles' former teacher Manes appears as though out of nowhere to challenge Empedocles in his resolution to take his life. To Manes's characterization of a "new Savior" (*der neue Retter*) whose suicide would be a justified sacrifice and to his insistent questions "Are you that man? The very same? Is that what you are? (*Bist du der Mann? derselbe? bist du diss?*)" Empedocles replies: "I know you in the dark word, and you/you all-knowing one, recognize me also (*Ich kenne dich im finstern Wort, und du,/Du Alleswissender, erkennst mich auch*)." But this assertion of knowledge is not enough for Manes, who demands that Empedocles *say* who he, Empedocles, is and who Manes is: "Oh say who you are! And who am I? (*O sage, wer du bist! und wer bin ich?*)." Empedocles says that he is indeed the new Savior, that he is who he is, by telling a story: what Hölderlin in his outline of the third version calls a "narrative of his history" (*Erzählung seiner Geschichte*). This story is one familiar not only to readers of Hölderlin but also to readers of romantic poetry. It is an autobiographical narrative telling the progress of his soul *from* the prereflective harmony of youth (*Ein Knabe war ich*) when he was at one with gods, men, and nature *through* the pain of separations caused by consciousness of others and consciousness of self *to* his recognition that his time and his people need a mediator whose self-sacrifice will simultaneously mark the dissolution of one epoch and the beginning of a new one. This is the same old story, and more important (for Empedocles, for Hölderlin, *and* for the reader) than its particulars is the act of reading Empedocles performs in order to tell it. Like Manes, we are less interested in *what* Empedocles says than in *how* he is able to say who he is. The "how" can be answered very quickly. Empedocles reads Manes by performing a certain literalization: in stating that he is indeed the new Savior, that he is who he is, Empedocles identifies himself with a character in a text. In short, he takes Manes literally. In doing so, he also has to take his past, his own story, literally, and this is explicit in his speech. His suicide will be the restoration of an original harmony, but with a difference:

whereas in youth life's enigma (*des Lebens Rätsel*) resolved itself for him in word and figure (*im Wort, im Bilde*), now he will find that which is living in death and no longer in image or figure (*nicht im Bilde mehr*). In other words, his sacrificial death will enable a *literal* possession of a state and a person (himself) that had previously been possessed only *figuratively*, and it is precisely the authority and the necessity of this literalization, this self-possession, that Manes comes to question. But we will not be able to find out what Manes *means* by his challenge and whether he is anyone to take literally merely from the content of his questions and Empedocles' response. In order to read this scene, it is necessary to play the role of Manes a little longer and read it *as* a scene of reading.

In this respect we get some help from the preceding scene, which explicitly sets the Manes-scene as a scene of reading. In addition, it drops some hints toward the identification of Manes, for it shows us Empedocles himself, in dialogue with his disciple Pausanias, playing the role that Manes will play in relation to him (Empedocles) in the last scene. If we begin to wonder "Who's who?" this may be no accident: at one point Pausanias begs Empedocles to "be who he is" (*Sei, der du bist*)—a master for a disciple, a father for a son—but Empedocles sends him off, saying "I am not who I am, Pausanias (*Ich bin nicht, der ich bin, Pausanias*)." In any case, the terms in which Empedocles challenges Pausanias and warns him against reading himself into a fate that is not his own (but Empedocles') are very much the terms that Manes uses in the last scene. He calls Pausanias "a foolish child" (*ein töricht Kind*) just as Manes says that "you Greeks are all children" to Empedocles; he puts Pausanias' discipleship in question by asking "How are you sure? (*Wie bist du sicher?*)"; and Pausanias says that Empedocles is "testing" him, that Empedocles speaks in riddles, and so on. But more important and more suggestive than these parallels is the final send-off wherein Empedocles, rather than giving the advice Pausanias wants, tells him to take an extraordinary trip: to Italy and Rome (*Italien. . . das Römerland*), the land of heroes and heroic martial feats; to Tarentum, where Empedocles once walked with his Plato (*einst mit meinem Plato ging*)—and then, Empedocles tells him, go to Athens itself and visit my old friend (Plato) there; and if your soul will still not rest, go ask in Egypt. "There they will open the book of fate for you./Go! Fear nothing! Everything returns./ And what should happen is already finished (*Dort öffnen sie das Buch des Schicksals dir./Geh! fürchte nichts! es kehret alles wieder./Und was geschehen soll, ist schon vollendet*)." Also sprach Empedokles. Now these parting words may be disconcerting for Pausanias—all we can be sure of is that he goes off (*Pausanias geht ab*)—but they are no less perplexing for us, especiallay since the uncanny figure of Manes appears directly after. Here is a Christian poet writing a tragedy about a pre-Christian, indeed pre-Socratic, hero who not only claims to be a Christlike Savior but sends his disciple off to a recognizably Imperial Rome and, in the same breath, to Plato.

In this quarrel both Ancients and Moderns get lost: everything returns, and with a vengeance. But if the Egyptian "book of fate" is a time machine as well as a space vehicle, we may get somewhere by following Empedocles' instructions for reading it. Since in the last scene Egypt in the figure of Manes comes to Empedocles, we have, finally, to ask: Who is Manes and what is his Egyptian wisdom?

Although he identifies himself (at length) in the last scene, Empedocles never does answer Manes's second question: "And who am *I*?" But if we follow his advice to Pausanias literally, as it were, and in fact go to Plato, we can go a long way toward identifying him and his story.[18] In Plato's *Timaeus*, a certain Critias tells of the tale that Solon brought with him from Egypt, where he discovered from the priests "that neither he nor any other Hellene knew anything worth mentioning about the times of old." Indeed, to make a long story short, when "on one occasion, wishing to draw them on to speak of antiquity, he began to tell about the most ancient things in our part of the world—about Phoroneus, who is called the 'first man,' and about Niobe, and after the Deluge, of the survival of Deucalion and Pyrrha, and he traced the genealogy of their descendants and. . .one of the priests, who was of a very great age, said, O Solon, Solon, you Hellenes are never anything but children, and there is not an old man among you."[19] Since these are the very words with which Manes scolds Empedocles and the Greeks, it may be worthwhile to find out what the Egyptian means by them. Unlike the Greeks, the Egyptians know that there were many destructions and many catastrophes arising out of many causes and that, indeed, where the Greeks now live other civilizations had risen, had flourished, and had perished many times over. According to the priest, the reason the Egyptians know this is that they have written down everything of note, preserved it in their temples, and no natural calamities have intervened to efface these memories. "Whereas," he says to Solon, "just when you and other nations are beginning to be provided with letters and the other requisites of civilized life, after the usual interval, the stream from heaven, like a pestilence, comes pouring down and leaves only those of you who are destitute of letters and education, and so you have to begin all over again like children, and know nothing of what happened in ancient times, either among us or among yourselves." In other words, what Solon thinks is a history with an origin, a development, and an end, what he thinks is a genealogy traceable to the first man, is actually a story that has been repeated many times and is more allegory than history. It is a story of inscriptions and effacements rather than a genetic history: more like the relationship between text and text than like the relationship between father and son. If we take this "allegorical vision" as the meaning of the seer's challenge to Empedocles' "historical vision," Empedocles' reading the book of fate (and the fate of the reader) comes into better focus. In identifying himself with a character (i.e., the new Savior) in Manes's text,

Empedocles tries to read himself into a text that does not allow for such a *self-inscription* (i.e., does not allow him to recognize himself in it *as* a self, but rather turns him into a text, a sign, an allegorical figure). Precisely at the moment when Empedocles thinks he will know the gods, men, nature, and himself no longer in image or figure (*nicht im Bilde mehr*), he knows *most* in figure and *becomes* a figure himself: that is, his narrative, which turns into an allegory of his inability to read himself (except, again [and again], as an allegory of unreadability). At the moment he reads himself best, he reads himself neither *as* a self nor as his own other but as a text that is for him radically unreadable because radically foreign: "A bolder, more foreign parable and example (*ein kühneres, fremderes Gleichnis und Beispiel*)."

Here we could come to an abrupt end and cut off further discussion by saying that Hölderlin could not finish his tragedy on account of this allegorical Egyptian insight, that in Manes he had created an opponent too strong for Empedocles, that the play founders—*scheitern* is the favorite German word to use at this point—from an excess of (ultimately sterile) self-consciousness. But such an end would be premature: it would be jumping to hasty analogies as well as to hasty conclusions. If the relation between Empedocles and Manes is a representation of the relation between the Greeks and that which is "national" (*das Nationelle*), "proper" (*das Eigene*), and "original" (*ursprünglich*) *for them*—to use the terms of the well-known "Böhlendorff-Brief"—this is no guarantee that the relation between Hölderlin, a "Hesperian" poet, and that which is national, proper, and original *for him*—that is, the Greeks, Greek *art*—is of the same order.[20] Perhaps we can go still further in identifying Empedocles, Manes, and their respective deaths, and thereby end up somewhat closer to home (than Egypt?). For, indeed, if Manes can be said to have the last word, as it were, it is only in a certain sense. For one thing, his Egyptian wisdom does not free him from the necessity of misreading and literalization. When Empedocles mocks Manes's powerlessless to heal his (Empedocles') spirit and challenges Manes's vision, all Manes can do is try to reimpose the father/son, master/disciple, relationship that his own teaching has made impossible: "Let us be still, son! And always learn (*Lass still uns sein, O Sohn! und immer lernen*)," he says, as though there were an internal necessity of literalization in the story that he tells, as though the catastrophes of effacement did not come from outside like floods and conflagrations but were (always already) inscribed in the book of fate. Like the good disciple he is, Empedocles replies by turning the tables: "You taught me, today you learn from me (*Du lehrtest mich, heut lerne du von mir*)." That a reversal indeed takes place and that Manes in fact becomes a disciple and reader of Empedocles is clear from a note Hölderlin wrote in notes for the unwritten fifth act: after Empedocles' death, Manes says Empedocles was indeed "the one who was called, who kills and gives life, in whom and through whom a world simultaneously destroys and renews itself (*der Berufene, der töte und belebe, in dem und durch den eine Welt sich zugleich auflöse und erneue*)." The next day, continues the note, he will proclaim what "the last will" (*der letzte Wille*) of Empedocles was. According to the executor of Empedocles' last will and testament, then, Empedocles has his own wisdom, whose unhappy science can be summarized in the one word "action": that is, Empedocles, precisely because he is *willing* to take Manes literally—"You will it, and so be it (*Du willst es, und so sei's*)," says Manes—is capable of action. That action may only be suicide, but, in the terms of the play, it is action *par excellence*, for it marks the transition, indeed, it is the condition of possibility for a transition from one world and one time to another world and another time—simultaneously radical forgetting and radical remembering. Empedocles' willingness to take Manes literally makes him a profoundly *historical* figure, for it is the catastrophic action that *founds* history, that makes it possible to distinguish periods of decline from periods of renewal, to trace genealogies, to recognize son in father and father in son, and so on. We could say—to continue reading the play's "own" metaphor—that rather than being just a misreader of Manes's book of fate, Empedocles *becomes* the book "itself": he becomes the (sacrificial) surface on which and through which the inscriptions and effacements of the history of his people take place.

This thematization in the play of the contradiction between the impossibility and the necessity of action is what makes Empedocles a properly tragic hero and what makes the Empedocles material, contrary to the assertions of many commentators, a properly tragic theme. It is also what brings Hölderlin's tragedy close to the Greeks, in particular the dramas of Sophocles. Manes, for instance, has been recognized as a Tiresiaslike figure, and there are many parallels between the scenes in which Oedipus and Empedocles confront their respective seers and (mis)read their respective fates. The most important parallel is that both scenes contrast a historical hero whose unselfconscious, literalizing knowledge makes him capable of action (and therefore tragedy) and a seer whose allegorically self-conscious vision not only makes him incapable of action but also prevents his knowledge from being of any use to anyone. Your knowledge is for the birds, Oedipus tells Tiresias, for when the riddling Sphinx came to your country you were unable to speak the word of deliverance, when it was, after all, clearly a prophet's task. "But I came, Oedipus, who knew nothing, and I stopped her./I solved the riddle by my wit (*gnōmē*) alone."[21] Just as Oedipus is the literalist who is nevertheless (or rather who is therefore) able to read the riddle of the Sphinx by saying "Man," so is Empedocles the literalist who is nevertheless (or rather who is therefore) able to read the riddle of the Egyptian book of fate by saying "I." That both (self-)recognitions and (self-)identifications bring along with themselves a necessary blindness is history. In any case, to say that Manes is right or that Empedocles is the name of a dead end that Hölderlin had to turn from would be like saying that Tiresias is proved to be right and that Oedipus was a "stage" in Sophocles' dramatic career. It would be, once again, to take literally what is only a figure and a moment in a play. And just because *The Death of Empedocles* is ostensibly unfinished does not mean that we must take it as the beginning of the end. Perhaps if we follow the fate of Tiresias in Hölderlin's writings a little further, we will be able to read the Manes scene not according to "impressions" (*Eindrücke*) but according to what Hölderlin in the late "Notes to Oedipus" calls "lawful calculation" (*der gesetzliche Kalkül*). A reading of this law and its calculation may help us finally identify the Manes scene *as* (tragic) scene, for, according to Hölderlin's notes, Tiresias or rather the speeches of Tiresias (*die Reden des Tiresias*) are essential to the working of the law of tragedy; indeed, in the case of Sophocles' *Oedipus* and *Antigone* they are what holds the plays together from beginning to end in that they make up the "caesura" (*die Zäsur*) of the tragedies.

Caesura: Hölderlin and the Egyptians

What Hölderlin means by "caesura" is a very peculiar "cutting off," for it is an interruption that, in brief, allows the tragedy to continue.[22] That is, since "the law" (*das Gesetz*), "the calculation" (*der Kalkül*), of the tragic lies more in the "balance" (*Gleichgewicht*) than in the "pure succession" (*reine Aufeinanderfolge*) of representations, an "anti-rhythmical interruption" (*gegenrhytmische Unterbrechung*) is necessary: it is what Hölderlin calls "the pure word" (*das reine Wort*), what in prosody is called caesura. This caesura, this pure word, has two functions, both of them crucial for an understanding not only of Hölderlin's readings of Sophocles but also for our understanding of the Manes scene. First of all, the interruption of the caesura marks the place where the succession and alternation of representations (*Wechsel der Vorstellungen*) in the tragedy—of plot, character, action, let us say—are cut off and where "representation itself appears (*die Vorstellung selber erscheint*)." In other words, like the Manes scene, the caesura is the place where the tragedy explicitly turns upon itself, where, in short, representation represents itself *as* representation. That this turning is not the reflection of a Subject (absolute or otherwise) but rather of a text is clear from Hölderlin's using explicitly linguistic terms to name it: that is, caesura, the pure word.[23] Indeed, rather than allowing the human subject to recognize himself in his own other, the caesura rips him out of his own sphere of life, out of the center of his own inner life, and carries him off into an other world and tears him into the eccentric sphere of the dead (*den Menschen. . . in eine andere Welt entrückt und in die exzentrische Sphäre der Toten reisst*). The second function of the caesura is that it protects one half of the tragedy from the other half (*so dass die erste Hälfte gleichsam gegen die zweite geschützt ist*), or, better, the beginning from the end

or vice versa. If the rhythm of the representations, for example, is such that the representations at the beginning of the tragedy are in danger of being over-whelmed (*hingerissen*) by those that follow, then the caesura, the antirhythmical interruption, comes toward the beginning, as is the case with the Tiresias scene in Sophocles' *Oedipus*. If we read the Manes scene from the point of view of these, some of Hölderlin's last, reflections upon tragedy—that is, as the scene in which the tragedy turns upon itself as representation and which is supposed to protect the tragedy's beginning from its (unwritten) end—a couple of particularly appropriate ironies become apparent. For one, the Manes scene, while carrying off Empedocles and his reader into an other world and into the eccentric sphere of the dead, would at the same time mark the return of that which is most original, most his own, for the Hesperian poet: that is, the Greeks and the problem of their imitation, Oedipus, father/son genealogies, and so on. Precisely where we should be farthest away, we are closest to home, and Empedocles has an Oedipus complex. For another—irony, that is—rather than *protecting* the beginning of Hölderlin's tragedy against its end, the caesura cuts the play off—indeed, the caesura cuts itself off—and, if anything, makes the "end" arrive too soon. We can shake our heads here (and books on Empedocles have been filled with such headshak-ing) and say "that's what happens when you try to be more Greek than the Greeks," but we should remember that even (and especially) caesuras (or, for that matter, "fragments") should not be taken literally (and that Hölderlin is always a few steps ahead of anyone else, particularly in his readings of the Greek tragedies). For perhaps when the (first) Böhlendorff letter says that "the *free* use of that which is *our own* [i.e., the Greeks, Greek *art*] is that which is most difficult (*der* freie *Gebrauch des Eigenen das schwerste ist*)," it means precisely *such* a return of the Greeks.[24] And perhaps the only tragic heroes a Hesperian (i.e., Christian) poet can create are pre-Socratic Greeks who have read Plato and perform an *imitatio Christi*. As far as the second irony is con-cerned, why should we take the "end" of the tragedy of Empedocles all that literally? Perhaps the effaced, unwritten end of the tragedy reinscribes itself in the speaking silence of Hölderlin's late hymns or in the monstrous translations of Sophocles (which would open the possibility that, at least in Hölderlin's work, Oedipus, like all (mis)readers, has an Empedocles complex)[25]—or even in the "final" caesura of Hölderlin's madness, whose silence also left traces. But lest we get carried off or carried away by this proliferation of endings, we would do better to remember that it is precisely the impossibility and the necessity of such analogies that is thematized in the Hölderlinian caesura. Although the caesura may be found everywhere in Hölderlin's text, its reading, its bridging by analogy, is always violent and always extorts a death *of* the reader: whether that death be put as a self-blinding or a long-deferred jump into a volcano. We are left, then, if not exactly with Empedocles' bronze slip-pers, with a trace resembling them: a caesura, a pure word, an antirhythmical interruption, which we can take neither literally nor figuratively—because it founds (and confounds) the difference between literal and figurative senses just as it founds (and confounds) history—and yet which we have to *keep* taking as both. But rather than ending with the many regrets and the pathos of undecidability, we would go back to the original version of Empedocles' final advice to Pausanias—the effaced or at least crossed-out lines over which Hölderlin inscribed the book of fate—and take them as instructions for us the readers: "There [i.e., in Egypt] much will become clear for you and great/And that we mortals, such as we stand/Before our very eyes (*Und dass wir Sterblichen, so wie wir* [*uns*]/*Vor Augen stehn*),/are only signs and figures (*nur Zeichen sind und Bilder*)/That you will nevermore regret! ([*Das*] *wirst du nimmermehr bedauern, lieber!*)" (4:671).

But how do we go to Egypt? How can we read the signs and figures that we ourselves are with no regrets? No doubt the question is analogous to asking (in an other respect): "How can I say: I! without self-consciousness?" Rather than answering—as though we could answer and as though we had not already answered—we would make two brief (we hope not too cryptic) suggestions toward a rereading of (particularly the late) Hölderlin. First, we return to Pausanias and his trip to Egypt, or, better, his return *from* Egypt. For what happens in the blank, the caesura, between the second scene and the Manes scene, between Pausanias's abrupt departure and Manes's equally abrupt return, is the detour through Rome, Greece (i.e., Plato), and Egypt; and Manes is, after all (or first of all?), only Pausanias come back from Egypt: the disciple become master, the master become disciple.[26] But if we can allegorize the three figures in terms of the first letter to Böhlendorff—with Manes representing the Orient (i.e., that which is proper, their own, original, *natural*, for the Greeks), Empedocles representing the Greeks (i.e., that which is proper, our own, original, *natural*, for us the Hesperians), and Pausanias representing us the Hesperians (i.e., that which is proper, their own, original, *natural*, for whom?)—then the uncanny return of Pausanias in the guise of Manes (and Manes in the guise of Pausanias) points to an impossible and yet inevitable (and inevitably catastrophic) identification of (or [impossible] analogy between) Egypt and Hesperia. In short, to put it as brusquely as possible, *we are the Egyptians*:[27] that is, in the terms of the first letter to Böhlendorff, the relation between nature and culture for us and the relation between nature and culture for the Egyptians is the same. For the Greeks, nature was the Oriental "fire from heaven," the "holy pathos," and culture (i.e., their art) was "Junonian sobriety," "the clarity of representation." For us, the Hesperians, according to Hölderlin, nature is precisely Greek art (i.e., Greek culture): "Junonian sobriety," "the clarity of representation." The implications are as follows: that for us (as well as for the Egyptians), culture, art, is the "fire from heaven," "holy pathos," and, to fill in the other blank, that for the Egyptians (as for us), nature is "Junonian sobriety," "the clarity of representation." Rather than a linear historical progression from Orient (i.e., Egypt) through Greece to Hesperia, this series of relations is read best in terms of chiasmic reversals that could be schematized as ˙in the accompanying diagram. In other words, the

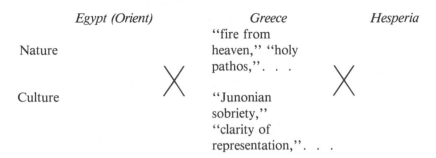

	Egypt (Orient)	Greece	Hesperia
Nature		"fire from heaven," "holy pathos,". . .	
Culture		"Junonian sobriety," "clarity of representation,". . .	

relation between the Egyptians and us is not any kind of dialectical process (or progress) from Orient to Hesperia, but rather more like, again, the "two" sides of a Möbius band—a non*orient*able surface.[28] But the problem is that we can never really, literally, say that "we are the Egyptians" without losing our orientation on this Möbius band of history altogether. In order to orient ourselves—(1) "to cause to face the east," (2) "to align or position with respect to a reference system"—we always look back at Egyptian culture and art through Greek eyes, we always reinvent Greek culture and art as a caesura, a cutting, on the Möbius band. We reinvent this Greece—that could never have been invented in the first place—not only to orient ourselves but also perhaps with a certain dark suspicion (not unlike Empedocles' reading of Manes's dark word, i.e., his suicide) that if we could ever really, literally, say that there were never any Greeks, we might have to admit that there were never any Egyptians either.[29]

To end on a less prophetic note, however—lest we take Empedocles' travel advice and make our (impossible) trip to Egypt too literally—it would be better to make the second suggestion toward a rereading of the late hymns. For such a rereading becomes necessary once we take Hölderlin's philosophy of history (understood as a textual history, a history of readings and rereadings) into account. What is wrong with most interpretations of Hölderlin's late hymns is that they are, in a sense, *too Greek* (whether they discover a late turning toward or away from Greece, toward or away from Hesperia). No matter how dialectically agile, they are all ultimately based on a reification, fetishization, better, *literalization* of the poems' "nature." Sooner or later these interpretations forget that our (Hesperian) nature is someone else's culture and art, that our (Greek, mimetic) representation of nature is just that: a representation, and insofar as it is a representation it is no more reliable or stable a ground than any other literalization.[30] Hence a rereading requires not only a reorientation but a "reorientalization"—a reallegorization[31]—of Hölderlin's Hesperian hymns and of us his Hesperian readers so that the returning of the late hymns may be seen in a different light (or, better, *read* in the black light of allegory). And yet the literalizations of the interpreters are not an aberration that comes from outside to disfigure Hölderlin's text but rather a necessity inscribed in the language of the late hymns, for these hymns are all, one could say, written in caesuras: they are all spoken by Manes/Pausanias (and Pausanias/Manes) and they are all turned toward Empedocles.[32] In other words, the late hymns name a place and a moment that could be understood as simultaneously pre- *and* post-reflective, and their language could be understood as simultaneously absolutely self-opaque and absolutely self-transparent (as long, of course, as we take all these words as *figures* to be read, for what the hymns name is a "placeless place" and a "momentless moment," and the "simultaneity" of their language's self-opacity *and* self-transparency is not any kind of unmediated or mediated presence-to-self but rather always the same return of the other in the same that nevertheless is never the other *of* the same, etc.—again, the impossible present of the caesura, what could be called the simulacrum of presence). In short, we could collapse Hölderlin's characterization of the "caesura" and Empedocles' characterization of Manes's speech, and say that the language of the late hymns is simultaneously "the pure word" (*das reine Wort*)—that is, purely word, nothing but word, nothing but language—and thereby necessarily also "the dark word" (*das finstere Wort*).

It is no wonder, then, that to interpret such a (radically self-divided) language means to literalize it: to take either the pre- or the post-reflective moment, either the self-opacity or the self-transparency of the language, as the meaning—or, at best, to take *both* of them (dialectically mediated in a history of self-consciousness) as the meaning. For, after all, really to *read* the caesura, to turn toward Empedocles—as disciple or as master, as disciple *and* as master, as both *and* as neither—would mean to turn toward a corpse, a ghost, a *revenant jamais venu*, or the like; it would require a vigil over a double death, over a sense doubly absent—always not yet come and always already gone. But perhaps it would be better not to belabor the "caesura," for like other (non)concepts of this sort—in the context of Hölderlin readings: like Heidegger's *Zwischen* (In-between), say, or Adorno's "parataxis"—the caesura is no master-word or slogan. Once one has found it, it is no great exploit to discover it everywhere in Hölderlin's work; henceforth the difficulty is to forget it.[33] But how do we forget this corpse, ghost, or *revenant*, this empty pyramid or empty tomb? How do we maintain a vigil over the absent sense? In a sense, all we need do is to follow Hölderlin, for the late hymns not only pose the "same" questions but also "answer" them by re-allegorizing Empedocles as Christ—or had Empedocles always already/always not yet been a Christ allegory?—and turning him into a "new Savior" who would, again, lead us out of Egypt.[34]

And just as the language that named the caesura was spoken simultaneously by Manes and Pausanias, Pausanias and Manes—the words "simultaneously" and "and" to be read as slashes, as marks of the caesura, and the word "spoken" to be read as a figure for "read and written"—so is the language that names this Savior spoken simultaneously by precursor and disciple, John the Baptist and John the Apostle (with John of Patmos figuring the impossible "synthesis" of the two).[35] It is what we would call a "parabolic" language, and it would require an analogously "parabolic" reading to follow it by maintaining a vigil over its doubly absent sense. "*Veillons sur le sens absent.*"[36]

Before returning to this doubly absent sense, in the following two chapters we will take a detour through its two philosophically most rigorous interpretations. The first is Peter Szondi's Hegelian interpretation; it has particular bearing on our first remark regarding Hölderlin's historical scheme. The second is Martin Heidegger's interpretation; it has particular bearing on our second remark regarding the rereading of the late hymns. As interpretations, both are, in a sense, too Greek. How do they (not) read the Egyptians in Hölderlin's work?

Chapter 2
Hölderlin in France

Ach, es sei die letzte meiner Tränen,
Die dem heil'gen Griechenlande rann,
Lasst, o Parzen, lasst die Schere tönen!
Denn mein Herz gehört den Toten an.
—"Griechenland" (1793)

In *The Tyranny of Greece over Germany*, E. M. Butler's chapter on Hölderlin begins, appropriately enough, with a long story of Hölderlin in France:

At the very beginning of the nineteenth century a girl of fourteen or so, who was later to become madame de S——y, was living very happily with her father in their castle near Blois. It was surrounded by a magnificent park in which was a great marble water-basin enclosed by a high balustrade. On this balustrade were ranged twenty-four statues of the greater and lesser Greek gods. One day the girl and her father, looking from an upper window, saw a sad and shabby stranger wandering aimlessly through the park. He caught sight of the statues and his whole demeanour changed. Approaching them enthusiastically, he lifted up his arms as if in worship and seemed, as far as they could tell, to be invoking them with words. Wondering who and what he might be, they came down to accost him. The girl found herself looking into a pair of dreaming, mournful eyes which she never forgot, any more than the strange things he said to her father:

"This water should be clearer, like the water of Cephissus or the spring of Erechtheus on the Acropolis. It is not worthy of the clear gods to be reflected in a darker mirror—but," he added with a sigh, "we are not in Greece."

"Are *you* a Greek?" questioned the count, only half in earnest.

"No, on the contrary, I am a German," and again the stranger sighed.

"On the contrary? Is the German the opposite of the Greek?"

"Yes," said the German shortly, and he added after a pause: "But

23

then we all are; you, the Frenchman as well; and your enemy the
Englishman too—all of us."
They begged him to accept their hospitality, and he entered the
castle, obviously in the last stages of exhaustion. Later they engaged
him in a conversation which, owing to the promptings of the young
girl's aunt, soon came to metaphysical subjects and the stranger began
to speak about immortality. "The beautiful gods of Greece are images
of the beautiful thoughts of a whole people," he concluded; "that is
immortality." "And are you too immortal in this way?" asked the
girl's aunt; for somehow they all felt curiously impressed by him.
"I?" he answered harshly: "I? The man who is sitting here now?
No indeed. My thoughts are no longer beautiful. But the I that was
mine nine years ago, that is immortal certainly." And after a pause
during which he seemed to reflect he repeated: "Yes, certainly, that I
is immortal." He could not or would not tell them his name, saying
with his head buried in his hands that he would do so tomorrow, but
that sometimes it was too hard to remember. He was easily persuaded
to stay over night; but after a terrifying outburst of insanity in the
small hours of the morning, he disappeared in a deep state of
depression next day.
This story was told by Madame de S——y to the journalist Moritz
Hartmann in 1852. It may or may not be apocryphal. It was probably
written up a good deal; but unless it is pure invention from beginning
to end, the hero was certainly Hölderlin. He was wandering half
demented through France in the summer of 1802; and even supposing
that some other countryman of his was in the same plight at the same
time, no one but the unhappy Hölderlin would have spoken as this
stranger did about the gods of Greece.[1]

Apocryphal or not—"1. Of questionable authorship or authenticity.
2. False; counterfeit" from Greek *apokruptein*, to hide away; *apo-* away +
kruptein, to hide[2]—this story is perfectly appropriate because it contains all the
received ideas that make up the myth of Germany's and Hölderlin's
Graecomania. For we get not only a pathos-ridden version of our modern,
sentimental, Schillerian alienation from and nostalgia for Greece and the
beautiful gods of Greece, but also the spectacle of a half-demented German
enthusing over cheap imitations of Greek sculpture—like some parody of Winckelmann in Rome. Indeed, if we believe E. M. Butler's book—and do not read
the texts—we would have to say that *any* German beside Hölderlin, any non-
Greek or any "Hesperian," if he would not have spoken quite as this stranger
did about the gods of Greece, he could nevertheless have told, would nevertheless have had to tell, *this* story, for it is a veritable allegory of how *one*
speaks about the Greeks and the Germans, Greece and Hesperia, Greek art and
Hölderlin's poetry. In other words, if this story were not "true," one would
have to invent it: that is, to invent a certain Greece and a certain Greek art, in

short, to invent the category of the aesthetic *as* Greek and the Greeks *as* the aesthetic moment in what is called the history of the West. So resilient and so persuasive is this invention of the Greeks that it is mechanically reinvented over and over again to serve as the point of reference for an interpretation of even those thinkers and poets who, like Hölderlin, do the most to undo and disarticulate this scheme and its ideology. Why this should be and what is the nature of its necessity are the questions that constitute the burden of our reading Hölderlin in France—a France that, according to Hölderlin's second letter to Böhlendorff (November 1802), which he wrote from his home town of Nürtingen upon his return from Bordeaux, allows him, oddly enough, better to understand the Greeks: "The athletic character of the southern peoples, in the ruins of the ancient spirit, made me more familiar with the character of the Greeks (*Das Athletische der südlichen Menschen, in den Ruinen des antiken Geistes, machte mich mit dem eigentlichen Wesen der Griechen bekannter*)" (6:432).[3]

The biographical details of Hölderlin's journey to and return from France are curious enough: he crosses the border at Strasbourg (where he is detained two weeks as a suspicious foreigner); he travels mostly on foot and by way of Lyon to Bordeaux, where he serves for a few months as tutor in the home of a German consul; and then, disappearing inexplicably, he travels on foot and probably by way of Paris back to Germany, where he arrives in a severely distraught and disturbed state (to find, among other things, that his "Diotima," Suzette Gontard, has died). But even though we know very little (aside from "apocrypha" like the above) about the "facts" of this episode of going over and returning—if not exactly to Greece, at least to the ruins of her spirit—its importance for an understanding of Hölderlin's work becomes clear once we take into account its *textual* frame. In a broader sense, the "before" of this frame consists of Hölderlin's so-called Homburg writings: the theoretical, "poetological" fragments (on the poetic process, a systematic theory of genre, the theory of the alternation of tones, etc.); the failed attempts to write the tragedy of Empedocles; and, directly before Hölderlin's departure for France in December 1801, a few completed and some only drafted versions of the late hymns, the so-called *vaterländische Hymnen*. The "after" of this frame consists of the completion of a number of these hymns (including some of the greatest, e.g., "Patmos") and the translations of Sophocles, accompanied by the maddeningly difficult "Notes to Oedipus" and "Notes to Antigone." A narrower and neater textual frame for the trip to France is provided by the two letters Hölderlin wrote to Böhlendorff: one directly before (4 December 1801) his departure and one shortly after his return (November 1802). The first letter is Hölderlin's most explicit and most complete statement about the relation between Greece and Hesperia, especially as it pertains to the (Greek in contradistinction to the Hesperian) poet's task. The second letter contains not only the remarks about Hölderlin's new familiarity with the Greeks but also some lines that are taken as evidence for his turning away from Greece and Greek art back to Hesperia and the *Vaterland*—that is, Hölderlin's so-called *abendländische Wendung* or *vaterländische Umkehr*: "Dear friend, I think we shall not gloss the poets up to our time, but that song altogether will assume a different character, and that we cannot make ourselves heard because we, after the Greeks, are beginning once more to sing nationally and naturally, that is, in a truly original way (*Mein Lieber! ich denke, dass wir die Dichter bis auf unsere Zeit nicht commentiren werden, sondern dass die Sangart überhaupt wird eienen andern Karakter nehmen, und dass wir darum nicht aufkommen, weil wir, seit den Griechen, wieder anfangen, vaterländisch und natürlich, eigentlich originell zu singen)*" (6:433). For all its would-be turning away from Greece—and for all its turning away from reading the manifest difficulty of these letters—such an interpretation nevertheless needs to reinvent that Greece if only as the opposite of us Hesperians. Whether we conceive of this Greece as something to turn away from or feel nostalgic about or whose absence we would mourn hardly makes a difference as long as we identify ourselves as Hesperians (like the hero of Madam de S——y's apocryphal story) in opposition to or as the negation of the Greeks. For such (albeit negative) self-identification always entails seeing ourselves from the Greek point of view, as it were, and defining our poetry on the basis of a Greek, mimetic, aesthetic model. It means, in short, to define our "sentimental," "romantic," *poetry* in terms of "naive," "classical," *art*. In the scheme of such an interpretation, it is once again the positing of the Greeks as *the* aesthetic moment that allows us to ground Hölderlin's poetics in his philosophy of history—to reconcile his poetics with what is taken to be his hermeneutics[4]—and thereby to make (historical) sense of Hölderlin's late lyrics and his project of translating and rewriting the tragedies of Sophocles. No matter to whom they are addressed, the ultimate destination of Hölderlin's letters to Böhlendorff turns out to be Greece, just as there is no coming home for Hölderlin or for his poetic destiny except to Greece—to her beautiful art and her beautiful gods, no matter how dead they may be.

But just as Hölderlin never quite comes home, the letters to Böhlendorff never quite arrive at their destination: the status of both addressor and addressee is problematic. The Greek, aesthetic and aestheticizing, interpretation of Hölderlin would do well to take a hint from the biographical details, which, as always with a poet whose life was as much a text as anything he wrote on paper, are instructive. Böhlendorff, whom Hölderlin met in Homburg in 1799, was a failed poet and dramatist who was unable to settle down professionally in Jena, Dresden, Bremen, or Berlin; who returned home in 1803, mentally disturbed (*geistig gestört*), as one says; and who after some years of unstable wandering ended his life by suicide. His biographer sums him up as a "wrecked idealist" (or "an idealist who foundered," *ein gescheiterter Idealist*).[5] In brief,

Böhlendorff is something like Hölderlin's weird shadow-self or double, and the two letters Hölderlin addressed to him could as well have been addressed to "himself." But he who would receive these letters—he who is well on the way to becoming "Scardanelli or Buonarotti or something like that" (as Hölderlin called himself after 1806)—is certainly not much of a self, just as the addressor Hölderlin who returns from his trip to France and to the ruins of the Greek spirit (only to find Diotima dead) does not return to his selfsame self. The fear of losing his head "in France, in Paris" (*Ich werde den Kopf ziemlich beisammenhalten müssen, in Frankreich, in Paris*), which Hölderlin expresses in the first letter to Böhlendorff, would certainly seem to have been justified. And the second letter to Böhlendorff confirms this: "The mighty element, the fire of heaven and the silence of the people, their life in nature, their confinedness and their contentment, moved me continually, and as one says of heroes, I can well say of myself that Apollo has struck me (*Das gewaltige Element, das Feuer des Himmels und die Stille der Menschen, ihr Leben in der Natur, und ihre Eingeschränktheit und Zufriedenheit, hat mich beständig ergriffen, und wie man Helden nachspricht, kann ich wohl sagen, dass mich Apollo geschlagen*)" (6:432). But these biographical details are only symptoms. Before deciding what they are symptoms of and before consigning these letters to the Dead Letter Office of psychopathology—"Hölderlin's madness," say—we would do better to determine the sense in which they can be neither delivered nor returned. We must examine the nature of the postal system, as it were, and in the case of Hölderlin's first letter to Böhlendorff this means reading more precisely the nature of the text's articulation of Greece with Hesperia. That it is indeed a question of a problematic articulation is clear from even cursory perusal of the letter, and it is difficult to understand how one could have ever interpreted this letter in terms of any simple turning—away from or toward Greece, to Greece or to an anti-Greece. Hölderlin begins by complimenting his friend's play (*Fernando*) and uses it as a pretext for an interpretation of Greek nature and our nature insofar as it bears on the predicament of the poet. It is worth quoting the crucial passages in full as much for what they do *not* say as for what they do:

> My friend! You have gained much in precision and in capable suppleness without having lost anything in warmth. On the contrary, like a good sword, the elasticity of your spirit has proved itself to be all the stronger in the school of constraint. This is what I congratulate you for above all. We learn nothing with more difficulty than to use freely that which is national. And I believe that it is precisely the clarity of representation that is originally as natural for us as the fire from heaven is for the Greeks. Precisely for this reason they will be more easily *surpassed* in beautiful passion, which you have also taken for yourself, than in that Homeric presence of spirit and gift of representation.

It sounds paradoxical. But I repeat it and leave it free for your examination and your use: in the progress of cultural formation (*Bildung*), the properly national will always be the lesser advantage. For this reason the Greeks are less masters of the holy pathos, because it was inborn for them, while on the other hand they are superior in the gift of representation from Homer on because this extraordinary man was soulful enough to capture for his Apollinian realm the occidental *Junonian sobriety* and thereby truly to appropriate that which is foreign.

For us it's the reverse. This is also why it is so dangerous to deduce the laws of artistic creation (*Kunstregeln*) solely and only from Greek splendor. I have labored long on it and know now that aside from that which has to be the highest for the Greeks and for us, namely the living relation and the skill (*Geschick*), we ought not to have anything *in common* with them.

But that which is one's own has to be learned just as well as that which is foreign. For this reason the Greeks are indispensable for us. Only we will not catch up to them precisely in that which is our own, national for us, because, as I said, the *free* use of *that which is one's own* [that which is proper, *das Eigene]* is the most difficult.

Mein Lieber! Du hast an Präzision und tüchtiger Gelenksamkeit so sehr gewonnen und nichts an Wärme verloren, im Gegentheil, wie eine gute Klinge, hat sich die Elastizität Deines Geistes in der beugenden Schule nur um so kräftiger erwiesen. Diss ists wozu ich Dir vorzüglich Glük wünsche. Wir lernen nichts schwerer als das Nationelle frei gebrauchen. Und wie ich glaube, ist gerade die Klarheit der Darstellung uns ursprünglich so natürlich wie den Griechen das Feuer vom Himmel. Eben desswegen werden diese eher in schöner Leidenschaft, die Du Dir auch erhalten hast, als in jener homerischen Geistesgegenwart und Darstellungsgaabe zu übertreffen seyn.

Es klingt paradox. Aber ich behaupt' es noch einmal, und stelle es Deiner Prüfung und Deinem Gebrauche frei; das eigentliche nationelle wird im Fortschritt der Bildung immer der geringere Vorzug werden. Desswegen sind die Griechen des heiligen Pathos weniger Meister, weil es ihnen angeboren war, hingegen sind sie vorzüglich in Darstellungsgaabe, von Homer an, weil dieser ausserordentliche Mensch seelenvoll genug war, um die abendländische Junonische Nüchternheit *für sein Apollonsreich zu erbeuten, und so wahrhaft das fremde sich anzueignen.*

Bei uns ists umgekehrt. Desswegen ists auch so gefährlich sich die Kunstregeln einzig und allein von griechischer Vortreflichkeit zu abstrahiren. Ich habe lange daran laborirt und weiss nun dass ausser dem, was bei den Griechen und uns das höchste seyn muss, nemlich dem lebendigen Verhältniss und Geschik, wir nicht wohl etwas gleich mit ihnen haben dürfen.

Aber das eigene muss so gut gelernt seyn, wie das Fremde.
Desswegen sind uns die Griechen unentbehrlich. Nur werden wir ihnen
gerade in unserm Eigenen, Nationellen nicht nachkommen, weil, wie
gesagt, der freie *Gebrauch des* Eigenen *das schwerste ist.* (6:425-26)

Although the letter certainly takes its origin from the *querelle des anciens et des modernes*, which continues in various guises in German thought of the latter half of the eighteenth century, it radically complicates the terms and stakes of that quarrel by introducing a doubleness into its adversaries. Both the Greeks and we are divided in terms of a distinction that for shorthand purposes may as well be called "nature" and "culture." That is, Greek nature—that which is "natural," "national," "original," "proper," "their own," *das Eigene*, for them—is "the fire from heaven" and "holy pathos." Greek culture—that which they had to appropriate, capture, booty, because it was *not* inborn but foreign (*das Fremde*) for them—is "the clarity of representation" and "Junonian sobriety." Our (Hesperian) nature, however—that which is natural, national, original, proper, *das Eigene*, for us—is precisely the (Greek) "clarity of representation" and "Junonian sobriety," whereas our culture—that which we have to appropriate because it is *not* our own but foreign (*das Fremde*) for us—is "the fire from heaven" and "holy pathos." In other words, there is a (chiasmic) reversal in the relation of nature and culture, that which is proper or one's own and that which is foreign, *das Eigene* and *das Fremde*, between the Greeks and us: what is *das Eigene* there is *das Fremde* here, and what is *das Fremde* there is *das Eigene* here. Both the doubleness (of *das Eigene* and *das Fremde*) and the reversal—"For us, it's the reverse (*Bei uns ist's umgekehrt*)"—are explicit. Now it is precisely on account of this doubleness that our relation (as poets) to the Greeks must also be double. On the one hand, we cannot simply imitate the Greeks, for rather than being nature, their culture is the reaction or response to a nature. It does indeed sound paradoxical, as Hölderlin notes, but it is rigorously consistent: precisely because the Greeks—their culture—are *our* nature, we cannot slavishly imitate them, for our poetry has to be the response to a different nature from theirs: we have to appropriate precisely that which was natural, inborn, for the Greeks ("the fire from heaven," "holy pathos") just as they had to appropriate that which (on account of their appropriation) becomes natural, inborn, for us ("clarity of representation," "Junonian sobriety"). And because it is more difficult, indeed the *most* difficult, to master that which is one's own, inborn, *das Eigene*, we shall not surpass the Greeks in the clarity of representation and Junonian sobriety that they had to appropriate and that we are born with. In order to be *like* them—at least insofar as the living relation (*lebendiges Verhältnis*) and the destiny (or "skill," *Geschick*) are concerned—we should not imitate *them* or abstract the rules of artistic creation (*Kunstregeln*) solely from the model of Greek splendor, but rather appropriate that which is not our own, foreign, *das Fremde*, for us. But this rejection of imitation—which amounts to a quite explicit rejection of Winckelmannian classicism—certainly does not allow us to speak of a turn away from Greece and back to the fatherland. The ideological motivations of such a (non)reading are clear, for if one insists on extracting a "turning" out of this letter, it would have to be a turning to that which is *not* our own, that which we have to appropriate, because it is *foreign*: *das Fremde*. Rather than any kind of turning away from Greece, the letter states quite explicitly that the proper, that which is one's own—in our case, the Greeks, Greek culture: "clarity of representation," "Junonian sobriety"—must be learned as well as that which is foreign, and that for this reason the Greeks are indispensable for us (*Aber das eigene muss so gut gelernt seyn, wie das Fremde. Desswegen sind uns die Griechen unentbehrlich*). If not imitated, the Greeks have nevertheless to be learned: we can't do without them. But what it would mean to *learn* the Greeks without yet imitating them, what it means for the Hesperian poet to have to reject the Greeks as models on the one hand and yet be unable to do without them on the other, is not easy to understand. How save the Greeks without imitating them? Peter Szondi's essay-long interpretation of the first letter to Böhlendorff, "The Overcoming of Classicism" (*Überwindung des Klassizismus*), is the most rigorous answer to this question.

Better than anyone before him, Szondi recognizes both the predicament into which Hölderlin has put the Hesperian poet (and the reader of the first letter to Böhlendorff) and its stakes. In order to wrest the interpretation of (particularly the late) Hölderlin out of the hands of the ideologically tainted "George-Kreis" interpretation and its descendants (of whom Heidegger can be taken as one[6]), Szondi makes the sloppy notions of *abendländische Wendung* and *vaterländische Umkehr* the main targets of his thorough argument. This is certainly a salutary correction, especially when one recalls the attempts to enlist Hölderlin's poetry (in particular the so-called *vaterländische Hymnen* like "Germanien") for stupidly nationalist ends. At the same time, however, Szondi understands better than anyone else the radical originality of Hölderlin's explicit anticlassicism: in short, that the Greeks were not nature but rather the response to a nature and that we can therefore dispense with having to imitate them. "No longer nature but rather the response to a nature that is not ours, the classical period appears to forfeit the ability to be the model for modernity (*Nicht mehr Natur, sondern Antwort auf eine Natur, die nicht die unsere ist, scheint die Klassik die Fähigkeit einzubüssen, der Moderne Vorbild zu sein*)."[7] Szondi's solution of this dilemma—save the Greeks without imitating them—takes the form of an attempt at a dialectical mediation of Greeks and Hesperians, that which is proper and that which is foreign, *das Eigene* and *das Fremde*. This solution is most neatly and rigorously stated in Szondi's summary:

Hölderlin's concern is to gain clarity about the difference between Greek and Hesperian art, the reason for which he recognizes as the difference between Greek and Hesperian nature. This differentiation dispenses him completely from the imitation of antiquity that Winckelmann's classicism had made a duty for him and at the same time allows him to gain insight into the reason that the Greeks nevertheless are *indispensable* for him. Hölderlin overcomes classicism without turning away from the classical. In this saving of the Greek for Hesperia, in the insight that the poetry of modernity will be able to distinguish itself through other means than that of antiquity, and in the recognition that freedom is necessary in art also in relation to that which is one's own, consists the conceptual content of Hölderlin's first letter to Böhlendorff.

The Greeks are *indispensable* for the Hesperian poet because in their art he comes up against his own origin as a foreign one. In this way he gains the distance in relation to that which is his own which is freedom.

Hölderlin geht as darum, sich über jenen Unterschied zwischen griechischer und hesperischer Kunst Klarheit zu verschaffen, als dessen Grund er die Verschiedenheit von griechischer und hesperischer Natur erkennt. Diese Unterscheidung dispensiert ihn vollends von der Nachahmung der Antike, die ihm der Winckelmannsche Klassizismus zur Pflicht gemacht hatte, und lässt ihn zugleich den Grund einsehen, aus dem die Griechen ihm dennoch unentbehrlich *sind. Hölderlin überwindet den Klassizismus, ohne von der Klassik sich abzuwenden. In dieser Rettung des Griechischen für Hesperien, in der Einsicht, dass die Dichtung der Moderne durch andere Mittel sich wird auszeichnen können als die antike, und in der Erkenntnis, dass auch dem Eigenen gegenüber in der Kunst Freiheit vonnöten sei, besteht der Ideengehalt von Hölderlins erstem Brief an Böhlendorff.*

Die Griechen sind dem hesperischen Dichter unentbehrlich, *weil er in ihrer Kunst dem eigenen Ursprung als einem Fremden begegnet. So gewinnt er zu dem Eigenen die Distanz, die Freiheit ist.*[8]

Szondi saves the Greeks (while giving them up as a model to be imitated) elegantly: Hölderlin would not have us surrender *das Eigene* at the cost of *das Fremde* or vice versa—they are of equal rank (*Gleichrangigkeit*), says Szondi—but rather would have us become ourselves, Hesperians, by recognizing ourselves in an other, the Greeks, which, because it *re*presents (in their art) that which is our own *as* foreign, allows us to gain a distance on it and thereby to appropriate it, master it, freely. This is how Hölderlin overcomes classicism

(*Klassizismus*) without turning away from the classical (*Klassik*). That this solution by dialectical mediation is rigorously Hegelian is clear from Szondi's mediating term: representation. In Greek *art* (*Kunst*) the Hesperian poet comes up against (*begegnet*) his own origin *as* (*als*) a foreign one: the word "as" (*als*) here to be invested with all the meaning of Hegel's *Vorstellung*. And just as art in Hegel's scheme marks a form of (self-)knowledge that precisely because it is still encumbered by (unreflected) representation (*Vorstellung*) needs to be overcome, sublated (*aufgehoben*), first by religion and then by (absolute idealist) philosophy, so Greek art can mark the aesthetic moment of Western history that we can sublate precisely by incorporating it *as* a moment in our story of how we became we—"Hesperian," "modern," the other *of* the Greeks. Utterly consistent in his argument, Szondi explicitly formulates the scheme in terms of Hegelian self and other later in the essay when he characterizes those things that can have a destructive effect on the poet—the given, positive, inherited, art of the Greeks—but which he should nevertheless not avoid, for "they are, in Hegel's terminology, his other, without which he is also not himself (*Sie sind, in Hegels Terminologie, sein anderes, ohne das er auch nicht er selber ist*)."[9] This scheme that is able to save Greek art (the *mimetic* art *par excellence*) by incorporating it as a moment—no matter how absent or how negative, for the greater the negation the greater the synthesis—in a history of self-consciousness, is even able to save sheer imitation of the Greeks, *as* a moment of the work of art: the Hesperian poet can even imitate Homer, what Hölderlin in his theory of the "alternation of tones" (*Wechsel der Töne*) calls the "naive tone" (i.e., clarity of representation, Junonian sobriety), if he installs this tone as *one* (momentary) tone in the total tonal structure that constitutes the poem.[10] In short, Szondi would assimilate even Hölderlin's poetics of tones—and elsewhere his poetics of genre[11]—to this interpretation of his philosophy of history in dialectical terms: that is, in terms of an opposition between *das Eigene* and *das Fremde* mediated by a history of self-consciousness that contains the aesthetic, self-representation in art, as an essential (and sublatable) moment.

But this eminently sensible interpretation—whose conception of the negative is powerful enough ultimately to totalize Hölderlin's biography with his poetry, his poetry with his poetics, his poetics with his philosophy of history, etc.—becomes questionable once we look more closely at the texts. If anything, it makes *too much* sense, and one begins to wonder whether Szondi can escape his own observation about preceding readers of the first letter to Böhlendorff: "It is as though the interpreters did not want to acknowledge Hölderlin's reflection, as though they were afraid to recognize it as his (*Es ist, als wollten die Interpreten die Überlegung Hölderlins nicht wahrhaben, als scheuten sie sich, sie als die seine anzuerkennen*)."[12] For in order to mediate the relations between *das Eigene* and *das Fremde* (and thereby between Greece and Hesperia), Szondi must interpret this relation as that of symmetrically opposed terms whose opposition is to be understood on the model of consciousness (i.e., in terms of self and other). Indeed, Szondi speaks of a "mirror-symmetry" (*Spiegelsymmetrie*) between Greek and Hesperian nature and art. On the basis of this "mirror-symmetry" he can interpret that which is our own (*das Eigene*) as Hegelian *das Positive* (given, immediate, abstract, etc.), the "freedom" of "the *free* use of *that which is our own*" (*der* freie *Gebrauch des* Eigenen) as meaning "with consciousness" (i.e., "with self-consciousness") and the task of the poet as "mediating the opposites" (*Vermittlung der Gegensätze*). Now although the (chiasmic) reversal—in the relation of that which is proper (*das Eigene*) and that which is foreign (*das Fremde*)—between the Greeks and us is certainly explicit enough in the letter, there is no evidence in the text to allow us to rewrite this reversal into a mirror symmetry of opposed terms. Indeed, what characterizes the relation between Greeks and Hesperians is a constitutive *a*symmetry—their nature is our culture, our nature is their culture—which can be taken as a (determinately) *negative* mirror symmetry only as long as we do not read the radical nature of the "negative" in this chiasmus: in a word, that which is foreign for us (*das Fremde*). That is, the Greeks can never serve as a (negative) mirror image in which we can recognize ourselves because they are divided against themselves; they contain a nature from which we are forever separated and which we can never make an object of (self-)consciousness. And what separates us from the *Greeks'* nature—"the fire from heaven," "holy pathos"—is precisely *our Greek* nature—"the clarity of representation," "Junonian sobriety." The ramifications of this asymmetry are far-reaching—especially once we recognize that the Greeks' nature was "Oriental," "Egyptian," culture—and we have elaborated them elsewhere.[13] All that concerns us here is Szondi's presupposition of there being an identity or at least an analogy between the *Greeks'* relation of nature and culture and *our* relation of nature and culture. This presupposition becomes questionable once we read the relation between the Greeks and us as an asymmetrical chiasmic reversal of terms, one of which (*das Fremde*) we have no access to because it cannot be the object of our perception or knowledge, not the object for a subject. If it is an object at all, it is somebody else's (the Greeks') object and not ours. The fact that our relation to the Greeks is structured not like the relation of consciousness to the object of its knowledge but like a trope—chiasmus, a reversal concerned only with the *relation* of terms and not their *constitution*—is already indicative of the problem, as is the fact that in Hölderlin's theory of tones the relation of one tone to another, of *Grundstimmung* to *Kuntscharakter*, is put not in terms of self and other but explicitly in terms of signification (*Zeichen*) and figuration (*Metapher*). If anything, it would have been easier to assimilate Hölderlin's philosophy of history to his poetics than vice versa. For instance, chiasmic reversals like the one between

Greece and Hesperia are an integral part of Hölderlin's theory of the alternation of tones—indeed, such a chiasmic reversal between the grounding tone, the meaning (*Bedeutung*), and the tone of the *Kuntscharakter* marks what Hölderlin calls the *Katastrophe* of an epic, lyric, or tragic poem.

In order to interpret Hölderlin's poetics on the basis of a philosophy of history that is conceived in terms of dialectizable oppositions of self and other—and in order to presuppose an identical or at least analogous relation between that which is proper (*das Eigene*) and that which is foreign (*das Fremde*) for us and for the Greeks—Szondi must invoke as his authority that which we, according to Hölderlin, *do* have in common (*gleich*) with the Greeks: that which is the highest (*das Höchste*), "namely the living relation and the skill (*nämlich dem lebendigen Verhältnis und Geschick*)." As is to be expected, Szondi has no trouble interpreting "living relation" as another name for the dialectical mediation of opposites—whether they be the different tones of a poem or the different natures of historical peoples—but his interpretation of *Geschick* is a loose end, as it were, which, once read, threatens to unravel the entire argument. Namely, Szondi quite correctly reads the *Geschick* that we are to have in common with the Greeks not as a common "destiny" or "fate"—for how could we have a common fate with the Greeks when their nature is not ours, and so forth?—but rather as "skill," "ability": in short, as Greek *techne*. In fact, he adds on the last page of the essay, the entire letter to Böhlendorff stands under the sign of this word; it is a letter from the workshop (Geschick *ist, mit dem griechischen Wort, techne. Im Zeichen dieses Wortes scheint der Böhlendorff-Brief insgesamt zu stehen, es ist ein Brief aus der Werkstatt*).[14] *Whose* workshop? one could rightly ask, and answer: the poet's. The first letter to Böhlendorff is a letter from the "workshop" of one poet to another poet about the (different) conditions of poetry writing for the Greeks and for "us." In short, the letter is about the *techne* of poetry conceived as the workmanlike *craft* of poetry. Hence Szondi is perfectly justified in bringing Hölderlin's poetics of the alternation of tones into the interpretation of this letter, since it clearly belongs among Hölderlin's "poetological" writings. But Szondi is not justified in turning this discussion of technique, of poetry as a craft, into a statement about aesthetics, into a pronouncement about *art*. Rather than being a letter about *ästhetische Praxis*—Szondi's words—the text is more properly about *poetische Praxis*. In short, it is the slippage by way of the Greek word *techne*—from art as craft to art as aesthetic object, from a category of *poetics* to a category of *aesthetics*—that allows Szondi to turn poetry into art. And that a *Greek* word should authorize this slippage is as little an accident as is the invention of the Greeks as *the* aesthetic moment of Western history. Poetry has to be turned into art if we are to have the mediating term—the possibility of representing ourselves in our own other—that can reconcile *das Eigene* and *das Fremde*, Greece and Hesperia.

One could say that Szondi has to save poetry for art in order to save the Greeks for Hesperia, but of course the reverse is also true: in order to save the Greeks for Hesperia, Szondi also has to turn poetry into art. The invention of the Greeks as the aesthetic moment of Western history is part of the same system that has to "aestheticize" poetry, reconstitute it on the basis of a model that is not linguistic but (dialectically) representational, that is, ultimately mimetic. Without *such* Greeks and without *such* poetry we might have to recognize not only that there were never any Greeks or any *Greek* poetry but also that poetry is not art and that we are not we (i.e., those who constitute themselves by telling the story of how "once" we were "Greeks" and "now" are "Hesperians," etc.). So that it is for "good reasons" that Szondi wants to save the Greeks for us and poetry for the aesthetic: he wants to save us for ourselves. What does *not* get saved in such a scheme, however, is Hölderlin's text—the text *as* text, poetry *as* poetry (and not as *art*). One symptom is the fact that the first letter to Böhlendorff never once uses the word "art" (*Kunst*). The closest it comes is in the word *Kunstregeln*, but it is clear from the context that it is indeed the *technical* rules of poetic making that are under discussion (just as in Hölderlin's theory of tones the term *Kunstcharakter* has more to do with a *made*, artificial, "character" [in the sense of "letter"] than with any aesthetic considerations). In short, the letter remains a letter from the workshop of the poet, and "art" as an aesthetic category is an importation necessary to the scheme of dialectical mediation of *das Eigene* and *das Fremde* in terms of self and other.

Szondi's (necessary) aestheticization of Hölderlin's historical scheme is most legible in the crucial sentence: "The Greeks are *indispensable* for the Hesperian poet because in their art he comes up against his own origin as a foreign one (*Die Griechen sind dem hesperischen Dichter* unentbehrlich, *weil er in ihrer Kunst dem eigenen Ursprung als einem Fremden begegnet*)." The introduction of both "mirror symmetry"—in the word *begegnet*, "comes up against," with its implication of opposition (*gegen*)—and aesthetics—in having the Hesperian *poet* come up against Greek *art*—in this sentence is clear enough. But it is also clear that a dialectical mediation of that which is our own and that which is foreign, *das Eigene* and *das Fremde*—in short, a representation of *das Eigene* as *das Fremde* ("our own origin *as* a foreign one")—is possible only as long as we do not read these words in Hölderlin's sense but transform them, translate them, as it were, into a Hegelian sense: that is, in order for us to recognize our origin, *das Eigene*, as our own in the art that represents it *as* foreign, *das Fremde*, we must translate Hölderlin's *das Fremde* into Hegelian *das Fremde*, a foreignness that is *not* our own (but is natural, their own, for the Greeks) into a foreignness that belongs to us, in short, we must translate that which is radically foreign into that which is foreign for us (i.e., not really foreign but our own—*das Fremde* into *das Eigene*). And if we understand Greek *nature* ("the fire from heaven," "holy pathos") as "Oriental" or "Egyptian"—as other

Hölderlin texts would authorize us to do—such a translation means transforming the Orient (the Egyptians)—that which is radically foreign for us because it
is not *our* foreignness—into Greece—that which is natural, national, proper,
our own, and so forth. (Another way to put this: Szondi Hegelianizes
Hölderlin's *fremd* to mean other, i.e., in opposition to a self, when for
Hölderlin it is precisely not *our* other.) No wonder, then, that Szondi needs to
bring art, as a mediating agent of self-representation, into the picture. But once
we read Szondi's sentence in a strictly Hölderlinian sense—"our own" to mean
"our own" (i.e., Greek) and "foreign" to mean "foreign" (i.e., Oriental)—it
begins to make weird but appropriately Hölderlinian sense: to come up against
that which is our own (*das Eigene*) *as* foreign (*das Fremde*) means to come up
against our Greek nature ("the clarity of representation," "Junonian
sobriety") *as* Oriental ("the fire from heaven," "holy pathos"); it means, in
short, to represent the Greek *as* the Oriental. This makes perfect Hölderlinian
(if not Hegelian) sense if we remember Hölderlin's own words about his
translations of Sophocles: he would foreground or "lift out" (*herausheben*) the
Oriental (*das Orientalische*), that which the Greeks had denied (*verleugnet*) or
repressed in their poetry, their Oriental nature. The trouble with Szondi's
interpretation, however, is that such a representation of "the clarity of
representation" or "Junonian sobriety" *as* "the fire from heaven" or "holy
pathos," of the Greeks *as* the Orientals (or the Egyptians), is not possible *as* a
representation but can take place only by way of translation: that is, by way of
a transposition, carrying-over, or *metaphor* that is based on a linguistic model
and not on a model of representation derived from the experience of
consciousness (i.e., self/other, subject/object, etc.). It is possible, again, only
in an orientalizing, allegorizing, translation of the Greeks like Hölderlin's own.
And Szondi's own story of how we invent the Greeks, Greek art, in order to
recognize ourselves in an other is itself a translation—of Orientals into Greeks,
of Hesperians into the opposite of the Greeks (i.e., it has more to do with how
Szondi reads Greek *words* than how he perceives Greek representations)—is
itself an allegory. It is a story of the invention and undoing of the aesthetic, of
art as aesthetic, which we tell in order to cover up the fact that there was never
any art in the first place, the fact that "in the first place" there was a self-
translation, self-signification, self-allegorization, and so on, which can never be
the activity of a self but which is always someone or something else's
encryptment in unreadable hieroglyphs, dead letters. In short, we invent the
Greeks in order to distinguish ourselves from an Orient and Egyptians—for
whom, after all, *das Fremde* ("culture," say) would be "the fire from heaven,"
"holy pathos" (i.e., the Greeks' nature, *das Eigene*) and, to fill in the other
blank, for whom *das Eigene*, nature, would be "the clarity of representation,"
"Junonian sobriety," for whom the relation of nature and culture would be exactly the same as ours—which for the German thought of the late eighteenth

century is synonymous with "a realm of death," as Hegel would put it—a death whose terror consists in its being not our own, not a negation, but someone or something else's, utterly foreign (*fremd*), a death without death.[15]

But we should not think that resorting to the (not so holy) pathos of Asia, the Orient, and Egyptians will let us escape the tyranny of Greece and all those who would turn poetry into art and words into pictures (or, to use a properly "romantic" vocabulary, allegories into symbols). We have only to recall the fate of Hölderlin in France: "and as one says of heroes, I can well say of myself that Apollo has struck me," he says in the second letter to Böhlendorff, words that gain a peculiar resonance once we remember that, according to the *first* letter to Böhlendorff, it was Homer's principal merit to have appropriated "the occidental, Junonian sobriety for his Apollinian realm (*die abendländische junonische Nüchternheit für sein Apollonsreich*)." The Apollinian fire from heaven (which corresponds to Nietzsche's *Dionysian*) is not something one can be *for*—which would be like being *for* encrypted death without death, say—just as the tyranny of Greek sobriety and representation is not something one can be *against*. A good example of the resiliency of the Greeks—and all the gifts they bring with them—is Hölderlin's most recent trip to France (Strasbourg no less) in two essays by Philippe Lacoue-Labarthe: "La Césure du spéculatif" and "Hölderlin et les Grecs."[16] In both of these essays Lacoue-Labarthe does not flinch from formulating Hölderlin's insights in all their radicality. Although taking over from Szondi the thesis of Hölderlin's "overcoming of classicism," Lacoue-Labarthe goes one better and rejects even the dialectical recovery of (an absent) Greece, by inscribing an irreducible doubleness in it (and therefore in *us*). What, he asks in "Hölderlin et les Grecs," can we decipher in Hölderlin's difficult texts? He answers: "Behind a thematics still coming for the most part from Winckelmann and Schiller (even if Hölderlin constructs completely new categories), above all the following, which is utterly unheard of during this epoch: namely that *the* Greece, as such, Greece *herself*, does not exist. But that she is at least double, divided—utterly torn. And that what we know about it, which is perhaps what she had been or what she had manifested of herself, is not what she was in reality—which, on the other hand, has perhaps never appeared. In the same way, correlatively, the modern West—that which Hölderlin never identifies simply with Germany but calls, more generally, Hesperia—does not yet exist, or is still only that which it is not (*Derrière une thématique encore largement tributaire de Winckelmann et de Schiller [même si Hölderlin construit de toutes nouvelles catégories], ceci, tout d'abord, qui dans l'époque est parfaitement inouï: à savoir que la Grèce, comme telle, la Grèce elle-même, n'existe pas. Mais qu'elle est au moins double, divisée—à la limite déchirée. Et que ce que nous en connaissons, qui est peut-être ce qu'elle a été ou ce qu'elle a manifesté d'elle, n'est pas ce qu'elle était en réalité—qui, en revanche, n'est peut-être jamais apparu. De même, cor-*

rélativement, l'Occident moderne—ce que Hölderlin n'identifie jamais tout simplement à l'Allemagne mais nomme, plus généralement, l'Hespérie—n'existe pas encore, ou n'est encore que ce qu'il n'est pas)."[17] No Greeks, no us, or at least no us *yet*—the point could not be clearer. And the Greece that never was is *"the* Greece as such, Greece *herself* (la *Grèce, comme telle, la Grèce* elle-même)"*: that is, the Greece as represented and as representing, Greece as the condition of possibility of (self-)representation (*comme telle*) and (self-)identification (*elle-même*), the aesthetic moment *par excellence.* Lacoue-Labarthe is also completely consistent in the consequences he draws from the nonexistence of this Greece: the labor of the poet turns out to be the task of the translator: *"The proper of the Greeks is inimitable because it had never taken place.* At the most, it is possible to have a glimpse of it or, at the very most, to deduce it from its opposite—art. And to introduce it, retroactively, in this art. Hence the work of *translation* (and I mean in particular the translation of *Antigone,* conceived as the most Greek of the tragedies of Sophocles), which consists in making the Greek text say what it never ceased saying *but without ever saying it.* Which consists in repeating the unproffered of the proffering itself (Le propre des Grecs est inimitable parce qu'il n'a jamais eu lieu. *Tout au plus est-il possible de l'entrevoir ou, à la limite, de le déduire de son contraire—l'art. Et de l'introduire, après coup, dans cet art. D'où le travail de* traduction [*et je pense plus particulièrement à la traduction d'*Antigone, *conçue comme la plus grecque des tragédies de Sophocle*], *qui consiste à faire dire au texte grec ce qu'il ne cessait de dire* mais sans jamais le dire. *Qui consiste à répéter l'improféré de sa profération même).*"[18] But how say the unsaid *of* the Greeks, that which they never ceased saying without saying it? How repeat the proffering of the unproffered? The task of translating the Greeks contains—is precisely the attempt *to contain*—a "negative" not easily accounted for by any conventional (mimetic or dialectical) logic, and one can read Lacoue-Labarthe's entire project as an attempt to find categories that would be able to formulate the radical nature of this peculiar Hölderlinian "negative" without compromising it. "La Césure du spéculatif" also formulates the vertiginous double bind of the Hesperian translator as uncompromisingly as possible—"It is altogether necessary to repeat that which is the most Greek among the Greeks. Begin the Greeks again. That is to say, no longer be Greek at all (*Il faut bel et bien répéter ce qu'il y a de plus grec chez les Grecs. Recommencer les Grecs. C'est-à-dire ne plus être grec du tout)*"[19]—and although it does not quite come up with "categories" that could master its peculiar "negativity," it is able to deploy the terms of a reading strategy that would make it readable, namely Derrida's: "In short, for Hölderlin it was necessary to make Greek art say what it had not said, not in the mode of a kind of hermeneutics aiming at the implicit of its discourse, but in an other mode—for which I believe we do not have a category—according to which it was a matter of making it say, quite simply, what had been said (but) *as that which had not been said*: the same thing, then, but in its *différance*. 'Hen diapheron eauto' (*Car en somme il fallait, pour Hölderlin, faire dire à l'art grec ce qu'il n'avait pas dit, non sur le mode d'une sorte d'herméneutique visant l'implicite de son discours, mais sur un autre mode—pour lequel j'ai bien l'impression qu'il nous manque une catégorie—par où il s'agissait de faire dire, tout simplement, ce qui était dit [mais] comme ce qui n'était pas dit: la même chose, donc, en différance. 'En diaphéron éautô*')"[20] That Heraclitus' "The one differentiated in itself" (and Hölderlin's translation of it in *Hyperion, Das Eine in sich selber unterschiedne*) is here not to be understood as the difference *of* the one or the same, but is to be read as a difference with a difference, as it were, is clear from its spelling: *la même chose.* . *.en différance.*

And yet almost in the same breath as they formulate rigorously the depth of Hölderlin's insight, Lacoue-Labarthe's readings nevertheless would attribute to Hölderlin a mimetic conception of translation and a sacrificial (dialectical) conception of tragedy. In doing so, they too would reinvent the Greeks—*la Grèce comme telle*. Hölderlin's theory of translation and his theory of tragedy are on the one hand speculative, dialectical, through and through, but at the same time they "disarticulate," "neutralize," "paralyze" the speculative and its sacrificial model of tragedy. Lacoue-Labarthe's solution is to formulate this simultaneity in terms of "oscillation," "alternation," "paralysis," and he invokes Hölderlin's theory of the alternation of tones and his concept of the "caesura" of tragedy to justify his formulation. Hölderlin would "oscillate" between articulating and disarticulating the speculative, his theory of tragedy as "the catharsis of the speculative" would "caesura" the speculative—that is, constitute it in its deconstitution and vice versa. But one could rightly wonder whether Hölderlin's "alternation" authorizes such an "oscillation" and whether his concept of "caesura" is easily assimilable to "catharsis." The fact that for Hölderlin the alternation of tones is a dynamic principle that, if anything, "animates" a poem (rather than paralyzes it) is one indication, as is the fact that Hölderlin's caesura has more to do with a text's (one could say "allegorical") self-signification—where "representation itself appears (*die Vorstellung selber erscheint*)," where representation represents itself *as* representation—than with any "catharsis" conceived on a sacrificial, ritualistic mimetic model of tragedy. (Indeed, in the theory of the alternation of tones, what Hölderlin calls the "catastrophe" of the poem [the caesura] is explicitly a [chiasmic] reversal between the tone of the *Kunstcharakter* and the tone of the *Bedeutung*, between, one could say, the tone of the signifier and the tone of the signified.) The problem with Lacoue-Labarthe's reading, we could say, is that he continues to use the discourse of mimesis, "mimetology," long after it has outlived its use: that is, to account for textual processes and a "negative" peculiar to language that it can by definition *not* account for. The essay's unproblematized coupling of mimesis and translation, art and poetry, is a symptom, as is Lacoue-Labarthe's having to use formulations like "the *echo* of that *unuttered speech* (*l'écho de cette parole imprononcée*)" to characterize the abyssal nature of the translator's task. How *echo* the *unspoken* without moving from *representation* to *signification* (or figuration), that is, to a model in which mimetic categories like "echo" are no longer pertinent? Perhaps the most pithy illustration of Lacoue-Labarthe's own double bind is the penultimate sentence of "Hölderlin et les Grecs": "Greece will have thus been this vertigo and this threat: a people, a culture, pointing to themselves, never ceasing to point to themselves, as inaccessible to themselves (*La Grèce aura donc été ce vertige et cette menace: un peuple, une culture s'indiquant, ne cessant de s'indiquer comme inaccessibles à eux-mêmes*)." If the Greeks indicate themselves, point to themselves, *signify* themselves *as* inaccessible to themselves, how are we to repeat or translate them by recourse to *any* mimetic, sacrificial, cathartic model of representation? For the discrepancy, the utter incommensurability, of the order of the *sign* (*s'indiquer*) and the order of *mimesis* (*comme*) is nicely visible, nicely *readable*, in this sentence. Indeed, one could say that the Greeks signified themselves precisely *as* (nonmimetic "as") that discrepancy: a people signifying themselves *as* what they are not, and therefore doomed to telling (over and over) the story of how they cannot read their self-signification, of how they cannot read themselves, an allegory of unreadability.

Why Lacoue-Labarthe needs—at least in "La Césure du spéculatif," which is the earlier essay—to force Hölderlin's texts back into mimetic, sacrificial, ritualistic, cathartic models of tragedy while all the time seeing its impossibility would require a lengthy argument. In brief, it is partly because he takes over too readily Szondi's Hegelian dialectical interpretation of Hölderlin's theoretical, poetological, writings: to do so, he, like Szondi before him, must ignore the explicitly linguistic (indeed rhetorical) framework and categories Hölderlin employs.[21] In greater part, however, it is because of his taking over from Bataille a conception of sacrifice—the representation of one's own death—based on an anthropologized interpretation of death in Hegel's *Phenomenology of Spirit*.[22] The trouble is, however, that the *Phenomenology* is *not* an anthropology—it is about *consciousness* and not about *man*, or if it is about man at all, it is about man as *aufgehoben* (sublated)[23]—and what Hegel would call the death *of* consciousness has nothing to do with natural, biological extinguishment. What makes consciousness a consciousness—that is, the condition of its being capable of *self*-consciousness—is precisely that it does *not* "die" like a dog or a cat but can represent its own death to itself. In Bataille's words: "In order that, in the end, man reveal himself to himself, he must die, but it is necessary for him to do it while living—in watching himself cease to be. In other words, death itself must become (self-)consciousness at the very moment when it annihilates the conscious being (*Pour que l'homme à la fin se révèle à lui-même il devrait mourir, mais il lui faudrait le faire en vivant—en se regardant cesser d'être. En d'autres termes, la mort elle-même devrait devenir conscience [de soi], au moment même où elle anéantit l'être conscient).*"[24] Bataille is quite right to say that to make one's own death a spectacle for oneself, a "subterfuge"—a theater, representation, in short, sacrifice—is necessary, but because he identifies *l'être conscient* with *l'homme,* the sacrifice he has in mind is more like the extinguishment of "man" than like the death of consciousness, more like the "death" of a cat or a dog than the death of consciousness. Insofar as Lacoue-Labarthe takes over from Bataille this anthropologized and mimetic interpretation of sacrifice—without taking over the radical (Nietzschean) consequences Bataille will draw from it—his reading of Hölderlin threatens to regress from its insights back into a mimetic model. But, of course, the "subterfuge" that will allow consciousness to represent its own death to itself, to survive its own death, as it were, to identify itself in the extinguishment of a dog or a cat, say, cannot be a *mimetic* operation. It must be a linguistic, indeed rhetorical, operation of self-signification or self-figuration—better, self-inscription—for its own death is not something (or a nothing) that can ever become an object of consciousness, just as we cannot *experience* death, we can only name it, impose a sense on it (by catachresis, say), give it a face, eyes, and a point of view (by prosopopoeia, as Hegel does when he speaks of *looking* into the *face* of the negative that is death *[dem Negativen ins Angesicht schaut]*).[25] And because it is a linguistic operation, such "representation" brings into the world still another death—what Blanchot calls "the death without death"—whose existence is "real" and determinate but which is completely out of the grasp of a self or a consciousness or a subject. When we *say* "I die," we suffer the death of the impossibility of dying; the "I" as a linguistic, grammatical subject can never die because it has always already died—it is always already dead. To say "I die" is to say "Death dies"—and death is not a self or a consciousness or a subject: death can *only* die and *never* die.[26] This third, other death—the first being "biological extinguishment," the second the "death of consciousness"—we could call with Blanchot the "death of writing" (or, for that matter, the death of reading): material inscription or the dead letter that kills *not* because it is immediate, sensuous, and the like—*not* because it kills the spirit in being opposed to it—but rather because it contains a death*ful* spirit, the death of spirit in a purely allegorical sign. It is *this* death, we claim, that the interpreters of Hölderlin cannot, will not, read in the first letter to Böhlendorff—where it is inscribed as the nature *of* the Greeks ("fire from heaven," "holy pathos") forever inaccessible to us, and which is figured elsewhere in Hölderlin's work as the Orient and the Egyptians—and its unreadability is why this letter can be neither delivered nor returned (except to the Dead Letter Office, i.e., a Greece that never was). And it is in order not to read this dead letter that both Szondi and Lacoue-Labarthe reinvent the

Greeks—the former by aestheticizing poetry and an-esthetizing the death *of* the Greeks, the latter by anthropologizing it—while knowing that they never were. Like all Greeks, they cannot read their own story.

But lest we take lightly this unwarranted return of (nonexistent) Greeks in an "allegory of unreadability"—in a story we tell to ourselves in order to (de)constitute ourselves as those who cannot (help but) read their own story—as an aberration peculiar to wrecked idealists, let us take an interpretation of art, of the so-called pictorial or visual arts, as a final example. In *Art and Illusion* E. H. Gombrich writes a chapter called "Reflections on the Greek Revolution" in which he characterizes the new mimeticism of Greek sculpture and painting, especially when it is compared to the eminently "pictographic," "hieroglyphic" art of the Egyptians. He attributes this "revolution" in representation to the classical sculptors' and painters' discovery of Greek narration, in particular Homer: "For what is the character of Greek narration as we know it from Homer? Briefly, it is concerned not only with the 'what' but also with the 'how' of mythical events."[27] His recognition of the constitutive difference between the natures of Egyptian art and Greek art leads Gombrich to caution us that "we must never forget that we look at Egyptian art with the mental set we have all derived from the Greeks. So long as we assume that images in Egypt mean much the same as they did in the post-Greek world, we are bound to see them as rather childlike and naive. Nineteenth-century observers frequently made this mistake. They described the reliefs and paintings in Egyptian tombs as 'scenes from the daily life' of the Egyptians. But recently it has been pointed out by Mrs. Frankfort-Groenewegen in her book *Arrest and Movement* that this habitual reading is due to our own Greek training. We are accustomed to looking at all images as if they were photographs or illustrations and to interpreting them as the reflection of an actual or imaginary reality."[28] For where the Egyptian may be concerned only with the "what" of his representation—he wants to represent the Pharaoh as the Pharaoh, say, whose posture or face may be the same, prescribed, codified, conventional posture or face for ten thousand years—the Greek artist wants to "convince" and asks about the "how" of the representation: "For as soon as the Greeks looked at the Egyptian figure type from the aspect of an art which wants to 'convince,' it undoubtedly raised the question why it looks unconvincing. It is the reaction we express when we speak of its 'rigid posture.' It might be argued that this reaction itself is due to our Greek education; it was the Greeks who taught us to ask '*How* does he stand?' or even 'Why does he stand like that?' Applied to a pre-Greek work of art, it may be senseless to ask this question. The Egyptian statue does not represent a man standing rigidly or a man standing at ease—it is concerned with the what, not with the how. To ask for more might have struck an Egyptian artist as it would strike us if someone inquired the age or mood of the king on the chessboard."²⁹ But this properly Hölderlinian admonition—we should not read allegorical signs as though they were symbolic representations—and the clarity of its distinction between Egyptian art and Greek art begin to waver vertiginously when Gombrich puts an Egyptian work of art alongside its Greek counterpart: "But there are indications in works of art to confirm that the Greeks of the archaic period were in fact inclined to read the pictograms of Egypt as if they were representations of an imagined reality. The most striking and most amusing example is the so-called Busiris vase in Vienna, of the sixth century B.C. There is little doubt that this humorous account of Herakles' exploits among the Egyptians was inspired by Egyptian renderings of some victorious campaign. We are familiar with the type of pictorial chronicle that shows the gigantic figure of Pharaoh confronting an enemy stronghold with its diminutive defenders begging for mercy. Within the conventions of Egyptian art the difference in scale marks the difference in importance. To the Greek who looked at pictures as evocations of a possible event, the type must have suggested the story of a giant among pygmies. And so he turns the Pharaoh into Herakles wreaking havoc among the puny Egyptians. The pictograph for a whole city becomes a real altar onto which two of the victims have climbed, and climbed in vain, stretching out their hands in comic despair. Many of the gestures of this vase could be matched in Egyptian reliefs, and yet their meaning is transformed: these men are no longer the anonymous tokens for a defeated tribe, they are individual people—laughable, to be sure, in their helpless confusion, but our very laughter presupposes an imaginative effort to see the scene enacted in front of us, to think not only of the 'what' but also of the 'how.'"³⁰

The Greeks' "mistake" is clear enough: they took Egyptian allegorical signs "as though they were representations of an imagined reality." Whereas in the Egyptian work the gigantic size of the Pharaoh in relation to the people he is conquering "marks only the difference in importance," in the Greek picture the larger size of Herakles in relation to the Egyptians he is conquering is a mimetic depiction of his superior size and strength. And in the case of the Busiris vase, at least, this literalizing misreading is far from a "mistake," for it allows the Greek artist not only to appropriate Egyptian art by taking it for what it is not (i.e., Greek) but also to turn it against the Egyptians (by turning a conquering Pharaoh among the people of Canaan into a Greek Herakles conquering Egyptians) and thereby mark the ascendancy of Greece over Egypt. (It is as though one were to take Giotto's allegorical "Charity" as the depiction of a girl cannibal offering a heart—a "mistake" one could make only by forgetting to *read* the inscription "Karitas" which Giotto fortunately supplied.) But one does not have to *see* these pictures in order to note the vicious circularity of Gombrich's argument and ask: how were we able to tell the difference between Egyptian allegorical art and Greek symbolic art in the first place?

Clearly enough, if the Greek picture looks more realistic, more mimetic, more concerned with the "how," in short, more like the representation of an imagined reality, this is only because we look at it with the mental set we have all derived from the Greeks: in other words, it is only because we look at it through Greek eyes—our Greek metaphysics, ontology, epistemology, and so on—that we are able to distinguish so-called Egyptian art from so-called Greek art. In distinguishing Greek art from Egyptian, we reperform the Greeks' literalizing misreading: we look at Egyptian (and Greek) art through Greek eyes. If we could look at the Busiris vase through Egyptian eyes, as it were, who knows what we would see—who knows what we would *read*? If we were to limit ourselves to the sheer difference in size of the figures in each of the works, we could say that Gombrich's distinction between Egyptian and Greek art amounts to the same things as seeing "A a" and "A a" and labeling the former "Egyptian" and the latter "Greek," the former a pictogram, the latter a representation of an imagined reality—and, in its (typically German idealist) ideological elaboration, the former as "primitive," "childish," "pre-reflective," etc., and the latter as "civilized," "adult," "self-conscious," etc.; the former "pre-art" (*Vorkunst*), as Hegel would put it, and the latter "art" (*Kunst*). In short, to tell his story of the passage from allegorical signification to symbolic representation, Gombrich, despite his caution, has precisely to forget that he looks at Egyptian art through Greek eyes. Even his story that would remember the Greeks' forgetting repeats their forgetting. The point is that such "looking" is an arbitrary (and ideologically motivated) allegorical reading: we do not *see* the difference between the Egyptians and the Greeks, we *read* it. It may be that the only way even for pictures to become pictures is for them to be turned into words—just as art can become art only if we forget that it is (Egyptian) poetry.

Chapter 3
Heidegger Reading Hölderlin

Jede Entscheidung aber gründet sich auf ein Nichtbewältigtes,
Verborgenes, Beirrendes, sonst wäre sie nie Entscheidung.
—Heidegger, *Holzwege*[1]

If Hölderlin's textual history disarticulates the (Hegelian) dialectical interpretation and the negative proper to it, it also disarticulates Heidegger's (fundamental ontological) "hermeneutic" interpretation and the negative proper to it.
This conclusion is by no means self-evident. As we have suggested in the
preceding two chapters, the Hegelian interpretation of Hölderlin depends upon
a certain ("Greek") aesthetification—turning poetry into art—indeed, an entire
"aesthetic ideology"[2] (i.e., an interpretation of art as that which makes it possible for the mind or spirit to know itself, to represent itself [its self-knowledge]
in phenomenal appearance, and thus as that which makes possible an articulation of [self-]knowledge with action in the world, of epistemology with ethics,
etc.). Since Heidegger's interpretation states quite explicitly that Hölderlin's
poetry is *not art*—that is, insofar as there is art in the strict Western sense only
as *metaphysical* art, Hölderlin's poetry is not art because it is not metaphysical
(and it is not metaphysical because it is not the sensuous representation of the
nonsensuous; it is not "symbolic" *[sinnbildlich],* as art in the metaphysical
[i.e., Platonic] conception is supposed to be)[3]—it cannot be charged with
aesthetification or "aesthetic ideology". Indeed, according to Heidegger's interpretation, Hölderlin's poetry is not to be thought in terms of the self-
knowledge of an infinite subject (coming to itself through self-consciousness).
Nevertheless, Heidegger's explicitly antiaesthetic, antiepistemological (and, as

many commentators have pointed out, antiphilogical) interpretation of Hölderlin uses his poetry to articulate ontology with history—both of these terms to be understood in a peculiarly Heideggerian sense: (1) "ontology" as fundamental ontology, in the sense of the project of *Being and Time*, asking the question of the meaning of Being; (2) "history" as *Geschick*, as the destiny of Being's self-forgetting (*Geschick der Seinsvergessenheit*). As the "founding of Being in words" (*die worthafte Stiftung des Seins*) (*E*, 41),[4] poetry, and Hölderlin's poetry *par excellence*, reveals and conceals Being; poetry is marked by, it *is*, the articulation of the ontological difference between *Being* and *beings, Sein* and *Seiendes*. In the remarks that follow, we would attempt to determine whether such an ontologizing interpretation of Hölderlin's poetry can account for Hölderlin's textual history and the negative (i.e., the "Egyptians," the "Orient") proper to it.

As the poet of the poet in a preeminent, in a signal, sense, Hölderlin, for Heidegger, "compels a decision," or, better, puts *into* the decision (*Hölderlin ist uns in einem ausgezeichtneten Sinne der Dichter des Dichters. Deshalb stellt er in die Entscheidung*) (*E*, 34). But if decisions are always guilty in one way or another (*Entscheidungen, die sich jederzeit so oder so schuldig machen*) (*E*, 35)—as the following page of "Hölderlin and the Essence of Poetry" states—then the decision *of* Hölderlin—in all senses, and reading the senses of the genitive is the burden of reading Heidegger on Hölderlin[5]—must necessarily also be guilty, lacking, in debt. Some commentators on Heidegger's "dialogue" with Hölderlin have prematurely identified this guilt, lack or debt as that of Heidegger's own interpretive procedure. But objections to Heidegger's "forcing" of Hölderlin's texts, his putting in things that are not "there," his ripping lines out of context, in short, his imposition of "philosophy" on "literature," especially when these objections base themselves on false conceptions of Heidegger's "Method"—"method" and "the path of thought" (*der Weg des Denkens*) are not at all the same thing, says Heidegger in a late text[6]—wind up being only so many refusals to read. Like his dialogue with the history of philosophy, Heidegger's dialogue with Hölderlin aims quite explicitly to think that which is unthought (*das Ungedachte*) or at least to "experience" that which remains unspoken in the poetry's saying,[7] to think, in short, that which is *not there* (in a radical sense that needs to be determined). Hence any attempt to follow that dialogue means to think a double unthought (Hölderlin's *and* Heidegger's), the unthought *of* the unthought, as it were—what Heidegger does not or cannot think in thinking the unthought (or, if thought, unspoken) of the poetry of Hölderlin, what his guilty decisions put in or leave out. This (perversely dialectical?) task is considerably complicated by the fact that one can with justice argue that "all" Heidegger does is to bring (back) to Hölderlin's poetry only what he had taken from it in the first place: already in *Being and Time* Heidegger's language is saturated by Hölderlin's so that Heidegger cannot easily be accused of forcing a "foreign" ("philosophical") language upon the ("literary") language of Hölderlin's poetry. But can such an economy of give and take between literature and philosophy, poetry and thought, *Dichten* and *Denken*, one language and another (or itself), ever be a balanced economy? And what (when? where?) is the guilt, lack, or debt, that unbalances it? Max Kommerell, in a letter to Heidegger (29 July 1942) that may very well be one of the best documents in the "Hölderlin and Heidegger" genre, poses the questions eloquently: "Where is the passage [or "crossing" or "going-over"] where your own philosophy flows into Hölderlin and where out of a description of the human situation it turns in so decisive a way into a metaphysical utterance and into absolute, ultimate certitude—where it finds this certitude out of itself and makes itself one with Hölderlin at this point—and where, finally, it approaches poetry in the specific nature of its utterance? (*Wo ist der Übergang, wo Ihre eigene Philosophie in Hölderlin mündet, und wo sie in so entschiedener Weise aus einer Beschreibung der menschlichen Situation zur metaphysischen Aussage und zur absoluten letzten Gewissheit wird—wo sie diese Gewissheit aus sich findet, und sich in diesem Punkt mit Hölderlin gleichsetzt—und wo sie endlich in der spezifischen Art der Aussage sich der Dichtung nähert?).*"[8] In his reply Heidegger (like the good teacher he is) corrects Kommerell's notions of "philosophy," "description," and "situation"—substituting "thinking" (*Denken*) and a "project" (*Entwurf*) "determined by Being itself" (*vom Sein selbst bestimmt*)[9] for these terms—but he never does answer the question of where the passage, crossing, going-over (*Übergang*), of poetry and thought takes place—or the question of their respective specific modes of utterance (*die spezifische Art der Aussage*). Toward the beginning of the lectures on Hölderlin's "Germanien," however, he indicates a direction toward thinking these questions by giving us Hölderlin's "own" answers in four separate passages: one from a dedication to the *Hyperion* and three from the novel itself.

By reading (1) Heidegger's (non)reading of these passages—like all (Greek) interpreters, Heidegger leaves out the Egyptians; (2) the pivotal passages in "Hölderlin and the Essence of Poetry"—namely, Heidegger's attempt to ontologize Hölderlin's negative (to interpret the presence and absence of the gods in Hölderlin's poetry as the concealment and dis-concealment of Being, i.e., in terms of the ontological difference); and (3) Heidegger's interpretation of "Germanien," in which the question of history and of its negative come together—all three texts from the middle 1930s—we would re-pose the questions of "Hölderlin and Heidegger"—the question of the "passage" between them and of its specific mode of utterance—and reread the decisions *of* Hölderlin.

Heidegger and the Egyptians

Heidegger's ostensible purpose is to determine the sway of poetry in the existence of a (historical) people (*Das Walten der Dichtung im Dasein der*

Völker) (*HH*, 20).[10] To this end, he quotes approvingly and without comment four related (very Schillerian) passages that assert the mediating roles of poetry, art, and philosophy. We will comment explicitly on the first three passages; the fourth is indirectly accounted for in this commentary. The first passage is from the well-known dedication (to the princess of Homburg) of the *Hyperion* and begins with "the poets": "Most often poets have been formed at the very beginning or at the end of an epoch. It is with song that the peoples descend from the heaven of their childhood into active life, into the land of culture. It is with song that they return from there into the original life. Art is the passage from nature to culture and from culture to nature (*Meist haben sich Dichter zu Anfang oder zu Ende einer Weltperiode gebildet. Mit Gesang steigen die Völker aus dem Himmel ihrer Kindheit ins thätige Leben, ins Land der Cultur. Mit Gesang kehren sie von da zurück ins ursprüngliche Leben. Die Kunst ist der Übergang aus der Natur zur Bildung, und aus der Bildung zur Natur*)" (*HH*, 20). As belonging with this passage (*Dazu gehört. . .*), Heidegger quotes Hyperion himself on the role of art in ancient Athens. The context in the *Hyperion* is a letter from Hyperion to Bellarmin that recounts a discussion—on the subject of the splendor of the ancient people of Athens, whence it comes, in what it consists (*von der Trefflichkeit des alten Athenervolks, woher sie komme, worin sie bestehe*) (3:77)[11]—between hero and friends (including the inspiring Diotima) on board a boat taking them to present-day Athens. According to Hyperion, Athenian art, religion, philosophy, and forms of government were the blossom and fruit of the tree, not the soil and roots, the effects rather than the causes. The cause of their splendor was the Athenians' growing up free of violent (external) influence of all kinds on measured, tempered fare, undisturbed in every respect: "'Thus the Athenian was a man,' I continued, 'and had to become one. Beautiful he came out of the hands of nature, beautiful, as one says, in body and soul' (*'So war der Athener ein Mensch,' fuhr ich fort, 'so musst er es werden. Schön kam er aus den Händen der Natur, schön, an Leib und Seele, wie man zu sagen pflegt'*)" (3:77). And yet, although Hyperion does not say so explicitly, something is lacking in this beauty, in this human-godly, natural state of equilibrium—self-knowledge—and art provides it.

The second passage quoted by Heidegger begins here: "'The first child of human, of divine beauty is art. In it the divine man rejuvenates and reproduces himself. He wants to feel himself, therefore he puts his beauty opposite himself. Thus man gave himself his gods. For in the beginning man and his gods were one, when, unknown to itself, eternal beauty reigned.—I speak mysteries, but they are true' (*'Das erste Kind der menschlichen, der göttlichen Schönheit ist die Kunst. In ihr verjüngt und wiederholt sich der göttliche Mensch sich selbst. Er will sich selber fühlen, darum stellt er seine Schönheit gegenüber sich. So gab der Mensch sich seine Götter. Denn im Anfang war der Mensch und seine Götter Eins, da, sich selber unbekannt, die ewige Schönheit war.—Ich spreche Mysterien, aber sie sind.')" (HH,* 20-21). Beauty's "second daughter," the passage continues, is religion, the love of beauty: the wise man loves beauty itself; the people love her children, the gods, who appear to them in manifold forms. In this characterization of the (self-)objectification and (self-)love of beauty in art and religion there would seem to be very little trace of the negative in the process of (self-)mediation—although one could already wonder about the "want" in the divine man's "wanting" to feel or sense himself *(Er will sich selber fühlen. .* .): what is the lack in beauty itself that makes it desire self-knowledge in self-representation? Self-sufficiency would seem to bring with it its own *in*sufficiency, one that can be filled only by self-duplication and self-reproduction—as though self-sufficiency could be truly self-sufficient, could be truly *itself,* only by mediating itself with its own self, by recognizing itself *as* self-sufficient in its own other. The Greeks, and the Athenians in particular, then, were splendidly, naturally, self-sufficient (adequate to themselves) not because they were *born* that way but because they reflected "that way," they *were* what they were because they *became* what they were in and through their art and religion:[12] *So* war *der Athener ein Mensch. .* .*so musst' er es* werden. Hyperion follows up these reflections on Greek art and religion with "historical" distinctions between the Greeks on the one hand and the "Egyptians" and "Goths" (or "Sons of the North") on the other, but then his Platonico-Schillerian (and, as always, proto-Hegelian) *Schwärmerei* is interrupted by a somewhat impatient interlocutor. It is worth quoting this suggestive exchange (Heidegger's third quotation) in full, not least of all because it articulates explicitly the question of the relation between poetry and philosophy: "'Good!' someone interrupted me, 'I understand that, but how this poetic religious people [the Athenians] should also be a philosophical people, that I don't see.' 'Without poetry,' said I, 'they would have never been a philosophical people!' 'What does philosophy,' he replied, 'what does the cold sublimity of this science have to do with poetry?' 'Poetry,' I said, sure of my thing, 'is the beginning and end of this science. Like Minerva from the head of Jupiter, philosophy springs out of the poetry of an infinite, divine Being. And so at the end the ununitable flow in her together again in the secret source of poetry' (*'Gut! unterbrach mich einer, das begreif ich, aber, wie diess dichterische religiöse Volk [die Athener] nun auch ein philosophisch Volk seyn soll, das seh' ich nicht. Sie wären sogar, sagt' ich, ohne Dichtung nie ein philosophisch Volk gewesen! Was hat die Philosophie, erwiedert' er, was hat die kalte Erhabenheit dieser Wissenschaft mit Dichtung zu thun? Die Dichtung, sagt' ich, meiner Sache gewiss, ist der Anfang und das Ende dieser Wissenschaft. Wie Minerva aus Jupiters Haupt, entspringt sie aus der Dichtung eines unendlichen göttlichen Seyns. Und so läuft am End' auch wieder in ihr das Unvereinbare in der geheimnissvollen Quelle der Dichtung zusammen')"*

(*HH*, 21). No philosophy without poetry; without poetry the Athenians would have never been a philosophical people—Hyperion's dictum can be read in at least two ways. If, on the one hand, poetry is the beginning and end of philosophy—source and sea of its river, as it were—then philosophy is dependent upon poetry for its own existence. But if we keep in mind the dialectical structure of nature's self-mediation and self-recognition in culture (through poetry and art), beauty's self-mediation and self-recognition in art and religion, then, on the other hand, the need *of* poetry can also be read as a *subjective* genitive. That is, poetry *needs* philosophy in order to know itself, in order to *become* what it *is*. In short, if art (and poetry) is the self-knowledge of nature (beauty, god, man), then *philosophy* is the self-knowledge of poetry (and art): "Beauty is truth, truth beauty" is true all right, but only when beauty itself knows itself—knows its self—*as* the truth; and such knowledge requires a narrative, a story, a history, of knowing (as the allusion to the story of Minerva's birth and the metaphor of the river would suggest), as though Keats's chiasmus had been narrativized, had to tell the story of beauty, in order to be true, in order that we know all we need to know.

But this story of beauty and truth, poetry and philosophy—so much a cliché of what critics call romanticism (and Hölderlin criticism in particular), it is no wonder that Heidegger feels no need to comment on it (especially, as we shall see, since it is a cliché he would undo)—is, of course, not the whole story. That there may be a tension in the happy relationship between poetry and philosophy is already suggested in Hyperion's metaphors for the beginnings and ends of philosophy: the birth of Minerva and the "secret source" (*geheimnissvolle Quelle*). In Hölderlin's not so secret philosophical source—the eighth letter of Schiller's *On the Aesthetic Education of Man in a Series of Letters* (1794)—the goddess of wisdom springs forth fully armed from the head of Jupiter in order to do battle with the senses: "It is not without significance that the old myth makes the goddess of wisdom emerge fully armed from the head of Jupiter; for even her first function is warlike. Even at birth she has to wage a hard battle with the senses, which do not want to be dragged from their sweet repose (*Nicht ohne Bedeutung lässt der alte Mythus die Göttin der Weisheit in voller Rüstung aus Jupiters Haupte steigen; denn schon ihre erste Verrichtung ist kriegerisch. Schon in der Geburt hat sie einen harten Kampf mit den Sinnen zu bestehen, die aus ihrer süssen Ruhe nicht gerissen sein wollen*).''[13] And the mysteriousness of the *secret* source would suggest that the itinerary of poetry back to itself by way of philosophy may be a crooked, an "eccentric path" (*exzentrische Bahn*) (like the path of man from and to natural "simplicity" *[Einfalt]* by way of culture *[Bildung]*, according to the famous opening of the "Thalia-Fragment" of *Hyperion*). That this is indeed true—that the analogy between the functions of, on the one hand, art and poetry—as that which enables *nature* (and beauty) to mediate itself with its self—and of, on the other hand, philosophy—as that which enables *poetry* to mediate itself with its self—is considerably less than strict; that, again, the apparent chiasmus "Beauty is truth, truth beauty" is not symmetrical—that is, contains a negative less easily recuperable (in a story of self-consciousness) than that of determinate negation—is borne out by a certain slippage between *art and poetry* (which then determines the nature of the relation between art/poetry and philosophy), which, although certainly at work in the quoted passages from *Hyperion*, is problematized (albeit in displaced form) in the connecting passages that Heidegger avoids by quoting selectively. What this slippage means for the understanding of Hölderlin and why Heidegger should (have to?) repeat it without reproducing that in the text which would unmask it is the burden of our reading. In Heidegger's first quotation, the slippage, for lack of a better word, consists of an assumption that art and poetry are parallel, homogeneous: of the same genre or kind. The assumption implies that poetry is just one particular kind of art, that there is nothing that would make poetry essentially different—different in *kind*—from arts like painting, sculpture, architecture. That something more is at stake, however, is suggested by the text's (in the third quotation) own calling attention to the slippage between art and poetry: that is, up to the point in the discussion where Hyperion's interlocutor abruptly interrupts him—with his "'Good'. . .'that I understand, but how this poetic, religious people (*diess dichterische religiöse Volk*) should also be a philosophical people, that I don't see"—there has been no mention of the Greeks as a *poetic* people. The discussion has mentioned only their *art* (and their religion). In this context, one would have expected the interrupter to say "this *artistic,* religious people" rather than "this poetic, religious people (*diess dichterische religiöse Volk*)." So that his interruption brings into the discussion not only philosophy but also poetry—as though precisely *in order to* bring in philosophy he *had* to change the terms somewhat and bring along with it the one particular art that is a *linguistic* art.

Now there would perhaps be no reason to think anything amiss in this change—after all, Diotima herself interrupts this interruption by saying that Hyperion and his interlocutor have wandered from the topic and reminds them of it: "But you are rambling. The talk is of Athens (*Aber ihr schweift mir aus. Von Athen ist die Rede*)" (3:81)—were it not for the peculiar "historical" reflections within which Hyperion frames his apparent Graecomania (and which, again, Heidegger neither quotes nor mentions). Since these reflections not only change the terms in which we understand Greek self-constitution by self-mediation (in art, poetry, and philosophy)—and complicate considerably any simpleminded notions of Hyperion's (or Hölderlin's or, for that matter, Heidegger's) Graecomania—but also lead directly to Hölderlin's most mature philosophy of history, it may be worthwhile to consider them in some detail. Namely, the talk is not just of Athens and the Greeks but rather of the Greeks as distinguished from two other peoples: the "Egyptians" and the "Goths" (or "the sons of the North [die Söhne des Nordens]" as Hyperion also calls them). Unlike the Egyptians and the Goths, who both go to extremes in their religion and art—whether it be toward the petty or the monstrous, the too sensuous or the too suprasensuous—the Greeks mark an equilibrium, a balance, a harmony, of all opposing drives and tendencies: "There [among the Greeks] is not the petty, not the monstrous of the Egyptians and the Goths, there is human spirit and human form. They stray less than others to the extremes of the suprasensuous and the sensuous. Their gods remains more than others in the beautiful middle of the human (Da ist nicht das Kleinliche, nicht das Ungeheure der Ägyptier und Goten, da ist Menschensinn und Menschengestalt. Sie schweifen weniger als andre zu den Extremen des Übersinnlichen und des Sinnlichen aus. In der schönen Mitte der Menschheit bleiben ihre Götter mehr, denn andre)" (3:80). Throughout Hyperion's long disquisition, the Greeks are characterized by a rhetoric of what one could call the "double not." That is, they are "not too this" and "not too that" but rather a mediation of the two: for instance, they are neither too servile nor too familiar (Nicht zu knechtisch und nicht gar zu sehr vertraulich) (3:80), unwilling to submit either to the "despotism of arbitrariness" (die Despotie der Willkür)—an Egyptian tendency—or to the "despotism of law" (die Gesetzesdespotie)—a tendency of the sons of the North.

The Egyptians and the sons of the North, in contrast, are victims of the "single not." The Egyptian is not reflective, never learns reflection, because he is driven (by his fiery climate, in part) outside himself: he is forced to kneel before he has learned to walk, to pray before he has learned to speak, and so on. Hyperion summarizes his plight: "The Egyptian is devoted before he is a whole, and hence he knows nothing of the whole, nothing of beauty, and the highest that he names is a veiled power, a terrible enigma; the mute somber Isis is his Alpha and Omega, an empty infinity out of which nothing reasonable has ever come. Even out of the most sublime nothing, nothing is born (Der Ägyptier ist hingegeben, eh er ein Ganzes ist, und darum weiss er nichts vom Ganzen, nichts von Schönheit, und das Höchste, was er nennt, ist eine verschleierte Macht, ein schauerhaft Rätsel; die stumme finstre Isis ist sein Erstes und Letztes, eine leere Unendlichkeit und da heraus ist nie Vernünftiges gekommen. Auch aus dem erhabensten Nichts wird Nichts geboren)" (3:82). The cold North, on the other hand, drives its children too much inside themselves and makes them too reflective too soon. In the North "one has to become reasonable, one has to become a self-conscious spirit, before one becomes a human being; one has to be a clever man before one can be a child; one does now allow the harmony of the whole being, beauty, to grow and ripen in him before he is cultivated and developed. Mere understanding, mere reason are always the kings of the North (man muss vernünftig, muss zum *selbstbewussten Geiste werden, ehe man Mensch, zum klugen Manne, ehe man Kind ist; die Einigkeit des ganzen Menschen, die Schönheit lässt man nicht in ihm gedeihn und reifen, eh er sich bildet und entwickelt. Der blosse Verstand, die blosse Vernunft sind immer die Könige des Nordens)"* (3:82-83). The Egyptians and the Goths, then, are both too early and too late: they cut off their natural education too soon and become old before they have ever been young. In short, they come both before and after their own childhood and its natural nurturing process: "for all discipline and art begin too early, where human nature has not yet become ripe. Completed nature must live in the human child before he goes to school so that the image of childhood may show him the return out of school back to completed nature (*denn jede Zucht und Kunst beginnt zu früth, wo die Natur des Menschen noch nicht reif geworden ist. Vollendete Natur muss in dem Menschenkinde leben, eh es in die Schule geht, damit das Bild der Kindheit ihm die Rückkehr zeige aus der Schule zu vollendeter Natur)"* (3:78). In short, because he had no (natural) childhood, neither the Egyptian nor the son of the North knows beauty; and because he does not know beauty, he has no philosophy. All he has is abject submission either to the nothing of an empty infinity or to the nothing of mere understanding and mere reasoning. In this characterization of the Egyptians and the Goths as peoples without a childhood, Hyperion sounds very much like the (later) Hegel of the *Philosophy of History*, who turns the Egyptian priest's complaint about the Greeks—"You Greeks are never anything but children—into a reason for the Greeks' splendor (and the Egyptians' misery): it is precisely *because* the Greeks were children that they had nature, beauty, art, and philosophy, whereas the Egyptians are always too old because they never became young.[14] And Hegel would certainly seem to be the right philosopher to invoke here since, according to Hyperion, that which makes it possible for the Greeks to remain (natural) children by becoming (cultured) children is the essence of beauty, as formulated by Heraclitus in terms Hegel would approve in that they express the principle of dialectical, self-conscious thought: "The great saying of Heraclitus—the *hen diapheron eautō* (the One differentiated in itself)—that only a Greek could have invented, for it is the essence of beauty, and before that was invented there was no philosophy (*Das grosse Wort, das* hen diapheron eautō *(das Eine in sich selber unterschiedne) des Heraklit, das konnte nur ein Grieche finden, denn es ist das Wesen der Schönheit, und ehe das gefunden war, gab's keine Philosophie)"* (3:81).[15] In line with his organic metaphors of growth and ripening, Hyperion compares Heraclitus's "divine *hen diapheron eautō*," the ideal of beauty (*das Ideal der Schönheit*), to a source of light and finally to the sun (*die Sonne des Schönen*)—suggesting that this Greek (philosophical) "sun" provided exactly the right amount of light and heat for the Greeks to grow, whereas the "sun" of the Egyptians was too hot and too close, and the "sun" of the Goths too cold and too far away.

Although the three peoples are not put in chronological order in these passages, there are enough indications elsewhere in the *Hyperion*, in Hölderlin's sources (from Herodotus and Plato to Winckelmann), and in Hölderlin's later work to let us take Hyperion's analysis as a *historical* scheme: in short, Egypt (or the Orient)/Greece/Hesperia. Indeed, Hyperion even figures the scheme for us in terms of the East to West[16] "solar trajectory" so dear to Hegel and the other German idealists (as well as to Nietzsche's Zarathustra—for whom it is dear in another sense). We have paraphrased these peculiar "historical" considerations at length, not just to give "equal time" to the Egyptians—whom every interpreter of Hölderlin leaves out, preferring, understandably enough (from an idealist standpoint), to concentrate on the Greeks and their meaning for us Hesperians—but also and especially to sketch the new historical scheme that emerges when we allow the Egyptians to enter the picture. To put it as starkly as possible: for Hölderlin, our history is not a story of Hesperians and Greeks, *us and them*, but rather a story of Hesperians, Greeks, and Egyptians, us, them, *and their them*. In other words, our "nature" is Greek culture and art—our nature is somebody else's culture—and the Greeks' "nature" was Oriental, Egyptian, culture and art. Even the mere recognition of this scheme forces us to pose questions about the (Hegelian) dialectical interpretation of our relation to the Greeks—and thus of the entire idealist, aesthetic interpretation of culture and art, poetry and philosophy, as the self-mediation of nature and beauty. That is, in order for us to define ourselves in opposition to, identify ourselves in, recognize ourselves in, the Greeks—our "completed nature" (*vollendete Natur*) and the image of childhood (*Bild der Kindheit*) to which we would return—we must assume that the relation between us and the Greeks is the same as or at least analogous to their relation to the Egyptians. But what if our nature (i.e., Greek culture and art) were radically divided against itself, contained within it an Egyptian "nature" from which we are radically separated by our inherited Greek nature, in short, our Greek metaphysics, ontology, epistemology, and so on? What if in positing the same or at least analogous nature for the Greeks we, like the tragic poet of Hölderlin's "Grund zum Empedokles," only transfer, carry over by metaphor, our personality, our subjectivity and objectivity into a foreign personality, subjectivity and objectivity—that is, someone else's subject/object relation, which may not be either the same or analogous to our own, which may bear no relation whatsoever to our own? What if the authority of such an analogy, such a metaphor, were only the authority of our will to power, which invents, which *must* invent, such Greeks and such Egyptians in order to identify ourselves (*as* selves) by distinguishing us from an Orient and Egyptians for whom we may speak, for whom we *must* speak, as though they had always already been spoken for?[17] To put these suspicions in the form of a statement: the Egyptians can never be *our* other because they are somebody else's (i.e., the Greeks') other—*our other's other*—and precisely because they are that, because our other (the Greeks) is divided against itself, it (the Greeks) in turn can never be *our* other. In other words, we invent our other—"our" Greeks—by suppressing *its* otherness (i.e., the Egyptians, the Orient) in it. Insofar as it names the radically other that we had to suppress in our other in order to make it our own, "the Egyptians" would be the name of that which asymmetricalizes, disarticulates, the self/other relation between us and the Greeks and thereby renders impossible any dialectical self-consciousness and self-recognition of ourselves in the Greeks or in the Egyptians or, for that matter, in *ourselves* (insofar as we can identify ourselves as Hesperians only in dialectizable opposition to the Greeks). Such an Egyptian (for lack of another name) reading of Hölderlin's historical scheme is not only possible but always already inscribed in an other possible (and necessary) rereading of the all-important *hen diapheron eautō*. That is, to read against Hyperion, or, better, to read with Hyperion against a Hegelianized Hyperion (or Platonized Heraclitus) we need only to alter the emphasis of his words: "*Only a Greek* could have invented the great saying of Heraclitus, the *hen diapheron eautō* (the One differentiated in itself), for it is the essence of beauty, and before that was invented, there was no philosophy (*Das grosse Wort, das* hen diapheron eautō (*das Eine in sich selber unterschiedne*) *des Heraklit, das konnte nur ein Grieche finden, denn es ist das Wesen der Schönheit, und ehe das gefunden war, gab's keine Philosophie*)" (3:81). If *only a Greek* could have invented the *hen diapheron eautō*, in this context it is not inappropriate to conclude that no Egyptian and no Goth, no Oriental and no Hesperian, could have.

Now such a conclusion raises the specter of vertiginous, unthinkable questions and possibilities. For one, if the *hen diapheron eautō* as the essence of beauty, the ideal of beauty, the sun of beauty, is that which made the Greeks Greek, how could a Greek (and only a Greek) have invented it? There were *no* Greeks before the essence of "Greekness"—the principle of dialectical mediation—was invented. Either a Greek did not invent it (because there were no Greeks before the invention), or it was never invented (because there were always Greeks—and hence there was no need to invent it). The problematic is contained within the nice ambiguity of the German verb *finden*, which can mean both "to invent" and "to find": perhaps the Greeks "invented" their Greekness by pretending to "find" it (as given, natural, etc.?) and "found" it by pretending to "invent" it. But more important are the consequences for us: if only the Greeks had beauty because only the Greeks could have invented the essence of beauty, the *hen diapheron eautō*—the principle that the One differentiated in itself must be a difference in (and *of*) identity, must be, if a negation, the (determinate) negation of the same or the One—then only the Greeks could have had art in the full sense of the dialectical interpretation. And when we try to make the mimetic, aesthetic, dialectical interpretation of art and history, we are only (pathetically) trying to be Greeks. But if we may not say with utter certainty that we are not Egyptians—who are we to say?—we certainly know that we are, alas, no Greeks. This fact provides reason for sadness, nostalgia, and various attempts (more or less dialectically agile) to recover (from) the loss only as long as we forget to take the Egyptians into account: once we do so, we find (*finden*?) not only that we are not Greeks but also that we are not even *non*-Greeks (i.e., the other *of* the Greeks).

But these "historical" questions lead too far afield (as well as [too?] straight to the heart of the matter). Like Hyperion and his interlocutor, who wander from the subject of Greece and its splendor when they discuss poetry and philosophy, we are straying from our topic—poetry and philosophy, Hölderlin and Heidegger—when we discuss the glory that was Greece (and that Greece could never have been). *Von Athen ist nicht die Rede.* What we want to know is why Heidegger, like all philosophical interpreters of Hölderlin[18]—and what interpreter *as* interpreter is *not* philosophical, at least as far as his presuppositions are concerned?—leaves out the Egyptians (and thus leaves out the considerations that lead directly to Hölderlin's philosophy of history). An immediate, superficial reason would be that he is more interested, at least in 1934, in what he can make of Hölderlin's "poetry of an infinite, divine Being (*die Dichtung eines unendlichen göttlichen Seyns*)" (3:81), but this is certainly not the whole story. Indeed, one would think that Heidegger, if anyone, would foreground the Egyptians, would express solidarity with the Egyptians, as it were, since to do so would mean to put in question the (Hegelian) dialectical interpretation of Hölderlin. If, as one could say, Heidegger chose Hölderlin in the first place precisely in order to rethink the dialectical interpretation of Being, to wrest what one could call an "irreflexive Being" (*irreflexives Sein*)[19] from the very "origin" of (Hegelian) dialectics, to stifle in the cradle, as it were, (Hegelian) dialectical thought, the "philosophy of infinite subjectivity" and all its works, then "Egypt" would in fact be the place of passage (*Übergang*) where, in Kommerell's words, Heidegger's thought "flows" into the poetry of Hölderlin. Why no Egyptians, then, why the silence about (or the enforced muteness of) the Orient? Perhaps the (textual) suppression of the Egyptians and the Orient contains more than merely "foreign matter" that does not have to be spoken about (because it has, again, always already been spoken for). That Heidegger, or at least his text, is to some extent aware of this is clear from a remark in the *Letter on Humanism* (1946):"We have still hardly begun to think the mysterious relations to the East, which became word [more idiomatically translated: "which found expression"] in Hölderlin's poetry (*Wir haben noch kaum begonnen, die geheimnisvollen Bezüge zum Osten zu denken, die in Hölderlins Dichtung Wort geworden sind*)."[20] If we *think* this statement in Heideggerian terms, its meaning runs somewhat as follows: we have hardly begun to think the mysterious relations to the East, which found expression in Hölderlin's poetry, because we have thought history only in terms of a self-conscious subject's coming to itself rather than thinking it in terms of the destiny of Being's self-forgetting. In short, the statement is calling for an extensive hermeneutic labor of reinterpretation. But to think Heidegger's sentence is not (yet) to read it, and reading may be what it is "really" about. That is, perhaps we can hardly begin to *think* the mysterious relations to the East—the Orient, the Egyptians—which have become *word* in Hölderlin's poetry—which have come to speech, to language—precisely because they *have* become *word*, and it can never be enough to think them, for they also have to be *read*. In other words, a reading of Heidegger's remark takes us directly to Kommerell's second question about the respective "specific modes of utterance" of poetry and philosophy, poetry and thought. Although Heidegger would reject the idealist, aesthetic, dialectical interpretation of art, poetry, and Hölderlin's poetry in particular, his having to suppress the Egyptians may nevertheless be a sign that he, like all philosophical interpreters, has to reperform the slippage between art and poetry, between art and that "art" which is essentially linguistic. Our claim is that the suppression of the Egyptians—the (necessary) refusal to read them or their suppression, once read—is the same thing as, or, better, is the (displaced) figure for or (effaced) trace of the slippage between art and poetry: that is, the effacement of that in poetry *as language* (and language as poetry) which puts in question *all* aesthetic interpretations of Western history, art, and poetry; that which puts in question all possibility of identifying ourselves—whether it be in a Hegelian or a Heideggerian sense—by recognizing ourselves in a *non*-self—whether that "non" be conceived as a Hegelian determinate negation or as a Heideggerian negativity whose sense we have yet to think and read. In other words, there are still other Egyptians (and, needless to say, still other Hesperians) than those seen (or thought) from the point of view of the Greeks, and we may—and may not (*whose* "not"? what is the "not" of the nonself that is Egyptian?)—be they.[21]

Chiasmus: Essence of Poetry/Essence of Language

Now the "slippage" between art and poetry is, of course, quite explicit and quite intended in Heidegger: as the "Origin of the Work of Art" (1935-36) articulates it, *all* art is "poetry," all art is "linguistic," in an ontological sense. Rather than assimilating poetry to art, Heidegger "linguisticizes" all art, turns it into poetry. Our task, then, would be to seek the equivalent of the systematic suppression of the "Egyptians"—the name of that, to recapitulate, which asymmetricalizes: (1) the historical scheme of "us and them"; (2) the homogeneity of art and poetry; and (3) the mutually constitutive relation of poetry and philosophy—in Heidegger's interpretation of poetry's linguistic nature, its "linguisticality." The best place to begin to read the question of poetry as language is the essay "Hölderlin and the Essence of Poetry" (1936), which explicitly focuses on the relation of poetry and language, indeed, which pivots on the relation between the essence of poetry and the essence of language. It is also a good place to begin to think Heidegger's peculiar "negativity" (for lack of a better word), since the "not" and the "nothing," the *Nicht* and the *Nichts, are* the pivot of the relation between the essence of poetry and the essence of language. As is well known, the essay consists of a five-step commentary on five "key words" or "pointers" (*Leitworte*) taken from various texts in Hölderlin's *oeuvre* and treated out of context. The first two are, in a sense, the most important for the argument of the essay. The first is a statement about poetry: "1. Writing poetry: 'That most innocent of all occupations' *(1. Dichten: 'Diss unschuldigste aller Geschäffte').*" The second is a statement about language: "2. 'Therefore has language, most dangerous of possessions, been given to man . . . so that he may affirm what he is' *(2. 'Darum ist der Güter Gefährlichstes, die Sprache dem Menschen gegeben. . .damit er zeuge, was er sei')" (E,* 33).[22] After quoting these two, apparently somewhat contradictory, key words, Heidegger asks how they go together—"Language, the field of the 'most innocent of all occupations,' is the 'most dangerous of possessions.' How can these two be reconciled? (*Die Sprache, das Feld des 'unschuldigsten aller Geschäfte,' ist 'der Güter Gefährlichstes.' Wie geht dies beides zusammen?*)" (*E,* 35)—but postpones a consideration of the question for later: "Let us put this question aside for the moment and consider three preliminary questions (*Wir stellen diese Frage vorerst zurück und bedenken die drei Vorfragen*)" (*E,* 35). When toward the end of the essay he returns to the question—"This brings us back to the question that we laid aside in the first instance (*Damit kommen wir zu jener Frage zurück, die wir zunächst beiseite stellten*)" (*E,* 42-43)—he does so by summarizing the essay's entire argument about the relation of poetry and language. Hence one could say that the question of how the innocence of poetry goes together with the danger of language organizes the argument of the essay and that the question's postponement motivates the argument's progress. But before we read Heidegger's "answer," we should first consider what the question means. The "innocence" of poetry is relatively straightforward and elicits only a half-page commentary. Since poetry appears in the modest guise of play, remains immersed in the imagined realm of play, it avoids the seriousness of decisions that always in one way or another create guilt. In short, "Poetry is like a dream, and not reality; a playing with words, and not the seriousness of action. Poetry is harmless and ineffectual. For what can be less dangerous than mere speech (*die blosse Sprache*)?" (*E,* 35).

The "danger of language," however, is considerably more complicated insofar as it is twofold: first of all, language is dangerous, indeed "the danger of all dangers" (*die Gefahr aller Gefahren*) (*E,* 36), because it creates the very possibility of a danger in the first place. It is clear that "danger" here is to be understood in the fundamental ontological terms of *Being and Time*: "Danger is the threat to Being from beings (*Gefahr ist Bedrohung des Seins durch Seiendes*)" (*E*, 36).[23] That is, since it is only by virtue of language that a world of "beings" (*Seiendes*) is opened to man in his existence (*Dasein*)—beings (*Seiendes*) that *as* existent (als *Seiendes*) afflict and enflame man and as nonexistent (*als Nichtseiendes*), that is, in the ontological sense, deceive and disappoint him—it is language that first creates the possibility of a threat to Being (*Sein*) and the possibility of a loss of Being (*die Möglichkeit des Seinsverlustes*) (*E*, 37). In other words, if danger is the threat to the ontological (Being) from the ontic (beings), then language, which creates the very possibility of the ontic for man—the world of individual entities of which he is one—also creates the possibility of a threat to Being. But, according to Heidegger, language also bears another danger within itself, namely, the danger *to* itself: "But language is not only the danger of dangers, but necessarily conceals in itself a continual danger for itself (*Aber die Sprache ist nicht nur die Gefahr der Gefahren, sondern sie birgt in sich selbst für sich selbst notwendig eine fortwährende Gefahr*)" (*E*, 37). Language endangers itself because both the purest and the most confused, the most hidden and the most ordinary, can come to word (*zu Wort kommen*) in it, and the word as word (*das Wort als Wort*) can never give an immediate guarantee as to whether it is "an essential word" (*ein wesentliches Wort*) or a "delusion" (*ein Blendwerk*) (*E*, 37). "Therefore language must constantly put itself into an appearance that it itself has generated, and hence endanger what is most its own, authentic saying (*So muss sich die Sprache ständig in einen von ihr selbst erzeugten Schein stellen und damit ihr Eigenstes, das echte Sagen, gefährden*)" (*E*, 37). Now if one remembers the nature of the first danger of language (i.e., of beings to Being), one cannot mistake this second danger for, say, some kind of idealist complaint like Schiller's "*Speaks* the soul, then it is no longer, alas, the *soul* that speaks (Spricht *die Seele, so spricht, ach! schon die* Seele *nicht mehr*)." No, the danger of language to itself—of its appearance (*Schein*) to its authentic saying (*das echte Sagen*), of its delusion (*Blendwerk*) to its "essential word" (*wesentliches Wort*)—is not a matter of the difference between thought and expression, essence and accidents, etc., but rather a question of, again, the ontological difference between Being and beings. Hence one could translate language's appearance (*Schein*) and language's essence, authentic saying (*das echte Sagen*), into ontic and ontological. That is, language presents itself as a tool man can wield, as just another being (*Seiendes*), but its essence, that which is most proper to it, is authentic saying (*das echte Sagen*), what Heidegger in the summary paragraph toward the end of the essay calls *poetry*: the founding naming of Being (*Dichtung ist das stiftende Nennen des Seins*) (*E*, 43). Now it is clear that—all the elaborations of the essay aside—a reversal has taken place. Heidegger had started out to determine the essence of poetry on the basis of an understanding of the essence of its "field" (i.e., language), and now it turns out that the essence of language *is* poetry (i.e., that in language which is most its own [*ihr Eigenstes*]—authentic saying, the founding naming of Being). In short, rather than thinking the essence of poetry on the basis of the essence of language, we should think the essence of language on the basis of the essence of poetry. This (chiasmic) reversal and the mechanism of its "ontologization" of language and poetry, language *as* poetry—a tortuous "negation" of the ontic we have still to read—is explicit in the essay and most visible in the summary paragraph, which also brings together the innocence of poetry and the danger of language.

Heidegger sets the paragraph off by introducing it as follows: "This brings us back to the question [the innocence of poetry/the danger of language] that we laid aside in the first instance. In now proceeding to answer the question, we will try at the same time to summarize and bring before the inner eye (*vor das innere Auge zu bringen*) the essence of poetry and of the poet" (*E*, 43). The metaphor of the "inner eye" recalls the beginning of the essay where Heidegger claims a determined order for his key words: "The necessary order in these sayings and their inner connectedness ought to bring before our eyes the essential essence of poetry (*Die bestimmte Ordnung dieser Worte und ihr innerer Zusammenhang sollen das wesentliche Wesen der Dichtung vor Augen stellen*)" (*E*, 34). The change suggests that "the eye" in having become the "inner eye" is now ready to think the necessity and the inner connectedness of the key words and to begin (reading?) the essay again: "*First of all* it appeared that the field of action of poetry is language. *Hence* the essence of poetry must be understood through the essence of language. *Afterward* it became clear that poetry is the founding naming of Being and of the essence of all things—not just any speech, but that particular kind which for the *first time* brings into the open all that which we *then* discuss and deal with in everyday language. *Hence* poetry never takes language as a raw material ready to hand, rather it is poetry that *first* makes language possible. Poetry is the primitive language of a historical people. *Therefore, in just the reverse manner*, the essence of language must be understood through the essence of poetry [my emphases] (*Zuerst ergab sich: der Werkbereich der Dichtung ist die Sprache. Das Wesen der Dichtung muss daher aus dem Wesen der Sprache begriffen werden. Nachher aber wurde deutlich: Dichtung ist das stiftende Nennen des Seins und des Wesens aller Dinge—kein beliebiges Sagen, sondern jenes, wodurch erst all das ins Offene tritt, was wir dann in der Alltagssprache bereden und verhandeln. Daher nimmt die Dichtung niemals die Sprache als einen vorhandenen Werkstoff auf, sondern die Dichtung selbst ermöglicht erst die Sprache. Dichtung ist die Ursprache eines geschichtlichen Volkes. Also muss umgekehrt das Wesen der Sprache aus dem Wesen der Dichtung verstanden werden)*" (*E*, 43).

The (chiasmic) reversal could not be clearer. We start with "the essence of poetry must be understood through the essence of language" and conclude with just the reverse (*umgekehrt*): "the essence of language must be understood through the essence of poetry." Equally clear is how Heidegger uses what one could call the language of syllogistic reasoning in order to effect the reversal: that is, the words we have underlined, "first," "then," "hence," "therefore," and so on. For what happens in the course of the paragraph is that the meaning of these words is itself reversed, or, better, that the meaning of these words is doubled: that is, when we begin by saying that "first of all" (*zuerst*) the field of action of poetry is language and that "hence" (*daher*) the essence of poetry has to be understood through the essence of language, we mean a priority and a consequence in the order of the ontic, in terms of the everyday understanding of poetry, language, and essence. But when we say that poetry is the speaking through which "first" (*erst*) comes into the open all that we "then" (*dann*) talk about and deal with in everyday language, we mean a priority and a consequence in the order of the ontological, in terms of an ontological understanding of poetry, language, and essence. In short, the first "first" is not the same as the second "first," and the difference between them is ontological. So that along with the (chiasmic) reversal comes a reversal in meaning from ontic to ontological: to say that the essence of language is to be understood through, on the basis of, out of (*aus dem*), the essence of poetry is not just a symmetrical inversion of saying that the essence of poetry has to be understood through, on the basis of, out of (*aus dem*), the essence of language, for the meaning of all the terms—especially the term that expresses the relation between the two essences: "through [etc.]" (*aus dem*)—has changed. In other words, the chiasmus is not a symmetrical chiasmus, and the asymmetry of its terms is, again, the asymmetry of the ontological difference between beings and Being. This (asymmetrical chiasmic) reversal has far-reaching consequences for an interpretation of the essay. It means, for instance, that we must read the essay both backward and forward, as it were: we must rewrite the claims of its beginning in ontological terms. For example, Heidegger's choice of Hölderlin as the poet of the poet is not, the essay would claim, an arbitrary, subjective decision but rather a necessity of thought: *we* do not decide to choose Hölderlin; he chooses us and in this sense is the poet who "puts into the decision" (*stellt er in die Entscheidung*) (*E*, 34). The same rereading would be required of Heidegger's claim of the "determined order and inner connectedness" of the key words: it would be an order determined not by a philosopher's caprice but rather by the matter of thought itself (*die Sache des Denkens*) as determined by Being itself (*vom Sein selbst bestimmt*), as the later Heidegger is fond of saying. But what we are interested in is the pivot of the reversal, that is, the negative that renders the chiasmus asymmetrical. In sheer grammatical terms, it is indeed a negative, a negation, that can be pinpointed in the paragraph: "*not* just any speech, *but* that particular kind which for the first time. . .(kein *beliebiges Sagen*, sondern *jenes, wodurch erst. . .)''*; or "Hence poetry *never* takes language as a raw material ready to hand, *rather*. . .(*Daher nimmt die Dichtung* niemals *die Sprache als einen vorhandenen Werkstoff auf, sondern. . .).''* This "not. . .but rather" locution is, of course, familiar to all readers of *Being and Time*: Heidegger uses it repeatedly in his analysis of the existential (*existentiale*) structures of *Dasein* to say, for instance, "When I say *Angst* I do *not* mean fear in the everyday (received, derived, deficient) mode—which is always fear of something—*but rather* the fear that is more original than and that is the condition of possibility of fear in the everyday sense—a fear of nothing.'' What the strategy of this locution amounts to, then, is a peculiar negation of the negation (that is, the everyday, the ontic, beings, *Seiendes*, as *non*existent in an ontological sense) for the purpose of determining, naming, or at least pointing toward, another "negation,'' another "Nothing'' (i.e., the ontological, Being, *Sein*, as *non*existent in an ontic sense). Small wonder, then, that poetry (as language) and language (as poetry) are both innocent and dangerous: if poetry is the founding naming of Being, it is certainly innocent, for it has nothing to do with beings; but, at the same time, it is certainly dangerous *to* beings, for it has to do with the Nothing *of* beings (i.e., Being). In poetry the (innocent and dangerous) "Nothing noths,'' as Kenneth Burke translates it, *das Nichts nichtet.*[24]

But in thinking this peculiar "negation of negation,'' Heidegger's other Nothing, we should avoid certain common (and perhaps inevitable) confusions. For one, Heidegger's *Nichts* is not to be understood as a determinate negation of beings (*Seiendes*) by Being (*Sein*), for then Being would in a sense need beings; it would be the negation *of* beings; and it would thus *belong* to beings (in the Hegelian senses of the double genitive, i.e., subjective as well as objective). This is *not* the nature of Heidegger's Not. But if the dialectician's understanding cannot account for Heidegger's Nothing, the logical positivist's critique—that such a Nothing is meaningless, senseless, contradictory, absurd, and that the sentence *das Nichts nichtet* is a pseudostatement that makes "syntactic nonsense''—is of even less help, for even the most logical of positivists would have to admit that when he talks about Heidegger and nothing else, about Heidegger's Nothing and nothing else, about nonsense and nothing else, he is also always already (and always not yet) talking about nothing (else).[25] In short, like all scientists, he cannot talk about anything without at the same time talking about Nothing. Even though positivism, like all science, wants to know nothing of the Nothing (*die Wissenschaft will vom Nichts nichts wissen*), as Heidegger wryly puts it in "What is Metaphysics?'' (1929), it still depends upon this Nothing, just as logical negation depends upon a more original Nothing, the Not depends upon the Nothing. "The Not does not originate through negation; rather negation is grounded in the Not that springs from the nihilation of the Nothing (*Das Nicht ensteht nicht durch die Verneinung, sondern die Verneinung gründet sich auf das Nicht, das dem Nichten des Nichts entspringt*).''[26]

"The Not does not. . . but rather. . ."—how think Not without negation, a "without" without the negation of the "without," *un "sans" sans "sans"*? For Heidegger, such thinking means evaluating, revaluating, as it were, the "positive" in the "privative" essence of truth as disconcealment, *a-letheia*: "First of all, the valuation of the 'positive' in the 'privative' essence of *aletheia* is necessary. First of all, this positive has to be experienced as the grounding trait of Being itself (*Zuvor bedarf es der Würdigung des 'Positiven' im 'privativen' Wesen der* aletheia. *Zuvor ist dieses Positive als der Grundzug des Seins selbst zu erfahren*)."[27] But, again, how think the "positive" of the "privative" without thinking in terms of oppositions like "positive" and "negative"? How think Heidegger's quotation marks (or italics, crossings-out, etc.) without first—what kind of priority, what kind of "without" would this be?—*reading* them?

One of the better attempts to think Heidegger's Nothing (without yet *reading* it) is that of Henri Birault in his *Heidegger and the Experience of Thought* (*Heidegger et l'expérience de la pensée*): "Double task, and a paradoxical task of thought. It is necessary to think without negativity the nihilating power of Being, for in truth this nihilating power shelters 'the best' of Being. It is the *lethe* of *aletheia*. But in another sense, it is necessary also to give an account of the advent of negativity on the basis of that which includes in itself the negative and the positive, all the time knowing that this pure inclusion definitively rejects these two terms. The refusal of negation without the refusal (or rather without the explanation) of that which makes the negation not only possible but necessary is only the refusal of a conclusion without premises. In its final effort, the thought of Heidegger is neither positive nor negative, nor indifferent to affirmation and negation. It is rather *suspensive*. It is the thought of the 'suspension' of Being which holds us suspended between earth and sky, between death and the gods (*Double tâche, et tâche paradoxale de la pensée. Il faut penser sans négativité la puissance néantisante de l'être, car en vérité cette puissance néantisante abrite 'le meilleur' de l'être. Elle est la* lethe *de l'*aletheia. *Mais d'un autre côté, il faut bien rendre compte aussi de l'avènement de la négativité à partir de ce qui inclut en soi le négatif et le positif, tout en sachant que cette inclusion sans mélange récuse en définitive ces deux termes. Le refus de la négation sans le refus [ou plutôt sans l'élucidation] de ce qui rend non seulement possible mais nécessaire la négation n'est que le refus d'une conséquence sans prémisses. Dans son dernier effort, la pensée de Heidegger n'est ni positive ni négative, ni non plus indifférente à l'affirmation et à la négation. Elle est plutôt* suspensive. *Elle est la pensée du 'suspens' de l'être qui nous tient en suspens entre la terre et le ciel, entre la mort et les divins*)."[28] Neither positive nor negative, nor indifferent to affirmation and negation—this characterization of Heidegger's "suspensive" thought of Nothing brings us back to Hölderlin and the essence of poetry—its innocence and its danger. For the authority of Heidegger's suspensive Nothing certainly seems to come from

Hölderlin: that is, from the double absence of the gods, what Heidegger calls the "double Not," in Hölderlin's (*our*) time of need. "Hölderlin, in the act of establishing the essence of poetry, first determines a new time. It is the time of the gods that have fled *and* of the god that is coming. It is the time of *need*, because it lies under a double lack and a double Not: the No-more of the gods that have fled and the Not-yet of the god that is coming (*indem Hölderlin das Wesen der Dichtung neu stiftet, bestimmt er erst eine neue Zeit. Es ist die Zeit der entflohenen Götter* und *des kommenden Gottes. Das ist die* dürftige *Zeit, weil sie in einem gedoppelten Mangel und Nicht steht: im Nichtmehr der entflohenen Götter und im Nochnicht des Kommenden*)" (*E*, 47). That Heidegger's Nothing is operative in this interpretation of Hölderlin's "double Not"—a kind of place-holder between past and future that creates a present, *our* present, as the time of need—is clear in the explicit asymmetry between one Not and the other: the time of need is the time of the god*s* that have fled and the go*d* that is coming. In other words, as in his interpretation of *aletheia*, Heidegger extracts a "positive" out of the "privative": that is, the (future) coming of the god out of the gods that have fled (in the past).[29] And yet is Heidegger's double Not also the double Not of Hölderlin? Are they the same? Of course, one cannot ask the question so simply, for it is evident that as long as we *think* this double Not in Heidegger's terms—that is, in terms of *aletheia*—it is indeed the "same"—*das Selbe* (the same) and *not das Gleiche* (the identical)—as Hölderlin's. Is there another Not, then? It is difficult to think what such an "other Not" could be, since Heidegger's Nothing (the *Nichts* that is the ground of his own and Hölderlin's *Nicht*) is *already* other, a *completely other* Nothing, as Heidegger puts it in "Zur Seinsfrage" (1955). Hence the "other Not" we are asking about would have to be an *un*thought "other Not," and *un*thought, again, in a sense other than Heidegger's "unthought" (*das Ungedachte*). It would have to be, in short (to break the chain of the endless return of Heidegger's "unthought," "other," "Not"), an unthought other Not that can nevertheless be *read* in Hölderlin's and Heidegger's text.[30]

Hölderlin and the Germans

> Wie ganz anders, anders war es da!
> —Schiller, "Die Götter Griechenlands"

> Wie anders ists!
> —Hölderlin, "Germanien"

Perhaps the best place to begin reading the "other Not"—of Hölderlin *and* of Heidegger—is Hölderlin's late hymn "Germanien," to which Heidegger devotes one hundred and fifty pages in the lectures from the *Wintersemester, 1934-35*. Appropriately enough, this poem that, according to Heidegger, is the perfect beginning (because it leads into the origin) begins with a Not—an apparent negation whose "object" is the Greek gods:

> Nicht sie, die Seeligen, die erschienen sind,
> Die Götterbilder in dem alten Lande,
> Sie darf ich ja nicht rufen mehr, wenn aber
> Ihr heimatlichen Wasser! jetzt mit euch
> Des Herzens Liebe klagt, was will es anders
> Das Heiligtrauernde?

> Not them, the blessed, who once appeared,
> Those images of gods in the ancient land,
> Them I may no longer call, but if,
> You waters of the homeland, now with you
> The love of my heart laments, what else does it want,
> The holily mourning (one)?[31]

Heidegger's entire project pivots on a reinterpretation of the poem's stark, abrupt, opening "Not." Indeed, says Heidegger, "This 'Not them. . .' with which our poem begins, is a decision of time (*Zeitentscheidung*) in the sense of the *original time* of the peoples" (*HH*, 51). One could say, then, that the question of the poem comes down to whether Heidegger can—whether *we* can, since the time decided *by* the poem is *our* time[32]—get past the first word of the poem. His complicated attempt to do so, his reinterpretation of the Not, of the refusal of the old, dead, Greek gods, is worth retracing.

The reinterpretation begins with a determination of the "grounding mood" (*Grundstimmung*) of the poem on the basis of the "holily mourning" (*das Heiligtrauernde*) heart of the opening lines: the mood is holy mourning (*heilige Trauer*). What does it mean? "Holy mourning" is not some sentimental subjective sadness or like physical pain—as we know from *Being and Time*, this is not what Heidegger means by mood—but rather something essentially other (*HH*, 82). This otherness is specifically determined by a threefold "not": the "holy mourning" is *not* (1) a despairing giving up of the old gods, indeed, as the first strophe says, these gods remain loved too much by the "I" of the poem—that is, the mourning does not exhaust itself in a sterile independence of the *subject*; nor (2) is it a rootless giving oneself up to the gods who have fled—that is, the mourning is not a losing of the subject in the *object*; nor (3) is it a refusal of both (1) and (2)—that is, the mourning is not an empty hovering between subject and object but rather "founds a new relation to the gods" (*HH*, 87).[33] This threefold "not" is what makes the mourning *holy*: it is not contingent and not poetic decoration, but "rather in it something groundingly essential is poetically said about Being pure and simple (*über das Seyn schlechthin*)" (*HH*, 90). In short, if the essential otherness of the holy mourning is that of Being, this grounding mood of the poem is an *ontological* category like the mood of dread (*Angst*) in *Being and Time* and "What Is Metaphysics?" And like the mood of *Angst*, which because it is fear of *nothing* rather than of something, discloses the Nothing, the *Nichts*, the mood of holy mourning, because it is a mourning over the present absence of the old Greek gods rather than over their (past) presence, discloses the Not, the *Nicht*. Hence the opening words, rather than any kind of refusal of the old gods or a nostalgic hanging onto them, are a recovering of the old gods *in* their absence, or, better, "the preservation of the divinity of the old gods in the mourning renunciation of them" (*HH*,93).

Heidegger's ontologization of Hölderlin's "Not" (*Nicht*) and "other" (*anders*) can be traced to its (textual) source in the pages he devotes to an extensive interpretation of the poem's opening. After the determination of the poem's grounding mood as holy mourning (the "holily mourning" heart), we can say the first strophe again with a now clearer knowledge, says Heidegger (*HH*, 96), who then quotes the entire first strophe (again), and comments: "Now we read nothing more of a refusal. We also gather that it is not at all a question of an external historical comparison of a previous state of the old world and the attitude to it with a later and contemporary world, not a question of humanism, but rather what holds sway here is the time of the peoples, and in question is the global destiny of the native earth" (*HH*, 96). The effacement of the opening "Not" could not be more explicit—now we read nothing more of a Not, we could paraphrase—but Heidegger makes it so: "But not only does nothing of a refusal happen in the first strophe. The 'Not' with which it begins is basically not at all an isolated negation, also not a renunciation, but rather. . ." (*HH*, 96). A peculiar torturing of language takes place here: *not* only does *not* a *not* happen in the first strophe, we could rewrite (*Nicht nur nichts von einem Nicht geschieht in der ersten Strophe. . .?*). If not only not a Not, what then? Heidegger's response is worth following to the end: "The 'Not'. . .rather finds its authentic [or proper] full meaning (*seine eigentliche volle Bedeutung*) in the 'what else does it want' (verse 5), the holily mourning heart. We have already pointed to the beginning of the second strophe and stated that, yes, the gods have themselves fled and hence a refusal of them is not necessary. With that, however, we do not broach the true import of the second strophe and its inner relation to the first. Rather we have to hold together in one both verse 5 and verse 19, 'what else does it want' with 'Nothing do I want to deny here and nothing do I want to plead for.' This line is the highest decisiveness (*höchste Entschiedenheit*), namely the taking over of the abandonment by the old gods. The grounding mood of holy mourning intensifies itself here to its innermost dominance. The mourning becomes a knowledge that the true taking earnestly of the gods who have fled as those who have fled is in itself precisely an awaiting of the gods, namely of their godliness as no longer fulfilled. The wanting-nothing-more and pleading-for-nothing is not the fall into a crude godlessness and an empty despair, no idle and clever coming to terms with death, rather this wanting is the wanting of verse 5—'what else does it want'—: turning to and pure self-maintaining in the space of a possible new meeting with the gods" (*HH*, 96-97). Rather than a despairing or facile refusal of the old gods, the poem's opening—read in the context of verses 5 and 19—would be the highest decisiveness, a mourning that is a knowledge of the gods who have fled *as* fled, and thereby a will to a possible new meeting of, with, the gods. ("All No [*Alles Nein*]," says the "Letter on Humanism," is only the affirmation of the Not [*ist nur die Bejahung des Nicht*].")[34] Perhaps here Heidegger could be more easily accused of "nostalgia" than in "Hölderlin and the Essence of Poetry" (for which the "Germanien" lectures are clearly a *Vorstudium*), for it would seem that the meeting we are awaiting is with the same old god*s* (whereas in "Hölderlin and the Essence of Poetry" there is an asymmetry between god*s* past and god to come). Nevertheless, we should remember that (1) it is a *new* meeting (*Neubegegnung*) with the gods, and, more important, that (2) it is not a *presence* that is mourned here but rather a *present absence* whose negativity is interpreted ontologically. Small wonder, then, that the "highest decisiveness" [or decid*ed*ness] (*höchste Entschiedenheit*) of this holy mourning—what we come up against under the name "Hölderlin"—puts us *into* the decision (*Deshalb stellt er in die Entscheidung*).

But such an understanding of the "Not *of* the Not" of Heidegger's "Poet *of* the poet" is nevertheless not yet a reading: how does Heidegger efface, erase, rewrite the poem's opening Not? If the Not finds "its proper, full meaning" (*seine eigentliche volle Bedeutung*) in line 5—"what else does it want?"—then what does this verse want? What does Heidegger want in reading the Not into it? In fact, Heidegger reads into it not only the Not but also the entire poem (indeed all of Hölderlin's poetry and all of poetry if we keep in mind Hölderlin's decisive exemplary position as the founder of "an other history"):[35] "Only when we measure the entire self-secured breadth of this holy mourning, which pushes away everything forced, do we meet and understand the deciding word (*das entscheidende Wort*) of the entire first strophe and thereby of the entire poem" (*HH*, 94). This "deciding word" (*das entscheidende Wort*), this "essential word" (*das wesentliche Wort*) (*HH*, 96), the word that turns "Not" to "Not" (of Being), "other" to "other" (of Being), beginning into origin, what does it say? As it turns out, this "word" does not say anything but asks (or does not ask?) a question: "The word has the linguistic form of the question and runs (verse 5): . . . what else does it want—it, the holily mourning heart. According to the usual characterization of forms of speech one can find here a so-called rhetorical question, a saying that despite having the form of a question is no question but rather an answering and assuring, the statement of a certainty and decidedness (*Das Wort hat die sprachliche Form der Frage und lautet (V.5): . . . was will es anders—es, das heilig trauernde Herz. Nach der üblichen Kennzeichnung der Redeform kann man hier eine sogenannte rhetorische Frage finden, ein Sagen, das trotz der Frageform keine Frage, sondern ein Antworten und Versichern, der Spruch einer Sicherheit und Entschiedenheit ist)"* (*HH*, 94-95). Although Heidegger seems to dismiss the "linguistic form"—a question, and, at that, a "so-called rhetorical question"—of his "deciding word" (as though because it were a question of *merely* linguistic *form* it could be effaced and rewritten—like a question mark, say—again and again), it is clear that he exploits this form and "the usual characterization of forms of speech" to the full: that is, he reads the question figuratively, *as* a rhetorical question (*une question de pure forme*, as one might say in French). Rather than asking "what else?" the question is really saying "nothing else": "The no longer being able to call the old gods, this self-submission to renunciation, what else is it—it is nothing else (*was ist es anderes—es ist nichts anderes*)—but the only possible resolved readiness for the awaiting of the godly" (*HH*, 95). It is this decision to read figuratively that allows Heidegger to rewrite the "Not" into "Not Not," as it were, and to take it (along with verse 19) as the "highest decidedness." And it is no use saying that Heidegger's *Nichts* comes before, is ontologically prior to, the question of literal and figurative, for here the decision of the question (literal/figurative?) comes before—that is, in terms of a temporality of reading and not a temporality of the destiny of the forgetting of Being—indeed, founds (and confounds) the question of the "Nothing" (*Nichts*).

Now the (first) problem with such a reading of the Not is that the question "what else does it want?" "what *other* does it want?" can, of course, also be taken literally as "what else is there?" That is, as asking what else besides *calling* (*rufen*) the mere *images* of the gods who *appeared*—gods who precisely *because* they appeared cannot be our gods because our culture is a response to a different, other nature from that of the Greeks. (Again, in the terms of Hölderlin's letter to Böhlendorff, our *nature* is Greek culture ["clarity of representation," "Junonian sobriety"]; and *Greek* nature is Oriental culture ["the fire from heaven," "holy pathos"].) This would be one possible reason why the "I" of the poem's opening fears that it is fatal, deathly, to *see* the beautiful countenances of the gods as though they were unchanged (as if *now* were *then: als wärs, wie sonst*): "To look upon your beautiful brows, as though/They were unchanged, I am afraid, for deadly/And scarcely permitted it is to awaken the dead (*Denn euer schönes Angesicht zu sehn, als wärs, wie sonst, ich fürcht' es, tödtlich ists,/Und kaum erlaubt, Gestorbene zu weken*)." In other words, the gods who appeared then are now, for us, dead not because they no longer appear but because for us, now, they *cannot* appear: that is, in the mode of Greek, mimetic representation, in the mode of appearance (*erscheinen*), images (*Bilder*), and so on. In short, perhaps the question is indeed asking for "other gods," whom it would be more appropriate to call (*rufen*): gods who can be called by a calling that is not a calling of images of *seen* (literally or figuratively) gods but a calling of, as it were, *heard* gods, a calling of calling. What other gods these could be and how they could be other is the question of the poem. Trying to "answer" this question—as though one could answer and as though we had not already answered (here and elsewhere)—would lead us too far away from (and too far into) the poem, but the implications (for Hölderlin and for Heidegger) can be indicated. The problem is not just that a literal reading of the question triggers another, opposed, reading of the poem—that is, it is not just that the poem is, as one says, "ambiguous"—but rather that (1) the two readings, figurative and literal, are mutually exclusive (better, mutually parasitical)—"the one reading is precisely the error denounced by the other and has to be undone by it"³⁶ (as Paul de Man puts it): *"Nothing but* them. . ." versus "Not *them*. . ."—and are not reconcilable, not mediatable (either by dialectics or by ontology), because (2) the difference between them is radically undecidable. There is no way to decide whether the poem is really asking or not asking for something else because the poem "itself" is *not* itself; it is divided against itself and does not know whether it is asking for something else or for more of the same. And the appeal to "tone" (or "context") is of no help here because, as Heidegger has so eloquently demonstrated, it is precisely this quesiton that decides the tone, the mood (*Stimmung*), of the poem in the first place; and if the question is itself undecidable, so is the tone or context by means of which we had hoped to decide the question.³⁷ In short, precisely the word, the phrase, that Heidegger calls the "deciding word" of the poem is itself undecidable and thus reproduces an other (de-ontologized) Not that cannot be effaced, that reproduces itself mechanically by self-quotation (which can never be the quotation of a self or a subject) like something merely recited by heart or repeated.³⁸ Rather than putting us into the decision, "Hölderlin" puts us into radical (i.e., subjectless, Beingless) undecidability.

To summarize, let us retrace Heidegger's interpretation of the question "what else does it want?" step by step in order to mark better how our reading of the question as undecidable diverges from Heidegger's path. Heidegger's effort is an attempt to efface the opening "Not" of the poem, to read "Not them" as "Precisely them," "Nothing but them," or *Not* "Not them." His interpretation accomplishes this on the basis of what he calls the grounding mood of holy mourning. This grounding mood (the mood of the ground) is an ontological category—like the mood of dread in *Being and Time*—and it provides the horizon of understanding against which the poem is to be read. It is the preunderstanding of the poem. The question "what else does it want?" is first read against the background of this horizon, in terms of the mood of holy mourning. But, on the other hand, the grounding mood of holy mourning is read on the basis of this question: that is, on the basis of the question read as not really a question but as an assertiveness and decidedness (*das entscheidende Wort*), in short, as a rhetorical question. Heidegger is explicit about this, but he dismisses the question of reading as only a question of *linguistic form*—a purely ontic concern, the ontic aspect of language, one could say. The circle in Heidegger's reading is explicit: the reading of the question as rhetorical is decided on the basis of the grounding mood; the grounding mood is decided on the basis of the reading of the question as rhetorical. And this is not some hermeneutic circle of part and whole but an ontologized circle of preunderstanding and understanding based on the existential structure of *Dasein*'s self-understanding: its always already being concerned with the question of the meaning of Being (see *Being and Time*, section 32). But what we are saying is that this circle is broken by reading. First of all, the question "what else does it want?" can also be read literally, and such a reading would give rise to an other history, one that plays itself out not as a story of us and them, of us and the Greeks, but as a story of us/them/ and *their* them, Hesperians/Greeks/and Egyptians (or the Orient). In such a history, the Greeks would be the name of a radical disjunction between us and. . .ourselves, the Egyptians (because, according to Hölderlin's letter to Böhlendorff, the relation of nature and culture for us and for the Egyptians is the "same"). We have already indicated what this other history would be like.[39] For our purposes here, it is more important that this (always possible) other literal reading is only the sign of a gap inscribed in the question: a gap not (just) between one (literal) meaning and another (figurative) meaning (masterable by a sufficiently rigorous hermeneutics that can hold both together) but rather a gap between meaning, the horizon of meaning, the grounding mood, the semantic pole, rhetoric. . .on the one hand, *and* the linguistic form of the question, syntax, grammar on the other—a gap, in short, between the meaning of words and the order of words, between the word as carrier of meaning and the word as place-holder or "syntactical plug." The question "what else does it want?" stands in the place of this gap—it makes a hole, as it were, in the text—and it is its status as mere placeholder, nonsignifying syntactical plug, that interferes with its semantic function as carrier of meaning. This mutual, asymmetrical interference—and not its lexical richness, polysemy, or ambiguity—is what renders the question truly undecidable in de Man's or Derrida's sense: undecidability is "the irreducible excess of the syntactic over the semantic." ("Its semantic void *signifies*, but it signifies spacing and articulation; it has as its meaning the possibility of syntax; it orders the play of meaning. *Neither purely syntactic nor purely semantic*, it marks the articulated opening of that opposition.")[40] And it is undecidability in this "sense" that always comes to interfere with Heidegger's attempt to reduce Hölderlin's syntax to ontological semantics, to questions of meaning that have nothing (ontological "Nothing") to do with questions of pure linguistic form, grammar, syntax. One could say that "linguistic form," syntax—and the necessity to dismiss it as ontic—mark an irreducible, necessary remainder of the technical (*Technik*) in any language (no matter how "ontologized") *as* language.[41]

Chapter 4
"Patmos"
The Senses of Interpretation

Auffallend müsste es aber dabei sein, dass eine Sprache dazu gekommen ist, ein und dasselbe Wort für zwei entgegengesetzte Bestimmungen zu gebrauchen. Für das spekulative Denken ist es erfreulich, in der Sprache Wörter zu finden, welche eine spekulative Bedeutung an ihnen selbst haben; die deutsche Sprache hat mehrere dergleichen.

—G. W. F. Hegel, *Wissenschaft der Logik*[1]

'Sinn' nämlich ist dies wunderbare Wort, welches selber in zwei entgegengesetzten Bedeutungen gebraucht wird. Einmal bezeichnet es die Organe der unmittelbaren Auffassung, das andere Mal aber heissen wir Sinn: die Bedeutung, den Gedanken, das Allgemeine der Sache. Und so bezieht sich der Sinn einerseits auf das ummittelbar Äusserliche der Existenz, andererseits auf das innere Wesen derselben.

—G. W. F. Hegel, *Vorlesungen über die Ästhetik*[2]

Hölderlin's "Patmos" lends itself readily to being treated as a religious document or a profession of faith. Interpreters of the poem have been particularly resourceful in tracing its many Biblical themes and allusions.[3] P. H. Gaskill sees "Patmos" as Hölderlin's closest approximation of the spirit of pietism.[4] But the determined effort to discover Christian doctrine in or behind the words of the poem has facilitated the covering of the poem's inconsistencies under the convenient labels of "mystery" and "paradox." Whether secular or religious, the interpreter is repeatedly forced into formulations like: "A secret. . .to grasp the God in the human word," "the magical properties of language," and "the divine power of the word."[5] This simultaneous recognition and magical dismissal of the poem's difficulties result in overly hasty oppositions and analogies between poetry and Scripture on the one hand and poetry and philosophy on the other.[6] The specificity of each disappears under an assumed likeness or unlikeness. This reduction is characteristic of interpretations of the dialogue between Hölderlin and philosophers, and it is not confined to Heidegger's readings of Hölderlin, which have caused some justified (if not always well-articulated) uneasiness among critics.[7] Interpreters of the relationship between Hölderlin and Hegel explicitly extoll one at the expense of the other and implicitly value literature over philosophy or vice versa.[8] Since the effort is always to demonstrate the discourse of one reducible to that of the other, Hölderlin has fared less well than Hegel—the author of the most subsuming discourse of all time—especially in regard to his poetry.[9] Yet the *rapprochement* of the two thinkers has already proved fruitful for an understanding of Hölderlin's theoretical writings and letters,[10] and this would indicate that a rigorous interpretation of the relationship between Hölderlin and Hegel may be the best route of access to Hölderlin. As such, it remains a route to be opened. This chapter cannot lay claim to such a project;[11] it does not even attempt to read "Patmos" in its "entirety."[12] Rather it is a preliminary essay toward: (1) a (re)reading of the late Hölderlin and (2) the (re)opening of a genuine dialogue between Hölderlin and Hegel.

> Zu lang, zu lang schon ist
> Die Ehre der Himmlischen unsichtbar.
> Denn fast die Finger müssen sie
> Uns führen und schmählich
> Entreisst das Herz uns eine Gewalt.
> Denn Opfer will der Himmlischen jedes,
> Wenn aber eines versäumt ward,
> Nie hat es Gutes gebracht.
> Wir haben gedient der Mutter Erd'
> Und haben jüngst dem Sonnenlichte gedient,
> Unwissend, der Vater aber liebt,
> Der über allen waltet,
> Am meisten, dass gepfleget werde
> Der veste Buchstab, und bestehendes gut
> Gedeutet. Dem folgt deutscher Gesang.
>   (2:171-72)[13]

Too long, too long now
The honor of the Heavenly has been invisible.
For almost they must guide
Our fingers, and shamefully
A power is wresting our hearts from us.
For every one of the Heavenly wants sacrifices, and
No good ever came of it.
We have served Mother Earth
And lately have served the sunlight,
Unwittingly, but what the Father
Who reigns over all loves most
Is that the solid letter
Be given scrupulous care, and the existing
Be well interpreted. This German song observes.

(475-77)

Usually supposed to state the poem's answers, strophe 15 can serve to pose the right questions. The poem ends with a hopeful affirmation of the poet's role in a time of need: German song observes the care of the solid letter and the interpretation of the existing. This two-sided activity of *pflegen* and *deuten* is presented as a contrast to the activity of serving "Mutter Erd'" (Mother Earth) and "Sonnenlicht" (Sunlight): whereas the relation of the strophe's "we" to these latter is described by the one, repeated verb *dienen*, two different verbs are used to describe the desired care and interpretation of "Buchstab" and "bestehendes." Since the former activity is unknowing ("Unwissend"), the passage from the identity of *dienen* to the difference of *pflegen* and *deuten* is one from ignorance to knowledge. Yet the relation of *pflegen* to *deuten* is not one of mere difference. That the two activities are simultaneously one activity is suggested by the "und" that links them and by German song's relation to them: "Dem folgt deutscher Gesang" is best understood as German song's observing simultaneous care and interpretation. The passage from unknowing, one-sided serving of Mother Earth and the sunlight to knowing service of the one Father who reigns over all is a movement from mere identity (or mere difference in the case of earth and sunlight) to the identity of identity and difference.

Yet such an identity is necessarily problematic, and its articulation cannot help but betray its difficulty. With each word, the difference between *pflegen* and *deuten* threatens to slide into radical (unsublatable) disjunction. Caring for the "veste Buchstab" (that of Holy Scripture) suggests an activity not unlike *dienen*, which calls for submission and self-effacement. Good interpretation of "bestehendes," on the other hand, requires considerably more self-assertion. The verb *deuten* has several meanings: to interpret, to point out or indicate, to bring the good into light,[14] to announce or prophesy. Unlike the blind submission to the solid letter implied by *pflegen*, all these meanings require knowledgeable participation by the subject, and the object of "Gedeutet" supports such a reading: like the fluid meaning of *deuten*, "bestehendes" could suggest something that was in movement,[15] which has come to a halt, perhaps only momentarily, as the word's grammatical status—nominalized present participle—would indicate. The dangers of both *pflegen* and *deuten* are clear: to submit slavishly to the letter may be to misinterpret the spirit—Grimm: *"nach dem buchstaben nehmen, fassen* geht auf strenge, wörtliche, den rechten sinn versäumende erklärung (*to take or grasp according to the letter* means strict, literal interpretation that misses the correct sense)"[16]—and to bring to light or interpret "bestehendes" may be to posit meaning arbitrarily. An additional meaning of *deuten* focuses the problem in a strikingly appropriate way: "da aber *ze diute* in der redensart *ze diute* sagen, reden night blosz deutlich, sondern häufig *zu deutsch* heiszt, zumal im gegensatz zu der lateinischen kirchensprache. . .*deuten* wäre so viel als dem volk, den Deutschen verständlich machen, verdeutschen"[17] (but since *ze diute*, idiomatically speaking, talking *ze diute* means not just clearly, but rather often *in German*, sometimes in contrast to the Latin church language. . .*deuten* would mean making understandable, Germanizing, for the people, the Germans). If to interpret "bestehendes" is also to make it understandable to Germans, the task of "deutscher Gesang" is translation: the suppression of the letter and its preservation in spirit. But in order for translation to be possible, the "veste Buchstab" cannot be regarded as *too* solid—that is, inseparable from its meaning—or disregarded as accidental: the translation must be simultaneously secondary and original.

The dilemma is contained in the verb *folgen*: to follow, physically or intellectually. Understood "literally," German song's following would mean its necessary belatedness in relation to the solid letter, its unavoidable secondariness. Understood "figuratively," following would mean German song's contemporaneity in spirit, its "Gleichursprünglichkeit." The former kind of following, however, would be unknowing, even blind, as the third and fourth lines of the strophe indicate: "Denn fast die Finger müssen sie uns *führen.*" Such following is the faith of the doubting Thomas. The figurative following, on the other hand, would be exposed to the dangers of *deuten*, the willful positing of meaning, and this may be the power ("Gewalt") referred to in the fifth line: "und schmählich entreisst das Herz uns eine Gewalt." "Der Einzige" ("The Only One," first version), the hymn closest to "Patmos" in most respects, expresses a similar difficulty as well as the hope for its resolution:

> Diesesmal
> Ist nemlich vom eigenen Herzen

Zu sehr gegangen der Gesang,
Gut machen will ich den Fehl,
Wenn ich noch andere singe.
Nie treff ich, wie ich wünsche,
Das Maas.

(2:155)

To One alone, however,
Love clings. For this time too much
From my own heart the song
Has come; if other songs follow
I'll make amends for the fault.
Much though I wish to, never
I strike the right measure.

(451)

These lines suggest another possible reading of "und schmählich / Entreisst das Herz uns eine Gewalt." Perhaps it is not a power that is wresting the heart from us, but the heart that is wresting a power from us: both "das Herz" and "eine Gewalt" can be either nominative or accusative, subject or object. *Gewalt* would be that of the father, "Der über allen *waltet*," and who demands the heart's sacrifice. In either case, the action of *entreissen* is disgraceful, uncalled for, and entails the omission of a necessary sacrifice: perhaps "das Herz" and "eine Gewalt" are one and the same.

But it is impossible to separate the "literal" and the "figurative" meanings of *folgen* because what German song follows is *dem*: singular article, both *pflegen* and *deuten*, both the identity and the difference of letter and spirit. The distinction of literal and figurative according to sensuous and spiritual meanings is commonly presupposed, but it is only that: a presupposition, and it may not be one shared by the poem: "Denn nichts ist gemein (For nothing is common)," according to strophe 13 (2:170). Before such distinctions can be made and before it can be known what the closing lines of the poem mean, it is necessary to know what meaning is: the poem calls for interpretation, but what is interpretation in its terms? More specifically, what is the nature of the distinction literal/figurative and what is the relation between its terms? Although the final strophe cannot answer these questions, it articulates the problematic of the poem in typically Hölderlinian fashion. The time in need of good interpretation is a time when the heavenly ones are invisible, when we are blind, when we omit just sacrifice, when we serve unknowingly, in short, it is a time *when*: a time in particular and time as such. The forces threatening good interpretation in such a time are also characteristic of Hölderlin. The dangerous extremes of blind subservience and willful self-assertion are the terms of the dilemma presented by the fragment "Der Gesichtspunkt aus dem wir das Altertum anzusehen haben" (The point of view from which we should regard antiquity): "Es scheint wirklich fast keine andere Wahl offen zu seyn, erdrükt zu werden von Angenommenem, und Positivem, oder, mit gewaltsamer Anmassung, sich gegen alles erlernte, gegebene, positive, als lebendige Kraft entgegenzusezen" (4:221) (There really appears to be almost no other choice open but either to be crushed by that which is received and the positive, or with violent presumption to oppose oneself as a living force to everything acquired, given, positive). The only possibility of resolution is offered by the distinction between blind, unknowing subservience and a more conscious activity: "Es ist nemlich ein Unterschied ob jener Bildungstrieb blind wirkt, oder mit Bewusstseyn, ob er weiss, woraus er hervorgieng and wohin er strebt" (4:221) (Namely there is a difference whether this formative power works blindly or with consciousness, whether it knows whence it came and whither it strives).

The burden of what is called "das Altertum" in this essay is called "das Inferieure" in "Reflexion," "Stoff" in "Über die Verfahrungsweise des poetischen Geistes" (On the procedure of the poetic spirit), and the given, "das Positive," of language in "Wink für die Darstellung and Sprache" (Indication on Presentation and Language). Each of these texts resolves the dilemma more or less successfully by dialectical mediation of the opposition's terms, which, in each case, could be called *Bewusstsein* (consciousness) and *Selbstbewusstsein* (self-consciousness) without doing too much violence to Hölderlin's conception.[18] But whereas the problem of the essays is primarily the exterior, positive, given side of the opposition, the last strophe of "Patmos," with its concern about *Gewalt* (violence), *Opfer* (sacrifice), and *deuten* (interpreting), suggests that the other side of the opposition—the reflecting consciousness—has become the more serious problem. This would certainly be true of the following lines from "Der Einzige" ("The Only One," second version), which are a negative reply not only to the prayer for achieving "das Maas" cited earlier but also to the resolution offered by "Der Gesichtspunkt":

> Seit nemlich böser Geist sich
> Bemächtiget des glüklichen Altertums, unendlich,
> Langher währt eines, gesangsfeind, klanglos, das
> In Maasen vergeht, des Sinnes Gewaltsames.
> Ungebundenes aber hasset Gott.
>
> (2:159)

> For since evil spirit
> Has taken possession of happy antiquity, unendingly
> Long now one power has prevailed, hostile to song, without
> resonance,

That within measures transgresses, the violence of the mind. But
                                                          God hates
The unbound.

                                                              (459)

"Das Altertum" has been mastered only too well, and the violence of the mind" ("des Sinnes Gewaltsames") proves to be as hostile to song ("gesangsfeind, klanglos") as slavish acceptance of antiquity's primacy. But it is not at all clear that the relation between the "we" or "I" of "Patmos" and Holy Scripture is identical to the relation between the poet and "Altertum" described in the essays and letters. Indeed, it would be surprising if dealing with the word of God—which includes retelling and re-forming the Gospel—were not even more problematic than coming to terms with Greek tyranny, for the Scriptures belong to a sphere that is absolutely different from the necessary relations of life, as Hölderlin insists in the essay "Über Religion": "Jene unendlicheren mehr als notwendigen Beziehungen des Lebens können zwar auch gedacht, aber nur nicht *blos* gedacht werden; der Gedanke erschöpft sie nicht" (4:276) (Those more infinite relations of life that go beyond mere necessity can of course also be thought, but not *only* thought; thought does not exhaust them). In "Der Einzige" ("The Only One," third version), Hölderlin is reluctant to compare Christ to Dionysus and Hercules—"Es hindert aber eine Schaam / Mich dir zu vergleichen / Die weltlichen Männer" (2:163) (But a shame hinders me / From comparing you / to worldly men)—nevertheless, his shame is not enough to prevent him from doing so, and it is clear that in being comparable the relations to *Altertum* and to Holy Scripture are at least similar in structure: an understanding of one would shed light on the other. So that the answers to the questions of interpretation and figurative language in a time of need would contain an aesthetics as well as an epistemology, theology, metaphysics, and perhaps even more than that. Good interpretation at a bad time: What is this?

Es ist der Wurf des Säemanns, wenn er fasst
Mit der Schaufel den Waizen,
Und wirft, dem Klaren zu, ihn schwingend über die Tenne.
Ihm fällt die Schaale vor den Füssen, aber
Ans Ende kommet das Korn,
Und nicht ein Übel ists, wenn einiges
Verloren gehet und von der Rede
Verhallet der lebendige Laut.
Denn göttliches Werk auch gleichet dem unsern,
Nicht alles will der Höchste zumal.
Zwar Eisen träget der Schacht,
Und glühende Harze der Aetna,

So hätt' ich Reichtum,
Ein Bild zu bilden, und ähnlich
Zu schaun, wie er gewesen, den Christ,

Wenn aber einer spornte sich selbst,
Und traurig redend, unterweges, da ich wehrlos wäre,
Mich überfiele, dass ich staunt' und von dem Gotte
Das Bild nachahmen möcht' ein Knecht—
Im Zorne sichtbar sah' ich einmal
Des Himmels Herrn, nicht, dass ich seyn sollt etwas,
    sondern
Zu lernen. Gütig sind sie, ihr Verhasstestes aber ist,
So lange sie herrschen, das Falsche, und es gilt
Dann Menschliches unter Menschen nicht mehr.

                        (2:169-70)

It is the sower's cast when he scoops up
The wheat in his shovel
And throws it, towards clear space, swinging it over the
                               thrashing-floor.
The husk falls at his feet, but
The grain reaches its end,
And there's no harm if some of it
Is lost, and of the speech
The living sound dies away,
For the work of gods, too, is like our own,
Not all things at once does the Highest intend.
The pit bears iron, though,
And glowing resins Etna,
And so I should have wealth
With which to form an image and see
The Christ as he truly was,

But if someone spurred himself on
And, talking sadly, on the road, when I was
Defenseless, attacked me, so that amazed I tried
To copy the God's own image, I, a servant—
In anger visible once I saw
The lord of Heaven, not that I should be something, but
To learn. Benign they are, but what they most abhor,
While their reign lasts, is falsehood, and then
What's human no longer counts among human kind.

                        (471-73)

Fortunately, all the questions are answered in one gesture: "Es ist der Wurf des Säemanns." This is no ordinary parable in that it is a synthesis of two New Testament parables: the parable of the sower and the separation of the wheat from the chaff. The latter is told by John the Baptist as he compares Christ to a winnower: "Und er hat seine Worfschaufel in der Hand; er wird seine Tenne fegen und den Weizen in seine Scheune sammeln; aber die Spreu wird er verbrennen mit unauslöschlichem Feuer" (Matthäus 3:12). The parable of the sower is told by Christ himself:

> Höret zu! Siehe, es ging ein Säemann aus, zu säen. Und es begab sich, indem er säte, fiel etliches an den Weg; da kamen die Vögel und frassen's auf. Etliches fiel auf das Felsige, wo es nicht viel Erde hatte, und ging bald auf, darum dass es nicht tiefe Erde hatte. Da nun die Sonne hochstieg, verwelkte es, und weil es nicht Wurzel hatte, verdorrte es. Und etliches fiel unter die Dornen, und die Dornen wuchsen empor und erstickten's, und es brachte keine Frucht. Und etliches fiel auf gutes Land und ging auf und wuchs und brachte Frucht und trug dreissigfältig und sechzigfältig und hundertfältig. Und er sprach: Wer Ohren hat, zu hören, der höre! (Markus 4:3-9)

Hölderlin's parable combines the two: the sower is winnowing; the throws of the sower and of the winnower are the same throw. Whether or not this presents a problem cannot be known before the parables are understood. The separation of the wheat from the chaff is relatively uncomplicated; John the Baptist is hearing confessions and preaching repentance: he baptizes with water, but Christ will baptize with the Holy Spirit and with fire at the Last Judgment when he will separate the saved from the damned. The parable of the sower, however, is more significant in that it is privileged in two ways. First, it is interpreted by Christ himself: "Der Säemann sät das Wort. Das aber sind die an dem Wege: wo das Wort gesät wird, und wenn sie es gehört haben, so kommt alsbald der Satan und nimmt das Wort weg, das in sie gesät war. Desgleichen die, bei denen auf das Felsige gesät ist. . ." (Markus 4:14-20). The seed is the word of God, and, depending upon the receptivity and faith of those who hear it, it either flourishes or perishes. In short, the parable of the sower is the parable of parable itself, and this, its second privilege, is stated by Christ: "Versteht ihr dies Gleichnis nicht, wie wollt ihr dann die andern alle verstehen?" (Markus 4:13). Yet whereas Christ's interpretation of the parable would suggest that the reception or rejection of the sown word depends solely on the nature of the terrain on which it falls—in other words, we understand or do not understand the figurative meaning because of the kinds of people we are—his own justification of speaking in parables uncovers a second election:

> Und er sprach zu ihnen: Euch ist das Geheimnis des Reiches Gottes gegeben; denen aber draussen widerfährt es alles durch Gleichnisse,

auf dass sie es mit sehenden Augen sehen und doch nicht erkennen,
und mit hörenden Ohren hören und doch nicht verstehen, auf dass sie
sich nicht etwa bekehren und ihnen vergeben werde. (Markus 4:11-12)

Those who neither see nor hear are separated from those who do—not only by
their own natures but also by Christ's expressed desire *not* to be understood by
everyone. As Jean Starobinski points out in his interpretation of this parable,
election is built into the form of the messsage as well as the destination of the
message.[19] This is the double election Hölderlin grasps in the synthesis of his
parable: the throws of the sower and of the winnower can be the same throw
because both are actions of election. The good word calls for good interpretation.

A concomitant totalization attempted by the parable is the erasure of
temporal distinctions. This is explicit in the fusion of sower and winnower and
implicit on an intertextual level: in being a synthesis of different parables told
or reported by different authors, Hölderlin's parable would be electing each of
them to contemporaneity. John the Baptist, the precursor of the Word; Christ,
the Word itself; the disciple who hears the Word at first hand and, as one of the
elect, comprehends and writes it down—all are united, contemporaneous, in
the throw of the sower. They all tell parables and each in his own way *is* a
parable: John the Baptist, whose function as precursor is to sacrifice himself
for his meaning, that is, Christ's coming; the disciple, whose meaning is to
point back to Christ; and Christ himself, the parable of parables, whose meaning is to point to the Father and sacrifice himself—letter for spirit—and whose
role as teacher is to send out his disciples, his parables, into the world, just as
the Father had sent him into the world. In stating the necessity of the repeated
"when's" of the preceding strophe—election: not all are saved, the parable's
fulfillment in time: "Nicht alles will der Höchste zumal" (Not everything does
the Highest One want at once)—Hölderlin's parable also affirms a level on
which the "when's" are meaningless, on which all are contemporaries in meaning. One could be called the level of literal meaning, the other the level of
figurative meaning. The parable of the sower is, in a sense, a figure for the
figure of figure(s). Strophe 10 is a text—"Wenn. . .wenn. . .wenn"
(When. . .when. . .when)—that demands a reading—"was ist dies?"
(what is this?). Strophe 11 replies, "It is the distinction between the literal and
the figurative sense."

What remains problematic, however, is the distinction itself: what is the
relation of figurative to literal in Hölderlin's parable, or, more important, is it
still possible to make the distinction? In synthesizing the two New Testament
parables and in sublating the temporal difference between the parable and its
fulfillment, the literal and the figurative, Hölderlin's totalizing parable has also
"literalized" the figure, or, better, it has placed literal and figurative on the
same level and thereby made it impossible to distinguish between them *as* literal

or *as* figurative. This is signaled by the easy transition the strophe makes between one sense and another: all that is necessary to pass from "Korn" to "Rede" and "lebendiger Laut" is an "und." It is not so much that the "figurative" has been "literalized" or vice versa but that the bridge which makes it possible to call one side literal and the other figurative, which grants one side temporal priority and the other eternal priority, has been collapsed. This collapse is even more "explicit" in a change Hölderlin made between this version of the parable and the sketch of a later version: "Es ist der Wurf das eines *Sinns*" (2:177) (It is the throw of a *sense*). The identity of sender, message, and destination is compressed into one word: the thrower (the Mind, the Meaning), the thrown (the sense: sensuous and spiritual, literal and figurative), and the receivers of the throw (the saved and the damned who are inscribed in the election of the message, who will hear or not hear depending upon their ability to distinguish literal and figurative) are all united in *Sinn*. It is possible to pass from sense to sense, but it is not possible to say which is literal and which is figurative: all senses are proper and all improper. So that when Hölderlin says his work is similar to divine work in not wanting everything at once—"Denn göttliches Werk auch gleichet dem unsern, / Nicht alles will der Höchste zumal" (For divine work also resembles ours / Not everything does the Highest want at once)—he is, in a sense, not telling the truth, for what his parable wants to say is the simultaneous necessity and impossibility of the distinction between literal and figurative. There is a name for such a founding and subverting figure—one that is both figurative and literal, proper and improper, and neither—and it is most appropriate to describe a parable that joins the actions of sower and winnower in a far-fetched (far-flung?) metaphor: catachresis, the violent, forced, or abusive imposition of a sign on a sense that does not have a proper sign in the language, the production of a sense, a meaning, and, as such, the condition of possibility of all meaning.[20] In not telling the truth, Hölderlin's catachrestic naming of the nameless, making sense of the senseless, founds the possibility of truth.

The lines that follow Hölderlin's parable of the sower meditate on the consequences of such a naming and the authority of its truth. Whereas the parable expresses confidence in the similarity of God's work and "our" work—it does not matter if some meaning is lost, misunderstood, because all will be made good in the fullness of time—the new parable declares a radical incompatibility between divine and human work as it switches from the problem of meaning in general to the truth or falsity of particular meaning in imitation. The poem's "ich" returns for the first time since the *Einkehr* (turning in) to Patmos in strophe 4 and, unlike the "wir" of the preceding lines, overtly asks for everything at once: "So hätt' ich Reichtum, / Ein Bild zu bilden" (so had I riches, / To form an image). The "ich" or "I" is not satisfied with the role of interpreter of parables, with being a parable himself, and would like to copy the image of Christ exactly as he was. That is, he wants to be more than a disciple contemporary in spirit (i.e., on the level of figurative meaning) and would be an immediate contemporary (i.e., on the level of literal meaning) as well. That this desire represents the same attempt to collapse the distinction between figurative and literal made in the parable of the sower is clear in its terms. The "so" of "So hätt' ich Reichtum" (So had I riches) implies the subject's comparing himself to (or drawing a conclusion from, in the sense of "therefore") the forces of nature: the pit that bears iron and the volcano. He would have the same resources and the same power for the task of creation as nature does; his drive is for spontaneous, natural, original creation: "das Ungebildete zu bilden" (To form the unformed) ("Der Gesichtspunkt" 4:221). But this kind of immediacy is youthful, illusory, self-destructive, and "Patmos" is well aware of it as is obvious in the explicit references to Hölderlin's earlier work: Aetna is the volcano into which Empedocles threw himself, and Hölderlin's *prayer* for *Reichtum* is remarkably similar to his *lament* for Empedocles: "hättest du / Nur deinen Reichtum nicht, o Dichter, / Hin in den gährenden Kelch geopfert!" (*Empedokles*, 1:240) (had you only, oh poet, not sacrificed your riches in the seething chalice). The appellation "Dichter" identifies more precisely the kind of riches that Empedocles sacrificed in committing suicide; it is his language, or, as the etymology of the word would suggest, his mastery over language: "die bedeutungsentwicklung von *reichtum* wurzelt in dem begriffe imperium, gewalt, herrschaft, herrlichkeit" (the development of the meaning of *reichtum* is rooted in the concepts *imperium*, force, mastery, splendor).[21] Herder, in the *Fragmente*, speaks of the poet's *Muttersprache* in similar terms as "eine Schatzkammer" (jewel room): "In ihr muss er also mit der grössten Leichtigkeit nachsinnen und Ausdrücke finden, in ihr den Reichtum von Bildern und Farben finden, der einem Dichter unumgänglich nötig ist: in ihr die Donnerkeulen und Blitzstrahlen finden, die er als Bote der Götter wirft" (In it he must therefore reflect with the greatest sensitivity and find expressions, in it he must find the riches of images and colors that are absolutely necessary for a poet: in it he must find the thunderbolts and flashes of lightning that, as messenger of the gods, he throws); and later: "Hier kann er in die Tiefe graben und Gold suchen und Berge aufführen und Ströme leiten, denn er ist Hausherr" (Here he can dig into the depths and seek gold and erect mountains and guide rivers, for he is lord of the realm).[22] To have *Reichtum*, then, would mean to have a mother language, to have enough mastery over *his own* language to be able to form an image of Christ.[23] The word *Bild* (image) is often used by Christ interchangeably with *Gleichnis* (parable): "Solches habe ich zu euch in Sprüchen und Bildern geredet. Es kommt aber die Zeit, dass ich nicht mehr in Bildern mit euch reden werde, sondern euch frei heraus verkündigen von meinem Vater" (Johannes 16:25).

But the youthful wish for immediacy and for *his own* language is complicated by the fact that here it is Christ who is to be seen and imitated immediately—as John the Evangelist, *der Seher*, saw him: "es sahe der achtsame Mann / Das Angesicht des Gottes genau" (the attentive man saw the face of the God exactly)—and the paradox of such an imitation is contained within the words *Bild* and *bilden*. *Bild* means likeness, image, parable, but the full import of the word is not conveyed until it is understood to signify the godly in man: "Und Gott sprach: Lasset uns Menschen machen, ein Bild, das uns gleich sei. . . Und Gott schuf den Menschen zu seinem Bilde, zum Bilde Gottes schuf er ihn" (Das erste Buch Mose 1:26-27). The godly in man would of course be the soul, and this is the origin of the verb *bilden*: "There is agreement now on its beginnings in the language of the mediaeval Mystics where *inbilden* meant 'to imprint God's image in one's soul.'"[24] To form a *Bild* of Christ, then, would present specific problems: (1) it would be *hubris* on the poet's part to compare himself to God in believing that he could make an image of that which is godly *in Christ*, (2) more interesting, to copy Christ exactly as he was ("wie er gewesen"), in time, would mean to copy his earthly, human, literal form—it would mean to form an image of an image. This is already implied in the redundant formulation "ein *Bild* zu *bilden*" (to form an image) and explicitly stated in "von dem Gott / das Bild nachahmen" (to imitate the image of God). The "ich" is fallen upon, and sees God in anger, as punishment for his attempt to imitate an image. The most serious consequence of this attempt and of its necessary failure is its disquieting implications about the natures of both God and man. If man cannot grasp the God because he cannot grasp an absolute difference and is therefore doomed to producing mere images of images, then all his conceptions of God, the Unknown, the absolutely different, are mere images of himself, anthropomorphisms: he creates God in his own image. But if man's images of God are false—and this is "das Falsche" in line 8 of strophe 12—then he, who is himself the image of God, is also false. That the possibility of forming a true image of man depends upon the possibility of forming a true image of God is conveyed by the penitent lines: "Im Zorne sichtbar sah' ich einmal / Des Himmels Herrn, nicht, dass ich *seyn* sollt etwas, sondern / Zu lernen" (In anger visible once I saw / The Lord of Heaven, not that I should be something, but / To learn). In trying to form an image of the God, he was also trying to *be* something himself. The entire problematic is compressed into the line "und es gilt / Dann Menschliches unter Menschen nicht mehr" (and then / What's human no longer counts among human kind), which also summarizes the imagery of money and counterfeiting begun in "So hätt' ich Reichtum" (So had I riches): if the coins the poet renders to God are counterfeit, the coins he renders to Caesar are no less so.[25] The attempt to construct an image of God has resulted in a deconstruction of both God and man.[26]

It is hardly necessary to demonstrate the similarity of this deconstruction to the sublation of the distinction between literal and figurative accomplished in the catachrestic parable of the sower, but, in addition, a relation may be established between them that simultaneously helps to focus their relation to the rest of the poem. There is a revealing interplay between the senses of sight and hearing in these strophes (as there is in the rest of the poem and in the quoted passages from Luther's Bible). As is clear from the parable of the sower, the mediated and mediating sense—the sense that accepts (at least apparently) difference and the postponement of truth—is hearing: "Und nicht ein Übel ists, wenn einiges / Verloren gehet und von der *Rede* / *Verhallet der lebendige Laut*." As is equally clear from the parable of the counterfeiter, the sense that demands immediacy—"ähnlich zu schaun, wie er gewesen, den Christ" (see the Christ as he truly was)—is sight. If hearing can be identified with the faithful figurative sense, and sight with the deluding literal sense, new meaning can be gained for the poet's being fallen upon on the road. Someone, "einer," spurs himself on and "talking sadly, on the way" falls upon the poet. This is an obvious allusion to the appearance of Christ to the disciples on their way to Emmaus: "Er sprach aber zu ihnen: Was sind das für Reden, die ihr zwischen euch handelt unterwegs? Da blieben sie traurig stehen" (Lukas 24:17). Less obvious, but equally significant, is the allusion to Saul's being struck down on the way to Damascus; later, Paul tells the story of his conversion: "und er erzählte ihnen, wie er auf dem Wege den Herrn gesehen und der mit ihm geredet" (Die Apostelgeschichte des Lukas 9:27). In both narratives there is a movement from blindness to sight to blindness: the disciples do not recognize Christ on the road as he speaks to them and interprets Holy Scripture for them, but, when he breaks bread with them at table, their eyes are opened and Christ disappears: "Da wurden ihre Augen geöffnet, und sie erkannten ihn. Und er verschwand vor ihnen" (Lukas 24:31); when he is struck down Paul does not recognize Christ until being told "Ich bin Jesus, den du verfolgst" and, afterward, is blind for three days: "Saulus aber richtete sich auf von der Erde; und als er seine Augen auftat, sah er nichts" (Die Apostelgeschichte des Lukas 9:8). Both the disciples in their weakness of faith and Paul in his being a persecutor of Christ see and do not see, "sehen und doch nicht erkennen," before their conversions. In both cases, the new physical blindness—Christ's absence from sight—marks a corresponding increase of spiritual sight, that is, in the sense of hearing: both the disciples and Paul go out and preach the word. The trouble with the "ich" of strophe 12, however, is that, although he too is on the way between senses, he is going in the wrong direction. On the way between the parable of the sower and the parable of the counterfeiter, between hearing and sight, figurative and literal, he is caught, defenseless, trying to literalize the figurative, to see that which can only be heard, to form that which can only grow in time.

At this point it is worthwhile to consider one of Hölderlin's most suggestive meditations on *Sinn*, the "Pindar-Fragment" known as "Von der Wahrheit" (Of Truth):

Furcht vor der Wahrheit, aus Wohlgefallen an ihr. Nemlich das erste lebendige Auffassen derselben im lebendigen Sinne ist, wie alles reine

Gefühl, Verwirrungen ausgesetzt; so dass man nicht irret, aus eigener
Schuld, noch auch aus einer Störung, sondern des höheren
Gegenstandes wegen, für den, verhältnissmässig, der Sinn zu schwach
ist. (5:282)

Fear of truth, on account of taking pleasure in it. Namely the first
living apprehension of it in the living sense is, like all pure feeling,
exposed to confusions; so that one does not err on account of any
disturbance but rather due to the higher object for which, proportionately speaking, the sense is too weak.

As in a great deal of Hölderlin's late work, there is a confusion among
epistemological, ethical, and eudaemonic levels: "Furcht" (fear), "Wahrheit"
(truth), "Wohlegefallen" (pleasure), "Auffassen" (apprehension), "Sinn"
(sense), "Gefühl" (feeling), "Verwirrungen" (confusions), "irret" (err),
"Schuld" (guilt), and so forth are interwoven in one enunciation, and it would
be impossible to unravel the strands of true/false, good/evil, and pleasure/pain
in these lines. As if this were not enough, the crucial words—*Auffassen* and
Sinn—are what may be called "speculative" or "dialectical" words: that is,
they carry two meanings, one referring to the sensuous, the other to the intellectual faculties.[27] Although the adjective in the formulations "lebendiges
Auffassen" and "lebendiger Sinn" (as well as the phrase "wie alles reine
Gefühl") would suggest that the senses are meant here, Hölderlin's peculiar use
of the word "lebendig" (e.g., to signify successful dialectical mediation as in
"lebendige Kunst" [living art], etc.) and the use of "Sinn" in the singular
would open other possibilities. One errs because (the) sense is too weak. Before
the senses of sense are unraveled, Hölderlin's emphases should be remarked:
one does not err because of one's own fault or because of a disturbance from
outside but because (the) sense is too weak proportionately, or in relation to the
higher object that is truth. A difference is posited between the levels or spheres
of truth on the one hand and (the) sense on the other. How this difference is
construed depends upon the reading of *Sinn*. If "der Sinn" is understood to
signify the sensuous faculties in general, then the implication is that the senses
are too weak, too low, to grasp truth because truth exists only on the level of
the mind. If "der Sinn" is understood to signify the intellectual faculties in
general, the mind, then the sense is too weak, too low, in that it is the mind of
man, a fallen creature, and therefore cannot grasp the spiritual, divine nature
of truth. In this reading the stress would be placed upon "eigener" in the
phrase "eigener Schuld"—that is, the weakness of the mind is not one's own
particular fault or lack but the fault of man in general, the condition of
man—and a radical (unsublatable), absolute difference between the realms of
(divine) truth and (human) sense would be implied. But this latter reading may

be reading in too much sense, and a translated version of it may be more satisfying: the sense, meaning itself, is too weak to grasp truth because *as* meaning it is a forgetting of differences and an arbitrary positing. In this case, a distinction would be suggested between "das *erste* lebendige Auffassen," "lebendiger Sinn," and "reines Gefühl" on the one hand, and the unmodified "der Sinn" on the other. That is, the first, living, immediate perception of truth in the living sense—in the metaphorical terms of "Patmos," this would be the sense of sight—*can* grasp truth, but this truth is just as immediately exposed to confusions because it appears in the form of "reines Gefühl." In Hölderlin's dialectic, *das Reine* (the pure) can never *appear as such*: "Das Reine kann sich nur darstellen im Unreinen" (Letter to Neuffer, 12 November 1798, 6:290). In other words, there is a transition, a translation, between the first *per*ception "im lebendigen Sinne" and the succeeding *con*ception in *Sinn*, in which (translation) the purity of truth in its completeness is lost. Error, then, would not be a mistake or a momentary disturbance but the very condition of meaning: "der lebendige Sinn" in its purity would be absolutely different, sheer exteriority, and "der Sinn," unable to grasp the totality of the truth presented by the living sense, would be an arbitrary imposition. Such an understanding of *Sinn* clarifies the fear of truth expressed in the introductory phrases. Truth is to be feared on account of taking pleasure in it because this pleasure, Kantian *Wohlgefallen*, uncovers the nature of truth; to take pleasure in truth is to know it in the only way it can be known: as a work of art, something that is "enjoyed" insofar as an interest is not taken in its existence, insofar as it does not exist. [28]

Nah ist
Und schwer zu fassen der Gott.
Wo aber Gefahr ist, wächst
Das Rettende auch.
Im Finstern wohnen
Die Adler und furchtlos gehn
Die Söhne der Alpen über den Abgrund weg
Auf leichtgebaueten Brüken.
Drum, da gehäuft sind rings
Die Gipfel der Zeit, und die Liebsten
Nah wohnen, ermattend auf
Getrenntesten Bergen,
So gieb unschuldig Wasser,
O Fittige gieb uns, treuesten Sinns
Hinüberzugehn und wiederzukehren.
(2:165)

Near is
And difficult to grasp, the God.
But where danger threatens
That which saves from it also grows.
In gloomy places dwell
The eagles, and fearless over
The chasm walk the sons of the Alps
On bridges lightly built.
Therefore, since round about
Are heaped the summits of Time
And the most loved live near, growing faint
On mountains most separate,
Give us innocent water,
O pinions give us, with minds most faithful
To cross over and to return.

(463)

Usually supposed to pose the poem's questions, strophe 1 also presupposes the "answers." The poem's "ich"—"So sprach ich"—asks for innocent water and wings, "treuesten Sinns," in order to go over and to return. "Unschuldig Wasser" may refer to Baptism with water, in which case it would be the Baptism performed by John the Baptist, and then the wings of truest sense would be the Baptism with the Holy Spirit performed by Christ: the poem would be asking for faith. But if water can be innocent, *Sinn*, as has been demonstrated, never is, and it may be worthwhile to consider the ways in which *Sinn* can be faithful. If *Sinn* is understood as immediate perception, then, in the metaphorical terms of the poem, sight would be the truest sense. But what was true for the parable of the counterfeiter and "Von der Wahrheit" holds for the rest of the poem: sight may be the most immediate sense, but, as such, it is also the sense most exposed to error. The "Asia" of "Patmos" is a realm of sight: it is described in visual images, resplendent with colors—"goldgeschmükte Pactol" (gold-bedded Pactolus) and "silberne Schnee" (silver snow)—its garden of flowers is "ein *stilles* Feuer" (a *still* fire), and its streets are "schattenlos" (without shade). Blinded, the "ich" is unused to such splendor and vainly seeks a point of reference: "und geblendet sucht' / Ich eines, das ich kennete" (and blinded I looked for one thing that I might know.[29] Unlike the "ich," however, the boatman—the "Genius," the truest sense—knows the islands ("Doch *kennt* die Inseln der Schiffer" [But the boatman *knows* the islands]) and it is through him that the "ich" *hears* about Patmos: "Und da ich hörte / Der nahegelegenen eine / Sei Patmos" (And when I heard that of the near islands one was Patmos). In contrast to Asia, Patmos is a realm of hearing: it hears gladly of the stranger's approach; its children are "Die *Stimmen* des heissen Hains" (the *voices* of the hot noon-day copse); its *sounds* hear the stranger ("die Laute / Sie hören ihn" [the sounds, they hear him]); and it cares for the strange visitor by echoing his lament. In coming from a realm of sight and immediacy where he was blinded, to turn in at the dark grotto of Patmos, the "ich" of the poem is like John—*der Seher* (the seer)—who in his youth saw the Christ directly: "es sahe der achtsame Mann / Das Angesicht des Gottes genau" (the attentive man saw the face of the God exactly). In other words, the only way to preserve the God in his absence from sight is precisely to preserve him *in* his absence: that is, in the realm of hearing. The truest sense, then, would be hearing—Herder's "Sinn der Sprache"[30]—which is coincident with thought. But if this sense is truest in preserving an absence, in forgetting the blinding differences of immediacy, then its status as most faithful is nothing less than paradoxical, and the attempt to formulate the paradox is evident in the characterizations of Holy Scripture in strophes 13 and 14: "*Stillleuchtende Kraft*" (still-glowing strength) falls from Holy Scripture; those afraid of the "sharp beam" practice upon the quiet gaze ("Am stillen Blike"). Each of these formulations can be understood as an attempt to convey in one word or phrase both the primacy and secondariness of Holy Scripture—its status as second origin—as well as the inability to posit a *first* origin, to decide whether it is sight or hearing, lightning or thunder, that is to be privileged. The truest sense would be neither sight nor hearing, neither senses nor intellect, but rather meaning: the preservation of the differences between senses, literal and figurative, letter and spirit.

Seen from this point of view (or "listened to in such a way"), strophe 1 is a series of attempts to formulate the identity of identity and difference: whether expressed in terms of the simultaneous nearness and farness of the God or "die Liebsten" (the most loved), simultaneous contemporaneity and secondariness in the spatialized temporality of "Gipfel der Zeit" (peaks of time) and "Nah. . .auf / Getrenntesten Bergen" (Near on mountains most separate), or simultaneous sight and hearing, literal and figurative, in *Sinn*, the problematic is the same (and different). In order to preserve the identity of identity and difference bridges, passages, and mediators are necessary; such a one is the poem that goes over and returns and whose beginning, middle, and end are *Sinn*: identical and different. The verb *wiederkehren* (returning) sums up the problem: if returning meant coming back to the same place, the verb *wiederkommen* (coming back) would have been more appropriate. But for that which is human such a coming back would be *mere* identity, sterile one-sidedness; only the God can *come* back: "Denn wiederkommen sollt es / Zu rechter Zeit" (2:168) (For it was to come back when / The time was due). The poem's *wiederkehren* is a re-turning: a going over and a turning again as the journey to Asia and the turning in (*einkehren*) at Patmos demonstrate. The asymmetry of "hinüberzugehen" (going over) and "wiederzukehren" (returning) is a loss of identity and a gain of meaning.

Maintaining the bridge between senses, between identity and difference, becomes increasingly difficult in the late Hölderlin as the most "insignificant" words, one by one, lose their innocence and gain a surplus of meaning. Such is the case of *Sinn* in "Von der Wahrheit." But this "Pindar-Fragment" and "Patmos," although both deconstruct the oppositions they would affirm, are still able to maintain the tension between senses and readings. In the late fragments of hymns even the hope for successful mediation, *Aufhebung* without excess, has to be abandoned. A passage in the fragment "Der Vatikan" contains the explicit plea for the familiar identity of identity and difference as well as a warning:

> Gott rein und mit Unterscheidung
> Bewahren, das ist uns vertrauet,
> Damit nicht, weil an diesem
> Viel hängt, über der Büssung, über einem Fehler
> Des Zeichens
> Gottes Gericht entstehet.
>
> (2:252)

> To preserve God pure and with differentiation
> That is entrusted to us,
> Lest, because much depends
> On this, on account of penitence, on account of an error
> Of the sign
> God's judgment break out.
>
> (my translation)

God has to be preserved in his purity and in his difference: "rein" could be understood as God the Father and "mit Unterscheidung" as Christ, but, in any case, the necessity of the identity of this identity and difference is clear from the "und" that links them, the one verb "be*wahr*en," which suggests a keeping *in truth*, and the singular "das" in the line "das ist uns vertrauet." As in "Patmos," our trust is to be *treu* to this dialectic, lest God's judgment arise over the failure of the sign. The sign's failure could be our error in misinterpreting it, in not keeping our trust, but it could also be the failure of the sign itself. This would be the election of the parable of the sower: those who hear are separated from those who do not according to their ability to hear the message, to understand the figurative meaning, but, also, their separation is always already inscribed in the form of the message itself. The failure, lack, or error of the sign—the necessity that some meaning be lost—is its condition, and this reading is supported by a corresponding passage later in the fragment, which could be construed as a reply:

> Der Kranich hält die Gestalt aufrecht
> Die Majestätische, keusche, drüben

In Patmos, Morea, in der Pestluft.
Türkisch. und die Eule, wohlbekannt der Schriften
Spricht, heischern Fraun gleich in zerstörten Städten.
  Aber
Die erhalten den Sinn. Oft aber wie ein Brand
Entstehet Sprachverwirrung.

(2:253)

The crane holds his form erect
The majestic, the chaste, over there
In Patmos, Morea, in the pestilential air.
Turkish, and the owl, well versed in the Scriptures,
Speaks like garrulous women in wasted cities.
  But
They keep the sense. But often like a
Fire confusion of tongues breaks out.

(my translation)

It is the familiar time of need; "der Kranich," Hölderlin's symbol for utter solitariness and desolation, holds the form upright in Patmos. This may be an allusion to the supposedly successful interpretation of Holy Scripture in the poem "Patmos," and the following lines would corroborate: unlike the crane of Patmos, the owl speaks, of the Scriptures, like garrulous women in wasted cities. Although the following lines ("Aber / Die erhalten den Sinn") would be the familiar expression of faith in a dialectical mediation—that is, in spite of the differences perpetrated by misinterpretation, the Scriptures keep their meaning—this time the mediation can be questioned at each word: what is the antecedent of "die"? Does "erhalten" mean to keep, preserve, or does it mean to get, procure, obtain? And the inevitable: what is "Sinn"? To start with the first question: "die" can refer to "Städten," "Fraun," or "Schriften." The first seems unlikely, but the second and third are equally possible: the Scriptures keep the sense, and the women, although misinterpreting, get the sense (although it may not be the same as that preserved by the Scriptures). But the simile must not be overlooked: the owl speaks, of the Scriptures, *like* garrulous women. If the "Die" who keep or get the sense are neither the Scriptures nor the women, and both, then the only one who keeps and gets the sense is the simile itself: they, the literal and figurative senses, keep *the* sense by preserving the difference within sense. Whichever reading is preferred, the line, rather than preserving sense, unleashes an excess of senses, and the following line can be understood as a commentary on this failure: "Oft aber wie ein Brand / Entstehet Sprachverwirrung." In a place where the earlier Hölderlin would have written a conciliatory, mediating *und* is now found another sharp, uncompromising *aber*; rather than being contained in any way, the excess of senses in the preceding line is repeated, exacerbated, and legitimated in a telling way by means of another simile: "wie ein Brand." The misinterpretations of Scripture, the confusions of sense, and *Sprachverwirrung* (confusion of tongues) are likened obliquely to the gift of tongues at the Pentecost. In Hölderlin's anti-Pentecost, the New Testament community of spirit becomes utter incommunicability, the failure of the sign, and God's judgment. Rather than going over and re-turning—from sense to sense—the late fragments collapse the bridge between sense and non-sense.[31]

II. Reading Hegel

Chapter 5
Pre-positional By-play

Men that, by custom, have got the use of a by-word, do almost in
every sentence pronounce sounds which, though taken notice of by
others, they themselves neither hear nor observe.
   —John Locke, *An Essay Concerning Human
   Understanding*, Book II, Chapter 9

The question of the meaning of meaning provides an exemplary beginning, for,
according to the *Philosophy of Religion*, it is a question of beginnings. To ask
what this or that means—"was bedeutet dies oder jenes" (XVI:32)[1]—is to ask
for two different, indeed opposed, meanings: *which one* depends upon the
question's point of departure. If "we" begin with the *Vorstellung* (representation) of an "expression, work of art, etc.," we are asking for the inner, the
universal, the thought (*Gedanke*). If we begin with the thought, we are asking
for the outer, the particular, the *Vorstellung*, an example of the thought's content (*ein Beispiel des Inhalts*). In each case, what we *want*—either *Gedanke* or
Vorstellung—depends upon what we *have*—either *Vorstellung* or
Gedanke—and meaning would be the passage from one to the other. Yet the
relation between these two passages is not (and in the System of Hegel *cannot*
be) one of symmetrical side-by-side coexistence, for then the question of meaning would be divided irrevocably against itself:[2] the one *two-sided* question
would disintegrate into two, mutually excluding, in Hegel's terms, abstract,
one-sided questions. That such a reading would indeed be incomplete is already
suggested by the strong wording at the end of the second passage: "through the
example the difficulty is cleared up, the spirit is in this way at last present to
itself in this content (*durch das Beispiel wird es [das Schwere] uns deutlich, der
Geist ist sich so erst gegenwärtig in diesem Inhalte*)" (XVI:33). The two
passages can be read as *one* narrative movement of spirit (*Geist*) from (one-
sided) *Vorstellung* through (one-sided) *Gedanke* to the recuperation of both
Vorstellung and *Gedanke* in the spirit's presence to itself. Such a movement

would be nothing less than the task of philosophy itself, as it is formulated succinctly in the *Encyclopedia of the Philosophical Sciences*: "The difference between representation and thought (*Der Unterschied von Vorstellung und von Gedanken*) has further importance because in general it can be said that philosophy does nothing else but transform (*verwandeln*) representations into thoughts—but of course from there the mere thought into the concept (*Begriff*)" (VIII:73-74). But if *Begriff* can be identified with the presence of spirit to itself, "das Absolute," then the passage of *Gedanke* to *Begriff* is already "present" in the first passage: "Consequently it means that the concept (*Begriff*) should be given, and hence the *concept* is the meaning; it is the absolute, the nature of God grasped in thought, the logical knowledge of the absolute, that we want to have" (XVI:32). In other words, by ending with the concept, the absolute, the presence of *Geist* to itself, each of the two passages—*Vorstellung* to *Gedanke* and *Gedanke* to *Vorstellung*—contains the entire narrative of the movement from the first to the second passage: from *Vorstellung* through *Gedanke* to their dialectical mediation in *Begriff*. Each movement—each meaning of meaning as point of departure—presupposes and posits the other: the entire narrative is always already and never yet present in each of its moments.

This double movement of position and presupposition is made possible by the work of two compound words—*Vorstellung* and *Beispiel*—and the play of their prepositions. That is, each of these words can play the rigorously dialectical roles of point of departure and end point on account of its peculiar status. Rather than being a merely outside—particular and sensuous—*representation* opposed to an inner—universal and spiritual—*thought, Vorstellung* is neither outside nor inside, neither particular nor universal, neither sensuous nor spiritual: although no longer mere representation, it is not yet real thought. Later in the *Philosophy of Religion* Hegel carefully distinguishes *Vorstellung* from both *Bild* (image) and *Gedanke*. Unlike *Bild*, which "takes its content from the sphere of the sensuous and depicts it in the immediate mode of its existence, in the particularity and arbitrariness of its sensuous appearance" (XVI:139), *Vorstellung* is *Bild* elevated to the form of universality: "the content is not grasped immediately in sensuous perception, not in the figural mode (*auf bildliche Weise*), but rather *mediated* through *abstraction*, and the sensuous, figural (*Bildliche*) is elevated to universality" (XVI:140). This elevation necessarily entails a negative relation to the figural (*mit dieser Erhebung ist dann notwendig das negative Verhalten zum Bildlichen verknüpft*) (XVI:140). But precisely on account of this (one-sidedly) negative relation to the sensuous and figural—*Erhebung* (elevation) is not (yet) *Aufhebung* (sublation)—*Vorstellung* is still essentially implicated (*wesentlich verwickelt*) with the sensuous: that is, *Vorstellung* needs the sensuous and this battle against it in order to be itself (*sie bedarf desselben und dieses Kampfes gegen das Sinnliche, um selbst zu sein*) (XVI:141). The sensuous belongs essentially to *Vorstellung* (*es gehört also wesentlich zu ihr*); only real thought can free itself absolutely from the sensuous and elevate the sensuous determinations of a content—and not merely negate them immediately—to the universal determinations of thought, to the certainty (*Bestimmtheit*) of the Idea. So that the position of *Vorstellung* is, in a sense, to have *no* position; its status is constant unrest (*Daher steht nun die Vorstellung in beständiger Unruhe zwischen der unmittelbaren sinnlichen Anschauung und dem eigentlichen Gedanken*) (XVI:141). This (non)status of being in-between, constantly on the way, is well conveyed by the word's meaning as a (spatial or temporal) "placing *before*": *Vorstellung* is a (posited) outside on its way to becoming a (presupposed) inside, or, more precisely, it is a movement *away* from exteriority and *toward* interiority. But it should not be forgotten that this movement *away* and *toward* would at the same time be a movement in the other direction: that is, in order to become *Begriff, Idee*, the presence of *Geist* to itself, and so on, thought also has to *come out* to *Vorstellung*. This is formulated in the first passage of the meaning of meaning: although we have the *Vorstellung* (*die Vorstellung haben wir wohl*) and are asking for the inner (*nach dem Inneren fragen wir*), what we must do is bring this inner *to Vorstellung* (*dies ist es, was wir zur Vorstellung bringen wollen*). In short, the movement toward the "inner" meaning would also always already be the movement toward the "outer" meaning. *Vorstellung* would be the name of this movement because it contains both (spatial) position and (temporal) presupposition: the question of—that is, the movement toward—meaning would be the dialectical mediation of the two meanings of *Vorstellung*.[3]

Although *Beispiel* would seem to function in much the same way as *Vorstellung*, its status in the text of Hegel is even more problematic. Like *Vorstellung*, *Beispiel* has a peculiar nonstatus, but the nature of this nonstatus is considerably different. Whereas the mediating function of *Vorstellung* is essential to the working of the System—it is hardly necessary to recall the crucial role played by *Vorstellung* in distinguishing the "places" of religion and philosophy (in the *Phenomenology*, the *History of Philosophy*, or the *Philosophy of Religion*, for example), or the role *Vorstellung* (subdivided into two layers of triads, one of which includes *zeichenmachende Phantasie* (sign-producing imagination) and the creation of linguistic signs) plays as a mediator between *Anschauung* (intuition) and *Denken* (thinking) in the *Encyclopedia*—*Beispiel* has no official place to fill or role to play: rather than in-between, *Beispiel* is to the side. But if its existence is marginal in relation to Hegel's System, *Beispiel* is nevertheless ubiquitous in Hegel's text:[4] not only every time that "Hegel"—the text—says "zum Beispiel" but in other, ostensibly more serious, contexts as well. The question of the meaning of meaning would certainly be one of these, for according to this text the spirit (*Geist*) can be present to itself—by implication "satisfied" (*befriedigt*) and "at home" (*zu Hause*) as it could *not* be in a pure (i.e., one-sided) determination of thought—only through an example of the thought-determination's content:[5] *Geist* would be truly "by itself" (*bei sich*) only by being "beside itself" (in a *Beispiel*). As with *Vorstellung*, the text makes use of prepositions indicating spatial direction to convey the double role of *Beispiel*: although it is an exterior example, it is the example of an interior content (*In-halt*); although by positing an example the spirit would seem to be going outside, it is only in this way that it can be inside (*in diesem Inhalte*). Once again this speculative wordplay on *Beispiel* accounts for itself by the word's *meaning*, for *Beispiel* means both "model" (*Vorbild, Muster*) and "example" or "illustration" (*veranschaulichendes Gleichnis*[6]). In other words, it both precedes and follows; it is both inside and outside, exemplary and derived: *Beispiel* would be "its own" *Beispiel*. Like the para- of parable, the *bei-* of *Beispiel* would mean both "at, toward, straight to" and "beside, to the side of."[7] The narrative of the meaning of meaning could be read as an interpretation of the "one" word *Beispiel*—a word that, like the question of meaning, is *one* only to the extent that it is different from, indeed opposed to, itself.

But all the questions have not been answered. If *Beispiel* can in fact play the role of *Vorstellung*, if it can be *in apposition to*, a stand-in (standby?) for, *Vorstellung*, then what would its status of systematic invisibility *mean*? Indeed, it would be something of a surprise if *Beispiel* turned out to be another "speculative word," for "Hegel"—the System—can admit any kind of presence "to the side" only by dismissing it as *one*-sided.

A good example—aside from the frequent complaints about the understanding (*Verstand*), which leaves its determinations "side by side" (*nebeneinander*) because it can link them only by the mere "also" (*Auch*)[8]—would be the list of pejoratives Hegel uses in the *Aesthetics* to put in its place "the conscious symbolism of the comparing form of art (*Die bewusste Symbolik der vergleichenden Kunstform*)": "accessory, ornament, decoration, supplement, mere by-play, marginal things, fleeting forms, that which stands on the side, the beside-the-point, that which plays to the side (*Beiwerk, Schmuck, Zierat, Zutat, blosses Beiwesen, Nebendinge, Nebenarten, zwitterhafte Gebilde, das nur*

Danebenstehende, das Nebensächliche, das Beiherspielende)" (XIII:486-91, 507). All of these (and others) proliferate within the space of a few pages, one next to the other, without apparent need to bring their disseminating meanings back to the one meaning: as though their metonymical disorder and lack of *system* were proof of their marginal status as excessive decorations—an *Unsinn* (nonsense) so insignificant as to need no sublation to *Sinn* (sense). But it is not insignificant that this exorcising rhetoric of the speculative philosophy is applied to a "conscious symbolism" that, to a great extent, means *figures of speech*: including *Fabel, Parabel. . .Rätsel* (riddle), *Allegorie, Metapher, Bild* (image), *Gleichnis* (parable).[9]

A better way to ask the question of *Beispiel* may be to ask the question of the meaning of meaning again, *a second time*: if a question of meaning is twofold, what would be the other, the *second*, meaning of meaning? The *Philosophy of Religion* provides two meanings of meaning, but they turn out to be *one* double (two-sided) movement of position and presupposition.[10] In other words, the text answers the question of the meaning of meaning *in the first sense only*: it tells what the inner, the universal, the thought, of the meaning of meaning is, but it does not give the example (*Beispiel*) to "house" that thought. What is the *Beispiel* of the meaning of meaning? What is the *Beispiel* of *Beispiel*? But the question cannot be asked so simply, for the System has a ready answer: *Beispiel* is its own *Beispiel*, and since the question of this context is the meaning of God, *Christ*—God's positing himself in his other—would be the *Beispiel* of *Beispiel*, as is suggested in the very next paragraph: "But this is God: not only in itself (*an sich*) but also essentially for itself (*für sich*), the absolute spirit that is not only the being that maintains itself in thought, but also one that *appears*, gives itself *objectivity* (*der nicht nur das im Gedanken sich haltende Wesen ist, sondern auch das* erscheinende, *sich* Gegenständlichkeit *gebende*)" (XVI:33). In *Reason in History* the nature of God—as the spirit able to produce himself by positing *his own* object—is in fact called "the most sublime example" (*das erhabenste Beispiel*). The same text, however, also provides a way to redefine the *second* question, for the sentence continues: "properly speaking it is not an example, but the universal, the true itself, of which all the rest is an example (*eigentlich ist sie nicht ein Beispiel* (*Bei-her-spiel*), *sondern das Allgemeine, das Wahre selbst, von dem alles Andere ein Beispiel ist*)."[11] What "we" want—and who would this (other) "we" be, if it cannot be a "we" included in the systematic play of the meaning of meaning?—would be precisely the *Beispiel* of the meaning of meaning, the *Beispiel* of *Beispiel*, that is *still* an example.[12] As the above sentence suggests, properly speaking such a *Beispiel* would not, *could* not, belong to the economy, the propriety of the "proper" (in *all* senses) sense, the two mutually positing and presupposing meanings of meaning. But, again, the question of the other meaning, the setting of the other scene (*ein anderer Schauplatz?*) for the play of *Beispiel*, is not an easy matter, for do "we," can "we," even know *what* "we" are asking? Or, for that matter, *when*? It is clear that asking the question of the meaning of meaning a second *time* cannot belong to the self-redeeming temporality of the movement *Vorstellung/Gedanke/Begriff*. What would it be like, such an other *Beispiel* and its other temporality? No doubt it would be like—yet it could not be "like" anything since it would be the condition of (im)possibility of *all* "like"—Hölderlin's parable of the sower,[13] but such thematic prejudicing of the question does not lead very far because *Parabel* is one of the figures assigned a not too prominent place in the equally peripheral conscious symbolism of the comparing form of art.

As with the "two" meanings of meaning, the status of a comparison (*Vergleichung*) within the system of this symbolism depends upon the point of departure (*Ausgangspunkt*): the artist—however, he is not (yet) really an artist because this form of art is not (yet), properly speaking, *art* but rather a "pre-art" (*Vorkunst*)—begins either with the outer representation or with the inner thought, the meaning (*Bedeutung*), to be represented. *Parabel* belongs to one of the former, less explicitly subjective, forms of comparison, and although Hegel mentions the parable of the sower as an example of Gospel parable (*die Parabel vom Sämann z.B.*), it is only in order to dismiss the story *itself* as of insignificant import (*eine Erzählung, für sich von geringfügigem Gehalt*). If the parables of the Gospel are "of the deepest interest," it is on account of their "meanings." The parable of the sower, for example, is "important only because of its comparison with the doctrine of the kingdom of heaven (*wichtig nur durch die Vergleichung mit der Lehre vom Himmelreich*)." In fact, the relation between the religious teachings and the human incidents that represent them in *Parabel* is somewhat like the relation between the human (meaning) and the animal (representation) in Aesop's fables.

But another use of parable, which Hegel mentions only "by the way," may be its jesting tone through which Goethe, for example, was able to write off from his soul that which is unpleasant in life (*durch welchen er sich das im Leben Verdriessliche von der Seele losschrieb*) (XIII:503). It would seem that Goethe, at least according to Hegel, made a practice of disburdening himself on the reader. The *Encyclopedia* tells of the beneficial effects of being able to exteriorize "overpowering feelings" and how Goethe, "especially through his *Werther*, was able to relieve himself, while subjecting the readers of this novel to the power of feeling (*Empfindung*)" (X:251).

A more promising way to formulate the question would be to concentrate on what was called the "textual"—as opposed to "systematic"—status of *Beispiel*: its systematically unrecognized presence in, or rather to the side of, the System. But the label "text" is no answer, for it presupposes that which is being sought: it assumes that the text has been *read* when it is precisely a question of *reading the text*. And how would *such* a text—a *Beispiel* of *Beispiel* in the other sense, the improper sense, the sense that is, properly speaking, unreadable—be read?

In the first place, it would probably be, would have to be, *mis*read. Two pages after the meaning of meaning, the *Philosophy of Religion* discusses the dangers, indeed necessity, of misreading a text in general and an "unsystematic" text in particular.[14] The words of the Bible, namely, are "a discourse that is not systematic (*ein Vortrag, der nicht systematisch ist*)," and a positive religion that takes the Bible for the essential foundation of doctrine is exposed to grave abuses. The danger lies not so much in the text or in the interpreter as in the nature of interpretation itself, or rather in what the nature of interpretation *brings along with it* (*mit sich*): that is, that the thought speaks along with it or by it (*dass der Gedanke dabei mitspricht*). While seeming to stay "with the sense (*bei dem Sinn*)," one "in fact develops further thoughts (*entwickelt in der Tat aber weitere Gedanken*)." In other words, as soon as the interpreter goes beyond "mere word-interpretation (*blosse Wortinterpretation*)"—which, strictly speaking, is not interpretation because it entails the substitution of one word by another of the same "compass" (*Umfang*)—he must misread the text because he always brings along thoughts conditioned by his own time. And yet it is neither the accompanying thoughts nor the necessity of bringing the sense of the Scriptures out "into consciousness, into representation (*Vorstellung*)" that is responsible for the misreading, but rather the "presentation of what the sense is supposed to be (*Darstellung dessen, was der Sinn sein soll*)" (XVI:36): it is *then* that the differently determined *Vorstellung* makes itself count, and this is why the commentaries on the Bible do not make us acquainted with its content but rather contain the attitudes (*Vorstellungsweise*) of *their own time*. This description of the necessity of misreading simultaneously completes and complicates the description of the movement through (from and to) *Vorstellung* described in the narrative of the meaning of meaning. On the one hand, it states explicitly the nature and the necessity of the difference between the two meanings of meaning (the difference *within* meaning): that is, it is a temporal difference which can be compared to, which is, the temporal difference separating the (*Vorstellung* of the) text and the (*Vorstellung* of the) interpreter. On the other hand—and this is the complication—it is not so much the interpreter or his *Vorstellung* that creates the difference of meaning, the difference of misreading, but rather the attempt to present the meaning of the text. In short, the temporal difference between text and interpreter can be called more precisely a difference between text *read* and text *written*. What kind of relation such a difference describes is difficult to say, for the relation between *Vorstellung* and *Darstellung* (presentation) in this passage is very much "like" the relation between *Vorstelling* and *Beispiel* in the meaning of meaning—a problematic *a*pposition that can turn into unsublatable *o*pposition if the "right" ("wrong," properly speaking) question is asked. Whatever the relation may be, the "writing" of *Beispiel* and *Darstellung* would make possible the reading of meaning and its (speculative mis)interpretation.

Yet the same—and can it ever be the same?—writing of *Beispiel* and *Darstellung* also makes reading impossible, for this writing cannot itself be read except when translated into the mediating language of *Vorstellung*; and such a translation always brings along with it the necessity of *Darstellung* and its writing: *Darstellung* would be its own condition of (im)possibility. Although the other question "What is the *Darstellung* of *Darstellung?*" leads to the "same" aporia as the other question "What is the *Beispiel* of *Beispiel?*" some progress toward the "right" question has been made. Hegel's presentation, example, of the difference between *Vorstellung* and *Beispiel*, *Vorstellung* and *Darstellung*, as the difference between text *read* and text *written* throws into better relief the precisely *textual* dimension of the problem: that is, the peculiar status of *Beispiel* cannot be thought as a merely spatial, appositional, (non)presence to the side of the System—such a *Beispiel*, if not sublatable, is nevertheless too easily deposited in the shadow-realm of *Nebending, Schmuck,* etc.—if the relation (between text read and text written) is intrinsically temporal. But since the peculiarly "textual" temporality of *Beispiel* and *Darstellung*—like the textual space they occupy—would not be that of the System, it cannot be thought *in terms of* either space *or* time: in order to become "itself" (undialectically) the text must clear an "other space" in which it may develop in an "other time" (and this somehow outside, different from, other than, the oppositions inside/outside, identity/difference, self/other). The necessity of misreading neither clears up nor develops how such clearing and development are possible, but it does indicate a direction: it is the interpretation of *Scripture* that leads to the most contradictory opinions; it is *Scripture* that all heresies as well as the Church invoke. And "Scripture" means not only the unsystematic discourse of the Bible: on the contrary, misreading is a necessity that holds sway even in the presentation of an "in itself already developed" philosophical *system*, that of Plato or Aristotle for example (*bei der Darstellung eines in sich schon entwickelten philosophischen Systems, z.B. des Platon oder Aristoteles*). Thanks to the (re)writing of *Darstellung*, even the text of a System, for example, may suffer the fate of so-called Holy Scripture (*sogenannte Heilige Schrift*) and be made into a waxen nose (*zu einer wächsernen Nase*).

Hegel's presentation of Aristotle's system in the *History of Philosophy* may serve a rereading of the question of *Beispiel*, for this presentation is, to a large extent, a question of (re)reading Aristotle's examples. If Aristotle has not been understood, it is because previous interpreters did not know how to read him, and for this reason to reread the text means also to tell *how* it should be read. For Hegel, nowhere is this more necessary than in the case of *De anima* and its examples. To illustrate the workings of sensation (*Empfindung*) Aristotle uses "that famous *comparison* which has so often been the occasion of misunderstanding, which has been so wrongly construed (*jene berühmte Vergleichung, die so oft Missverständnis veranlasst hat, so schief aufgefasst worden ist*)" (XIX:207). It is not immediately apparent *why* this should be so, for Hegel has no problem stating directly what Aristotle says: "He says namely that sensation is the taking up of the perceived forms (*die Aufnahme der empfundenen Formen*), without the matter; in sensation only the form comes to us, without the matter." Such behavior is to be distinguished, according to Hegel, from practical behavior like eating or drinking, when we act as particular individuals who, as materially existent, relate to the material in a material way. For Hegel, there is no need to dwell on *such* activity, and he dismisses what Aristotle has to say about the vegetative soul (*die ernährende Seele*) as insignificant: "What Aristotle says about feeding (*Ernährung*), 'whether like on like or on the opposed (*ob Gleiches vom Gleichen oder vom Entgegengesetzten*),' is insignificant (*unbedeutend*)" (XIX:205). Sensation is "more interesting" since in its taking up of the form (*Formaufnahme*) the material is "consumed" or (more "correctly," especially in regard to etymology) "effaced" (*vertilgt*). Obviously, such a consumption would be more of an "effacement" and is not to be confused with the consumption that occurs in nourishment, for "form is the object as universal (*die Form ist der Gegenstand als Allgemeines*)" (XIX:208); in sensation we relate only to the form and take it up without the matter. To tell *how* this occurs is the task of the misread example: "'as the wax takes in only the sign of the golden signet ring, not the gold itself, rather purely its form (*wie das Wachs nur das Zeichen des goldenen Siegelringes an sicht nimmt, ohne das Gold selbst, sondern rein seine Form*)'" (XIX:208). But if it is possible to repeat the meaning of the example[15] without difficulty—and Hegel does so several times (even before citing it)—then what has gone wrong in its interpretation?

Hegel is expansive on this matter, and it is worthwhile to follow him: the unnamed misinterpreters—*man* (one), *jeder* (everyone)—have stopped in a crude way with the coarseness of the comparison (*Man bleibt roherweise beim Groben des Vergleichs stehen*). When one holds on to the example (*bloss an dies Beispiel hält*) and goes over (*übergeht*) to the soul, one says that the soul behaves (*verhalte sich*) like the wax, that representations (*Vorstellungen*), sensations, all things are only impressed into the soul; the soul is a *tabula rasa*, empty, and exterior things make only an impression, as the material of the signet ring works on the material of the wax. This is the misreading, and it is the lot of most philosophers when they "adduce a sensuous example (*ein sinnliches Beispiel anführen*)" because "everyone understands this and takes the content of the comparison in its entire compass (*Umfange*)—as though everything that is contained in this sensuous relationship were also valid for the spiritual" (XIX:208). In the wax/ring example, the comparison applies only (*nur*) to the determination that in sensation only (*nur*) the form is taken up, only (*nur*) the form is for the perceiving subject, only (*nur*) the form comes to the subject; only in regard to this side is a comparison being made (*nur nach dieser Seite ist verglichen*). Hegel's repeated "only" stresses the distinction to be made, the overlooked difference (*Unterschied*) between the image (*Bild*) and the behavior of the soul. In short, Hegel's ability to tell the difference between the two "sides" of the example—the side meant to be compared and the side meant not to be compared, the side of similarity and the side of difference—is what makes it possible for him to read it: he can tell the difference between the material and the form because he can tell the difference between the sensuous and the spiritual sides of the example. In order to read the example Hegel uses the difference that the example is meant to read: it is as though he were able to read a difference between matter and form, sensuous and spiritual—the differene between the interpreters who see only the similarity and overlook the difference and Hegel who sees both—inscribed in the *Beispiel* of that difference. But if in order to be read the *Beispiel* has always already *to have been read*—if reading is a rereading—then how is it possible to read *in the first place*? In other words—and the problem is precisely the impossibility of finding *other words* to read the words of the *Beispiel* of *Beispiel*—how can Hegel claim to read a text that his own reading has rendered, properly speaking, unreadable? Indeed, it would not be improper to ask "Who is reading whom?" in the case of a text that has its (mis)readers (including Hegel) inscribed within "itself": perhaps Aristotle has as much of a claim to reading Hegel as Hegel has to reading Aristotle.[16]

But Hegel's rereading of the *Beispiel* does not stop with a reading of the difference inscribed in the example: if he has a claim to rereading the text, it is because he *rewrites* it. What previous interpreters overlooked in the example is that the wax in fact does *not* take up the form: "the impression remains an exterior figure, a design on it, but not a form of its essence (*dieser Eindruck bleibt eine äusserliche Figur, Gestaltung an ihm, aber keine Form seines Wesens*)"; "if this form became the form of its essence, it would cease to be wax" (XIX:209). The soul, on the other hand, takes up the form into its own substance, *assimilates* it, and in such a way that the soul is in itself, to a certain extent (*gewissermassen*), everything that is perceived (*alles Empfundene*). The example means to say that *only* the form comes to the soul, but *not* that the form is and remains exterior to the wax and that the soul, like wax, has no form in itself. In short, the soul neither is nor behaves like wax, and Hegel repeats the denial several times: "In no way is the soul supposed to be passive wax and to receive determinations from the outside." He goes so far as to say that the taking up of the form (as the universal) is *not* like that of the wax (*Die Seele ist die Form, die Form ist das Allgemeine; und das Aufnehmen desselben ist nicht wie das des Wachses*). Since the wax/ring example too easily suggests the passivity of the soul in sensation, Hegel proposes his own version: although it cannot be denied that passivity is a moment in sensation, this passivity is *sublated*, the soul *holds away* (*hält. . . ab*) the material, *repels* (*repelliert*) it, *relates* (*verhält sich*) only to the form, and *transforms* (*verwandelt*) the form of the exterior body into its own. Just as Hegel's rereading of Aristotle's example was a repetition of the soul's behavior in sensation, so is his new version of the soul's behavior in sensation a repetition of his rewriting of Aristotle's example: that is, the soul is supposed to hold away, repel, the material just as Hegel holds away the material of Aristotle's example by denying that the soul behaves like wax. Unlike the misreader who stays with the coarsely material of the comparison and *holds on* to the *Beispiel* (*an dies Beispiel hält*), Hegel relates (*verhält sich*) only to the form and transforms, appropriates, Aristotle's example by rewriting it. Such a rewriting is active in its relation to the material whereas the taking up performed by the misreader is merely passive. By holding on to the material, the wax, of Aristotle's example, the misreader becomes like wax himself: he who attempts to read the writing of *Beispiel* without *re*writing it risks being turned into a waxen nose. In being able to write off the unpleasantness of the material, Hegel would be like Goethe: just as Goethe was able to disburden himself of excess *Empfindung* by writing *Werther* and subjecting the *readers* of this novel to the power of feeling, so Hegel disburdens himself of the material excess of Aristotle's example by rewriting it and subjecting the *readers*—the waxen *mis*readers inscribed in his text. But if such rewriting can take place only at the expense of the (mis)reader, does it not also occur at the expense of Aristotle's text? Is not Hegel doing precisely what he blames other readers for doing: that is, turning the text into a waxen nose? Is Hegel's new example—a process of *aufheben* (sublating)/ *abhalten* (holding away/*sich verhalten* (relating to)/*assimilieren* (assimilating)/*verwandeln* (transforming)—simply to the side of Aristotle's wax/ring example, a case of mere metonymical substitution? Whence comes the authority of rewriting and its new—its other—*Beispiel*?

Since to a certain extent—and the question is precisely to *what* extent—Hegel's new example substitutes a *digestive* model for Aristotle's *mimetic* model, another way to formulate the question would be to ask: how can the *form* be eaten? If the soul "assimilates" and "transforms" the *form* of the exterior body into its own, the question of feeding, "'whether like on like or on the opposed,'" would apparently not be as insignificant as Hegel would have it. But Aristotle's explanation of the body's digestion in *De anima* is indeed not of too much help because it is very much like Hegel's version of the soul's digestion: that is, as long as the food remains undigested, the body feeds on that which is opposed to it; as soon as the food is digested, it feeds on something like itself.[17] The two moments would correspond to the succeeding moments of passivity and activity in Hegel's version of sensation. But since in sensation the soul digests not the material but only the form of its object, the digestive analogy cannot explain *how* that process takes place. Indeed, as Hegel emphasized at the beginning of this passage, sensation is to be undertood precisely in its *difference* from nourishment. To stay with the analogy of nourishment would be once again to stay with the *wax* of the comparison. Aristotle compares the relation between body and soul to that between wax and its form, and Hegel quotes this example earlier in his presentation: "'One should therefore not ask whether soul and body are one,'"—and Hegel paraphrases (i.e., rewrites) this to mean "one ought not to say this, that they are one"—"'just as one does not ask whether the wax and its form are one'" (XIX:201). But if the digestive model cannot satisfy the appetite of Hegel's new *Beispiel* ("L'Homme ne vit pas seulement de pain" [Man does not live by bread alone], says Georges Bataille in the course of rewriting another [or the same?] Hegel text, "mais des comédies par lesquelles il se trompe volontairement" [but by the comedies through which he voluntarily deceives himself],[18] all that remains is the model of rewriting—to "eat" the form would be to rewrite it—and why should this model have any more authority than digestion? In fact, rewriting would seem to be even more questionable as an analogy than nourishment, for it puts in question *all* models, analogies, comparisons, by substituting (active) *production* (in particular *textual* production) for all (passive) mimetic models. The authority of the new example produced by Hegel's text would be the authority of its own production: rewriting (as the activity that denies authority) would be its own authority. But the authority of Aristotle—or that of Hegel—is not written off so easily. In order to explain the difference between potentiality and reality, passive and active knowledge, Aristotle introduces the example—one not cited (explicitly[19]) by Hegel—of three men: the first can be said to be "knowing" because man as such is a knowing creature; another can also be said to be knowing because he understands the art of "(reading and) writing" (*grammatikēn*); but only he who really thinks, who actively practices his knowledge, can be properly said to be knowing.[20] If Hegel can rewrite Aristotle's example—or should it be: "If Aristotle can rewrite Hegel's example"?—it is because he has read Aristotle's text—or should it be: "it is because he has read Hegel's text"? Hegel's distinction between passive "taking up" and active, appropriating, rewriting is always already inscribed in Aristotle's distinction between passive and active knowledge. So that the authority for rewriting Aristotle's *Beispiel* comes from Aristotle himself—but if the *Beispiel* can be only *re*written, if it can *be* only *as* rewritten, who writes the *Beispiel*? Who is "Aristotle" that he may write the *Beispiel*? For that matter, who is "Hegel"?—or, more precisely, it comes from the authority of *thought* itself. Although Hegel does not cite the example of the "three" men, his other example, which takes the place of Aristotle's "famous" example, does comes from "an other, infamous example (*ein anderes berüchtigtes Beispiel*)" (XIX:214): the *Beispiel* of thought.

Aristotle's treatment of thought in *De anima* is "essentially speculative" (*wesentlich spekulativ*), and it marks the place where his language most coincides with Hegel's: "In our language the absolute, the true, is only that whose subjectivity and objectivity are one and the same, are identical; this is precisely contained in Aristotle as well (*In unserer Sprache ist das Absolute, Wahrhafte nur das, dessen Subjektivität und Objektivität ein und dasselbe, identisch ist; dies ist ebenso auch im Aristoteles enthalten)"* (XIX:218). Aristotle's *nous* thinks the identity of identity and difference, "it is the thought of thought, the thinking of thought (*Er ist der Gedanke des Gedankens, er ist das Denken des Gedankens)"*(XIX:219). As such, it can be summarized only in superlatives: "This is the highest peak of Aristotelian metaphysics, the most speculative that can exist (*Dies ist so die höchste Spitze der Aristotelischen Metaphysik, das Spekulativste, was es geben kann)"* (XIX:219). As the very peak, what Aristotle says about thought is to be elevated above its context. That Aristotle simply "goes over" (*geht. . . über*) (XIX:212) from sensation to thought—as Hegel states at the beginning of his presentation (of Aristotle on thought)—is mere appearance, for thought is not "beside" and does not come after anything: "It only appears as though thinking is discussed beside other things; this form of succession of course appears in Aristotle. But what he says about thinking is for itself the absolutely speculative and does not stand beside something else, sensation, for example, which is only *dynamis* for thinking (*Es hat nur den Schein, als ob von dem Denken gesprochen würde neben anderem; diese Form des Nacheinander erscheint allerdings bei Aristoteles. Aber was er über das Denken sagt, ist für sich das absolut Spekulative und steht nicht neben anderen, z.B. der Empfindung, die nur* dynamis *ist für das Denken)"* (XIX:219). If Aristotle's presentation of thought is so close to the truth of the speculative philosophy, a great deal would be at stake for Hegel in the proper understanding of the infamous *Beispiel* of thought: "'The *nous* is like a book, on the pages of which nothing is really written (*Der* nous *ist wie ein Buch, auf dessen Blätter nichts wirklich geschrieben ist)'"* (XIX:214). This is the well-known example of the *tabula rasa*, and Hegel had signaled its misreading at the very beginning of his presentation of Aristotle's philosophy: common opinion believes that "according to Aristotle the soul is a *tabula rasa*, that it receives its determinations passively from the exterior world (*Aussenwelt*), that his philosophy is empiricism, the worst Lockeanism, and so on" (XIX:133). This misreading of the *tabula rasa* was also denounced proleptically in Hegel's reading of the wax/ring example. So that the scene for the drama of *Beispiel*, misreading, and Hegel's rereading is set in advance, and there are no surprises in the manifest plot: exteriority and passivity are once again the principal villains. As the misreaders of the wax/ring example held on to the coarsely material of the comparison and overlooked the *difference*, so here "one overlooks all thoughts (*ubersieht alle Gedanken*) of Aristotle and grasps only such an exterior comparison (*und fasst nur solche äusserliche Vergleichung auf)"* (XIX:214-215): according to the misreading "Aristotle says that the spirit (*Geist*) is a *tabula rasa* on which exterior objects (*äussere Gegenstände*) are first supposed to write." "Such accidental comparisons are grasped (*aufgefasst*) particularly by representation (*Vorstellen*), instead of holding on to the concept (*statt sich an den Begriff zu halten*), as though they expressed the fact (*als ob sie die Sache audrückten*)." The key to a proper reading is once again the recognition of a difference, a limit to the breadth of the comparison: "Aristotle does not at all mean (*ist gar nicht gemeint*) the comparison to be taken in its entire extent (*in ihrer ganzen Ausdehnung*); understanding is not a thing, does not have the passivity of a writing tablet (*Schreibtafel*) (for then we forget all concept)." Thought is active, and hence "the comparison limits itself (*beschränkt sich*) only to this, that the soul has a content only insofar as one really thinks"; just as a book in potentiality contains everything but in reality nothing before one writes in it (*ehe darauf geschrieben ist*).

Like the example of sensation, the example of thought is bound (even more?) inextricably to its reading: that is, if to think means to write in the blank book of thought, to *think* the *Beispiel* means to write in the blank book *of* the *Beispiel*. Like the thinking soul, the *Beispiel* of thought contains everything in potentiality but nothing in reality until it is written. And "everything" includes the misreaders who fail to write in, to think, the blank book of the *Beispiel*: *everyone* can understand a book on which nothing is written (*Ein Buch, auf das nichts geschrieben ist, kann jeder verstehen*). As long as one does not write in the book of *Beispiel*—as long as one does not put the "book on which nothing is written" *within quotation marks* and understand it *as* a *Beispiel*—one remains an anonymous (every)one—"man," "jeder"—inscribed in the book that in reality contains nothing: the misreader would be a passive writing tablet waiting for exterior things to write on it. The "book on which nothing is written" and which *everyone* can understand because *no one* has read it—that is, because no one has rewritten the "nothing" of the book of *Beispiel* (on which "nothing" *is written*) so that it would mean something—would be like *Also sprach Zarathustra*: "Ein Buch für Alle und Keinen." Hegel, on the other hand, precisely because he is able to distinguish between the thought, the concept, the *Sache* (the real thing), of the example and its "nothing" (i.e., the exterior, accidental comparison, the extent to which the example is *not* to be taken) can write in the blank book of the *Beispiel*: that is, he writes in the book in which "nothing" is written by rewriting it (i.e., by reinscribing the "nothing" within his own text so that it may mean something)—by negating the negation. Unlike the misreader—everybody—who passively accepts the book on which nothing is written and thereby becomes a blank book himself— nobody—Hegel actively rewrites the book on which nothing is written and thereby becomes a real book himself—somebody—(and simultaneously allows Aristotle to become a real book—himself). By rewriting and rereading Hegel turns the one—unwritten, unread—book of Aristotle into *two* books: the one unwritten and unread; the other rewritten and reread. But the relation between these two books remains problematic. It is not just that Hegel once again presupposes the reading of the example in order to read it—that is, he can understand the example of *thought* because he can distinguish between the *thought* and the excess passivity and exteriority of the example—even if the assumption may seem less immediately justifiable than his rewriting of the example of sensation on the authority of thought. Presupposing what it posits is, after all, the very truth of a dialectical scheme, and where could it be more true than in the movement of thought thinking itself? If in rewriting the "nothing" of Aristotle's example Hegel renders it unreadable, it is a *determinate* unreadability. Nevertheless, another unreadability may accompany the other *Beispiel*, and a way to begin its reading may be to ask another question: how is it possible to think, to *(re)write*, nothing? But if this question is not to be taken as an invitation to the (re)writing of the big *Logic*,[21] it needs to be reposed (deposed?), and repositioning the apposition may help: how is it possible to think nothing *as* (re)written? Or, again, what is the "nothing" *of thought*, that it may be (re)written?

The other *Beispiel*—Aristotle's *or* Hegel's?—replies of itself: the "nothing" of thought is the *Beispiel* of thought, and it cannot be thought *except* as (re)written. That is, the *Beispiel*—the excess exteriority and passivity of the comparison, its *non-thought*—is that which thought needs to posit in order that it may presuppose itself. But if *Beispiel* is the "nothing" of thought, or, to put it in more Hegelian terms: if *Beispiel* is the "negation" of thought, the negation *within* thought without which thought cannot negate the negation, then a reinscription of its two excesses—passivity and exteriority—is necessary. Hegel's difference between an exterior and passive *Beispiel* and an interior and active thought is more problematic than mere (sublatable) opposition, for the two sides contaminate one another by means of an (chiasmic) exchange of properties. In order to become the interior activity that it is, thought must first be an interior *passivity* in that a passive taking up, *reading*, is necessary for a (re)writing of *Beispiel*: in this case a reading of the *difference* between *Beispiel* and thought. But if this "interior passivity" alone can be relegated to the status of a moment in the dialectical movement, together with its complement (its crossing) it presents more of a problem: namely the writing read by the interior passivity, the difference between the interior thought and the exterior comparison, between the extents to which the comparison is and is not to be taken, is inscribed *in* the *Beispiel by* the Beispiel. Rather than merely passive exteriority, the *Beispiel* is an *active* exteriority: the *Beispiel* "itself" inscribes the difference between the "extents" of the comparison, between thought and nonthought. That "the comparison limits itself only to this. . . (*die Vergleichung beschränkt sich aber nur darauf. . .*)" means that the comparison *limits itself*. The *Beispiel* produces the excess (passivity and exteriority) of *Beispiel*: the simile *dis*sembles, *dis*simulates (*die Vergleichung vergleicht*?[22]). If *Beispiel* is the "nothing," the *nonthought*, of thought, it is nevertheless—also always already—a nonthought that *thinks*: a thinking nonthought that cannot itself *be* *thought*—"la non-pensée pensante, cette réserve de la pensée qui ne se laisse pas penser."[23] To say that "it makes no difference," that then *Beispiel* may as well be called thought, is no answer because this is precisely the problem: in order that the difference between thought and *Beispiel* may make sense, what is called thought and what is called *Beispiel must* make a difference. The real problem is not that thought needs to presuppose itself as different from *Beispiel* in order that it may be thought, but that it cannot do so without rendering itself *indistinguishable* from *Beispiel*: *in*different to *Beispiel in terms of* identity and difference. If there is a difference between thought and *Beispiel*, it is an undecidable and therefore excessive difference. In the same movement that produces sublatable passivity and exteriority, the excess of *Beispiel* produces an unsublatable interiority and activity. And this excess, rather than coming from anywhere outside thought, is inscribed within thought itself: *not* as the "nothing," the "other," the "excess" *of* thought, but as the unthinkable non-thought whose thinking makes thought (im)possible. Thought would be the dissimulation of *Beispiel*. To rewrite and reread the blank book of *such* a *Beispiel* would be to become *nobody* in a different way from those—"man," "jeder"—who became nobody by leaving the blank book unread and unwritten. The reader who (re)writes the "nothing" of *Beispiel* only allows the blank book to write itself, to write itself as always already written. Unlike the *History of Philosophy*, the excess of *Beispiel* needs neither (the thought of) "Aristotle" nor (the thought of) "Hegel" to be written. Indeed, it would be more correct to say that the excess of *Beispiel*, just as it dissimulates (as) thought, just as it writes the fiction of the authority of thought, writes the fictions of "Aristotle" and "Hegel," the dissimulations of authority and authorship. The book of *Beispiel*—as the book in which nothing *is* written—is a book for all and for none: a book that is unreadable and unwritable because it can be read and written (only) by nobody.

Chapter 6
Parentheses
Hegel by Heidegger

On ne saurait 'lire' Hegel, sauf à ne pas le lire. Le lire, ne pas le
lire, le comprendre, le meconnaître, le refuser, cela tombe sous la
décision de Hegel, ou cela n'a pas lieu. Seule l'intensité de ce non
lieu, dans l'impossibilité qu'il y en ait un, nous dispose pour une
mort—mort de lecture, mort d'écriture—qui laisse Hegel vivant,
dans l'imposture du Sens achevé. (Hegel est l'imposteur, c'est ce
qui le rend invincible, fou de son sérieux, faussaire de Vérité.
—Maurice Blanchot, ''Fragmentaire''[1]

—from the beginning and in the end, the question of the text—its writing and
its reading, its beginnings and its ends—is difficult to avoid. '' 'Science of the
Experience of Consciousness' is [or, better, ''sounds'' or ''resounds'' (*lautet*)]
the title that Hegel, at the publication of the *Phenomenology of Spirit* in the
year 1807, puts at the beginning (*voranstellt*) of the work'' (*H*, 105)[2] If the title
placed at the beginning of the ''work'' (*Werk*) is indeed the title of the work,
what is the ''Phenomenology of Spirit''? If the ''Phenomenology of Spirit'' is
the ''work,'' what does Hegel mean by prefacing it with another title? The

---

The following text begins with an introductory section, but we hope that some additional
prefatory remarks on its subject and method will be of help to the reader. What we would do is to
reread the question of self-consciousness in the text of Hegel by reading the ''genesis'' of the
''we''—the so-called philosophical consciousness, the scientific observer who watches the education of natural consciousness to real knowledge—in the ''Introduction'' to the *Phenomenology
of Spirit*. A number of commentators have recognized self-consciousness as the ''principle'' of

attempt to read the two titles has a long history—so long, in fact, that it has become legend—and it is not surprising that it often takes the place of an attempt to read the work, for the existence of the two titles puts in question the very existence of the work *as* work: that is, as *one* book with a beginning, middle, and an end. According to the legend, it is either a science of the experience of consciousness or a phenomenology of spirit—or both or neither. From the beginning, interpreters of the "work" have noticed a discrepancy between the route mapped out in the "Introduction" (*Einleitung*) and the route that the text follows: the Introduction outlines a "transcendental-psychological" analysis of consciousness, but "we have hardly stepped over the threshold of self-consciousness when we begin to meet up with historical forms" and by the time "we" arrive at the section on "reason" (*Vernunft*), the book has left its beginnings (the analysis of consciousness) behind altogether.[3] Here where the book divides itself into two books, the one legend becomes

---

the *Phenomenology*, but none has been able to read this principle because none has recognized the extent to which he or she, the reader of the *Phenomenology*, is inscribed in the text as the "we." As long as the status of this "we," the reader of the text, is assumed to be unproblematic, no critique of or going "beyond" Hegel is possible, for such an assumption forever relegates the interpreter to a decidedly pre-Hegelian position: that is, already accounted for, and disposed of, by Hegel. In order to do a rigorously Hegelian reading of Hegel, it is necessary to read the reader *of* the text of Hegel, and one such exemplary reader is Heidegger in his "Hegel's Concept of Experience"—a paragraph-by-paragraph analysis of the "Introduction" to the *Phenomenology*. By reading Heidegger's reading of Hegel, we hope to shed some light not only on the "we" of Hegel's text but also on the question of the possibility of an "other we" that would not be the other *of* the "we" of Hegel. We begin by reading Heidegger's short introductory paragraph, go on to read the first paragraph and then the "rest" of Hegel's "Introduction," continue by reading Heidegger's commentary (on Hegel's first and sixth paragraphs in particular), and end with an example from Heidegger's *Identity and Difference*.

Just as the "subject" of this reading is precisely the question of the subject of reading, so the "method" is the question of the method of reading, or, in other words, the question of the senses in which reading can or cannot be called a "method." The question of reading—which is the question of the text—is dealt with in its proper place and at the proper time. Nevertheless, since one of the main points of the text is that the "relation" or whatever happens between Hegel and Heidegger cannot be understood, cannot be thought, merely in terms of a difference in their "ideas" or in terms of a mere "misunderstanding" of Hegel by Heidegger, but rather has to be thought in terms of "reading and writing," it may be of help if we provide a preliminary clarification (not to say justification) of our introduction of these terms. In introducing the terms "reading and writing," we are doing no more—and it is this "no more" that is most in need of being read—than accepting the text as it appears, as it presents itself, to us: that is, as a written text to be read. In other words, the beginning is in Hegel's terms strictly phenomenological: in accepting the text as it appears and presents itself to us—that is, as a text written to be read—we accept its own standard (*Massstab*). But it is precisely this beginning—its appearance, self-presentation, and acceptance, its reading and its writing—that is most in question and least given. If we could see what is given in the acceptance of the appearance and self-presentation of such a beginning—what is at stake in the reading (and writing) of Hegel by Heidegger—then perhaps reading (and writing) would become a serious task for us.

many: since the effort is always to reconcile the text with itself—its beginning (*Einleitung*) with its end (*Das absolute Wissen*), or, better, the one beginning (*Einleitung*) with the other beginning (*Vorrede*)—the solution usually takes the form of a genetic pattern. That is to say, Hegel started out to write a "Science of the Experience of Consciousness," but in the process of writing, in fact in the process of *publishing*, the book "something" happened (and it is the burden of interpretation to determine what this "something" is) to make him "change his mind" and, in effect, write another book: a *Phenomenology of Spirit*. Some interpreters go so far as to claim that it was not so much a matter of changing his mind as of Hegel's losing all control over his book in the act of writing it. Hegel's own testimony in letters to his publisher and others goes far to support this thesis: he repeatedly speaks of the difficulties and confusions attendant upon the writing and the publishing of the book and complains about the "unformed" character of the last sections (*der grösseren Unform der letzten Partien*). In fact, it seems Hegel wanted to have the "first" title page ("Wissenschaft der Erfahrung des Bewusstseins") cut out of the book in order that the other title page ("Phänomenologie des Geistes") could stand alone, and it is only on account of the printer's inability or failure to carry out these instructions to the letter that the title destined for doom ever saw the light of day. But, versions of the legend continue, what importance can a title, and at that an (incompletely) suppressed title, have? More important is the fact that Hegel let the Introduction stand as it was, and the naively genetic interpretation cannot account for it: in all rigor, it ought to demand that the Introduction insofar as it is an introduction to a "science of the experience of consciousness"—in fact, an interpretation of *that* title—be suppressed along with the title. Speaking "sharply" (or "with a threatening undertone": *um es ein bisschen zugespitzt auszudrücken*),[4] one interpreter suggests just that: after all, if Hegel lost his head, as it were, during the writing of the book, it would only be an act of mercy to finish the cutting operation he began but the recalcitrant printers thwarted. More dialectically sensitive interpreters shy away from such violence and prefer a more delicate operation: Hegel may very well have changed his mind while writing the book, but it is our job as interpreters to read the text as it has come down to us, and that means to demonstrate how the beginning and the end of the book do in fact hold together, how one part of the book grows out of the other, how one title completes, enhances, and explains the other. In short, despite appearances, the book is one book by one author, and if it seems to become other than itself, this is only more proof of its ultimate selfsameness, that is, proof that the book itself undergoes the dialectical process it presents: a process of formation (*Bildung*) in which it becomes itself by turning into that which is its other. Rather than creating a monstrosity, the turn from an analysis of the forms of consciousness, from a narration of the manifestations of consciousness, to an analysis of the historical forms of spirit (*Geist*) is shown to be a development necessary for the unity and integrity not only of Hegel's thought but of the book as book. Needless to say, this more humane strategy brings along with it a violence of its own—even if it is, as it would claim, only the violence that "Hegel" inflicts upon himself, the violence proper to the dialectical movement. In this case, rather than being cut out, the "Introduction," still the biggest obstacle to a reconciling reading, is banished more subtly and more effectively by decree: it will not be read. There is a corollary to this law that is applied to those who, like Heidegger in "Hegel's Concept of Experience," disobey the law of nonreading and read anyway: you will not be read. Although in the third sentence of his text Heidegger would seem to subscribe to the reconciling dialectical interpretation by identifying "experience" and "phenomenology"—"'Experience' names that which 'the Phenomenology' is (*'Die Erfahrung' nennt das, was 'die Phänomenologie' ist*)"—he makes it clear that this reconcilement and this identity are problematic and in need of being read: "What does Hegel think when he uses the word 'experience' in this emphatic way? (*Was denkt Hegel, wenn er das Wort 'die Erfahrung' in dieser betonten Weise gebraucht?*)" In order to know what the "Phenomenology" *is* or, in other words, what "experience" *names*—to know the difference between and the identity of "naming" (*nennen*) and "being" (*sein*)—it is necessary to read the text of the "Introduction": "The answer is given to us by the piece with which, after the Preface, the work begins (*Die Antwort gibt uns das Stück, mit dem nach der Vorrede das Werk beginnt*)." Heidegger proceeds by citing and then reading the text. Because Heidegger's citing not only cuts the introduction out of its context, but also reinscribes it in the new context of his reading, it has fallen under the law of nonreading. This does not mean it has been ignored. On the contrary, like the victimized title ("Science of the Experience of Consciousness") and the Introduction that reads it, Heidegger's text returns again and again with an uncanny insistence to haunt the texts of its nonreaders—as though ever in need of ever new refusals to read. A good example is provided in the editors' Foreword to the useful volume *Materialien zu Hegels 'Phänomenologie des Geistes'* (Materials for Hegel's *Phenomenology of Spirit*).

The editors summarize Heidegger's "detailed, paragraph by paragraph meditation": rather than seeking to make Hegel's text "accessible to the uninitiated reader (*dem unvertrautem Leser zugänglich zu machen*) or to present ["actualize" (*vergegenwärtigen*)] its content in the medium of Marxist or existentialist conceptions," Heidegger sees it "as a basic text of Western metaphysics (*als einen Grundtext der abendländischen Metaphysik*)." "He wants to discover within it the concealed presuppositions [or "prejudices" or, better, "pre-opinions" (*Vormeinungen*)] that determine the understanding of the basic concepts, organize the thought progression, and allow Hegel to formulate sentences whose sense is yet to be thought and whose claims are still to be judged but which can be neither opened nor decided by Hegel's own thought. For both Hegel and ourselves these presuppositions (*Vormeinungen*) have become destiny (*Geschick*), and our terminologically hardened philosophical language of concepts (*Begriffssprache*) does not allow these presuppositions to be recognized. Rather, according to Heidegger, they must be sought in early texts, in which they still speak themselves as themselves (*in denen sie sich noch als solche aussprechen*). For this reason Heidegger works hard to hold Hegel's lines, so to speak (*gleichsam*), against a bright light source (*eine helle Lichtquelle*) in order to make visible between them as though in a secret writing ["coded writing" (*Geheimschrift*)] the formulations of Aristotle and to read the lines of each in the context of the other's lines. In order to be able to think Hegel—this is the law of the interpretation—one must think Aristotle *in Greek*."[5]

As a summary paraphrase of Heidegger's text, this nonreading is fair enough, even if it is not all that certain that all Heidegger does is to read Hegel in the context of Aristotle (and vice versa), and even if it is still less certain that such a reading could be a reassuring operation: since, according to Heidegger, the groundlessness of Western thought (*die Bodenlosigkeit des abendländischen Denkens*) begins with the translation (*Übersetzen*) of Greek experience into an other way of thought—"by no means the harmless operation it is still thought to be these days (*keineswegs der harmlose Vorgang, für den er noch heutigentags gehalten wird*)" (*H*, 13)—retranslating Hegel's *Grundtext* into Aristotle's (and vice versa) would be an abysmally precarious activity.[6] But more important and more symptomatic for the forms in which the refusal to read—Hegel and Heidegger, Hegel *by* Heidegger—manifests itself is the paragraph that follows, for in refusing to read the text, in fact, in apologizing for not reading the text, the editors compound the first refusal by another one: they attempt to prevent anyone else from reading the text. "It is clear," say the editors without saying to whom it is so clear, "that it cannot be the business (*Sache*) of a handy collection of study texts for the *Phenomenology* to present the Heideggerian paradigm of this micrological procedure of decipherment, as profound as it is arduous (*dieser ebenso tiefsinnigen wie mühseligen, mikrologischen Entzifferungsverfahrens*). Heidegger's commentary requires a metacommentary. But it is hardly an accident that among the imposing number of Heidegger interpretations none is to be found that would fill this need [do justice to this requirement (*die diesem Bedürfnis Rechnung trägt*)[7]]. Above all, an argument with such an essay should not take place within the framework of a Foreword. Nevertheless, Heidegger's essay (*Aufsatz*) on Hegel's concept of experience possesses a great power of attraction (*grosse Anziehungskraft*) for many who turn to the *Phenomenology of Spirit*. Therefore it recommends itself (*empfiehlt es sich*) to warn of a misunderstanding to which it [Heidegger's *Aufsatz*] lies near. The 'Introduction' to the *Phenomenology* is no basic text

(*Grundtext*) of Hegelian philosophy, but rather the prolegomenon emerging from the philosophical presuppositions of the time of composition (*das von philosophischen Vormeinungen der Abfassungszeit ausgehende Prolegomenon*) to a work that according to its idea forbids using the author's terminology (*die Terminologie des Autors*) in its full, for the author "standard-giving" meaning (*in ihrer vollen, für den Autor massgeblichen Bedeutung zu gebrauchen*) right at the beginning. Out of the context of this Introduction one cannot yet glean, for example, what Hegel understands by 'knowing' (*'Erkennen'*), 'Absolute,' 'true,' or 'to will.' It is also not sensible [that is, full of sense (*sinnvoll*)] to ask for this in this context. Sentences that make global claims—precisely those that Heidegger puts in the center of his interpretation—do not express Hegel's final judgment (*Hegels abschliessendes Urteil*), but rather representative views (*repräsentative Ansichten*). Hegel relies on them for a preliminary explanation and justification of his undertaking a presentation of apparent knowledge. The text that Heidegger interprets was supposed to create an exoteric approach to the work. To teach (*unterrichten*), uninhibitedly if possible (*möglichst unverkrampft*), about it [the text] is therefore the most fitting end (*Zweck*) that it serves. On the basis of this point of view, the text from J. E. Erdmann's history of philosophy was chosen."

It is hardly an accident that in attempting to do honor to the difficulty of Heidegger's text while protecting both the reader and Hegel from its dangerous (because seductive) misunderstanding, the editors end up by devaluing and excluding all three: Heidegger's text, for despite being "detailed," "profound," "arduous," it does not provide unproblematic access to the work insofar as it requires a metacommentary, insofar as it has to be read; Hegel's text, for it grows out of "pre-opinions" (*Vormeinungen*), expresses merely "representative views," and therefore should be "taught uninhibitedly"—by teacher to student, by master to slave—rather than being read; and the reader, the "uninitiated reader," for he or she is one of the many who turn to the *Phenomenology* but are easily seduced by misunderstanding, one who needs to be warned against futile, indeed senseless, attempts (like Heidegger's) to read texts whose meaning is not full, to fill with meaning texts that are better summarized and dismissed. Some questions can be asked about the presuppositions (*Vormeinungen*?) of this threefold dismissal: (1) Is the best access to Hegel provided by commentaries that are so transparent as to be in no need (no danger?) of being read? (2) How can a text that introduces meaningless "representative views" on the basis of unthought, unread, presuppositions explain or justify anything? (3) How can the uninitiated reader become one of the elect—how can the nonreader learn to read Hegel (or Heidegger for that matter) if to teach him means to teach strategies of nonreading? It is no accident that the text with which, after the Preface, the "work" begins—the original (non)beginning that reads the original (non)title: the (non)introduction that introduces either the introduction to the "System of Science" or its first part or both (dialectically) or neither(?)[8]—it is no accident that this text not only provides the "answers" but, more important, poses the questions: (1) The problem of the "uninitiated reader" and his education is inscribed in the text as the natural consciousness and the problem of its education (*Bildung*) to a standpoint—absolute knowledge—where it can know itself absolutely, that is, read the text of its own experience. (2) The question of the introductory text and the validity of its presuppositions is inscribed in the introduction as the explicit rejection of critical examinations that would presuppose (*voraussetzen*) the meanings of words like "absolute," "true," and so on, examinations that would base themselves on dry assertions (*Versicherungen*) and empty opinions (*Meinungen*)—but, of course, it is also reinscribed as the introduction of another—valid and necessary—presupposition (of a point of departure, of an end point [*Ziel*], of a route marked out by stations, and of a standard [*Massstab*] against which to measure the truth of these presuppositions). (3) Last—but, needless to say, also first—the question of the status of the "commentator," the initiated reader, he who already knows how to read and who by reading (and writing) a text plays a role—active or passive, opaque or transparent—in the education of the uninitiated reader, is inscribed in the text as the question of the "we": the "we" too easily and too readily identified as the "philosophical consciousness," the teacher, the seer who is able to see what natural consciousness cannot see, who not only can read the text that is the experience of natural consciousness but can also select and reproduce it, rewrite it, in the form of a (dialectically) coherent narrative with a beginning, middle, and an end, and who can then present this narrative—the presentation of apparent knowledge, the science of the experience of consciousness, the phenomenology of spirit—this biography of (natural) consciousness to consciousness so that it may recognize and read its own autobiography: *und so erzählte ich mir mein Leben* (and so I narrated my life to myself).[9] If finally and first of all it is the reading and the writing of the "we" that makes the text of the experience of consciousness possible, a reading of Hegel's text is impossible without a (re)reading and a (re)writing of this "we." In other words, as long as the commentator, teacher, editor of study texts for the *Phenomenology* refuses to read this inscription of his role, his self, his "we," in the text of the Introduction (just as the "we" is inscribed in the text of the experience of consciousness)—as long as he refused to read the *subjective* as well as the objective genitive in the phrase "the reading and the writing of the 'we' "—he remains a nonreader *of* Hegel. By refusing to inscribe himself in Hegel's text as the "we," he is forever inscribed in it as the natural consciousness or worse: as one of those (nonreaders) who presupposes (*voraussetzen*), asserts (*versichern*), and opines (*meinen*). Small wonder that the text has proved to be uncannily unreadable.

The text of the Introduction "sounds" in the original edition: "It is a natural representation that . . .(*Es ist eine natürliche Vorstellung, dass.* . .)." If the sentence is in fact allowed to sound in the "original" (German), it resounds as the "original" echoed by, and the unoriginal echo of, a sentence toward the beginning of the section *Selbstbewusstsein:* "It is a *self-consciousness for a self-consciousness* (*Es ist ein* Selbstbewusstsein für ein Selbstbewusstsein)" (*PhG,* 140). Just as the status of the "Es" in this sentence—ostensibly a pronoun with an antecedent in the "Selbstbewusstsein" of the preceding sentence: "It is. . ."—is rendered problematic—that is, perhaps it is (also?) an "impersonal" formulation meaning "There is. . ."—by still another echo on the following page—"There is for self-consciousness an other self-consciousness (*Es ist für das Selbstbewusstsein ein anderes Selbstbewusstsein)*" (*PhG,* 141)—so is the first sentence of the Introduction (retroactively? dialectically? metaleptically?) rewritten by these latter sentences to include (always already and always not yet) self-consciousness: according to "natural representation," in order to know what truly is, it is first necessary to know what knowing is. But precisely to the extent that the bending back—reflection—of knowing upon itself is in this sentence inscribed in *Vorstellung* ("placing in front of," "representation"), it is inscribed in a doubly *un*selfconscious medium. As a "placing in front of," *Vorstellung* places knowing *before* that which is known and *in front of* the knower. In so doing, it presupposes that there is (1) someone who knows, a *knower*; (2) something to know, a *known*; and (3) a relation between them, *knowing*. Such a presupposition of the subject, object, and indeed method of the examination makes a real examination of knowing impossible, for in positing a static object and a static subject of knowledge, it separates them by a knowing that is forever separated from itself (like the subject from the object), that cannot know itself because it wants to make knowing the object of the examination while forgetting that it is also the *subject* of the examination. By placing its object—knowing—in front of itself, *Vorstellung* would want to know knowing itself *without* knowing itself: again, in order to know "the thing itself (*die Sache selbst*)," it is necessary to know one's self *as knowing* and not as a medium—not as something that stands between knower and known—not as a tool (*Werkzeug*) or as a means (*Mittel*).

Just as *Vorstellung* as "presupposition" was insufficiently self-conscious precisely because it placed knowing in front of, before (*eh, vorher*), knowing, so *Vorstellung* as "representation" is insufficiently self-conscious because it sees (*betrachtet*) knowing as (*als das Werkzeug. . .als das Mittel*) other than itself: it does not see its seeing as seeing but rather (represents it) as tool and as means. In other words, it *re*presents a knowing (already constituted, already presented, in the past) not as itself, not as representing, but as active tool or passive medium: in not being able to represent representation as representation, it is unable to know knowing as knowing. *Vorstellung*, then, as "presupposition" and as "representation," cannot approach the "thing itself," cannot really know what is in truth (*das wirkliche Erkennen dessen, was in Wahrheit ist*), because it *is* as *pre*supposition—and thereby places itself (its being in truth) in front of, before, itself—and as *re*presentation—and thereby places itself (its being in truth) in back of, after, itself: always wanting to know itself *before* knowing itself or *after* knowing itself, it is unable to know what *is* in truth because it is unable to *be* in truth.[10] Insofar as its "nature"—as "presupposition" and as "representation"—prevents *Vorstellung* from being itself, it is a "natural" *Vorstellung*—(*Es ist eine natürliche Vorstellung),* and insofar as it *is* a natural *Vorstellung*—that is, insofar as it is not *Vorstellung* itself—it is always a natural *Vorstellung that* (*Es ist eine natürliche Vorstellung, dass.* . .). That is, since *Vorstellung* can never be for *Vorstellung,* for itself, but must always be before or behind itself, it cannot stand alone (for itself) as self-consciousness can (*Es ist ein Selbstbewusstsein für ein Selbstbewusstsein*) but must always be a *Vorstellung that* (*dass*), a *Vorstellung* that is other than itself.

In a first, preliminary, sense, *Vorstellung* is a word, a text, that is unreadable (and unwritable) precisely to the extent that it is a word *that*, a text *that*, cannot read (or write) itself. And yet the text (of the Introduction) reads (and writes): "It is a natural representation that. . ." The text can read (and write) natural *Vorstellung*, for what it does in the first sentence is precisely to presuppose (*Es ist eine natürliche Vorstellung*) and represent (*dass.* . .) natural *Vorstellung* (presupposition, representation): in doing so, it presupposes and represents natural *Vorstellung* (presupposition, representation) *as* presupposing and representing. In other words, although *Vorstellung* may be unable to know knowing, read reading, because it can neither know itself (as knowing) nor read itself (as reading), the text is able to know and to read *Vorstellung* as *Vorstellung.* This knowing, this reading, of the text, however, is not (yet) enough to recover *Vorstellung* in its truth, for the only way that *Vorstellung* could *be* what it is in truth would be to know and to read itself the way that the text knows and reads it. But what is the way that the text knows and reads *Vorstellung,* and who is the reader (and writer) of the text that he may read (and write) the text itself as reading (and writing)? The way that the text knows and reads *Vorstellung* is as a way of recovering the truth of natural *Vorstellung* through a process of education, as the way of the natural consciousness that penetrates to true knowing (*der Weg des natürlichen Bewusstseins, das zum wahren Wissen dringt*) (*PhG,* 67), as the education of consciousness to science (*Bildung des Bewusstseins selbst zur Wissenschaft*)—in short, as the "Science of the Experience of Consciousness," as the "Phenomenology of Spirit." But if the text that is able to read the text (of the experience, the education) of natural *Vorstellung*—that is able to presuppose and represent presupposition and representation as presupposing and representing—is precisely the text of natural *Vorstellung,* it would mean that the text (of natural *Vorstellung*) has in some way—but *what* way, if the way is always the way *of* the text?—(always already) to be read and written as the text *before* being read and written. In other words: on the one hand the "text"—the text that reads (and writes) *Es ist eine natürliche Vorstellung, dass.* . ., that presupposes and represents presupposition and representation as presupposing and representing, etc.—on the one hand the text would save natural *Vorstellung* from its inability to read itself and would educate it to a standpoint where it could read itself; on the other hand the (same?) text would doom natural *Vorstellung* to another (or the same?) unreadability, for it cannot read natural *Vorstellung* before reading itself, and since the text is itself the text of natural *Vorstellung*, it cannot read itself before reading the text of natural *Vorstellung*. Again: in order to presuppose and represent a natural *Vorstellung* as (yet) unreadable, the text presupposes and represents itself as (always already) read; but since it cannot do one without doing the other, the text always presupposes and represents, reads and writes, itself as *two* texts: the one unread and unwritten; the other (re)read and (re)written. The text cannot write or read its unread and unwritten beginning—- *Es ist eine natürliche Vorstellung, dass.* . .—without already having written and read its (re)read and (re)written end: "Das absolute Wissen" (Absolute knowing). The text—its beginnings and its ends, its writing and its reading—is doubly inscribed—doubly presupposed and doubly represented—in the presupposition and representation of the first sentence: as the unread, unreadable nonreader, the natural *Vorstellung*; and as the already read, already readable reader, the "we." The "we," although still "invisible," is inscribed in the text from the beginning—along with the absolute (knowing): *die Sache selbst.* . .*das wirkliche Erkennen dessen, was in Wahrheit ist.* . .*wodurch man des Absoluten sich bemächtige.* . .—as the reader and writer of the text that reads and writes natural *Vorstellung*. This may be the sense in which the absolute is always "near to us," "with us" (*bei uns*), but it may also be the sense—and the forgetting of this sense is the forgetting of natural *Vorstellung*[11]—in which "we" as well as the absolute are always near to, with, natural *Vorstellung*.

But if the double inscription of the text—and the relation between the two inscriptions: natural *Vorstellung* and the "we'," natural *Vorstellung* and the absolute—is to be read, a double reading is necessary: a reading of the "we" as well as a reading of natural *Vorstellung*. Although the "we" is (doubly) inscribed in the text from the beginning (as the reader [and writer] [un] able to read [and write] both the beginning and the end of the text), it takes some time to "appear" in the first paragraph as the active "we" who wields the tool of knowing—in the sentence that begins "Or if knowing is not the tool of *our* activity.* . .(Oder ist das Erkennen nicht Werkzeug unserer Tätigkeit.* . .)" (*PhG*, 63)—and as the passive "we" who allows the light of truth to reach it through a passive medium—"but rather, so to speak, a passive medium through which the light of truth reaches through to *us* (*sondern gewissermassen ein passives Medium, durch welches hindurch das Licht der Wahrheit an uns gelangt*)." Neither the one nor the other (reading of the) "we" is able to attain its end—its final goal (*Endzweck*), the heaven of truth (*Himmel der Wahrheit*), the absolute (*das Absolute*), the absolute essence (*das absolute Wesen*), the light of truth (*das Licht der Wahrheit*), etc.—for in both cases the "we" uses a means that produces the opposite of its end (*Wir gebrauchen in beiden Fällen ein Mittel, welches unmittelbar das Gegenteil seines Zwecks hervorbringt*): the application of a tool changes the object, and the interposition of a medium allows the object to appear only as it is in and through the medium and not as it is in itself (*an sich*).

And yet neither the tool nor the medium is really at fault in "our" inability to attain "our" end, but rather "our" very attempt to serve ourselves by means of a means (*oder das Widersinnige ist vielmehr, dass wir uns überhaupt eines Mittels bedienen*). If the problem were only what the tool and the medium *did* to the absolute in presenting it through *Vorstellung*, in representing it to us in representation, it would appear possible to grasp the absolute by subtracting the effects of the tool and the medium from the result of the operation (*den Teil, welcher in der Vorstellung, die wir durch es vom Absoluten erhalten, dem Werkzeuge angehört, im Resultate abzuziehen und so das Wahre rein zu erhalten*). The real problem—and the reason such a subtraction can never deliver the absolute—is what *we* do to the absolute and to ourselves in presupposing and representing knowing as tool and as medium (*Vorstellungen* von dem *Erkennen* als einem *Werkzeuge* und *Medium*) (*PhG*, 65). That is, such a *Vorstellung* of knowing presupposes and represents a knower—"we"—who is forever separate from the (to be) known—the absolute—and thereby makes it impossible for either ever to *be* in truth: a knower—"we"—who is separated from the known—the absolute—by his own knowing—his own being—can never know—or be—in truth; and a known—the absolute—that is separated from its knower—"us"—by it being (un)known—by its being—can never be known—or be—in truth.

The trouble with "our" using a means to grasp the absolute is precisely *our* using a means: by presupposing and representing knowing as a means, we are presupposing and representing an already known—one, unified, constituted—known; by serving ourselves to the absolute by means of a means, we are only serving ourselves to our (self-serving) selves. A knower who presupposes and represents knowing as a means also presupposes and represents himself not as a knower but as a means: that is, in falsifying knowing, he falsifies both himself as knowing subject and the absolute as (the to be) known object. He who wants to know knowing by means of a knowing that is a means does not want to know knowing at all, for he wants to know an object that is himself without knowing the object as himself. In other words, "we" are back in the position of the reader (and the writer) of the texts of natural *Vorstellung* in the first sentence who wants to read (and write) the (unread, unwritten) text of natural *Vorstellung* without recognizing that insofar as he is himself the already read (and written) text of natural *Vorstellung*, he cannot read (or write) the text of natural *Vorstellung* without (re)reading and (re)writing the text that he is (always already and always not yet) himself. In the same way, we want to read the text of the absolute without recognizing that insofar as we are (in truth) readers, we (the readers) are inscribed in the text of the absolute (the true, that which *is* in truth) and therefore cannot read the text of the absolute without reading the text that we are ourselves.

But just as the false presupposition and representation of knowing as means falsified both the knower and the (to be) known, so the false model of reading as means falsifies both the reader and the text (to be read), for as long as reading is presupposed and represented as a means that separates us from the text of the absolute, we can read neither the text of the absolute nor the text of ourselves. If the absolute were in fact separate from us, if the absolute were not and did not want to be in and for itself already with us (*wenn es nicht an und für sich schon bei uns wäre und sein wollte*) (*PhG*, 64), it would mock the ruse that seeks to bring the absolute closer to us without changing it, the ruse that we are ourselves when we pretend that we can bring an absolute separate from us closer to us without already having presupposed and represented the absolute as near to us, as with us. The absolute—were it not already with us—would mock us just as the text mocks the reader who would read the text better than the text reads itself without being able to read himself as reader of the text. So that on the one hand when the "we" appears in the first paragraph as a "we" that presupposes and represents knowing as tool or medium, it also presupposes and represents itself—the knower—as a tool or a medium and therefore appears as natural *Vorstellung*. To the extent that the "we" appears as such—that is, as the unread, unreadable nonreader that is the natural *Vorstellung* of the first sentence—its relation to the absolute would appear to be the same as the relation of natural *Vorstellung* (in the first sentence) to the "text"—that is, the text that is able to read (and write) the text of natural *Vorstellung* because it has (always already) read (and written) it(self). But, on the other hand, this does not mean that the "appearance" of the "we" in the first paragraph is a mere repetition of the appearance of natural *Vorstellung* in the first sentence, for a (chiasmic and, in this case, rigorously dialectical) reversal has taken place between the two "appearances." In other words, to the extent that in the first sentence the "text" can be identified, can be *read*, as the read, readable, and reading reader—the "we" who can read (and write) the beginning of the text because he has (always already) read (and written) the end:

namely, absolute knowledge—the appearance of the "we" in the first paragraph as natural *Vorstellung*—that is, as the presupposition and representation of knowing and therefore itself, the knower, as tool and as medium—is a *dis*appearance of the knowing—read, readable, reading—"we" and a (re)appearance of the unknowing—unread, unreadable, nonreading—"we" (of natural *Vorstellung*). But—and this is the crossing of the chiasmus—if natural *Vorstellung* disappears as natural *Vorstellung* to (re)appear as the unknowing "we" of natural *Vorstellung*, the knowing "we" (of the text of the first sentence) disappears as the knowing "we" only to (re)appear as the knowing absolute. In other words, what natural *Vorstellung* was in the first sentence (i.e., appearing)—"we" are now; and what "the text," the "we" of the text, was in the first sentence (i.e., not appearing) "the absolute" is now. Again: when the reader of the text—the "we" who does not appear in the first sentence but is nevertheless "present" as he who presupposes and represents, reads and writes, the text of natural *Vorstellung*—when the reader of the text appears in the first paragraph as the "we" he cannot but disappear as a reader capable of reading the text, for appearing means appearing in the element of natural *Vorstellung* (i.e., as presupposing and representing). And when natural *Vorstellung*—the text that appears in the first sentence but remains unread and unreadable as long as it cannot read (and write) itself—disappears in the first paragraph as natural *Vorstellung*, it cannot help but (re)appear as a text capable of reading itself, for disappearing as natural *Vorstellung* (as presupposing and representing) means (re)appearing in the element of thought (i.e., absolute knowing, the absolute).

So the appearance (and disappearance) of the "we," and the disappearance (and [re]appearance) of natural *Vorstellung*, in the first paragraph are by no means a simple repetition but rather a rereading (and a rewriting) of the first sentence: the text (the nonappearing "we") appears, presents itself, as appearance, as presentation, by disappearing as text and reappearing as (the "we" of) natural *Vorstellung*—or, later, as apparent knowing (*erscheinendes Wissen*)—but, on the other hand and at the same time, natural *Vorstellung* disappears as appearance, as (re)presentation by (re)appearing as the text (of the absolute) and disappearing as natural *Vorstellung*. The text—but *which* text: natural *Vorstellung* or the "we"? the "we" of natural *Vorstellung* or the absolute?—cannot say, cannot read or write, that the absolute is already with us (*bei uns*)—the absolute *as* already with us—for such saying, such reading and writing, would not be the appearance, the self-presentation, of the absolute but rather the appearance of the absolute as natural *Vorstellung* (as presupposition and representation) and therefore the disappearance of the absolute as the absolute. The text cannot say that the absolute is already with us because the text as the read, readable, and reading reader of the first sentence has become the unread, unreadable, and nonreading "we" of the first paragraph: in other words, it is no longer the "we" who is the text but rather the absolute; it is no longer natural *Vorstellung* that is the unread, unreadable, nonreader but rather the "we." The text in fact does *not* say that the absolute is already with us but rather reads (and rewrites): if the absolute were not and did not want to be in and for itself already with us (*wenn es nicht an und für sich schon bei uns wäre und sein wollte*). That is, "we" and our self-deceiving efforts to bring the absolute closer by means of the ruse of a means would indeed be mocked by the absolute, would indeed be driven back to "our" point of departure—in short, would indeed be only repeating the first sentence of the text—if the absolute were not already with us: if the absolute had not already "appeared" as the nonappearing reader (and writer), the "we," of the text of natural *Vorstellung* in the first sentence of the text. The dependent clause—if the absolute were not and did not want to be in and for itself already with us (*wenn es nicht an und für sich schon bei uns wäre und sein wollte*)—cannot and does not "presuppose" or "represent" or "posit" or whatever the presence of the absolute as with us but rather rereads and rewrites the first sentence of the text. The non-appearance of the "we" in the first sentence is reread and rewritten in the first paragraph as the absolute that does not appear because it has always already (and always not yet) appeared (as nonappearing) in the first sentence of the text. The only way that the text—and the absolute is now the "text": the non-appearing reader (and writer) of the appearing (unread, unreadable) text of natural *Vorstellung*, which "we" have become in the first paragraph—can make the absolute—that is, itself—appear, can present the absolute, can read and write the absolute, is by not making the absolute appear as appearing (but as having already appeared), by not presenting the absolute as present (but as having already been present), by not reading and writing the absolute as reading and writing (but as already read and written). The text does so and needs already to have done so, for if the absolute *were not* already with us, "we" could not have presupposed and represented natural *Vorstellung* (presupposition and representation) as presupposing and representing, "we" could not have made natural *Vorstellung* appear as appearing while making ourselves "present" without appearing, "we," the text, could not have read or written the first sentence of the text.

If the first paragraph of the text—the appearance of the "we," the non-appearance of the absolute—rather than being an arbitrary and futile repetition of the first sentence, is a necessary narrative that rereads and rewrites the first sentence of the text, then the narrative of the text as a presentation of the appearing of apparent knowing—as the presentation of apparent knowing (*Darstellung des erscheinenden Wissens*) (*PhG*, 66)—is a self-presentation (*Selbstdarstellung?*) of the text (of apparent knowing), a self-reading and self-writing of the text. But such a self-reading and self-writing of the text is more than just problematic, for it is an operation—a narrative movement—in which the self that reads and writes itself can do so only by *not* reading and writing itself as reading and writing itself but only as having already read and written itself. The "we" can appear as the "we" of absolute knowing only when it does *not* appear, that is, only when it does not appear as the "we" of natural *Vorstellung*, only when it does not appear *as* the "we" that must appear as the "we" of something other than itself. But how can the "we" appear as not appearing and not appear as appearing when both—appearing *and* not appearing—entail appearing and not appearing *as* and therefore always bring along with them the "we" of natural *Vorstellung*, that is, of presupposition and representation of something *as* something? And how can the text read and write itself as *not* reading and writing but as already read and written when both—(not) reading and (not) writing *and* (not) having read and (not) having written—entail reading and writing *as* and therefore always read and write along with themselves the nonreading and nonwriting of natural *Vorstellung*? Since it would appear impossible for the "we" of the text to appear as itself without appearing as the "we" of natural *Vorstellung*, to read and write itself without reading and writing the text of natural *Vorstellung*, it would appear impossible for the "we" of the text either to appear or to read and write itself in the first place—as though the first sentence of the text could have been neither read nor written, and as though the first paragraph's using words like "absolute," "knowing," and so on were a fraud (*könnten sie [unnützen Vorsellungen und Redensarten von dem Erkennen als einem Werkzeuge. . . oder als einem Medium] als zufällige und willkürliche Vorstellungen geradezu verworfen und der damit verbundne Gebrauch von Worten als dem Absoluten, dem Erkennen, auch dem Objektiven und Subjektiven und unzähligen andern, deren Bedeutung als allgemein bekannt vorausgesetzt wird, sogar als Betrug angesehen werden*) (*PhG*, 65-66). Indeed, the text and its "we" would have remained unreadable and unwritable—in the first and preliminary sense—if the self-reading and self-writing of the first paragraph had not already read and written the answer to the question of the impossibility of the text's reading and writing itself. As the first paragraph's rereading and rewriting of its first sentence (i.e., the text's self-reading and self-writing) demonstrates, the "text" is precisely that which reads and writes the narrative of the impossibility of reading and writing, the narrative of the impossibility of reading and writing except as a reading and a writing of the text of natural *Vorstellung*—except as reading and writing *as*. But to the extent that the text can read and write the narrative of the impossibility of reading and writing itself, it can make this impossibility of reading and writing itself an object *for itself*, that is, for its reading and writing itself. The answer of the text is—as always in the text of "Hegel": "This is what deals the wound and also what heals it (*Dieses ist es, welches die Wunde schlägt und dieselbe auch heilt*)"[12] (VIII:88)—self-consciousness: the text turns its condition of impossibility into its condition of possibility by turning its self—as the impossibility of the text—against itself, by turning an object in itself (*an sich*) into an object for itself (*für sich*). So the reader and writer of the text, the "we" of the text—in spite of being unable to appear except *as*, except as appearing in the element of natural *Vorstellung*, in spite of being unable to read and write the text except *as*, except as the text of natural *Vorstellung*—the reader and writer of the text turns against himself— just as real knowing, science (*Wissenschaft*), in order to free itself from the appearance that is its appearing, turns against its appearance, against the *Schein* (semblance) of its *Erscheinung* (appearance); and science can do this only by turning itself against its illusory appearance (*und sie kann dies nur dadurch, dass sie sich gegen ihn [den Schein] wendet*) (*PhG*, 66)—the reader and writer of the text turns against himself by making the appearance of apparent knowing appear, by reading and writing the impossibility of reading and writing (except *as*). This turning (*wenden*) of the text against (*gegen*) itself in order to turn itself into an object (*Gegenstand*) for itself is the turning point of the text whether it occurs in the first sentence or in the first paragraph of the Introduction—or, for example, in the last sentence of the introduction to the section "Selbstbewusstsein": "In self-consciousness as the concept of spirit consciousness finally has its turning point, on the basis of which it may step out of the colorful illusory appearance of the sensuous given and out of the empty night of the suprasensuous beyond into the spiritual day of the present (*Das Bewusstsein hat erst in dem Selbstbewusstsein, als dem Begriffe des Geistes, seinen Wendungspunkt, auf dem es aus dem farbigen Scheine des sinnlichen Diesseits und aus der leeren Nacht des übersinnlichen Jenseits in den geistigen Tag der Gegenwart einschreitet*)" (*PhG*, 140).[13]

But if in order to step into its present (*Gegenwart*) the text has to turn against (*gegen*) itself and thereby turn itself into its own object (*Gegenstand*), the turning point of its self-presentation always entails a moment of self-*re*presentation: *Selbstdarstellung* is not possible without *Selbstvorstellung*. So that the text's representations of knowing *as* tool and *as* means, of the "we" as tool and as means, not only stake out the beginning of the text—by posing the question of the text as that which is at stake—but also have already staked out the end of the text—by responding to the question of the text as that which has always been at stake. Rather than "sticking" in the system of opinion and prejudice (*im Systeme des Meinens und des Vorurteils zu stecken*) (*PhG*, 68), the text gives up its opinions—which insist on that which is "mine" (*meinen*)—and follows through the stations staked out for itself by its own nature—its nature *as*: *as* natural consciousness, that which has staked out itself (as that whose [im]possibility has always been at stake)—just as the presentation of apparent knowing can be seen as the way of the soul that travels through the series of its forms as though through stations staked out for it by its own nature (*als der Weg der Seele, welche die Reihe ihrer Gestaltungen, als* *durch ihre Natur ihr vorgesteckter Stationen, durchwandert*) (*PhG*, 67) and whose end, goal, is staked out just as necessarily as the series of forms of its progression (*Das Ziel aber ist dem Wissen ebenso notwendig als die Reihe des Fortganges gesteckt*) (*PhG*, 69). The possibility of sticking, of being stuck (*stecken*), in the system of opinion and prejudice—the possibility of sticking in the element of natural *Vorstellung*, the possibility of not being able to go past the first sentence of the text because unable to read and write that sentence—remarks what is at stake in (self-)staking out (*vorgesteckte Stationen, das Ziel ist. . . gesteckt*): namely, the possibility of sticking in the system of opinion and prejudice, in that which is one's own in its immediacy, is a possibility limited to that which is limited to a "natural life"—"That which is limited to a natural life cannot by itself go out above its immediate existence (*Was auf ein natürliches Leben beschränkt ist, vermag durch sich selbst nicht über sein unmittelbares Dasein hinauszugehen*)" (*PhG*, 69). But "natural life" is not the same as natural *Vorstellung*. Whereas the former, in order to go beyond the limits of its immediate existence, needs to be driven out, ripped out, by something other than itself—"but it is driven out above it [its immediate existence] by an other and this being ripped out is its death (*aber es wird durch ein anderes darüber hinausgetrieben, und dies Hinausgerissen werden ist sein Tod*)" (*PhG*, 69)—the latter, natural *Vorstellung* (the presupposition and representation of which "natural consciousness" is capable because it is *not* limited to a "natural life"),[14] insofar as it is always in front of, before, and always in back of, after, itself, always stakes itself out as its own (im)possibility, as the impossibility of its being present to itself except as a staking out of—always already and always not yet stak*ed* out—turning points (at which it turns against itself as its own impossibility). Unlike that which is limited to a "natural life," natural *Vorstellung* is constantly driven out, ripped out, to go beyond the limits *of* itself *by* itself because the "other"—"the beyond" (*das Jenseits*), the goal (*Ziel*) of the movement, the absolute—is always posited, staked out, along with itself *as its* other, as an other belonging to it—"the beyond is always posited for consciousness along with the particular (*mit dem Einzelnen ist ihm zugleich das Jenseits gesetzt*)" (*PhG*, 69). In other words, natural consciousness, presupposed and represented as natural *Vorstellung* (i.e., as presupposing and representing itself), always carries a death within itself, always carries *its own* death within itself, and therefore can never achieve the rest (*Ruhe*) of self-sufficiency, for it is always suffering violence at the hands of itself to go beyond itself. Its staked-out route, as well as its beginnings and ends, is nothing else than, can be nothing else than, a way of doubt and despair on which it can do nothing but constantly die to itself in order that it may continue to follow the route of its dying to itself.

   Staking out this route, then, is a matter of life and death; the only way that the route (and its beginnings and ends) can be staked out is as (always already and always not yet) staked out: that is, natural *Vorstellung* (as the representative of consciousness) must conceal (*verstecken*?) the staked-out route (and its beginnings and ends) all the more carefully in order to discover its staked-out stakes all the more surely. It must die to itself as staking out in order to be staked out, in order to discover that it has already been staked out. The movement of the text—the text as it presupposes and represents itself, the text as it dies to itself, in natural *Vorstellung*—is, in a sense, a movement that recuperates the senses of the word *stecken*—a movement that rereads by rewriting and rewrites by rereading the "one" word *stecken*: a word that signifies "to conceal, to hide" most insistently in those places where it would mean "to stake out, to mark out" most clearly.[15] *Selbstdarstellen* is a *Selbstvorstellen* is a *Selbstvorstecken*. But in order to rise to the level of real knowing, science (*Wissenschaft*), this movement of the text of natural *Vorstellung* requires a scientific observer: a reader who can read the text of natural *Vorstellung*—the narrative of turning points at which consciousness turns upon itself to die to itself—a reader who can read the text as not only a series of discrete moments, of objects in themselves (*an sich*), but as a necessary and necessarily complete narrative of the forms of consciousness presented as the presentation of apparent knowing and appearing *for* someone: for us (*für uns*). But this "someone," this "we" of the reader of the text, insofar as he is the "other" that natural *Vorstellung* presupposes and represents along with itself—insofar as he is the always already read, readable, and reading reader of the text that haunts the unread, unreadable, and nonreading text of natural *Vorstellung*—this reader would be the death of consciousness *to* consciousness: rather than a "someone," he would have to be a "no one." Insofar as consciousness—presupposed and represented as natural *Vorstellung*—stakes out for itself its route—its beginnings and its ends, and its beginnings are always its ends insofar as it cannot stake out its beginning without also staking out its end (its death to itself)—as well as the standard, the measuring staff (*Massstab*), against which it can measure its stakes—for in measuring its staking out against its already having been staked out it is measuring itself against itself—insofar as the text of natural *Vorstellung* would read and write itself as the reading and writing of its own impossibility, it would have no need of "us," of a "we" other than the text who would measure the text against something other than the text, for the text of natural *Vorstellung* has "us," its own "we," inscribed in itself (as its own death to itself) from the beginning (and in the end).

It is not necessary for "us" to bring along standards, a measuring staff, and to apply *our* notions and thoughts in the examination (of the text of natural consciousness as presupposed and represented in natural *Vorstellung*)—*und hiemit nicht nötig haben, Massstäbe mitzubringen und* unsere Einfälle und Gedanken *bei der Untersuchung zu applizieren*) (*PhG*, 71-72)—because: in examining the truth of apparent knowing we are examining an object in itself (*an sich*), but insofar as *we* are examining it we are examining that object not as it is in itself (*an sich*) but as it appears for (*für uns*)—rather than examining *its* truth we are examining *our* knowing of its truth; but the examination becomes a dialectical movement (necessary and complete) only when we can turn this knowing "for us" against ourselves, that is, only when we realize that the object we are examining—knowing—has a moment "for itself" already inscribed within it to the extent that this object—knowing—is also a knowing *of something*, that this object knows something for itself (*für es*). Hence both moments—being in itself (*Ansichselbstsein*) and being for another (*Füreinanderessein*)—fall into the object—knowing (*Wissen*)—that "we" are examining, and our task is to leave out *our* notions, *our* thoughts, *our* standards, in short, to leave out *ourselves*, because "we" have to become the death of consciousness by dying to ourselves—to that which is ours—and falling into consciousness. Only in this way will we be able to see the thing as it is in and for itself (*dadurch, dass wir diese [unsere Einfälle und Gedanken] weglassen, erreichen wir es, die Sache, wie sie an und für sich selbst ist, zu betrachten*) (*PhG*, 72). A contribution from us becomes therefore superfluous—*wird eine Zutat von uns überflüssig* (*PhG*, 72)—or, better, a contribution *of us*, of ourselves, is superfluous. And yet this superfluous reader, this "we," who dies to himself and falls into the text in order that the text may read (and write) itself—who becomes a no one in order that the text may become a "we" (his "we")—is absolutely necessary, for he is able to see (*betrachten*) the *turning of consciousness* upon itself (*eine Umkehrung des Bewusstseins selbst*). This seeing—"our" contribution, the contribution of the "we"—is what elevates the series of experiences of consciousness to the level of a scientific (i.e., knowing in truth) progression, and what consciousness cannot do so long as it has not seen with "our" eyes (*Diese Betrachtung der Sache ist unsere Zutat, wodurch sich die Reihe der Erfahrungen des Bewusstseins zum wissenschaftlichen Gange erhebt, und welche nicht für das Bewusstsein ist, das wir betrachten*) (*PhG*, 74). Our contribution, the contribution of the reader (and writer) of the text, is to leave out (*weglassen*) that which is ours, to leave out ourselves: we contribute ourselves by leaving out the contribution of ourselves. We read (and write) the text only by dispossessing ourselves of our already having read (written) it and thereby allow the text—the experiencing consciousness for whom the process of our reading (and writing), the process of our self-dispossession, takes place, so to speak, behind its back (*gleichsam hinter seinem Rücken vorgeht*) (*PhG*, 74)—to read (and write) itself. The narrative that the text reads (and writes) when it is finally (and preliminarily) able to read (and write) itself as the history of its own becoming, the history of how "we," the text, became ourselves by dispossessing ourselves of ourselves, is the narrative of its own, of *our* own, acts of dying to ourselves. So in the end and from the beginning we may read and write: *Und so haben wir uns unseren Tod* (*immer schon und immer noch nicht*) *erzählt* (and so we have [always already and always not yet] narrated our death to ourselves). Rather than being a spectator who watches the drama (comedy or tragedy) of consciousness at a distance, or a spectator who alternates detachment and sympathy by sometimes donning the comic mask of natural consciousness and acting out its role all the more convincingly while disavowing it all the more completely, "we," the text, would be more like the comic actor who lets his mask fall only to reveal underneath another, the same, mask, the mask into which he has always already fallen apart: a death mask.[16]

If the reading (and the writing) of the text of "Hegel" is a rereading (and a rewriting) of the reader (and writer) of the text himself, or, better, "ourselves," then "we," the (reader and writer of the) text, are also (always already and always not yet), for example, the reader (and the writer) of the text of "Heidegger." But who can be the reader (and the writer) of the text of "Heidegger" if "no one" can read (and write) the text of "Hegel" because only no one can dispossess himself of his self and fall into the text as the reader (and writer) already inscribed in the text? The reader (and the writer) of the text of "Hegel"—that is, more precisely, of the text of "no one"—as the self-dispossessed (first) person (plural) "we," finds himself, "we" find "ourselves," in a double bind: on the one hand, if the only way "we," the text, "we" the reader (and writer) of the text, can appear in truth is by disappearing *as* ourselves, *as* readers (and writers) of the text (and reappearing in the text as the text); if the only way we can read (and write) the text is by not reading (and writing) as reading (and writing) but as always having read (and written) the text, then "our" reading (and writing) of the text cannot take place precisely to the extent that it takes place as *our* reading (and writing). But even if our reading (and writing) of the text does take place as not taking place, not as *our* reading (and writing) but as the reading (and writing) of no one, then it still takes place as already having taken place in, as already inscribed in, the text of "Hegel" (i.e., in the text of no one). Our reading (and writing) of the text cannot take place either as our reading (and writing) or as our not reading (and writing). On the other hand, if "our" reading (and writing) of the text takes place not as the reading (and writing) of the text of "Hegel"—that is, not as already inscribed in the text of no one—but rather as the reading (and writing) of an *other* text—"our" own, "Heidegger's," somebody's, anybody's—then to the extent that this "other" text reads (and writes) itself as the other of the text of "Hegel" (i.e., no one), it remains inscribed in that text as *its* other, as the death to itself that the text of no one carries within itself, and therefore it cannot take place. Whether it takes place as the reading (and writing) of the text of "Hegel" or as the reading (and writing) of an "other" text, the reading (and the writing) of the text cannot take place in the first place.

And yet the text of "Heidegger" takes place as both the reading (and writing) of the text of "Hegel" and the reading (and writing) of an other text; or rather it would read (and write) the double bind as "both. . .and" in order to reread (and rewrite) it as "neither. . .nor." The reading of "Heidegger" begins—but, of course, it has already begun—by rewriting the text of "Hegel": "Only in passing [by the way, by the by] and so that he hides it in a dependent clause [literally, "side-clause"], Hegel nevertheless says this (*Nur beiläufig und so, dass er es in einem Nebensatz versteckt, sagt Hegel jedoch dieses*)" (*H*, 119-20). By turning what Hegel says "in passing" (*beiläufig*) about the absolute's being with us (*bei uns*) into the *Leitmotiv* of the reading, by staking out in a main clause (*Hauptsatz*) what Hegel hides in a side-clause (*in einem Nebensatz versteckt*), the text of "Heidegger" also rewrites what Hegel says into what Hegel does not say. Namely, Hegel does not say: "The absolute is in and for itself already with us and wants to be with us (*Das Absolute ist schon an und für sich bei uns und will bei uns sein*)" (*H*, 120); but rather: "if the absolute were not and did not want to be in and for itself already with us (*wenn es nicht an und für sich schon bei uns wäre und sein wollte*)" (*PhG*, 64). Turning a conditional dependent clause in the subjunctive mood into a declarative independent clause in the indicative mood is not an unproblematic act of rereading and rewriting—"But mere reversing [overturning] is always a suspect activity (*Aber das blosse Umkehren ist jedesmal ein verfängliches Tun*)," says Heidegger in "Zur Seinsfrage" (Toward the question of Being)[17]—for in making "visible" that which is "invisible," in revealing that which is concealed—in the text of "Hegel"—the text of "Heidegger" also conceals that which is revealed and makes invisible that which is visible: in turning *Nebensatz* into *Hauptsatz*, Heidegger also turns *Hauptsatz* into *Nebensatz*.[18]

But what (or whom) does the text of "Heidegger" conceal in revealing what can be called an "other" text—the text of what Hegel does not say: the unthought (*das Ungedachte*) of "Hegel"? In reading (and rewriting) the *bei uns* of the first paragraph, what it conceals is precisely the text of what Hegel says, or, better, the narrative movement that takes place between the first sentence and the (non)appearance of the absolute *bei uns*, for to turn *Nebensatz*—"a dependent [literally, "unindependent"] clause, which is dependent on a main clause, and which by itself cannot make sense (*unselbständiger, von einem Hauptsatz abhängiger Satz, der allein nicht sinnvol bestehen kann*)"[19]—into *Hauptsatz* means to suppress that on which the dependent clause depends for its meaning: or rather, as in this case, it means to "read into" the dependent clause the meaning that is "elsewhere"—in the *Hauptsatz*, in the context, in the narrative of the text. By saying "the absolute is in and for itself already with us and wants to be with us," Heidegger collapses the narrative movement *from* the "invisible" absolute—the "we" who can begin to read and write the text of natural *Vorstellung* because he has already read and written its end (i.e., absolute knowing)—and the "visible" natural *Vorstellung*—the text that cannot begin to read and write itself because it cannot (yet) read and write itself—of the first sentence *to* the absolute "visible" only as "if it were not already with us" (i.e., if it had not already appeared as nonappearing in the first sentence) and the "invisible" natural *Vorstellung* that reappears as the visible "we." In other words, Heidegger both reads and does not read the text—that is, reads both "Hegel's" text and an "other" text. On the one hand, to say that the absolute is already with us is to read "Hegel," for if the absolute were not already with us, we could not have written the first sentence of the text; on the other hand, to say that the absolute is already with us is *not* to read the text of "Hegel," for in the text of "Hegel" the absolute can never appear as already with us as *appearing* but only as (always already and always not yet) *having appeared*.

Again: if the movement of Hegel's narrative, the text of Hegel, is read, or rather reads *itself*, as a movement, a process of becoming, that seeks to recuperate the meaninglessness of the *Nebensatz*—the meaninglessness of the absolute's being already and not yet with us—that seeks to read its own unreadability—the unreadability of its always already and always not yet having been read—then Heidegger's strategy in suppressing this movement, this process of becoming, is a suppression of the text. Or, more precisely, it suppresses the text by collapsing, superimposing, the beginning of the text and the end of the text. This strategy renders the text of Hegel *more* readable insofar as it makes visible that which is invisible, allows the nonappearing to appear, makes the implicit explicit, thinks the unthought—in short, reads the unread and unreadable—but it also renders the text of Hegel *less* readable *as the text of "Hegel"* insofar as in order to read the text it needs to suppress precisely that which makes the self-reading and self-writing of the text possible, that which has to remain unreadable and unwritable if the reading and writing of the text is to take place. This strategy of reading and not reading would be an attempt to let the reading and the writing of the text of Hegel take place but take place not as the reading and the writing of the text of Hegel but as the reading and the writing of an "other" text. But what "other" text this could be and how it could be "other"—that is, to what extent it is the "other" of the text of Hegel and therefore remains inscribed in that text, takes place as not taking place—cannot be read without a reading of the text of "Heidegger," without a reading of the reader of the text of "Heidegger": Heidegger's "we."

Just as collapsing the beginning and the end of Hegel's text allowed the text of Heidegger to read and not to read the text of Hegel, so collapsing the two "we's" of the text of Hegel—the nonappearing reader and the appearing nonreader—allows the text of Heidegger to say "we" without saying it, to read (and write) the "we" of Hegel's text without reading (and writing) it(self). That is, on the one hand, all Heidegger's text does is to "cite" the "we" of Hegel's text as it paraphrases the first paragraph of that text. To say, for example, "this being-with-us (*parousia*) is already in itself the way that the light of truth, the absolute itself, irradiates us (*Dieses Bei-uns-sein* (parousia) *ist in sich schon die*

Weise, wie das Licht der Wahrheit, das Absolute selbst uns anstrahlt)" (*H*, 120) is to do little more than to make more "explicit" the relation between the "absolute" and "us" in the first paragraph of Hegel's text. But, on the other hand, the collapsing of the narrative between the invisible "with us" of the first sentence and the visible "if it were not already with us" of the first paragraph—the turning of an invisible *Nebensatz* into a visible *Hauptsatz*—allows the text of Heidegger to put the "we" of the (reader and writer of the) text of "Hegel" into a context where it no longer reads (and writes) the text of Hegel. That is, having collapsed the narrative—having suppressed the text—between the "nonappearance" of the absolute in the first sentence and the "appearance" of the absolute as having already appeared in the first paragraph, Heidegger's text can turn the absolute's being with us into a "substantive"—something "having independent existence; independent"[20]— and thereby can turn that which appears only as not appearing (i.e., only as having already appeared) into that which appears as appearing: the *parousia* of the absolute. Just as Hegel's text, the "we" of the (reader and writer of the) text of Hegel, cannot and does not say that the absolute is with us, so it does not and cannot say that this "being-with-us" (*Bei-uns-sein*) is anything "in itself" (*in sich*), for in the text of Hegel anything "in itself" (*in sich*) is really, in truth, *nothing* "in and for itself" (*an und für sich*). Either the "in itself" (*in sich*) is the (as yet) unthought, the (as yet) unselfconscious, and therefore *is* only to the extent that it is *not* (yet) in truth—that is, only to the extent that it appears (in natural *Vorstellung*) and, in Hegel's terms (text), appears as an *an sich* that has not (yet) become *an und für sich*—or it is nothing at all, the ineffable, the one-sidedly abstract, sheer opinion, and so on. In the text of Hegel, something is either as not yet true, as not yet being in truth, or as already true, as already being in truth: it can be either *an sich* or (*für sich* or) *an und für sich*, but it can never *be in sich*.[21] And yet Heidegger's text—as it turns *Nebensatz* into *Hauptsatz*, as it leaves out Hegel's narrative by collapsing its beginnings and its ends, as it cites Hegel's "we" while collapsing the invisible and the visible "we's" of the text of Hegel—introduces not only a substantive appearance of the absolute with us (*Bei-uns-sein*) and an *in sich* that claims to be and yet cannot be "in" the text of Hegel (except as *an sich*) but also along with them a whole chain of appearances that cannot appear in the text of Hegel (except as apparent), a whole other context in the place of the suppressed context of Hegel's text. In the context of Hegel's text, formulations like "the absolute itself (*das Absolute selbst*)," "the absolute in its absoluteness, that is, in its being-with-us (*das Absolute in seiner Absolutheit, d.h. in seinem Bei-uns-sein*)," the actual itself in its truth (*das Wirkliche selbst in seiner Wahrheit*)," "the absolute in its *parousia* (*das Absolute in seiner Parusie*)"— formulations like these are *meaningless* in the text of Hegel except as expressions of an (as yet) unthought—unread, unreadable, nonreading— point of departure that nevertheless contains within itself its thought—read, readable, reading—end point and therefore needs to turn against itself in order to (re)read (and [re]write) its own history, the narrative of which it is the result. Equally meaningless in the text of Hegel is any *als* other than the *als* of natural *Vorstellung* (as representation): to say "philosophy as knowing of the absolute (*die Philosophie als Erkennen des Absoluten*). . .what it [philosophy] is as such knowing (*was sie als solches Erkennen ist*)" (*H*, 120) is not to say anything (as yet) about philosophy, knowing, or the absolute, for as long as these are represented in the element of (presupposition and) representation *as*, they do not present themselves in truth. So when the text of Heidegger rewrites the (non)appearance of the absolute in the text of Hegel to read "This presence-with-us, *parousia*, belongs to the absolute in and for itself (*Dieses Bei-uns-an-wesen, die Parusie, gehört zum Absoluten an und für sich*)," it is no longer reading the text of Hegel—or, more precisely, the text*s* of Hegel, the double inscription of the two texts: the one unread and unwritten, the other (re)read and (re)written—but rather inscribing it in an other text—a text in which formulations like *in sich, Bei-uns-sein, das Absolute in seiner Absolutheit*, and words like *parousia, als, bei, gehört* have meaning[22]—by reinscribing its double inscription as inscribed *once, in sich,* neither in the text of natural *Vorstellung* nor in the text of the "we."

When the text of Heidegger, then, reads and writes that "at the beginning and in the course of the first paragraph it looks as though Hegel were trying to meet the critical demands of natural representation for an examination of knowing (*Im Beginn und Verlauf des ersten Abschnittes sieht es so aus, als versuche Hegel den kritischen Ansprüchen des natürlichen Vorstellens auf eine Prüfung des Erkennens zu entsprechen*)" (*H*, 120), it needs to be asked: to *whom* does it look that way? And when it continues to read and write that "in truth what is important for him [Hegel] is to indicate [to note] the absolute in its *parousia* with us (*In Wahrheit liegt ihm daran, auf das Absolute in seiner Parusie bei uns hinzuweisen*)," it needs to be asked: in truth for *whom*? If this appearing (*sieht es so aus*)—for whom?—and this truth—whose truth?—are to have any meaning, if they are to be readable, they must presuppose (and represent) an other text, an other context, in which appearance and truth appear in truth not as presupposed and represented, not as already having appeared in truth, but as *other*—other than presupposing and representing as presupposed and represented. In other words—and the question is: in *whose* words?—in order to read and write itself (but not as the "self" of the text of Hegel: self-consciousness), in order to be read and written (but not by the "we" of the text of Hegel), the text of Heidegger, the text of Heidegger's "we," has to presuppose and represent an other text, an other "we"—an other presupposition and representation—in which it has already read and written itself neither *as* reading and writing nor *as* already read and written. It does so—but, of course, not as doing so—and has already to have done so—but, of course, not as already having done so—by introducing an other "we"—but whose "we" can it be if it cannot *be* except as the "we" of Hegel (i.e., of no one)?—in the place where it collapses the two "we's" of Hegel. That is, although it appears as though "all" Heidegger's text does is to superimpose the "we" of Hegel's end (absolute knowing) over the "we" of Hegel's beginning and thereby to read one by reading the other, to read *both* of them by suppressing, by not reading, the narrative between them that produces both of them, actually, in truth (*in Wahrheit*?)—but *whose* truth?—the text of Heidegger, by reading and writing both, reads and writes neither the one "we" of Hegel's text nor the other "we" of Hegel's text but another, its own, "we": the "we" of the text of Heidegger. In other words, saying the two "we's" of Hegel at once makes it possible for Heidegger to introduce his own invisible "we," to say "we" without saying it "himself": Heidegger makes a contribution of his self by leaving out his self or, better, by leaving out that which makes the "self" of Hegel's text possible, by leaving out Hegel's text. Again: when Heidegger reads and writes "Through this we are only really [properly] bidden into the relationship to the absolute, in which we already are (*Dadurch werden wir nur eigens in das Verhältnis zum Absoluten gewiesen, in dem wir bereits sind*)" (*H*, 120), he is no longer, not only, rereading and rewriting the text of Hegel—no longer and not only citing the two "we's" of Hegel as one "we"—but also introducing the (other) "we" that makes it possible to leave out that which makes the "we" of Hegel possible. Thus "we" can be bidden into the relationship to the absolute—"we" can rewrite and have rewritten Hegel's *Nebensatz* into "our" *Hauptsatz*—in that, insofar as, "we" already are; in that, insofar as, "we" are already "we"; in that, insofar as, *in dem wir bereits sind* can be rewritten to read *indem wir bereits sind*. So Heidegger's introduction of a new context for the text of Hegel's Introduction is no arbitrary replacement of Hegel's text by his own text but rather an attempt to allow the reading and the writing of the text of Hegel to take place—but to take place not as already read and written in the text of Hegel but as already read and written in an other text: the text of Heidegger. Heidegger, like Hegel, first prepares the examination—*Hegel bereitet die Prüfund erst vor* (*H*, 120)—the examination of Hegel's text as the text of an other who is nevertheless *not* the other *of* the text of Hegel. Hegel writes: if the absolute were not and did not want to be in and for itself already with us, we, the text, could not have written the first sentence of the text; Heidegger rewrites: if we, the text, had not already written our text (*Being and Time*, for example), if we had not already inscribed Hegel's text (Hegel's "we") in our text (in the text of our "we"), we could not have (re)written: the absolute is and wants to be in and for itself already with us.

But if the first step of Heidegger's preparation for the reading of Hegel's text—not unlike Hegel's preparation for the examination of knowing: "The first step of the preparation consists of our giving up the usual notions about knowing (*Der erste Schritt der Vorbereitung besteht darin, dass wir die gewöhnliche Vorstellung vom Erkennen aufgeben)"* (*H*, 120)—consists of our giving up "our" notions, our *Vorstellung*, of reading as the reading of the text of Hegel, as the reading of the "we" of Hegel, in order that "we" may read the other "we" of the text of Heidegger, then this first step should be distinguished from the first step of the text of Hegel, for that text also begins with a self-appropriation by means of (by means of a nonmeans: neither tool nor medium, neither active nor passive, and both) a self-dispossession. That is, as long as Heidegger's "we" appears (by not appearing) in the guise of the doubly inscribed "we" of Hegel, it is in danger of writing itself not as the other text but as the other *of* the (doubly inscribed) text of Hegel: its replacement of Hegel's narrative by Heidegger's would be a mere displacement, its first step a detour. In order to appear as the other "we"—and to disappear as the (double) "we" of the text of Hegel—Heidegger's "we" has to appear as itself—and to disappear as the self of self-consciousness—in terms ("appear," "as," "itself") different from the terms of Hegel's "we"—that is, not in terms of identity and difference, self and other, and the like—so that Heidegger's text may replace its displacement of Hegel's text—and take place as the text of Heidegger—and end the detour of the first step (*der erste Schritt*) by turning it into the step back (*der Schritt zurück)—out* of "metaphysics" (i.e., the text of Hegel as the self-recuperation by self-alienation of spirit [*Geist*] in, specifically, the history of philosophy) and *into* the "essence of metaphysics" (i.e., the text of Heidegger as the revealing and concealing of Being in, specifically, the history of philosophy as the destiny [*Geschick*] of the forgetting of Being [*Seinsvergessenheit*], or, of the ontological difference).[23] The displacement is replaced, the detour of the first step ends when—when else?—Heidegger's "we" can no longer go around its own beginnings: "In this place an explanation [clarification] of the linguistic usage [use of language], which has meanwhile [in-between-time] become necessary is no longer to be gone around (*An dieser Stelle ist eine inzwischen nötig gewordene Klärung des Sprachgebrauches nicht mehr zu umgehen)"* (*H*, 141). "In this place"—that is, if this place, the reading and the writing of the text of Heidegger, is to be a place, is to take place—"an explanation of the linguistic usage"—that is, a reading (and a writing) of *our* reading (and writing) of certain words like "being," "we," etc., in contradistinction to the reading (and the writing) of the "same" words by Hegel's "we"—"which has in-between-time become necessary"—that is, which has become necessary during the course of *our* narrative as the narrative that arises in the place where we have suppressed the narrative *between* the two "we's" of Hegel's text and which has become necessary because we do not want our narrative, our "we," to take place as the text of Hegel (i.e., not to take place) but as the other text that is nevertheless not the other of the text of Hegel—"is no longer to be gone around"—that is, this reading (and writing) of our "we" as the detour of the first step has to end if it is not to be confused with, if it is not to be inscribed in, the reading (and the writing) of the double "we" of Hegel's text. The suggestion is that up to now, up to this place, the "in-between" of Heidegger's narrative has been a detour around this clarification, around this reading of his own reading in its difference from the reading of Hegel. "In contrast to Hegel's use of language we use"—and this using of the "we" is the "first" time that Heidegger uses his own "we," that is, in contrast to, in its difference from, the "we" of Hegel—"in contrast to Hegel's use of language we use the name 'Being' both for that which Hegel along with Kant calls objectness and objectivity as well as for that which he represents as the truly actual and calls the actuality of the spirit (*Im Unterschied zum Sprachgebrauch Hegels gebrauchen wir den Namen 'Sein' sowohl für das, was Hegel mit Kant die Gegenständlichkeit und die Objektivität nennt, als auch für das, was er als das wahrhaft Wirkliche vorstellt und die Wirklichkeit des Geistes nennt*)" (*H*, 142).

Since this clarification of the difference between Hegel's use of the word "Being" and Heidegger's use of the same word marks the place where his text, the "we" of the reader (and the writer) of the text of Heidegger, explicitly turns upon itself, nothing less is at stake in this turning than the difference between Hegel and Heidegger: the turn to a reading of their different uses of the same word is a turn to the reading of their different uses of sameness. In question *here*, in this place—at the turning point where Heidegger's "we" turns upon itself *as* the reader of Hegel's "we" (i.e., in its difference from the "we" of Hegel)—is both the turning and the sameness: the same word returns in the texts of Hegel and Heidegger, but this return of the same is read (and written) differently. On the one hand, "all" Heidegger does is to take a step back in his reading, in the reading of the reader (and the writer) of the "we" of Heidegger, by explicitly turning upon the detour of his first step. Namely, in "our" reading of Hegel's first paragraph, "we," the reader (and the writer) of the text of Heidegger, were able to collapse the two "we's" of Hegel's text—the (thought) "we" that does not appear in the first sentence and the (unthought) "we" that appears later in the first paragraph—by suppressing the (two-way) narrative between them because, in contrast to Hegel, "we" use the same word (*Sein*) *both for that which* (*sowohl für das, was*) he thinks as not yet true and calls "objectness and objectivity" *as well as for that which* (*als auch für das, was*) he represents as the truly actual and calls the actuality of the spirit. In other words, "we" were able to say "we" without saying it "ourselves" because *then* we said the two "we's" of (the beginning and the end of) Hegel's text *once*, simultaneously, in the same word, just as *now* "we" say the (unthought) beginning and the (thought) end of the text of Hegel in one and the same word: *Sein* ("Being").

In contrast to this use of one and the same word in two different senses, for Hegel—and it is worthwhile to paraphrase *this* Hegel, the Hegel inscribed in the text of Heidegger—"since the time of his decided terminology (*seit der Zeit seiner entschiedenen Terminologie*)" (*H*, 141), the word *Sein* is the name for that which is in truth not yet the true and the real (*was eigentlich in Wahrheit noch nicht das Wahre und Reale ist*): "for Hegel 'Being' is valid always with the restriction of 'only Being' (*'Sein' gilt Hegel stets in der Einschränkung des 'nur Seins'*)" (*H*, 142). It is in accordance with this restrictive use of "Being" as "only Being," as a "still untrue reality (*noch unwahre Realität*)," that Hegel interprets the philosophy of antiquity: "because it had not yet set foot on the land of philosophy, that is, self-consciousness, in which the represented object as such first is, it thinks the real only as the existent (*Weil sie [die antike Philosophie] noch nicht das Land der Philosophie, das Selbstbewusstsein, worin das vorgestellte Gegenständliche erst als ein solches ist, betreten hat, denkt sie das Reale nur als das Seiende*)" (*H*, 142). "The truly existent is only the *ens actu*, the actual, whose *actualitas*, actuality, lies in the knowing of self-knowing self-certainty (*das wahrhaft Seiende ist das ens actu, das Wirkliche, dessen actualitas, Wirklichkeit, im Wissen der sich selbst wissenden Gewissheit besteht*)" (*H*, 142): only such knowing can in truth claim to *be* all of reality, *the* reality (*Nur diese kann in Wahrheit, d.h. jetzt stets aus der Gewissheit des absoluten Wissens, beanspruchen, alle Realität zu 'sein'*) (*H*, 142). But, as Heidegger notes, "here where it should have disappeared, Being returns (*So kehrt freilich hier, wo es verschwunden sein sollte, das Sein wieder*), but the absolute knowing of science takes no notice of this return (*Aber das absolute Wissen der Wissenschaft nimmt davon keine Kenntnis*)." Indeed, "according to the way in which Hegel uses the word Being he ought, strictly speaking, no longer call that which for him is the true actuality of the actual, the spirit, by a name that still contains the word being (*Nach der At, in der Hegel das Wort Sein gebraucht, durfte er streng genommen das, wis ihm die wahre Wirklichkeit das Wirklichen, der Geist, ist, nicht mehr mit einem Namen benennen, der noch das Wort 'sein' enthält*)." Nevertheless, "this occurs all over insofar as the essence of spirit remains self-consciousness (*Das geschieht jedoch überall, insofern das Wesen des Geistes das Selbstbewusst-sein bleibt*)." This reading of the return of the same word in the text of Hegel (in its difference from the return of the same word in the text of Heidegger) is—and this is (finally) the "other hand" of "all" that Heidegger does in explicitly turning upon the detour of his first step—nothing short of "perverse" ("from Latin *pervertere*, to turn the wrong way, turn around: *per-* completely + *vertere*, to turn"),[24] for, as Heidegger recognizes here (at the turning point) and elsewhere,[25] Hegel also—but it is precisely this "also," the meaning of this "also," that Heidegger would rewrite and reread—Hegel also uses the very same word *Sein* ("Being") in two senses.

The next to last page of the big *Logic* explicitly reads the word "Being" as both the beginning and the end of thought: "Thus logic, too, in the absolute

Idea, has gone back to that simple unity which is its beginning; the pure immediacy of being, in which at first every determination appears to be extinguished or left out by abstraction, is the Idea that has reached through mediation, that is, through the sublation of mediation, a likeness that corresponds to itself. The method is the pure concept that relates itself only to itself; it is therefore the *simple self-relation* that is *being*. But now it is also *fulfilled* being, the concept that comprehends itself, being as the concrete and also absolutely *intensive* totality (*So ist denn auch die Logik in der absoluten Idee zu dieser einfachen Einheit zurückgegangen, welche ihr Anfang ist; die reine Unmittelbarkeit des Seins, in dem zuerst alle Bestimmung als ausgelöscht oder durch die Abstraktion weggelassen erscheint, ist die durch die Vermittlung, nämlich die Aufhebung der Vermittlung zu ihrer entsprechenden Gleichheit mit sich gekommene Idee. Die Methode ist der reine Begriff, der sich nur zu sich selbst verhält; sie ist daher die einfache Beziehung auf sich, welche Sein ist. Aber es ist nun auch erfülltes Sein, der sich begreifende Begriff, das Sein als die konkrete, ebenso schlechthin intensive Totalität*)" (VI:572). As this exemplary passage states, taking notice (*Kenntnis nehmen*) of the return of Being, knowing (*erkennen*) Being, recognizing (*wiedererkennen*) Being—in short, the movement of self-comprehension of the concept *from* the pure immediacy of Being (*die reine Unmittelbarkeit des Seins*) or, as the beginning of the *Logic* puts it, "*Being, pure Being*. . .It is pure indeterminacy and emptiness (*Sein, reines Sein*. . . *Es ist die reine Unbestimmtheit und Leere*)" (V:82), *to* what "is now also *fulfilled* Being (*es ist nun auch* erfülltes *Sein*)"—would be the dialectical process itself, and hence not only is it no wonder that *Sein* (Being) returns in the name of that which is the true actuality of the actual (i.e., self-consciousness [*Selbstbewusst-sein*]), but it is absolutely necessary that it do so.

How can "Heidegger"—but it is only *here*, at this turning point, that "we" (who, "we"?) are going to be able to read who "Heidegger" is, who the "we" of the reader (and the writer) of the text of "Heidegger" is—how can Heidegger write—and this writing would be precisely that which distinguishes the writing (and the reading) of Heidegger from the writing (and the reading) of Hegel—how, then, can Heidegger write that *Sein* "ought" (*sollte*) to have disappeared where, for Hegel, it *must* appear, that, "strictly speaking," Hegel ought (*durfte*) not to use a word containing the word "being" where, strictly speaking (Hegel's speaking), Hegel *must* use a word containing "being," and that, finally, the absolute knowing of science takes no notice of the return of *Sein* when the absolute knowing of science is *nothing but* the process of taking notice, knowing, re-cognizing, the return of (the same and different) *Sein*? Since Heidegger's reading quite explicitly takes notice of the return of *Sein* in the text of Hegel—never mind its acute sensitivity to all the double uses of words in the Introduction (e.g., earlier in the reading of the very same sixth paragraph Heidegger takes notice of the difference between Hegel's writing "nur Begriff" [mere concept] and "realisierter Begriff" [realized concept])—it cannot be charged with *mere* perversity[26]—that is, turning the "wrong way," a charge that leaves the texts of both Hegel and Heidegger, of Hegel *by* Heidegger, unread—but rather has to be read precisely *at* this turning point that does and does not take notice of the return of *Sein* in the text of Hegel. That is to say, it should be recognized that the reason Heidegger can charge Hegel with using the word *Sein* in one sense only is that he refuses to recognize the taking notice, knowing, recognizing, of the return of *Sein* in the text of Hegel *as* a taking notice. In other words, the taking notice of the return of *Sein* performed by the absolute knowing of science is not a *true* (for Heidegger)—and "we" are about to read what *is* true for Heidegger—taking notice, for the *Sein* that returns at the end (as the knowing of self-knowing self-certainty, as *Selbstbewusst-sein*, as *erfülltes Sein*) of the dialectical process is the "same" *Sein* with which it started out: that is, a *Sein* thought as "the being-ness of being, which since the beginning of Greek thought up to Nietzsche's teaching of the eternal return of the same took place as the truth of being (*Die Seiendheit des Seienden, die seit dem Beginn des griechischen Denkens bis zu Nietzsches Lehre von der ewigen Wiederkunft des Gleichen sich als die Wahrheit des Seienden ereignete*)" (*H*, 142). In short, Hegel's taking notice of the return of *Sein* is not a true taking notice, for when *Sein* returns in the text of Hegel it is still the same empty *Sein* with which the text started out: a *Sein* thought on the basis of *Seiendes*, a *Sein* whose difference from *Seiendes* remains unthought. This is the sense in which Hegel uses the word *Sein* in one and the same sense only, and this is the sense in which absolute knowing takes no notice of the return of the one and the same word *Sein*: "The *einai*, Being of the Greeks, we interpret not, as in Hegel's view, on the basis of the objectness of immediate representation of a subjectivity that has still not come to itself, that is, not on the basis of this [i.e., objectness] but rather on the basis of Greek *aletheia* as the presence from and into disconcealment (*Das einai, Sein der Griechen, deuten wir nicht wie Hegel aus seiner Sicht als die Gegenständlichkeit des unmittelbaren Vorstellens einer noch nicht zu sich gekommenen Subjektivität, d.h. nicht aus dieser, sondern aus der griechischen aletheia als das Anwesen aus der und in die Unverborgenheit*)" (*H*, 142). What remains unthought, then, and what has to remain unthinkable in absolute knowing's taking notice of the return of the same word *Sein* is precisely the return of the sameness, the sameness of that which returns because it *is*—*das Sein*—and this sameness of the same always has to remain unthought and unthinkable because its return is always thought in the same way on the basis of *Seiendes* and not on the basis of the disconcealment and concealment of *aletheia*. This is why when the same word *Sein* returns in the text of Hegel where it ought to have disappeared, where, strictly speaking, Hegel ought not to name with a word still containing "sein," it "is not the consequence of an imprecise and inconsequential terminology but rather it is grounded in the hidden way in which Being (*Sein*) itself reveals and conceals itself (*ist freilich nicht die Folge einer ungenauen und inkonsequenten Terminologie, sondern er gründet in der verborgenen Weise, in der das Sein selbst sich enthüllt und verbirgt*)" (*H*, 142-43).

What Heidegger's perverse reading of the same (and different) word *Sein*—his reading *in* of (a different) *Sein* and his reading *out* of (the same) *Sein*—does is once again to flatten out the difference between the "empty" *Sein* of Hegel's beginning and the "full" *Sein* Hegel's end by superimposing the one *Sein* onto the other *Sein* and calling both of them the same (empty) *Sein* insofar as both are thought on the basis of *Seiendes*. The "flattening out" of this superimposition is accomplished by Heidegger's inscription of the history of Western metaphysics thought on the basis of *aletheia* as the destiny (*Geschick*) of the forgetting of *Sein* (*Seinsvergessenheit*) in its difference from *Seiendes* into the text of Hegel's history of philosophy as the self-recuperation by self-alienation of spirit, as the movement of the self-comprehending concept from empty *Sein* to full *Sein*. This inscription is necessarily a double inscription insofar as Hegel's philosophy is the same as his history of philosophy (except—and books have been filled to account for this exception—except that the former moves "purely in the element of thought (*rein im Elemente des Denkens*)" (VIII:59). In other words, Heidegger in one and the same gesture, in one and the same turn, inscribes the one unthought and unthinkable *Sein* in both the text of Hegel's history of philosophy and the text of Hegel's philosophy: just as *Sein* is forgotten in Hegel's text, so is *Sein* forgotten in Hegel's text of the history of philosophy, for both texts, both histories, think *Sein* on the basis of *Seiendes*. What remains most perverse about the turn of this double inscription—this double rereading and double rewriting of the (same and different, same for Hegel but different for Heidegger) word *Sein* in the text of Hegel (and in the text of Heidegger)—is Heidegger's claim, the claim of the "we" of the reader (and the writer) of the text of Heidegger, that this turning, this double inscription, this rereading and rewriting of the word *Sein* in and out of the text of Hegel, is *not* Heidegger's turning but rather the (re)turning performed by "Being itself" (*das Sein selbst*) (*H*, 143).[27] In other words, when Hegel's "we" says *Sein*, it is indeed Hegel's "we" that says it (and yet does not take notice of *what* it is saying); when Heidegger's "we" says *Sein*, it is "Being itself" (*das Sein selbst*) that says it. Heidegger is able to say this—Heidegger is able to say this (*Sein*) while not saying it himself—because in superimposing the *Sein* of the destiny of the forgetting of Being upon the *Sein* of the history of philosophy, in flattening out the difference between the *Sein* of Hegel's end and the *Sein* of Hegel's beginning, he is performing the same movement as he did in the reading of Hegel's first paragraph: namely, just as superimposing the "we" of Hegel's end upon the "we" of Hegel's beginning by suppressing the narrative, the history, that produces them allowed Heidegger to say "we" once without saying it "himself," so superimposing the destiny of the forgetting of Being upon Hegel's history of philosophy (and thereby upon Hegel's text as a dialectical movement of Being's taking notice of itself)—in short, collapsing the difference between the beginning and the end of Hegel's philosophy of the history of philosophy by calling both (the beginning and the end) the return of the same—allows Heidegger, here at the turning point, to say *Sein* (twice as well as once) and yet *not* to say it himself: as "Being itself" (*das Sein selbst*).

But the "self" that appears at the turning point to take notice of the return of "Being itself" (*das Sein selbst*) by saying Being without being the sayer of Being itself, the "we" that appears to turn upon its self in order to say "we" without saying it(self), the reader (and the writer) of the text of Heidegger who appears to reread (and rewrite) the return of the same in the text of Hegel without rereading (and rewriting) it himself—the "self," the "we," the "reader (and the writer)," of the text that appears without appearing itself—all remain unread and unreadable as along as Heidegger's reading of the text of Hegel—the narrative of the movement from the nonappearing "we" to the appearing "we," from the reading of Hegel's first paragraph that is the detour of the first step to the reading of Hegel's sixth paragraph that is the (re)turning upon the detour of the first step—all remain unread and unreadable as long as Heidegger's reading of the text of Hegel is thought, is read (and written), only on the basis and in the terms of the destiny of Being as the self-revelation and self-concealment of Being itself. For what remains unthought, unread, and unreadable on the basis of *aletheia* and in the terms of the *Geschick* of *Seinsvergessenheit* is precisely the *self* of the "we" of the reader (and writer) of the text of Heidegger who is able to say Being itself without saying Being itself, who is able to be "we" without being "we" himself, who is able to be the reader (and the writer) of Being itself in the text of Hegel without being the reader (and the writer) of the text of Hegel himself: in short, who is able to be a self without being a self, who is able to speak for Being *it*self without being *him*self. In other words, when Heidegger inscribes the history of Western metaphysics—thought as the destiny of the forgetting of Being in its difference from beings—in Hegel's text of the history of philosophy—thought as the history of Being's coming to itself by way of the turning of self-consciousness—he is on the one hand thinking that which remains unthought in the text of Hegel, reading (and writing) that which remains unread (and unwritten) in the text of Hegel. But, on the other hand, he is able to do so only by returning the turn of self-consciousness: that is, in order to inscribe the history of philosophy as the destiny of Being in Hegel's text, what Heidegger has to do is to find himself, recognize himself, inscribed in the text of Hegel not as a self that speaks for Being itself but rather as a self that speaks for Being itself without being itself. In short, in order to say Being itself without saying it himself *as* a self Heidegger has to recognize that *his* (self-less) Being—the Being of his rereading (and rewriting) of the history of philosophy as the destiny of the forgetting of Being in its difference from beings—always already and always not yet says itself (but not as a self) in the text of Hegel.

The point at which the reader (and the writer) of the text of Heidegger turns upon himself and takes notice of his self as inscribed in the text of Hegel is the turning point of the text where Heidegger in order to inscribe Hegel's text into his own text—*Being and Time*, for example—can do so only by inscribing his own text in the text of Hegel. He does so and has already to have done so by recognizing himself, *his* Being itself, in the text of Hegel and thereby dispossesses himself of his self (of "his" Being itself) and falls into the text as the reader (and the writer) *of* the text of Hegel. Again: when Heidegger's "we," the reader (and the writer) of the text of Heidegger, appears as itself—as his own "we" in its difference from the "we" of (the reader and the writer of the text of) Hegel: "In contrast to Hegel's use of language *we* use. . ."—it can do so only by making the turn of self-consciousness and recognizing itself as its own other in the text of Hegel. In other words, Heidegger's "we" in turning upon the detour of its first step (when it was present without appearing) by explicitly turning upon itself (and appearing without being present itself) repeats the same movement, the same narrative, the same history, that takes place between the nonappearance of the "we" in Hegel's first sentence and the appearance of the "we" in Hegel's first paragraph. "One chooses dialectics only *(Man wählt die Dialektik nur)*," says Nietzsche, and Nietzsche (and, fortunately or unfortunately, Heidegger's *Nietzsche*) is never very far away when we speak of the (eternal or not) return of the same, "when one has no other means *(wenn man kein andres Mittel hat)*."[28] So that Heidegger's double reading(s)[29]—that is, of both Hegel's text as well as his own text and neither—and double inscription(s)—that is, of both Hegel's text in his own text and his own text in Hegel's and neither—is (are) necessarily double in a double sense: on the one hand his rereading and rewriting of the text of Hegel (which text is nothing but the history of its own self-[re]reading and self-[re]writing) thinks the unthought and unthinkable, reads (and writes) the unread (and unwritten) and unreadable (and unwritable) of that text, but on the other hand and in the same turn of the "re-" of this rereading and rewriting—and *whose* sameness, *whose* turn, and *whose* rereading and rewriting would, could, this *be*?—Heidegger can do so only by being himself, having his self—the unthought and unthinkable, the unread (and unwritten) and unreadable (and unwritable) of the text of Heidegger—thought, read, and written by the text of Hegel. If the unthought of Hegel—the unread and unreadable (and the unwritten and unwritable) of the reader (and the writer) of the text of Hegel—is the "Being" *(das Sein)* of "Being itself" *(das Sein selbst)*, then the unthought of

Heidegger—the unread and unreadable (and the unwritten and unwritable) of the reader (and the writer) of the text of Heidegger—is the "self" (*das Selbst*) of "Being itself" (*das Sein selbst*).[30] The point is—and a vertiginous turning point it is—that "Heidegger" cannot think one without "Hegel's" thinking the other, that he cannot think that which is different from Hegel without Hegel's thinking that which is the same. In (not) thinking the same, Heidegger's reading of Hegel—and this also always already (and always not yet) reads: Hegel's reading of Heidegger—would meet his own (*whose* own?) understanding of how correct interpretation understands a text, but this understanding would be a meeting, so to speak, with a vengeance: "A correct interpretation never understands the text better than its author understood it but, to be sure, otherwise. Only this other must be such that it meets with the same that the interpreted text thinks (*Eine rechte Erläuterung versteht jedoch den Text nie besser als dessen Verfasser ihn verstand, wohl aber anders. Allein dieses Andere muss so sein, dass es das Selbe trifft, dem der erläuterte Text nachdenkt*)" (*H*, 197).[31]

But if Heidegger's thinking of Hegel's unthought turns out to be the same as Hegel's thinking of Heidegger's unthought, who is it who takes notice of the double reading (and writing) of this double unthought? And whose taking notice—whose turning, whose sameness, whose Being—allows this reader (and writer) to read (and write) the text of this double unthought? And, above all, who calls it reading (and writing)? The questions are more and less than rhetorical, for once "we" recognize—and it is this recognition (*whose* recognition?) that is "our" condition of (im)possibility—that Heidegger's double reading and double inscription of the unthought of the text of Hegel turns out to be the same as Hegel's double reading and double inscription of the unthought of the text of Heidegger, we also must recognize that in this mutual (chiasmic) double reading Heidegger and Hegel play the roles of *both* (Hegel's) natural consciousness and (Heidegger's) ontological (non)consciousness *and* (Hegel's) "we" and (Heidegger's) ontic consciousness. That is to say, when Heidegger reads the unthought of Hegel as the latter's necessary inability to think the "Being" of "Being itself" except on the basis of "being" (*Seiendes*), he is playing the role of the knowing, ontological (non) consciousness (and the natural consciousness) and relegating Hegel to the role of the ontic consciousness (and the knowing "we"), which uses the word "Being" in only one sense (because, in Heidegger's terms, it does not take notice of the return of *Being*, it is trapped on the level of the *ontic*); and when Hegel reads the unthought of Heidegger as the latter's necessary inability to think the "self" of "Being itself" except on the basis of *aletheia*, he is playing the role of the knowing "we" (and the ontic consciousness) and relegating Heidegger to the role of the natural (and ontological non)consciousness that uses the word Being in only one sense (because, in Hegel's terms, it does not take notice of the turn of self-consciousness that allows empty Being to become full Being). But if

Heidegger and Hegel can and have to play (chiasmically) *both* roles— in short-hand, the ontological (non)consciousness and the natural consciousness, the ontic consciousness and the "we"—then that would leave no role for "us" to play: "we" are superfluous; "we" leave out "our" contribution.

And yet this leaving out of "ourselves" by no means solves "our" problem or answers "our" questions—*whose* questions?—for an other "we" (always already and always not yet) makes an other return to ask yet an other question: If in this re-turning (*Wieder-Umkehrung*?) of the same in the double reading and double inscription of Hegel and Heidegger, of Hegel *by* Heidegger, we can leave out the contribution of ourselves, which or rather *whose* leaving out are we—*who*, we?—talking about? Do we—the (other) reader (and writer) of the text(s) of Hegel by Heidegger—leave out ourselves by falling into the text(s) in a turning of self-consciousness or do we leave out ourselves by saying "Being itself" without saying "Being itself" ourselves? And how can we leave out ourselves by one without leaving out ourselves by the other if both are—in Hegel's terms or in Heidegger's terms—the same? Again: if the texts of Hegel and Heidegger read (and write) themselves—either as Being thought on the basis of the turning of self-consciousness or as Being thought on the basis of the unthought return of *aletheia* and as both and as neither—then who are we that we may leave out ourselves as the (other) reader (and writer) of the text(s) of Hegel by Heidegger? And who are we that we may call it reading (and writing)? We can answer the question(s) of the other "we" only by rereading (and rewriting) the question of the text's reading (and writing) itself as the text of the other we: that is, we turn upon ourselves by taking notice that in our reading (and writing) of the text(s) of Hegel by Heidegger the contribution that we make as our leaving out the contribution of ourselves is precisely *our* reading (and writing). In other words, reading (and writing) the text(s) of Hegel by Heidegger is what we add, *is* the "we" that we add, in our allowing the texts of Hegel and Heidegger to read (and write) themselves (i.e., their own "we's"). But just as Heidegger's using of the word "Being" both for the appearing of apparent knowing and for the absoluteness of the absolute may at first look like arbitrariness, so our using of the words "reading (and writing)" for both Heidegger's (re)reading (and [re]writing) of Hegel's self-reading (and self-writing) and vice versa may appear to be an arbitrary imposition: as though we had imposed "literature," as though we had imposed, say, Blanchot's "terms" upon the "relation," upon whatever "happens"—what can *we* call it?—between Hegel and Heidegger. And our turning upon ourselves to (re)read (and [re]write) the contribution of our "reading (and writing)"—insofar as it *must* be both the (re)turning of self-consciousness and the (re)turning of *aletheia* and yet at the same time *can* be neither—would appear to be the death of reading and the death of writing (*mort de lecture, mort d'écriture*) that leaves the text(s) of Hegel by Heidegger unread (and unwritten) because self-read (and self-written).

Here, in this place, at the turning point, a clarification of the use of language that has been (absolutely?) necessary from the beginning (and in the end) as the question of the "we" of the text—our reading and our writing, our beginnings and our ends—is no longer to be gone around. Only in passing and so that he hides it in a context whose "self-evidence" renders the words invisible Heidegger nevertheless says: (1) that "from a literary point of view," "seen literarily" (*literarisch gesehen*), the fifteen paragraphs preceding the next-to-last one-sentence paragraph of Hegel's introduction contain the interpretation of the title "Science of the *Experience* of Consciousness" (*Die voraufgegangenen Abschnitte enthalten, literarisch gesehen, die Auslegung dieses Titels*) (*H*, 178); (2) that "Literarily, we can take the sixteen paragraphs as the interpretation of the title that then fell away (*Literarisch können wir die sechzehn Abschnitte als die Erläuterung des Titels nehmen, der dann wegfiel*)" (*H*, 190); and (3) that this "title is not understood so long as one reads it according to the habits of natural consciousness (*bleibt der Titel unverstanden, solange man ihn nach der Gewohnheit des natürlichen Bewusstseins liest*)" (*H*, 182), that is, so long as one reads it only forward and does not recognize that the genitives are subjective as well as objective genitives. There are some obvious anomalies in this view of the relation between Hegel's title and Hegel's text. For one thing, the status of a title that exists both inside and outside the text and yet at the same time *neither* inside *nor* outside the text is, to say the least, problematic: if the movement of Hegel's text is understood as an interpretation of the title ("*Science* of the *Experience* of Consciousness") that the text finally reaches, finally earns, in the next-to-last one-sentence paragraph of the text—that is, "Through this necessity [the dialectical necessity of natural consciousness' moving from one object of knowing to a new object of knowing while not knowing itself what is happening] this way to science is already itself *science*, and according to its content science of the *experience of consciousness* (*Durch diese Notwendigkeit ist dieser Weg zur Wissenschaft selbst schon* Wissenschaft, *und nach ihrem Inhalte hiemit Wissenschaft der* Erfahrung des Bewusstseins)" (*PhG*, 74)—then this title truly exists only *after* the text of the Introduction has been read (and written). In this case the text of the Introduction is an interpretation of a title that is not (yet) fully entitled to its status as title, and this would be one (dialectical) way to understand its dropping away: that is, *before* the reading (and writing) of the text of the Introduction, the title is *impossible*; *after* the reading (and writing) of the text of the Introduction, the title is *unnecessary*. In any case, the relation between a title that can exist as title neither before nor after the text—a title that contains the text of its interpretation and is at the same time contained by it, a title that cites the text of its interpretation and at the same time is cited by it—and a text that can exist as text neither before nor after the title is hardly covered by seeing one as the interpretation (*Auslegung, Erläuterung*) of the other:[32] there would be more involved in "literary seeing" than, as it were, meets the eye. A symptom of the unsettling character of this "more than meets the eye" is Heidegger's explicit cutting out, dropping, of the next-to-last one-sentence paragraph—the paragraph that "contains" the (dropped) title—of Hegel's text. That is, while recognizing that the sentence forms a paragraph in its own right—and, at that, a paragraph that summarizes the results not only of the fourteenth and fifteenth paragraphs but of the entire text—Heidegger nevertheless (first) treats it within his reading of the "fifteenth" paragraph when it is actually (literarily speaking?) the *sixteenth* paragraph; and, when he comes to the last paragraph of Hegel's text (i.e., the *seventeenth* paragraph), he calls it *"The sixteenth paragraph,* with which the piece closes (Der sechzehnte Abschnitt, *mit dem das Stück schliesst)"* (*H,* 180). To boot, Heidegger's extensive reading of Hegel's speculative titles takes place in an additional eight-page section that follows (after a space) his reading of the "sixteen" paragraphs: in short, Heidegger's reading of the next-to-last paragraph—we cannot call it the sixteenth paragraph because Heidegger has given that "title" to the last paragraph—as both inside and outside the text, as both necessary to and necessarily dropped from the text, repeats Hegel's (re)reading (and [re]writing) of "his" title. Again, even a brief look at the relation between title and text cannot help but discover unsettling possibilities of reading (and writing) that cannot be stabilized by treating "literary seeing" as self-evident. The translators' uneasiness with these unsettling possibilities of reading (and writing) is mirrored in their being uncertain as to the *meaning* of "literary seeing" in Heidegger's text. The American translator writes "In literary terms" for *literarisch gesehen* and "Textually we may regard" for *Literarisch können wir. . .nehmen,* whereas the French translator is at least consistent in writing *philologiquement* for both.[33]

What seeing "in literary terms," "textually," "philologically," "literarily," means in the text of Heidegger, in the text(s) of Hegel by Heidegger, would be of more than just passing interest to us, for such "seeing" presents us with another possibility of (re)reading (and [re]writing) the question of the text's reading (and writing): that is, Heidegger's (non) introduction of "literary seeing"—and let us call it "reading," for what other name could *we* give it?—provides us with an alternative to the double reading and double inscription of the text(s) of Hegel by Heidegger. In other words, this alternative, this other reading, is a peculiarly textual operation that takes place—"And does it take place?" is the question of the text—*neither* on the basis of the turn of self-consciousness *nor* on the basis of the self-revelation and self-concealment of Being (thought as *aletheia*) and yet at the same time bears some peculiar (textual?) relation to *both* of these readings. The "neither. . .nor" is explicit enough: just as "reading" (*lesen*) is identified as the activity of natural consciousness and opposed to "thinking"—"we have to think the title through the middle of the mediating word [i.e., *Erfahrung*] and always simultaneously backward and forward (*müssen wir den Titel durch die Mitte des vermittelnden*

Wortes hindurch jedesmal zugleich von rückwärts und nach vorwärts denken)" (*H*, 182)—so taking the title "literarily" is identified as lacking and again opposed to thought: "Literarily we can take the sixteen paragraphs as the interpretation of the title, which then fell away. But thought on the basis of the thing itself, it is not a matter of a book title but rather the work itself (*Literarisch können wir die sechzehn Abschnitte als die Erläuterung des Titels nehmen, der dann wegfiel. Aber aus der Sache gedacht, handelt es sich nicht um einen Buchtitel, sondern um das Werk selbst)"* (*H*, 190).

Heidegger's distinctions line up as oppositions: "reading" is opposed to "thinking" as "taking literarily" is opposed to "thinking on the basis of the thing itself" as the "title" is opposed to the "work" or, more precisely, as "reading" or taking "literarily" the relation between the title and the work is opposed to "thinking" that relation. In short, the activity of "reading" or taking "literarily" is sufficient neither in the terms of Hegel—insofar as it is an activity of natural consciousness—nor in the terms of Heidegger—insofar as it is not (yet) thinking on the basis of the thing itself. And yet in spite of this explicit "neither. . .nor"—or perhaps because of it—"reading" and taking "literarily" is an activity that haunts Heidegger's text from the beginning and in the end. That is, "literarily," we can take Heidegger's text—from its first paragraph and its explicit demand for a reading of Hegel's title(s) (backward and forward, subjective as well as objective genitives)--as *nothing but* the interpretation (*Auslegung, Eräuterung*) of the text of Hegel's introduction *as* an interpretation (*Auslegung, Erläuterung*) of the title(s). In short, just as a tying onto the opinion of natural *Vorstellung* characterizes the style of Hegel's paragraphs and their hanging together (*Dieses Anknüpfen an die Meinung des natürlichen Vorstellens kennzeichnet den Stil der Abschnitte des Stückes und ihres Zusammenhanges*) (*H*, 190), so does it characterize the "style" and the coherence of Heidegger's text. Hence not only is literary "seeing," "taking," or *reading* an activity that is correct in its reading of the relation between the title and the text, between Hegel's text and Heidegger's text, but it is also an activity that, in a sense, makes the interpretation (*Auslegung, Erläuterung*) of the text(s) possible insofar as *no* interpretation (of the text)—neither one of the double readings and double inscriptions of the text(s) of Hegel by Heidegger—is possible *without* such literary seeing, taking, and reading. Unless we can read (and write) Hegel's text *as* a (re)reading (and [re]writing) of the title(s)—forward and backward—and Heidegger's text *as* a (re)reading (and [re]writing) of the title(s)—backward and forward—we can interpret (*auslegen, erläutern*) neither the text of the one nor the text of the other. In other words, although literary seeing, taking, or reading may be unable to think on the basis of the thing itself, it is nevertheless able to simulate, to mimic, the movement of thought thinking itself in an interpretation, and this simulation, this mimicry, of thought is far from innocent insofar as *every* movement of thought and its interpretation is exposed to it. That is, insofar as every movement of thought and its interpretation is vulnerable to being seen, taken, or read literally, this vulnerability would be the condition of possibility of every movement of thought and every interpretation.

But this condition of possibility is also (always already and always not yet) the condition of impossibility of every movement of thought and its interpretation in that no interpretation of a movement of thought can ever gain mastery over the simulation, mimicry, of literary reading (and, we might add, writing) by subsuming it under the activity of its interpretation: no matter how rigorously and how vociferously it protests, denounces, or disowns the simulation and mimicry of literary reading (and writing), every interpretation of a movement of thought necessarily exposes itself to that very simulation and that very mimicry precisely to the extent that the very language, text, terms, *words*, of that protest, denunciation, or disowning can always be (re)read (and [re]written) literally. In short, not only does literary reading (and writing) always come *before* the text of the interpretation (*Auslegung, Erläuterung*) as its condition of possibility, but it also always goes *after* the text of the interpretation as its condition of impossibility: the text of the interpretation and the interpretation of the text are always divided, parasitized, by the (literary) reading (and writing) that comes before to give life to the text and goes after to kill it in a coming and going that has no end (and no beginning). Reading (and writing)—the title(s), for example—would be a parasite that gives and takes the life of interpretation. And Maurice Blanchot would be, for example, the life and death (*mort de lecture, mort d'écriture*) of the text(s) of Hegel by Heidegger. To the extent, then, that (literary) reading (and writing) is always already (and always not yet) present in the text of Heidegger's reading of Hegel—and that means: of Hegel's reading of Heidegger—our use of these words (from the beginning and in the end) to name that which remains unthought and unthinkable, unread and unreadable, in the "interpretation" of Hegel by Heidegger—what we have called the double reading and the double inscription of the text(s) of Hegel by Heidegger—is not an arbitrary imposition but rather an attempt to make visible that which is invisible, to think the unthought and unthinkable, to read the unread and unreadable, in short, to allow the reading (and the writing) of the text to take place. But lest it be thought that we have smuggled in (literary) reading (and writing)—literature—into the double reading and double inscription of the text(s) of Hegel by Heidegger much, *too* much, in the same way that Heidegger smuggles the *parousia* of the absolute into the text of Hegel's first paragraph—"Only in passing and so that he hides it in a side-clause"—let us give an example of the way in which (literary) reading (and writing) precedes and follows—haunts, parasitizes, gives life to and kills—the double reading and the double inscription of the text(s) of Hegel by Heidegger. But it should be noted from the start that there can be no example of reading (and writing) if reading (and writing) is the name of the mutual undoing of one text by another, for such an example could not itself read (and write) this mutual undoing without at the same time undoing itself and would therefore remain itself unreadable (and unwritable). In short, the example of reading (and writing) would have to be an example of the impossibility of reading (and writing) itself; it would have to be an example of the impossibility of example itself: an example, as always, of example.

About fifteen years after his reading of "Hegel's Concept of Experience," Heidegger, in the second essay of *Identity and Difference* ("The Onto-theological Constitution of Metaphysics")—"an attempt to begin a dialogue (*Gespräch*) with Hegel" (*ID*, 31)—opens a parenthesis and gives an example. The status of both the parenthesis—where, when, and upon what does it open?—and the example—what is it an example of?—is problematic. It is worthwhile to follow the logic of the parenthesis and of the example separately before reading the writing of the one within the other. "Here a parenthetical remark is indeed required concerning what we said about the matter of thinking. . .(*Hier bedarf es freilich einer Zwischenbemerkung, die unser Reden von der Sache des Denkens angeht. . .*)" (*ID*, 57), writes Heidegger to interrupt his text with an "incidental remark, a digression, an aside" (*Zwischenbemerkung*)[34]—let us call it, along with the French translator,[35] "parenthesis"—"a remark thrown in without having been asked for; keep your parentheses to yourself!; may I allow myself a parenthesis?[36] (*eingeworfene Bemerkung, ohne dass gefragt worden ist; behalte deine Zwischenbemerkungen für dich!; darf ich mir eine Zwischenbemerkung erlauben?*). Although this parenthesis may be a "digression," it is far from being an "incidental remark," for it is "a remark that demands our attention, our marking, ever anew, again and again (*eine Bemerkung, die immer neu unser Aufmerken verlangt*)": "When we say 'Being,' we use the word in the widest and most indeterminate universality [or generality]. But already then when we speak only of a universality, we have thought Being in an inappropriate way. We represent Being in a way in which It, Being, never gives itself (*Sagen wir 'das Sein,' so gebrauchen wir das Wort in der weitesten und unbestimmtesten Allgemeinheit. Aber schon dann, wenn wir nur von einer Allgemeinheit sprechen, haben wir das Sein in einer ungemässen Weise gedacht. Wir stellen das Sein in einer Weise vor, in der Es, das Sein, sich niemals gibt*)" (*ID*, 57). In terms of "context," the remark that demands our attention, our re-marking, again and again would be a reference to an earlier parenthetical remark (and its re-marking) on the use of the word "Being": on the second page of the essay Heidegger opens a parenthesis—"(In the seminar, the manifold and yet unified use of the word 'Being' was discussed. Being for Hegel means first of all, but *never only*. . . [(*Im Seminar wurde der mehrfältige und doch einheitliche Gebrauch des Wortes 'Sein' erörtert. Sein besagt für Hegel zunächst, aber* niemals nur. . .]" (*ID*, 32-33)—and closes it, but then comes back to it again later: "The remark on Hegel's use of the ambiguous key word 'Being' shows that. . . (*Die Bemerkung über Hegels Gebrauch des mehrdeutigen Leitwortes 'Sein' lässt erkennen, dass*. . .)" (*ID*, 41). But the parenthesis is a remark that demands our re-marking again and again in terms of still another "context": that is, insofar as the parenthesis is a re-marking of the use of the word "Being"—whether it be in the text of the history of philosophy in general or in the text of the *History of Philosophy* as read (and written) by Hegel, and, for Heidegger, as we have seen and as we shall see again and again, there is no *difference* between the two (precisely because the difference *as* difference has been forgotten)—it is no mere digression, incidental remark, or aside, but it is rather a re-marking that marks Heidegger's entire enterprise *from* the project of fundamental ontology *through* the step back (out of metaphysics and into the essence of metaphysics) *to* the thinking of Being on the basis of *Ereignis* ("taking place," "self-appropriating event"). In other words, in terms of the other context, the parenthesis is no interruption of the text of the essay but rather it *is* the context: rather than being inscribed in the text of the essay as an incidental remark, the parenthesis is that in which the text of the essay is inscribed. This is the sense in which the parenthesis demands our re-marking it again and again, and this may also be the sense in which the parenthesis may never be closed (or, for that matter—the matter of thinking [*die Sache des Denkens*]?—opened). In any case, if the parenthesis, rather than being an incidental remark interrupting the text of the essay, is instead (or at the same time) the very context of the text, that in which the text is inscribed—the *thesis* rather than (or as well as) the parenthesis—then a great deal would be at stake for Heidegger (and for Hegel and for Hegel by Heidegger) in the (re)reading (and [re]writing) of the example that the exemplary parenthesis gives.

Just as the question of the context of the parenthesis was, as always, a question of the difference—not only the difference between Hegel's use of the word "Being" and Heidegger's use of the same word, and the difference between Being thought on the basis of "beings" (*Seiendes*) and "Being thought on the basis of the difference (*Sein gedacht aus der Differenz*)" (*ID*, 57), that is, the (ontological) difference between Being and beings, but also the difference between mark and re-mark, thesis and parenthesis—so the question of the context of the example (*Beispiel*) is a question of difference: not only the difference between Hegel and Heidegger, between beings and Being, but also the difference between the example and that of which it is the example, between *Beispiel* and *Spiel*, between giving and not giving the example, between reading and rereading (writing and rewriting) the example—in short, between reading and not reading (writing and not writing) the example of reading (and writing). This would indeed be an example to end, as it were, all examples, but since we have to begin somewhere let us begin with the difference between the example and that of which it is and is not, that of which it can and cannot be, the example, for if we can circumscribe this difference we may be better able to read the inscription of the other differences (and the other difference) in the *Beispiel*: "The way in which the matter of thinking, Being, comports itself remains a unique state of affairs. Our customary way of thinking can at first clarify it always only insufficiently. This is attempted through an example while it should be noted from the start that nowhere in beings is there an example [a by-play, a by-spell] for the essence of Being, presumably because the essence of Being is the exemplar itself [the spell itself, the play itself] (*Die Art, wie die Sache des Denkens, das Sein, sich verhält, bleibt ein einzigartiger Sachverhalt. Unsere geläufige Denkart kann ihn zunächst immer nur unzureichend verdeutlichen. Dies sei durch ein Beispiel versucht, wobei im voraus zu beachten ist, dass es für das Wesen des Seins nirgends im Seienden ein Beispiel gibt, vermutlich deshalb, weil das Wesen des Seins das Spiel selber ist)*" (*ID*, 58).

Before we give the *Beispiel*, before Heidegger gives the *Beispiel*—and who are we that we may give the *Beispiel*, who is Heidegger that he may give the *Beispiel*, when there can be no *Beispiel* to be given?—let us leave aside the parenthetical questions of what is given, by whom, etc., and first consider what the *Beispiel* about to be given can be an example of. What the giving of the example will attempt is to clarify (*verdeutlichen*) the unique state of affairs (*einzigartiger Sachverhalt*)—that is, the way (*Art*) in which the matter of thinking, Being, comports itself (*sich verhält*)—which our usual way of thinking (*Denkart*) can clarify, at least at first, always only insufficiently. But this clarification by giving an example is not to be understood as the clarification of the essence of Being, as an example for the essence of Being, because there can be no such clarification, no such example: nowhere in beings is there an example for the essence of Being to be given. That is, the example about to be given has to be very precisely an example *only* of how Being comports itself (*sich verhält*) and *not* of Being itself. In other words, the example about to be given has to be an example of how Being does *not* give itself, for to give an example is to give in a way that Being does *not* give itself, that is, in beings, on the level of the ontic. Again: the example about to be given has to be an example of how Being does not give itself in an example, an example for the lack, absence, impossibility, of example: a *Beispiel* for the impossibility of a *Beispiel* (for the essence of Being). This lack, absence, impossibility, of the example is exemplified in Heidegger's play on the etymology of the word *Beispiel*: etymologically speaking, *Beispiel* does not mean "by-play," a playing on the side, but rather "by-spell," a *saying* on the side.[37] If the essence of Being, then, is "the play itself (*das Spiel selber*)," no *Beispiel* can exemplify Being because no *Beispiel* can play on the side of Being insofar as every *Beispiel* is a saying on the side, a by-spell, and *not* a playing on the side, a by-play. But even if we were to take *Beispiel* to mean "by-play," it would still not be an example for the "play itself" insofar as the relation between the essence of Being (i.e., the play itself) and beings (i.e., the by-play) is *not* a relation of main event to sideshow, play to by-play. To think of the essence of Being in this way, to put Being into such a relation, into any relation (i.e., *next to* beings), is precisely to think Being inappropriately in a way it never gives itself. When we give *Beispiel* as by-spell, Being gives itself as the play; and when we give *Beispiel* as by-play, Being gives itself as the spell. Whether we give a *Beispiel* as a "by-spell" or as a "by-play," we can never give a *Beispiel* for the essence of Being precisely to the extent that we give a *Beispiel*.

Again, the only *Beispiel* we can give is a *Beispiel* for the impossibility of a *Beispiel* (for the essence of Being), and what better way to give *such* a *Beispiel* than to give the example of (Being as) the universality of the universal, to give the example of how Being *never* gives itself? And who could think Being in a way inappropriate to it, in a way in which it never gives itself, better than Hegel: that is, the exemplary giver of Being in a way in which it never gives itself? "Hegel once mentions the following case to characterize the universality of the universal [the generality of the general]: someone would like to buy fruit in a store. He demands fruit. One offers him apples, pears, offers him peaches, cherries, grapes. But the buyer rejects that which is offered. He would have fruit at any price. Now that which is offered to him each time *is* fruit and yet it turns out: fruit is not for sale (*Hegel erwähnt einmal zur Kennzeichnung der Allgemeinheit des Allgemeinen folgenden Fall: Jemand möchte in einem Geschäft Obst kaufen. Er verlangt Obst. Man reicht ihm Äpfel, Birnen, reicht ihm Pfirsiche, Kirschen, Trauben. Aber der Käufer weist das Dargereichte zurück. Er möchte um jeden Preis Obst haben. Nun ist aber doch das Dargebotene jedesmal Obst und dennoch stellt sich heraus: Obst gibt es nicht zu kaufen*)" (*ID*, 58). Although we may wonder about Heidegger's giving Hegel's example rather than his own, the example itself would appear to be above suspicion and its straightforwardness beyond reproach. Nevertheless, even aside from the question of its being Hegel's example—and that *is* a question—Heidegger's giving, shall we say "offering," of the example remains problematic. If no example of the essence of Being can be given, Heidegger, in nevertheless giving an example, gives an example that necessarily gives in a way that Being does not give itself. And such a (not) giving would be the same as the fruit vendor's giving and not giving fruit: in offering an example of the impossibility of example, Heidegger is repeating, as it were, the gesture of the fruit vendor who offers us fruit while at the same time telling us that fruit is not for sale. In other words, in saying "that nowhere in beings is there an example for the essence of Being (*dass es für das Wesen des Seins nirgends im Seienden ein Beispiel gibt*)" and then giving an example of the impossibility of giving an example, Heidegger inscribes his (not) giving in the example of giving—"Now that which is offered to him each time *is* fruit (*Nun* ist *aber doch das Dargebotene jedesmal Obst*)"—and not giving fruit—"and yet it turns out: fruit is not for sale (*und dennoch stellt sich heraus: Obst gibt es nicht zu kaufen*)."

But "Heidegger"—and at stake here and now (as everywhere and always) is both the name and the quotation marks—is inscribed in the example not only as the fruit vendor who gives and does not give fruit, for the parenthesis continues: "It remains infinitely more impossible to represent 'Being' as the universal in relation to particular being. There is Being only at all times and every time in this or that destined coinage: *Phusis, Logos, Hen, Idea, Energeia,* Substantiality, Objectivity, Subjectivity, the Will, the Will to Power, the Will to Will. But that which destines is not given lined up like apples, pears, peaches, lined up on the counter of historical representing (*Unendlich unmöglicher bleibt es, 'das Sein' als das Allgemeine zum jeweilig Seienden vorzustellen. Es gibt Sein nur je und je in dieser und jener geschicklichen Prägung*: Phusis, Logos, Hen, Idea, Energeia, *Substanzialität, Objektivität, Subjektivität, Wille, Wille zur Macht, Wille zum Willen. Aber dies Geschickliche gibt es nicht aufgereiht wie Äpfel, Birnen, Pfirsiche, aufgereiht auf dem Ladentisch des historischen Vorstellens*)" (*ID*, 58). In other words, Heidegger is also inscribed in the example that he has just (not) given as "the buyer" (*der Käufer*) who would have fruit and yet refuses the fruit that is offered him: in saying that it is infinitely more impossible to represent Being as the universal in relation to particular beings—and this is the relation that the example characterizes (*zur Kennzeichnung der Allgemeinheit des Allgemeinen*)—Heidegger says that the example he has just given of the way in which Being does not give itself is still insufficient, indeed *infinitely* insufficient, to characterize the (not) giving of Being. In short, he refuses the example he has given and not given as an insufficient example of giving and not giving. And yet Heidegger—the text, the parenthesis—does not just refuse the example he gives without giving, for in repeating, as it were, the gesture of the buyer of fruit (just as he had repeated the gesture of the fruit vendor) Heidegger once again and very precisely inscribes his refusal in the *Beispiel* of the refusal: that is, just as that which is offered each time *is* fruit, so there *is* Being in this or that destined coinage; but just as it turns out that fruit is not for sale, so it turns out that that which destines is not given lined up like apples, pears, and so on. The sequence *Es gibt Sein / Aber dies Geschickliche gibt es nicht* is always already (and always not yet) inscribed in the example's sequence *Nun* ist *aber das Dargebotene jedesmal Obst / Obst gibt es nicht zu kaufen.* Insofar as his refusal of the example is inscribed in the example itself—and we are getting to the reading (and the writing) of the example "itself"—Heidegger cannot but accept the example of the impossibility of accepting the example just as he could not but give the example of the impossibility of giving the example. But if the give-and-take of the example is always already inscribed in the example, the distinction between Heidegger's (not) giving and (not) taking of the example and the example's (not) giving and (not) taking of "Heidegger," of the text of Heidegger's parenthesis, is impossible to maintain. Just as it turned out that the parenthesis on the use of the word Being rather than being the interruption of the text was itself the context of the text, so it turns out that the example (*Beispiel*) rather than being given or taken by the text of the parenthesis itself gives and takes the text of the parenthesis. Rather than Heidegger's (not) giving and (not) taking *Beispiel*, what we have is the *Beispiel's* (not) giving and (not) taking "Heidegger."

And these inscriptions—the text of the essay in the parenthesis, the parenthesis in the *Beispiel*—are not fanciful "literary" reading (and writing) but rather a necessity inscribed (from the beginning and in the end) in the text of Heidegger: that is, "Heidegger" can and *must* be both the fruit vendor who gives and does not give fruit and the fruit buyer who takes and does not take fruit because he has inscribed (but without inscribing "himself") the entire history of Western philosophy thought as the destiny (*Geschick*) of Being's giving and not giving itself on the basis of *aletheia* in the example of the fruit *as* the fruit itself. From *phusis* to "Will to Will," the destined coinages of Being are so many apples, pears, and peaches lined up on the counter of historical representation, but insofar as they give themselves in this way they do not give Being in the way that that which destines gives Being. Hence if Heidegger's text is not to suffer the same fate (*Geschick*?) and wind up on the counter of historical representation as another apple or pear, as another destined coinage of Being that nevertheless gives Being in a way that Being does not give itself, all it can do is to give and take fruit while saying that fruit is neither to be given nor to be taken, and it does so by giving and taking the coinages of Being as thought on the basis of beings (*Seiendes*) but at the same time *not* giving and *not* taking them because they are given in a way (i.e., on the basis of *Seiendes*) that Being does not give itself. Heidegger's text may be unable to give Being in the way that Being gives itself, but it can at least *not* give Being in the way that Being does not give itself, and it does so by inscribing all the exemplary coinages of Being, all the exemplary ways in which Being does not give itself, in its own exemplary text of the destiny of Being's self-forgetting. These exemplary ways in which Being does not give itself have recognizable names: for examples, Anaximander, Heraclitus, Parmenides, Plato, Aristotle,[38] even if in some cases they would most appropriately have the names of several philosophers: for example, "subjectivity" would cover the coinages of Being from Descartes through Hegel. In short, by inscribing himself in the example as the fruit vendor and fruit buyer, Heidegger would keep from being inscribed in it as an apple or pear while at the same time inscribing in it all the destined coinages of Being—"Hegel," for example—as apples, pears, and so on. Hegel would be one of the (forbidden) fruit (not) given and (not) taken by Heidegger.

Again: as the exemplary giver-and-taker of *Beispiel* who gives and does not give, takes and does not take, the example of the way in which Being does not give itself—the example of the impossibility of giving an example—Heidegger would keep from becoming an example of such (not) giving himself. And yet the fact that "Heidegger"—the text, the parenthesis, the *Beispiel* (not) given and (not) taken—is able to do so only by inscribing the entire destiny of the forgetting of Being (in its difference from beings)—and hence his own text as a rereading (and rewriting) of that destiny—in the example of fruit should make us wary, for Heidegger used the same strategy in "Hegel's Concept of Experience" in order to inscribe Hegel's reading of the word Being in his own text. That is, Heidegger superimposed the entire destiny of the forgetting of Being—*his* text—upon the history of philosophy—Hegel's text—in order to collapse the difference between empty Being and full Being and thereby read "his own" unthought Being (*das Sein selbst*) inscribed once in the text of Hegel. But just as that self-inscription turned out to be not only Heidegger's thinking of Hegel's unthought but also Hegel's thinking of Heidegger's unthought, so Heidegger's self-inscription of the entire destiny of Being in the example of the fruit—in the example of the impossibility of example—is not just any act of rereading (and rewriting). The example that Heidegger rereads (and rewrites) as the example for the impossibility of example and, to this extent, for the way in which Being does not give itself is—and it is no accident—the example of Hegel: "Hegel once mentions. . .(*Hegel erwähnt einmal*. . .)."

Or rather the example of example, the example to end all examples, if it is not exactly Heidegger's, is not exactly Hegel's either. The difficulty of identifying the example and its author begins with Heidegger's *einmal*: "Hegel once mentions. . .(*Hegel erwähnt einmal*. . .)" and the translators' uncertainty about its meaning is, as always, symptomatic: the American translator writes "at one point" and the French translator writes *quelque part*. How are we to read the "oneness" of the "once," the "where" of the "somewhere," inscribed in *einmal*? If we are to believe the translators, Heidegger's "once" is a case of mere academic, professorial, forgetfulness or even carelessness: it does not matter where, when, and how many times Hegel mentions this example, and, besides, I don't remember exactly anyway. But just as the forgetting of Being is not quite like a philosophy professor's forgetting his umbrella—"The 'forgetting of Being' has often been represented as though, to say it in an image, Being were the umbrella left standing somewhere due to a philosophy professor's forgetfulness (*Die 'Seinsvergessenheit' hat man denn auch vielfach so vorgestellt, dass, um es im Bilde zu sagen, das Sein der Schirm ist, den die Vergesslichkeit eines Philosophieprofessors irgendwo hat stehen lassen*)"[39]—so the forgetting of the example to end all examples is not quite covered by academic, professorial, forgetfulness. Rather than being translated by the professor's "at one point" or "somewhere," Heidegger's *einmal* would be better covered—and it is indeed a question of a cover-up (*whose* cover-up?) that we are trying to uncover and recover—by the storyteller's "once upon a time," for Hegel mentions this example not "somewhere at one point" but rather (at least) three times in three places: (1) in the introduction to an early version of the *Encyclopedia*[40] which is then (2) rewritten (with very slight changes) in the "final" version of the *Encyclopedia*, and (3) mentioned again with considerable changes and a reference back to the *Encyclopedia* in the introduction to the *History of Philosophy*. In none of these mentions is it a case (*Fall*) of a buyer of fruit in a store. Indeed, the first two mention an offering and a refusing of fruit without characterizing either the giver or the taker of fruit, and the third version characterizes the "giver" as a physician (*Arzt*) who prescribes fruit (*Obst*) for the "taker," his sick patient, who is offered "cherries or plums or grapes" but refuses them all in "a pedantry of the understanding (*in einer Pedanterie des Verstandes*)" "because none of these fruits is fruit (*weil keine dieser Früchte Obst sei*)" (XVIII:37). Hence Heidegger's "once" (*einmal*) is an active forgetting of Hegel's examples in that it allows him to rewrite them as given *once*, somewhere, sometime, by "Hegel." The fact that earlier in the essay (*ID*, 32) Heidegger mentions and quotes from (and gives the reference to) a famous passage in the *Encyclopedia* (paragraph 14) that follows directly upon Hegel's fruit example (in paragraph 13) would be an indication of the active nature of this forgetful rewriting.

But Heidegger's rewriting of the example(s) is not limited to his giving an example that is not exactly the example of Hegel: in rewriting the examples, Heidegger also rewrites that which they exemplify. Namely, at stake in Hegel's text is not exactly, not merely, the "characterization of the universality of the universal (*Kennzeichnung der Allgemeinheit des Allgemeinen*)" (*ID*, 58) but rather a more subtly dialectical distinction between the universal and the particular, especially as it has bearing on the distinction between "philosophy" as such and particular philosophies as they appear in history. For our first example, let us give (and take) the one in the final version of the *Encyclopedia*: "With the aspect of so many *different* philosophies, the *universal* and the *particular* has to be distinguished according to its proper determination. The universal, taken formally and placed *next to* the particular, becomes itself also something particular. Such a placing would of itself attract attention as inappropriate and clumsy with objects of ordinary life, as for example if one who demanded fruit should rule out cherries, pears, grapes, and so on because they were cherries, pears, grapes, but *not* fruit. But in regard to philosophy one allows oneself to justify scorning philosophy because there are so many philosophies and each one is only *one* philosophy, not *the* philosophy—as though cherries were not also fruit (*Bei dem Anschein der so vielen, verschiedenen Philosophien muss das* Allgemeine *und* Besondere *seiner eigentlichen Bestimmung nach unterschieden werden. Das Allgemeine, formell genommen und* neben *das Besondere gestellt, wird selbst auch zu etwas*

Besonderem. Solche Stellung würde bei Gegenständen des gemeinen Lebens von selbst als unangemessen und ungeschickt auffallen, wie wenn z.b. einer, der Obst verlangte, Kirschen, Birnen, Trauben, usf. ausschlüge, weil sie Kirschen, Birnen, Trauben, nicht *aber Obst seien. In Ansehung der Philosophie aber lässt man es sich zu, die Verschmähung derselben damit zu rechtfertigen, weil es so verschiedene Philosophien gebe und jede nur* eine *Philosophie, nicht* die *Philosophie sei,—als ob nicht auch die Kirschen Obst wären)"* (VIII:59). At stake in Hegel's fruit example is, on the one hand, the *difference* between universal and particular: that is, he who demands fruit and expects it to be given like cherries or pears is turning the universal into a particular by putting it next to the particular. But also at stake in this example is, on the other hand, the *identity* of universal and particular: that is, he who demands fruit and then rejects cherries and pears because they are particular fruits and not fruit itself does not recognize that the only way to the universal is through the particular. In other words, what he who demands and then refuses fruit does is not to understand the identity of the identity and difference of universal and particular: since there is no road to philosophy as such that does not lead through particular philosophies what one has to do is to accept, to think, these particular philosophies in their particularity in order to discover that which is *universal in them.* To put the universal—philosophy—*next* to the particular—philosophies—or to put it inaccessibly *beyond* the particular is inappropriate and clumsy. The only way to have fruit is to eat particular fruits: cherries, pears, and so on.[41]

This necessity of eating the fruits of particular philosophies by recognizing the identity of the identity and difference of universal and particular is stated even more insistently in the version of the fruit example given by the introduction to the *History of Philosophy*: "That loose talking and rationalizing which holds onto the mere difference and out of disgust or fear of the particular in which a universal is actual does not want to recognize or grasp this universality I have compared elsewhere to a sick man for whom the doctor prescribes eating fruit and whom one offers cherries or plums or grapes, but who in a pedantry of the understanding does not take hold because none of these fruits is fruit but rather some are cherries, others plums or grapes (*Jenes Ausreden und Räsonnement, das sich an die blosse Verschiedenheit festhält und aus Ekel oder Bangigkeit vor der Besonderheit, in der ein Allgemeines wirklich ist, nicht diese Allgemeinheit ergreifen oder anerkennen will, habe ich anderswo mit einem Kranken verglichen, dem der Arzt Obst zu essen anrät und dem man Kirschen oder Pflaumen oder Trauben vorsetzt, der aber in einer Pedanterie des Verstandes nicht zugreift, weil keine dieser Früchte Obst sei, sondern die eine Kirschen, die andere Pflaumen oder Trauben)*" (XVIII:37).

"Hegel's" example of fruit rereads (and rewrites) "Heidegger's" example of fruit so "explicitly" that we need hardly make a contribution to the reading (and writing) of the example. The example in which Heidegger has inscribed the entire destiny of the forgetting of Being—Western metaphysical thought—is not just any example in the history of philosophy but rather the example of the History of Philosophy (as read and written by the text of Hegel) itself. For what is involved in the reading of the fruit example—as the example that would illustrate how the relation between philosophy and particular philosophies is to be taken and not taken—is nothing short of the meaning of the entire history of philosophy: "The interpretation of this [i.e., the differences of many different philosophies] will open for us the meaning of the entire history of philosophy (*Die Erläuterung hierüber wird uns die Bedeutung der ganzen Geschichte der Philosophie aufschliessen*)" (XVIII:37). And what this interpretation amounts to in Hegel's *History of Philosophy* is, to make a long story short, an explanation of the concept of "development" (*Entwicklung*): that is, the self-recuperation by self-alienation and self-recognition of spirit in its own historical manifestations. "The development of spirit is going out, self-rending, and simultaneously coming to self (*Die Entwicklung des Geistes ist Herausgehen, Sichauseinanderlegen und zugleich Zusichkommen*)" (XVIII:41). In terms of the relation between philosophy as such and particular philosophies, this means philosophy's—the spirits's, the Idea's—becoming conscious of itself in particular philosophies, and the way we participate in this movement of self-consciousness is by ourselves becoming self-conscious. We turn upon ourselves by recognizing that we who contain within ourselves the identity of the identity and difference of universal and particular are already inscribed in the particular object confronting us insofar as that object—in this case a particular philosophy—already contains that (*our*) identity of the identity and difference of universal and particular. In other words, we have to recognize that just as our demand for fruit is both universal and particular, so is the fruit we are offered both particular and universal: just as we can never demand the one without demanding the other, so we can never be given the one without the other. But if the only way to seize the universal is to seize the particular, such seizing (*ergreifen*) always entails a process of self-exteriorization, falling into the object, recognizing the self as the self in its own other, etc., in short, it always entails a movement, a development (*Entwicklung*), of self-consciousness in *history*. Hence the sick man's refusal to seize particular fruits because they are not fruit—particular philosophies because they are not philosophy—would be not only a disgust with and fear of the particular in which a universal is actual, but also a refusal of the movement of self-consciousness in history—in short, of history *as* self-consciousness.

So the difference between Hegel's reading (and writing) of the fruit example and Heidegger's reading (and writing) of the fruit example is, as always, a difference between two histories or, better, between history (*Geschichte*) and destiny (*Geschick*). This is why Heidegger's rewriting of Hegel's example has to take on the character of refusal. The most obvious refusal is Heidegger's rejection of precisely that which Hegel's example illustrates: namely, whereas Hegel uses the example of (not) giving and (not) taking fruit to "clarify" the speculative identity of universal and particular, Heidegger uses the "same" example to "clarify" (*verdeutlichen*), but only insufficiently, the way in which Being does not give itself as a universal in relation to particular beings. That is, since the relation between Being (that which destines Being) and the destined coinages of Being is not one of universal and particular, not to give or take Being is like the (not) giving and (not) taking of fruit only insofar as that (not) giving and (not) taking of fruit is *not* thought as a relation of universal and particular: Being can be neither put *next to* beings nor put *beyond* beings as a universal in relation to beings. Insofar as Heidegger's rewriting of the example is an inscription of an other difference, a difference other than the difference between universal and particular, and an other identity, an identity other than the speculative identity of universal and particular, his rewriting is necessarily not only a refusal of all that the example exemplifies—the speculative identity of universal and particular that brings along with it an interpretation of history (and therefore of the history of philosophy) as a movement of self-consciousness, in short, history as self-consciousness—but also (always already and always not yet) a refusal of the example itself. That is, in order to show that the difference between Being and beings, between that which destines Being and the destined coinages of Being, is not to be thought in terms of the difference between universal and particular, Heidegger has to institute an other difference between his writing of the example of the difference and Hegel's writing of the example of the difference. And the way Heidegger does so is to rewrite Hegel's example for the necessity, for the absolute necessity, of giving and taking an example into his own example for the impossibility, for the destined impossibility, of giving and taking an example (except as *not* giving and *not* taking an example).

Again: by rewriting Hegel's example of the necessity of example into his own example of the impossibility of example, Heidegger is able to reinscribe Hegel in the fruit example as one of the apples, pears, etc., insofar as Hegel is precisely one of those who gives and takes an *example* of Being and to the extent that he does so (i.e., gives and takes an *example* of Being) necessarily gives and takes Being in a way it never gives and takes itself. And yet if the only way Heidegger can inscribe Hegel in the example *as* he who gives and takes the example (and thereby becomes an apple or a pear) is by inscribing himself in it as he who refuses to give and take the example (and thereby keeps from becoming an apple or a pear), then he inscribes himself in the example not only as the fruit vendor and fruit buyer but also (always already and always not yet) as he who refuses the medicine of Hegel's example—the speculative identity of universal and particular (and, we might add, of *Spiel* and *Beispiel*), the development

(*Entwicklung*) of spirit, the Idea, in a movement of history of self-consciousness, etc.—because it is a *Beispiel* and not *das Spiel selber* (the play itself). In short, by refusing Hegel's example—by rewriting the necessity of the example into the impossibility of the example—Heidegger inscribes himself in it as the sick man for whom the doctor prescribes fruit. Heidegger may be able to rewrite Hegel's example and inscribe Hegel in it as one of the fruit neither given nor taken on Heidegger's fruit stand, but he cannot do so without at the same time inscribing himself in it as Doctor Hegel's recalcitrant patient. But if Heidegger cannot reread (or rewrite) Hegel's example without Hegel's also rereading (and rewriting) Heidegger's example—and this is the example of the double reading and double inscription of the text(s) of Hegel by Heidegger— then who can read and write the example itself?

The answer, as always, reads and writes (as though by) itself: if the example can be only *re*read and *re*written, no one can read and write the example itself, for there is no example itself to be read and written. And yet the reading and the writing of the example is also necessary in that no rereading and no rewriting of the example is possible without it. In other words, we should recognize that in giving the example of the double reading and double inscription of the text(s) of Hegel by Heidegger, that in giving the example of reading and writing itself, we have given the example of the necessity and impossibility of giving an example, insofar as the example of reading and writing—Hegel by Heidegger for example—is not ours to give (or take). In short, we too are inscribed in the example of the necessity and impossibility of reading and writing the example of reading and writing itself: we too give (and take) and cannot give (and cannot take) the example of reading and writing; we too can only reread and rewrite the example of reading and writing without being able to read and write the example of reading and writing itself ourselves. We could say—who says?—that just as reading (and writing) was the parasite of interpretation, so the example of reading and writing itself is the parasite of reading and writing: the example has always already and always not yet come before the reading and the writing to give it life and has always already and always not yet gone after the reading and the writing to kill it in a coming and going that has no end (and no beginning). But if the example has (from the beginning and in the end) always already and always not yet reread (and rewritten) not only the texts of Hegel and Heidegger but also our reading (and writing) of the double reading and double inscription of the text(s) of Hegel by Heidegger, what does that leave us with? That leaves us with(out) an exemplary reading (and writing) and parentheses without end[42]—

Chapter 7
Reading for Example
"Sense-certainty" in Hegel's
Phenomenology of Spirit

Il y a dans la dialectique un piège: alors qu'elle est le mouvement même du contenu, tel qu'il le réalise par autoconstitution, ou l'art de retracer et de suivre les rapports de l'appel et de la réponse, du problème et de la solution, alors que la *dialectique* est par principe épithète, elle devient, dès qu'on la prend pour devise, dès qu'on en parle, au lieu de la pratiquer, une puissance d'être, un principe explicatif. Ce qui était la manière d'être de l'Etre devient un malin génie. O Dialectique, dit le philosophe, quand il s'aperçoit que peut-être la vraie philosophie se moque de la philosophie. Ici, la dialectique est presque quelqu'un, comme l'ironie des choses, c'est un sort jeté sur le monde qui fait que nos attentes sont tournées en dérision, une puissance rusée, derrière notre dos, qui nous déconcerte, et qui, pour comble, a son ordre et sa rationalité; pas seulement un risque de non-sens donc, mais bien pire; l'assurance que les choses ont *un autre sens* que celui que nous sommes en mesure de leur reconnaître.
—Maurice Merleau-Ponty, *Le Visible et l'invisible*

"Sense-certainty; or the 'this' and 'meaning' (*Die sinnliche Gewissheit; oder das Diese und das Meinen*)," the first part of the first chapter of Hegel's *Phenomenology*, has exemplary status in the book and in commentaries on the book. Not only is it the first example of the dialectical movement at work in a particular content—that is, the first figure of apparent knowing—and as such can be taken as a model for the figures to follow, but, as the beginning, it is in Hegelian terms necessarily also the (as yet unreflected) end. That is, just as on the first page of the *Phenomenology* proper we begin with "immediate knowing, *knowing* of the immediate (*unmittelbares Wissen,* Wissen *des Unmittelbaren*)*,*" so on the next-to-last page we end with immediacy, the only difference being the difference in the former that has become identity in the latter: "For the self-knowing Spirit, just because it grasps the Concept, is the immediate identity with itself, which, in its difference, is the *certainty of immediacy,* or sense-consciousness—the beginning from which we started (*Denn der sich selbst wissende Geist, ebendarum dass er seinen Begriff erfasst, ist er die unmittelbare Gleichheit mit sich selbst, welche in ihrem Unterschiede die* Gewissheit vom Unmittelbaren *ist, oder das sinnliche Bewusstsein—der Anfang, von dem wir ausgegangen*)" (*PhG,* 563).[1] Insofar as this beginning that is also an end is *Being*—"and sense-certainty's truth contains nothing but the sheer *being* of the thing (*und ihre Wahrheit enthält allein das* Sein *der Sache*)" (*PhG,* 79)—it is analogous to the itinerary of the big *Logic,* which also goes from empty, pure Being (*Sein, reines Sein*) to "*fulfilled* Being" (*nun auch erfülltes Sein*) (VI:572). It is no wonder, then, that for commentators the dialectic of sense-certainty has "exemplary and normative value" and is "decisive for the interpretation of Hegel's philosophy."[2] Jacques Derrida's *Glas,* one exemplary reading of that philosophy and of this beginning, would seem to agree, for it too begins with Hegel's sense-certainty: "what besides remains today, for us, here, now, of a Hegel? / For us, here, now: that is what will have been impossible henceforth to think without him. / For us, here, now: these words are quotations, already, always, we will have learned it from him (*quoi du reste aujourd'hui, pour nous, ici, maintenant, d'un Hegel? / Pour nous, ici, maintenant: voilà ce qu'on n'aura pu désormais penser sans lui. / Pour nous, ici, maintenant: ces mots sont des citations, déjà, toujours, nous l'aurons appris de lui*)."[3] Now this beginning—like Hegel's, a double beginning—has received much attention, but its peculiar doubleness has not been remarked. For if this beginning is, as Eugenio Donato puts it, "emblematic" of all beginnings, it is not because it just repeats Hegel "to indicate the necessarily mediatized nature of representation" and because it "tells of the absence of privileged origins"[4]—such representation and such absence are eminently dialectizable—but because rather than just deferring the beginning, it introduces into it an unsublatable asymmetry. That is, there is a difference between the first and the second reading of "For us, here, now" (*Pour nous, ici, maintenant*): in the first reading, these words are "what" (*ce que*) one (impersonal *on*) will henceforth not be able to "think" (*penser*) without Hegel; in the second reading, these words are precisely "these words" (*ces mots*)—"already, always" quotations—we will have learned from Hegel. In other words, to *think* the "here," the "now," and the "we" of "for us" is still an activity mastered by the system of the old Hegel: that is, it is still inscribable into a history of self-consciousness whether it be that of the

READING FOR EXAMPLE □ 165

Phenomenology or of the *Logic*. But to learn that the "here," the "now," and the "we" of the "for us" are words that are already always quotations requires a different activity, one not as easily (or not at all) recuperable for the System. The repetition of the word "we" (*nous*) in the second reading indicates the problematic nature of such learning: if we will have learned from Hegel that the word "we" (in "for us") is a quotation, we have to recognize that whenever we say "we"—for example, when we say that "we will have learned. . ."—we are indeed not recognizing ourselves but quoting ourselves. And such self-quotation—and can quotation ever be that of a self, a subject?—requires another "we," another "Hegel," another "here" and "now," and an other activity to read them. That such reading is not a given and not to be taken for granted is clear from Derrida's double beginning: both Hegel's and his own *and* neither his own nor Hegel's. Hence before asking what it means for us—who, we?—to learn that these words ("here," "now," "for us") are always already quotations—that is, asking what it means to read them—let us first ask what it would mean to think these words.

Thinking the "here," the "now," and the "we" would mean, from the beginning, engaging in a dialogue, a question-and-answer session, in which we hold our thinking, our conceptualizing (*das Begreifen*), at a distance, or at least apart from mere taking up (*Aufnehmen*) and apprehending (*Auffassen*): "The knowing that is first of all or immediately our object can be none other than that which is itself immediate knowing, *knowing* of the *immediate* or of that which is. We have to behave just as *immediately* or *receptively*, that is, not to change anything in the object as it offers itself and to hold conceptualizing apart from apprehending (*Das Wissen, welches zuerst oder unmittelbar unser Gegenstand ist, kann kein anderes sein als dasjenige, welches selbst unmittelbares Wissen, Wissen des Unmittelbaren oder Seienden ist. Wir haben uns ebenso unmittelbar oder aufnehmend zu verhalten, also nichts an ihm, wie es sich darbietet, zu verändern und von dem Auffassen das Begreifen abzuhalten)*" (*PhG*, 79). As always, we begin with a redoubling of the beginning: the first words of the opening sentences introduce the partners in the dialogue—a knowing (*Das Wissen*) and the "we" (*Wir*)—as well as the relation between them. That is, just as (*ebenso*) the first figure of apparent knowing is an immediate knowing, knowing of the immediate, so our relation to it has to be equally (*ebenso*) immediate in order that we may allow it to examine itself, to test itself against its own standard of truth. In other words, our relation to our object—immediate knowing—is the same as that object's relation to its own object—that is, the immediate, that which is—and this symmetrical sameness is expressed in the word *ebenso* (just so, just as, equally, etc.). But there is a negative already built into this relation in that we can behave (*verhalten*) immediately and add nothing to our taking up (*Aufnehmen*) of the object only if we leave out, forget, negate, put down, as it were, what we already know and act as though we knew only as much and in the same way as sense-certainty knows. But, of course, in order to leave out ourselves, our knowing, our contribution (*Zutat*), we must have been there in the first place: this knowing "is first of all or immediately *our* object (*zuerst oder unmittelbar unser Gegenstand ist*)." In other words, as the Introduction (*Einleitung*) to the *Phenomenology* had announced, the examination of apparent knowing appears from the beginning under the double aspect of the natural consciousness—here "sense-certainty"—and the "we"; the question is not so much *what* sense-certainty or we know but rather the redoubling of this knowledge, that is, what we have here is knowing *of* knowing, knowledge of knowledge (i.e., self-conscious knowing, knowing turning upon itself). Sense-certainty, however, does not know that, and we cannot *tell* it what it does not know but rather have to let it discover on its own what it is in truth—what its truth (Being, *Sein*) *is* in truth, what *is* is in truth—through a process of experience (which is, in a sense, a *re*experience for us, without which reexperience we would not be in truth "we"). In short, for sense-certainty and for us experience would mean answering the question contained in the opening sentences and its rhetoric of being and nothing ("can be none other [*kann kein anderes sein*]")—that is, "What *is* sense-certainty?"—and answering that double question twice: once for sense-certainty and once for us.

The (double) answer to this question is given in the opening sentence of the next-to-last paragraph of "sense-certainty": "It is clear that the dialectic of sense-certainty is nothing else but the simple history of its movement or of its experience, and sense-certainty itself is nothing else but just this history (*Es erhellt, dass die Dialektik der sinnlichen Gewissheit nichts anders als die einfache Geschichte ihrer Bewegung oder ihrer Erfahrung, und die sinnliche Gewissheit selbst nichts anders als nur diese Geschichte ist*)" (*PhG*, 86). If the answer to the question "What is sense-certainty?" reads "Sense-certainty is (its own) history," this answer calls for a double reading—by us and by sense-certainty—and a rewriting of both question and answer. In spite of (or rather because of) its rhetoric of being and nothing (*nichts anders als. . .nichts anders als*), which echoes the first sentence, this answer forces us to reread Being—the "is," the copula—and thus the truth of sense-certainty. That is, Being—as object and as subject—has turned out to be the name not of the richness of immediacy but rather of an empty abstraction, a contentless universality, which in order not to mean *nothing*, to distinguish itself from nothing, has to be thought as mediated, as having and *being* a history: a history of sense-certainty's movement from one object of knowing to a new object of knowing. But whereas we realize that this movement is also an inversion of consciousness itself, that the new object of knowing—perception (*Wahrnehmung*), say—is also a new *subject* of knowing, natural consciousness forgets this, its own, history and has to begin the movement all over again and test its knowing against a new object that it takes as found, given, immediate, and not as what it *is*: that is, the result of a history (of knowing). "Natural consciousness also always reaches this result, which is what is true in it, and makes the experience of it; but it also forgets it again and again and begins the movement all over again (*Das natürliche Bewusstsein geht deswegen auch zu diesem Resultate, was an ihr das Wahre ist, immer selbst fort und macht die Erfahrung darüber; aber vergisst es nur ebenso immer wieder und fängt die Bewegung von vorne an*)" (*PhG*, 86). What this answer amounts to, then, is that the question "What is *X*?" is the wrong question and "*X* is. . ." is the wrong answer so long as we think the "is," the copula, undialectically, unspeculatively (i.e., in terms of the one-sided identities of formal logic). If in the dialectical movement that is its history sense-certainty learns (incompletely) how to read itself—that is, how to answer the question "What is. . .?"—we learn how to reread the question *of* that question—that is, to answer the question "What is the 'what is. . .?' "

Before we ask about the conditions of this speculative dialogue, the *scene* framed by such speculative question and answer, some more general remarks on the exemplary predicament of sense-certainty are in order. Commentators go astray when they take the "sense" in "sense-certainty" at face value and interpret this section as Hegel's critique of a "radical empiricism."[5] For rather than beginning with some kind of ineffable unity of knower and known, subject and object, we begin with a division that already marks the titles of this section: sense/certainty, the this/meaning. In short, we begin with certainty and not with the senses; any pristine, original experience untainted by the language of knowing has been discarded as soon as we introduce the word "consciousness" (*Bewusstsein*), which, in Hegel's thought, is always consciousness *of* something (and therefore always entails the given oppositions of knower/ known, subject/object, self/other, etc.). As we have already suggested in our remarks on the question of sense-certainty, Hegel's critique is directed not so much at sense-certainty as at its language, its rhetoric, a certain misreading of the verb "to be." In being unable to read the copula speculatively, sense-certainty is very much in the position of what Hegel calls *Vorstellung*—representation, sometimes translated as "conception" or "picture-taking." *Vorstellung* is an in-between activity or faculty of the mind that takes its content both from the senses and from thought. In a general sense, it is what we do everywhere and always (except when we read philosophical texts speculatively, i.e., except when we read *as* the "we"). In paragraph 20 of the *Encyclopedia of the Philosophical Sciences*, Hegel tries to distinguish this (picture-) thinking of *Vorstellung* from the thinking of thought. This is not such an easy matter, for "there are conceptions constituted by materials emanating from self-conscious thought, such as those of law, morality, religion and even of thought itself, and it requires some effort to detect wherein lies the difference between such conceptions and thoughts having the same import (*hat jedoch die Vorstellung auch Stoff zum Inhalt, der aus dem selbstbewussten Denken entsprungen ist, wie die Vorstellungen vom Rechtlichen, Sittlichen, Religiösen, auch vom Denken selbst, und es fällt nicht so leicht auf, worin der Unterschied solcher* Vorstellungen *von den* Gedanken *solchen Inhalts zu setzen sei*)" (VIII:72-73). The fault in *Vorstellung* is that it leaves the determinations of thought side by side in a relation of contiguity and is stuck either in empty and sterile tautology, saying that Right is Right, God is God, and so on, or it disperses itself in a multiplicity of isolated determinations again related to one another by mere contiguity, saying that God is the creator of the world, all-wise, almighty, and so on. In short, *Vorstellung* is torn between the one of an empty subject and the many of dispersed predicates, and it is in this sense like sense-certainty, which can only say that "this is this," "now is now," "here is here," and "sense-certainty is sense-certainty" on the one hand, or that "this (now and here) is the night, the day, a tree, a house," that "sense-certainty is this and that, now and then, here and there," on the other hand. According to paragraph 20, the reason *Vorstellung* leaves its determinations, its predicates, side by side is that it disregards the binding, linking, indicated to them in their subject (*der Verbindung ungeachtet, die ihnen in ihrem Subjekte angewiesen ist*) (VIII:73). What such an indicating, pointing, *sign*, that points to the binding of subject and predicate in the subject would be like is not clear from this context, but its nature is certainly problematic: that is, it would be a sign that points to itself, but the self that it points to would be less like a subject and more like an act, a binding contract (*Verbindung*), as it were, of the subject with itself. In other words, this sign-subject would be like an utterance whose status as either constative or performative cannot be decided: like the utterance "I am sorry," which may *state* that "I feel bad" or may *perform* the act "I apologize." In order to bind the two utterances of *Vorstellung*—"I am I" and "I am *A* and *B* and *C* and so on"—the subject has to say "I am sorry" to itself. Before deciding whether it has anything to apologize for (or feel bad about), let us determine more precisely the structure of the subject's dialogue with itself, for it may help us return to the speculative dialogue of "sense-certainty" and the "we."

In distinguishing conceptual, philosophical thinking (*begreifendes Denken*) from mere rationalizing, argumentation (*das Räsonnieren*)—a purely formal thinking (*formales Denken*) that can be identified with a *Vorstellung* that takes its content from thought—the Preface (*Vorrede*) to the *Phenomenology* distinguishes their readings of the proposition: whereas argumentation takes the subject as a fixed basis that it leaves behind when it goes over to its predicates, conceptual thinking reads the predicates as negations *of* the subject, that is, as negations belonging to the subject, which it uses to return to the subject in a movement of reflection. But this movement of reflection is by no means simple: "Usually, the Subject is first made the basis, as the *objective*, fixed self; from here the necessary movement to the multiplicity of determinations or predicates proceeds; here the knowing I itself steps into the place of the former subject and is the linking of the predicates and the subject holding them. But since that first subject enters into the determinations themselves and is their soul, the second subject, namely the knowing one, still finds in the predicate that which it thought to have finished with and through which it wants to return into itself, and instead of being able to be the agent as argumentation in the movement of the predicate, whether to attach this or that predicate, it rather still has to do with the self of the content, and should not be for itself but rather together with it (*Sonst ist zuerst das Subjekt als das* gegenständliche *fixe Selbst zu Grunde gelegt; von hier aus geht die notwendige Bewegung zur Mannigfaltigkeit der Bestimmungen oder der Prädikate fort; hier tritt an die Stelle jenes Subjekts das wissende Ich selbst ein und ist das Verknüpfen der Prädikate und das sie haltende Subjekt. Indem aber jenes erste Subjekt in die Bestimmungen selbst eingeht und ihre Seele ist, findet das zweite Subjekt, nämlich das wissende, jenes, mit dem es schon fertig sein und worüber hinaus es in sich zurückgehen will, noch im Prädikate vor, und statt in dem Bewegen des Prädikats das Tuende als Räsonnieren, ob jenem dies oder jenes Prädikat beizulegen wäre, sein zu können, hat es vielmehr mit dem Selbst des Inhalts noch zu tun, soll nicht für sich, sondern mit diesem zusammensein*)'' (*PhG*, 50-51).

If we seek enlightenment of this tortuous last sentence (of paragraph 60 of the Preface), and go to J. N. Findlay's commentary to the *Phenomenology* in the back of Miller's translation, we are thrown back, disappointed, onto this sentence. After a rather unhelpful paraphrase, the commentator adds, in parentheses, suddenly switching to telegram style: "(Paragraph very difficult owing to identification-in-distinction of the conscious with the logico-grammatical subject)." If the identification-in-distinction of the knowing with the "logico-grammatical subject" is what this sentence is about, it is no wonder that this sentence is so difficult, for its *subject* is precisely the dialectical movement itself. To paraphrase, after the second subject, the knowing "I" (*das wissende Ich*), steps into the place of the first subject (i.e., the subject of the proposition)—that is, after the proposition is understood, given a meaning, read, supported by an understanding subject who thus binds subject and predicates—it finds another subject which new subject is neither (1) simply the subject of argumentation (because that first subject has gone over into the predicates), nor (2) simply the addition of new predicates (because those predicates have been filled by the first subject's entering into them and becoming their soul), but rather (3) the self or the subject of the content itself. In other words, the second or knowing subject recognizes itself in the first subject, but because that first subject has gone over into its predicates, this recognition is not sterile tautology but the absorption of the second subject by the subject of the content itself. This falling of the second subject into the subject of the content is what makes this movement rigorously dialectical: the immanent movement of the content itself. If we reduce this properly dialectical sentence to the form of a proposition—for example, "the second subject finds the first subject in the predicate (*das zweite Subjekt findet das erste Subjekt noch im Prädikate vor*)" or "the second subject *is* the first subject (in the predicate) (*das zweite Subjekt ist das erste Subjekt [im Prädikate]*)"—we find that in order to read it we have to reperform the very movement that is its subject: that is, as readers of this sentence, *we* are the second subject who puts itself in the place of the (first) subject of the proposition; but just like that second (knowing) subject, what we find in the predicate of *this* proposition (i.e., "the first subject") is precisely the (first) subject that has entered into these predicates (i.e., "the second subject"). In short, neatly (and dialectically) enough, we, the second subject, find in the predicate ourselves, the second subject (which *was* the subject of the proposition but had entered into the predicate), and thereby become the subject of the content itself, in this case the (speculative) proposition itself. We cannot read Hegel's sentence (speculatively) without this sentence's reading us (speculatively).

If this movement is the general structure of the dialogue that takes place between the subject and itself, consciousness and self-consciousness, natural consciousness and the "we," "sense-certainty" and the "we," then two of its essential moments should be remarked: (1) the substitution of the first subject by the second knowing subject, which is in this case put in terms of a theater metaphor—"here the knowing I steps into the place of the first subject (*hier tritt an die Stelle jenes Subjekts das wissende Ich selbst ein*)"; and (2) the coming together of the second subject with the self of the content, which is here put in terms of the *ought*, the *should* ("ought, should, not be for itself but rather together with the self of the content [*soll nicht für sich, sondern mit diesen zusammensein*]"). When Hegel later illustrates this movement by the example "God is being (*Gott ist das Sein*)," the identification of the second subject with the subject of the content is again put in the mode of the "ought": "it [the subject] is still immersed into the content, or at least the demand is there that it be immersed into it (*ist es in den Inhalt noch vertieft, oder wenigstens ist die Forderung vorhanden, in ihn vertieft zu sein*)" (*PhG*, 51). In regard to the first moment, we ask: (1) what is the theater, the play, and the scene in which the second subject takes the place of the first? and (2) what is the nature of this substitution of one subject for the other? In regard to the second moment, we ask: (1) is the identification of the second subject with the subject of the content only one that *should* take place, a demand, or is it one that does take place? and (2) if it is a demand, what is its guarantee, its necessity? In short, does a recognition take place or only a demand for or claim to a recognition? If we try to answer the questions in regard to the first moment by going from the reading of the speculative proposition to the reading of the speculative presentation of sense-certainty, for example, the answers are clear: the theater in which the play of substitutions (of one subject for another) takes place is language, which, according to the last paragraph of sense-certainty, "has the divine nature of immediately inverting [converting, perverting] the meaning and making it into something else and thus not letting it *get into words at all (welches die göttliche Natur hat, die Meinung unmittelbar zu verkehren, zu etwas anderem zu machen und so sie gar nicht* zum Worte kommen *zu lassen)" (PhG*, 88-89). This *inversion* (*verkehren*) performed by language is very much like the inversion (*Umkehrung*) of (natural) consciousness itself as it travels the road of despair (*Weg der Verzweiflung*) from one figure of apparent knowing to the next; it is an inversion that "we" observe and indeed accomplish insofar as it "takes place, so to speak, behind the back of natural consciousness (*gleichsam hinter seinem Rücken vorgeht)" (PhG*, 74). As such, this inversion (*verkehren*) would be better translated as *conversion*, as Hans-Georg Gadamer interprets it in an essay on Hegel's passage on the "inverted world" (*verkehrte Welt*) in the *Phenomenology*: he notes "that ordinary German usage quite confidently distinguishes between *falsch* (false) and *verkehrt* (inverted or backward). Of course an answer that inverts things or gets them twisted is not correct, but the elements of truth are recognizable in it and only need to be put right. A false answer, on the other hand, contains no such possibility of making it right. Thus, for example, the information someone gives you can be called *falsch* if it is deliberately given with the intent of deceiving—but in such a case it could not be called *verkehrt*. For an answer that is *verkehrt* is always one that was meant to be correct and that turned out to be false. In this sense too the *malum* is the *conversio boni*."[6]

The dialectical conversion that takes place whenever the "we" confronts the "I" of natural consciousness, language confronts mere "opining" or "meaning" (*Meinung*), is structured like an exemplary moment of conversion in the New Testament: Christ's combat with Legion.[7] After Christ has crossed the sea and come ashore in a foreign land, "a man with an unclean spirit (*ein Mensch mit einem unsaubern Geist)"* (Markus 5:2) approaches him: "Who had his dwelling among the tombs; and no man could bind him, no, not with chains (*der seine Wohnung in den Grabhöhlen hatte. Und niemand konnte ihn mehr binden, auch nicht mit Ketten)"* (Markus 5:3). This man is unbound in a figurative sense as well, for when Christ asks him his name, the reply is: "My name is Legion: for we are many (*Legion heisse ich; denn wir sind viele)"* (Markus 5:9). That is, because he is possessed by many devils, the one man is simultaneously, metonymically, as it were, an "I" and a "we" that he/they cannot bind on his/their own: he is a walking anacoluthon. The *dénouement* of the story is well known: Christ allows the devils to be driven out of the man and into the swine (which are thereupon driven off a cliff and into the sea), thereby restoring him to his right reason and converting him into a disciple. This combat is for us exemplary of dialectical conversion on account of its essential moments: both symmetrical and asymmetrical. What we have here is a confrontation of Logos and Legion (etymologically, logologically, related to one another) with a one and a many on each side of the struggle, the difference being the difference on each side: Christ, the Logos, being bound (by the "Holy," as opposed to the "unclean," Spirit) to the many in the mystery of the Holy Trinity; Legion, the anti-Logos, completely unbound. If Christ is able to convert Legion into Logos or at least into a sign that points to the one Word, it is because he is able to read the anacoluthon of the "I" and the "we." This reading is properly speculative, properly dialectical, in that it takes place by means of an asymmetry in the combat, which amounts to a properly determinate negation. That is, whereas Christ does not give his name and yet, and therefore, is recognized immediately by Legion—as though there were an immediate understanding or contract between the god and the demon, Word and anti-Word—Legion's having to give his/their name can be taken as the moment and the sign of his/their falling into the power of the Logos. Christ here is, and wields the power of, the Negative: because he does not give his name, he is the no one who can bind Legion to himself ("and no one could bind him [*und niemand konnte ihn mehr binden*]"); Christ dis-possesses Legion of his "we" (the demons) and re-possesses Legion with his own "we" (the good Word, etc.). This story of dispossession and repossession is very much the story of *Vorstellung* and thought, the first subject (of argumentation) and the second (knowing) subject, "sense-certainty" and the "we"; and like these dialogues, it has for a condition the essential symmetry of the partners: Logos and Legion (the speculative "we" and the "I") share the terrain and the universe of discourse, no matter how negative the realm into which the Logos has to descend, how negative the negation. Indeed, the greater the negation— the land of the tombs, or death, ultimately—the greater the positive synthesis.

But not only can the story of Logos and Legion serve to illustrate—as by example—dialectical con-version, but it may also help us re-pose our question about the second moment of the dialectical movement—the coming together of the second subject wth the subject of the content, that is, whether it takes place or only a claim to it is made. Namely, is there another *verkehren*—one more like *per*version than *con*version—in language and by language that is not merely the inversion of the correct answer, that does not come up against it in the same universe ("turned into one") of discourse as other of the same? Is there an other Legion whose anacoluthon is not unbound and re-bound quite as easily—a Legion who does not give his/their name? Posing the question is not an easy matter, for we cannot simply take the side of Legion—with some kind of polytheism, pluralism, schizophrenia, or schizo-culture—but rather need an other point of view entirely. Perhaps one way to begin reading this story and

Hegel's story is, as it were, from the point of view of (pardon our saying so) the swine sacrificed for the glory of the Logos and determinate negation—a pure loss (about two thousand head, according to Mark), sheer excess. Finding the equivalent of this pure loss, sheer excess, in the play of substitutions, the dialogue, between sense-certainty and the "we" is also not an easy matter, for we cannot, again, simply take the side of sense-certainty (as some commentators have done). And since this excess (or lack?) would be a Legion that does not give his/their name—an unreadable anacoluthon, as it were—the task becomes more difficult because *language* is the theater in which this play (of substitutions, conversions, perversions) is staged. What is another Legion in the Logos? we ask, and try to remember that the "answer" to this "question" would be one that disarticulates such question and answer, such dialogue.

If we return to the dialogue of "sense-certainty" and the "we," we cannot help but remark a number of disquieting elements: first of all, the downright ludicrousness of the dialogical proceedings. Few commentators have failed to note the arbitrariness, unfairness, indeed bullying that victimized sense-certainty undergoes at the hands of the "we." Nietzsche mercilessly criticized Socrates' dialectical questioning—the bully Socrates surrounded by beardless youths and senile old men asks "What is the beautiful, the good, the just, and so on?" and receives an answer, for example, "Agathon is beautiful, good, just, and so on"—because the nature of his questions ("What is. . .?") already decided the matter beforehand (i.e., in metaphysical terms, in terms of essence and accidents, etc.). Nietzsche would be equally scornful of Hegel's procedure in sense-certainty.[8] For not only do we ask sense-certainty the same old question—for example, "What is the Now? (*was ist das Jetzt?*)"—but we do not even wait for it to answer—"we answer, for example: *the Now is night* (*antworten wir also zum Beispiel*: das Jetzt ist die Nacht)" (*PhG*, 81). The proceedings—especially in the case of the question "What is the Here?"—bear a suspicious resemblance to games played in a school playground at recess—for example, tapping someone's shoulder behind the back, causing him to turn his head that way, and then looming up on the other side: "*The Here is not a tree*, but rather *a house* (Das Hier ist nicht ein Baum, *sondern vielmehr* ein Haus)" (*PhG*, 82). This indecorousness—matched in the *Phenomenology* only by the crass humor of the section "Physiognomy and Phrenology" (*Physiognomik und Schädellehre*)—is somewhat distressing for anyone expecting "the earnestness, the pain, the patience and work of the negative (*der Ernst, der Schmerz, die Geduld und Arbeit des Negativen*)." Equally disquieting is all the textual paraphernalia in this episode of consciousness: for example, in order to test the truth of sense-certainty ("Now is the night"), we write it down and return, later, with this inscription to sense-certainty; and in the final paragraph there is even mention of "*this* piece of paper on which I write *this* or rather have written this (dieses *Stück Papier, worauf ich* dies *schreibe oder vielmehr geschrieben habe*)" (*PhG*, 88). And never mind the usual Hegelian surfeit of puns and wordplays—not only on *aufheben* (sublating) but on *mein* (possessive adjective) and *Meinung* (opinion), *wahr* (true) and *aufbewahren* (preserving), and so on. All this rampant "textuality" is certainly made to order for what is called "deconstructive" reading, and one could go far with it; in particular, the two skits on the "Now" and the "Here" lend themselves to readings that could be called "grammatological" and "rhetorical" (or "tropological") respectively. A good example of the former is Werner Hamacher's reading of the double inscription of the "Now." He shows that the very test, the very proof, of sense-certainty's inability to say *what* it means when it says "Now"—that is, its inability to say one, particular, self-identical, self-simultaneous "Now"—is based on another, one, self-identical, self-simultaneous moment of reading and writing during which the "we" is able to compare the first inscription ("Now is the night") and the second (implied) inscription ("Now is the day").[9] In other words, the question is precisely the question of Hegel's own text: the necessarily self-identical piece of paper on which he writes this and this, and is able to compare them (i.e., is able to read himself). The example of the "Here" lends itself well to a "tropological" reading insofar as it is put in terms of turning: "*The Here* is, e.g., the *tree*. I turn around, and this truth has disappeared and turned into its opposite (Das Hier *ist z.B. der* Baum. *Ich wende mich um, so ist diese Wahrheit verschwunden und hat sich in die entgegengesetzte verkehrt*)" (*PhG*, 82). The turning here plays the same role as the writing in the example of the "Now": it both suppresses a (particular) "Here" and preserves a (universal) "Here," but, at the same time (and in the same place), it presupposes a fixed point, a posited literal meaning, against which the turning or troping can be measured. In both readings, the *writing* and *turning* are constitutive (undialectically, untranscendentally) and can be taken as just different words for *Aufhebung* (sublation, supercession, or "elation" as Geoffrey Hartman translates it); what the deconstructive reading shows is that in the case of this one key word Hegel's System depends ultimately (undialectically) on the possibility of reading two mutually excluding meanings at once, simultaneously, and that this reading "at once" in a nonparticular and nonuniversal here and now is the condition of dialectical space and time and not vice versa. In short, to paraphrase too quickly, the only thing that cannot be *aufgehoben* (sublated) is *Aufhebung* (sublation) "itself," and Jean-Luc Nancy's *La Remarque spéculative* is a good example of the strategies of such readings.[10]

What we are seeking, however, is a less tangible, as it were, textual (stage?) "property," something less imposing than *Aufhebung* and ostensibly less scandalous and less visible than the example of writing. That is, we are less interested in the examples than in the strategy of example, exemplification, in this section, for examples—both visible and invisible—are ubiquitous in sense-certainty. For one thing, they mark the interplay between the "we" and sense-certainty, indeed, the passage from questions posed by the "we" to answers that *we* give, for example, in the place of, in the voice of, the "I" of sense-certainty. This is already a bit unsettling insofar as it provides a slightly different picture of the dialogue between the "I" and the "we" than we have been led to expect by the passage in the Preface on the first and the second subjects: not only do we, the knowing subject, step dramatically into the place of sense-certainty, but we do not even let it state that first proposition of the argumentative subject. But, again, it is not so much the victimization of the first subject (here of sense-certainty) that is the problem, but rather the linguistic nature of our speaking for it. That is, "for example" (*zum Beispiel*) here marks a shift between literal and figurative senses. When we ask "What is the Now?" and answer for sense-certainty, for example, "Now is the night," what we do is to take the question literally, as it were, as though we (playing the role of sense-certainty) did not hear the (invisible) quotation marks around the "Now." In short, playing the role of sense-certainty for example is not so much a matter of putting on and taking off masks as it is a question of reading and misreading. And this question cannot be spirited off the stage as easily as we dispose of the body of sense-certainty. One clue is the text's effacement of the act of reading (the example, for example) at the end of the passage on the "Now": when, at noon, we come back to the truth ("Now is the night") we have written down, we do not *read* it, according to the text, but we *look* at it: "If *now, this noon*, we look again at the written-down truth, we shall have to say that it has become stale (*Sehen wir* jetzt, diesen Mittag, *die aufgeschriebene Wahrheit wieder an, so werden wir sagen müssen, dass sie schal geworden ist*)" (*PhG*, 81). In any case, the question is: can we step up to sense-certainty and step back without losing or gaining anything while taking those steps? Can one assume the language of another without being tainted or contaminated or parasitized by it? The question, as always, is that of translation. In order to test the truth of translation, a simple experiment is sufficient: translate something into another language, German for example, and then try to get it back by *translating* back into English. A certain opacity, a certain asymmetry, is part of that process, an opacity and asymmetry that has nothing to do with the "faithfulness" of the translation or with particular and universal, immediacy and mediation, and the like, but rather with a shift of reading: that is, distinguishing literal and figurative senses. In short, if the passage between the knowing "we" and sense-certainty takes place for example (i.e., by the translation of example), then the (dialectical) symmetry of that relation is in question: that is, the relation is not one of a subject and an object who can come up against one another in the same space at the same time, but rather is a relation determined by the reading (and writing) of example, the translation of *Beispiel*.

Now, on the surface, Hegel's text is not at all bothered by example, by the translation of *Beispiel*. Indeed, it gives us a genetic history of the word as converted (like Legion) for the ends of the speculative "we." In the third paragraph of this section, Hegel's text makes a first distinction between the essence and the excess in sense-certainty: "But when we look at the *pure being* which makes up the essence of this certainty and which it pronounces as its truth, we see that much more is involved. An actual sense-certainty is not only this pure immediacy but an *example* of it (*An dem reinen Sein aber, welches das Wesen dieser Gewissheit ausmacht und welches sie als ihre Wahrheit aussagt, spielt, wenn wir zusehen, noch vieles andere beiher. Eine wirkliche sinnliche Gewissheit ist nicht nur diese reine Unmittelbarkeit, sondern ein* Beispiel *derselben*)" (*PhG*, 80). It is hard to tell exactly what the word "example" (*Beispiel*) means here, but the context and the first sentence of the following paragraph, which puts "example" (*Beispiel*) in opposition to "essence" (*Wesen*)—"This distinction between essence and example . . . (*Diesen Unterschied des Wesens und des Beispiels . . .)*"—makes it clear: *Beispiel* refers to that side of the knower/known, subject/object, relation which is taken to be inessential, accidental, that which is not the truth of knowing. As such, the word *Beispiel* seems to derive from Hegel's homemade verb *beiherspielen* (in the passage quoted above), which Miller renders as "is involved"—when we look at this pure being, "we see that much more is involved (*beiherspielt*)"—but which could be translated literally as "to play on the side"—that is, when we look at this pure being, we see that more is in play, that more is playing to the side of this essence like an excessive ornament or decoration. In short, sense-certainty not only is some pure immediacy but rather is made up of essence and accident, main event and side-show, play and by-play. But that the translation of *beiherspielen* (playing on the side) into *Beispiel* (example) is not unproblematic becomes clear when we look more closely at the translators' hesitancies in rendering *beiherspielen*: for *spielt noch vieles andere beiher*, Miller writes "much more is involved"; Baillie writes that "there is a good deal more implied in that pure being"; and Jean Hyppolite comes closest to the "literal" meaning with: *Mais dans ce pur étre. . . .il y a encore bien autre chose en jeu.* The translators are equally uncertain when the verb *beiherspielen* returns (twice) later in sense-certainty. In stating that the "Now" as universal is indifferent to particular "Now's" (like "Night" and "Day"), the text uses the formulation "*gleichgültig gegen das, was noch bei ihm herspielt* (indifferent to what plays to the side of it)" (*PhG*, 81); and later to express the indifference of the universal "I" to its particular apprehensions (of a house or a tree, etc.), the text says again "*gleichgültig gegen das, was noch beiher spielt* (indifferent toward that which plays to the side)" (*PhG*, 83). Miller renders these two as "indifferent to what happens in it"; Baillie, "indifferent to what is still associated with it"; and Hyppolite is again most "literal" in writing "*indifférent à ce qui se joue encore près de lui*" and "*indifférent à l'égard de tout ce qui est encore en jeu.*"

If we list these examples of properly untranslatable examples, it is to point out not only their ubiquity in the text of sense-certainty but also the fact that the translators do not know, cannot tell, what is involved, implied, associated with, or what happens, or is *en jeu* in Hegel's text when the verb *beiherspielen* makes its entrance. And it is important to know what or who is in play (or at work) when this verb enters, for it names that extra, accidental, inessential excess that at each stage of the argument is to be distinguished from the essence or truth of sense-certainty. The distinction between essence and example (*Beispiel*) is from the beginning clearly marked and clearly meant to govern the following reversals: sense-certainty begins by taking its object as the essence and its knowing as the example (*Beispiel*), but then finds that the object is impermanent and inessential, so it asserts that the subject, the "I," is the essential and the object is the example. But the problem is not just the meaning, the translation, of the verb *beiherspielen* (to play on the side) but rather its transformation into *Beispiel* (example)—the derivation of "example" from "playing on the side." Jean Hyppolite's footnote to the first occurrence of the verb and its translation into *Beispiel* helps pose the question: "Here Hegel uses the words 'Beispiel' and 'beiherspielen.' The example is what plays *to the side of* the essence. The particular and the universal do not interpenetrate (*Hegel emploie ici les mots 'Beispiel' et 'beiherspielen.' L'exemple est ce qui se joue* à côté de *l'essence. Le singulier et l'universel ne se pénètrent pas*)." Now Hegel is certainly entitled to play on the word *Beispiel* and to give it the meaning "paticular, inessential, excess" in opposition to "universal, essential, truth"—in short, as though it meant side-show, by-play—but the trouble is that he cannot reconcile this meaning with the meaning the word has in the two dialogues between the "we" and "sense-certainty": that is, an illustration, a story, a parable, a speaking on the side, by-spell. How mediate between playing on the side and saying on the side, by-play and by-spell, except by a pun, paronomasia (an other naming, naming besides)?.And the problem is serious insofar as in Hegel's original "derivation" of *Beispiel* from *beiherspielen*, the word *Beispiel* has both meanings: by-play and by-spell. That "an actual sense-certainty is not only this pure immediacy, but an example (*Beispiel*) of it" means both "by-play"—particular, inessential, and so on—and "example" as it later appears in the text (and as in its "normal" usage). And these two meanings are not reconcilable, not mediatable, because they are not symmetrically opposed: just as the relation universal/particular is of a different order and a different kind from the relation literal/figurative. Perhaps it is no accident, as one says, that "by-spell," the English cognate of *Beispiel*, meant not only "parable, proverb," but also "one whose worthlessness is proverbial, who becomes a byword" and "an illegitimate child, a bastard." Rather than a genetic history of *Beispiel*, the text's pun (as nontranslation) tells a story more like a "genealogy" in Nietzsche's sense: one that reveals an illegitimacy and a usurpation at and *as* the "origin."

Again, the problem is not the pun or Hegel's carelessness in choosing his words but rather the disarticulation of the dialogue of sense-certainty that the word *Beispiel* covers up. For rather than being any kind of carelessness, the wordplay on *Beispiel* becomes a (nondialectical) necessity as soon as we pose the question "What is sense-certainty?" and answer "Sense-certainty is sense-certainty and an example (*Beispiel*) of sense-certainty." That is, if we continue this line of questioning and ask "What is the question 'What is. . .?'?" we have to answer "The question is the question and an example of the question" and, again, "The answer is the answer and an example of the answer." Now all the examples in this chain are eminently dialectizable in that each is the name of a particular, immediate, sublatable excess—a too much by-play—that comes up against the Logos on the same terrain (even if the Logos has to descend among the tombs to convert it). But the logic of this self-questioning and self-answering Logos demands that we finally ask still another question—"What is the example?"—and find that we have to answer it: "The example is the example and an example of example." And this answer—this second (or third?), other example, the example *of* example—is one that "asymmetricalizes" the dialogue of speculative question and answer: that is, in the phrase "example of example," the word "of" marks a genitive whose ambiguity is not confined to the possibility of reading it as either objective or subjective genitive (and, dialectically mediated by a history of sense, as *both*) but rather one that disarticulates such (subjective or objective) genitive appropriation altogether. An example can never represent or exemplify itself enough *as* example to recover its own excess, the excess of example "itself," for there will always be one more (or less) as yet unreflected and forever unreflectable and unmediatable example left over or missing: + *Beispiel*.

The text's punning on *beiherspielen* and *Beispiel*—its (impossible) translation of one into the other (when each is not the other *of* the other)—is one mark of *this* example (of example), *Beispiel* of *Beispiel*, but its traces are disseminated throughout Hegel's text in that to ask a question and to give an answer is not just to ask a question and give an answer but also to give an example of asking a question and giving an answer. In short, insofar as we can never question and answer without giving examples of question and answer, all questions and all answers are always already parasitized by the question (and the "answer") of the example of example, *Beispiel* of *Beispiel*. In other words, when "Hegel," the text, in the third paragraph of sense-certainty says "example" (*Beispiel*), he says example—better, reads and writes example—*for* example, and that ("for") in two senses: (1) he says example in place of example "itself" in that he usurps the one (usual) meaning of the word (parable, illustrating narrative, by-spell) and puts in its place another meaning (playing on the side, by-play); and (2) he says "example" *for* example (i.e., *as* example, as example of saying "example"). And because to say this latter example *for* example always means to give the example *of* example, it is impossible to *say* it. We cannot speak *for* example without the example's speaking *for* us, that is, without the example's turning us into an example (of saying "we"), so that we do not know whether we are *saying* "we" or *quoting* "we" (i.e., giving an *example* of saying). In short, speaking for example is always in danger of speaking *against* itself, but nonoppositionally; hence it would be better to say (read or write) that speaking *for* example is always in danger of speaking *by* itself. And such a speaking, such a saying of the example *for* example, of the example *for* us, is not what the Preface had in mind when it demanded that we the knowing subject fall into the text and become one with the subject of the content, for *this* speaking is not that of a self or a subject but of example, *Beispiel*, "itself." Reading (and writing) for example would be the simulacrum of "conceptual thinking" (*begreifendes Denken*). The fact that our speculative reading of the sentence on the first and the second subjects cannot take place unless in addition to distinguishing the identity and the difference of the first and second subjects we also read (and write) the first and the second subjects as within or without quotation marks would be a reminder of the claim of *Beispiel* and reading for example. Like Legion, *Beispiel*, example, says (reads and writes): "Example is my name, for we are many (*Beispiel heisse ich; denn wir sind viele*)"—a sentence in which the asymmetry of calling, naming (*heissen*), and being (*sein*) is to be read as a mark, the signature, of *Beispiel*, example, "itself," the one and the many that does/do not give its/their name. If "Hegel" had been able to read *this* example, if he had known what "we"—who, we?—know, he would not have been able to write (the *Phenomenology of Spirit*, for example), but he would perhaps have written something else (for example, Nietzsche's *Zarathustra*?). In other words, what we do—when we read not as a "we" but for example—here and now, everywhere and always, is to read the Hegel (a Hegel? *un Hegel*?) who could not, did not, write (except for example, except the *Phenomenology of Spirit* for example) but who nevertheless (always already and always not yet) wrote something else for example.

Epilogue

Epilogue
Dreadful Reading
Blanchot on Hegel

No rereading of Blanchot in the 1980s can take place without coming up against what a fragment from "Fragmentaire" calls "the dread of reading" (*l'angoisse de lire*): "The dread of reading: it is that every text, no matter how important and how interesting it may be (and the more it gives the impression of being so), is empty—it does not exist at bottom (*il n'existe pas dans le fond*); it is necessary to clear an abyss, and if you don't jump, you don't understand."[1] If in order to understand (reading and the dread proper to it) we have to clear the abyss of the text's essential nonexistence, it may be good to know what this nonexistence comes down to. Rather than proceeding directly to the text of Blanchot and its nonexistence—and thereby risking a too immediate answer to the question of (the existence or nonexistence of) his text—we would take a detour and begin by way of the question of reading: as a pretext, then, Blanchot's reading of Hegel, in particular the *Phenomenology of Spirit*—an apparently existent text if there ever was one. Another fragment from "Fragmentaire" provides us with something like a kit for rereading Hegel through Blanchot: "One cannot 'read' Hegel except by not reading him. To read him, not to read him, to understand him, to misunderstand him, to refuse him, falls under the decision of Hegel, or it does not take place. Only the intensity of this nonplace, in the impossibility that there be one, disposes us for a death—death of reading, death of writing—that leaves Hegel living, in the imposture of the finished Sense. (Hegel is the impostor, that is what renders him invincible, crazy for his gravity (*fou de son sérieux*), counterfeiter of Truth.)"

On the one hand, this fragment formulates the dread of the reader in the face of Hegel's System: whether you read Hegel or do not read him, you will regret it because in either case you will have been read *by* Hegel. That is, to read Hegel—the *Phenomenology of Spirit*, for example—means to follow at a distance and immerse oneself in the dialectical movement of knowing's (*das Wissen*) examining itself as the philosophical observer who is both superfluous and necessary, who puts himself in by leaving himself out, the "we" of the text. In short, the reader of Hegel—objective genitive—inscribes himself, is already inscribed, in the *Phenomenology* as the book's own "we" and thereby becomes the reader of *Hegel*—subjective genitive—Hegel's own reader. But even *not* to read Hegel—to misunderstand him, to refuse him—falls under the decision of Hegel precisely to the extent that it defines and identifies itself as the refusal *of*, or in opposition to, Hegel, the System. That is, the refusal to read Hegel, like all (mere) negations, has a positive content—it is always the negation *of* something, in this case the negation of Hegel and therefore still belongs to him, Hegel's own negation. The familiar work of determinate negation ensures that reading or not reading Hegel will not make a difference. And yet, on the other hand—and this would have to be a third, other, hand since both one and two turned out to be the hands of Hegel—the writing of the fragment begins to make an imperceptible difference once we begin reading it. For the text gives us not only the difference between reading Hegel and its negation, but also the difference between reading and "reading"—in quotation marks. However we read this third, other, neuter (*neither* one, reading, *nor* the other, not reading) reading in quotation marks, it is clear that its difference is not easily masterable by a thought whose motor is determinate negation: for "reading"—in quotation marks—cannot be thought as the negation (of reading or not reading), it can only be. . .read. Whatever else it does, such a reading opens up a space for the reading of this fragment and a rewriting of its terms differently, otherwise. For one thing, we can now read the "or" in "or it does not take place" (*ou cela n'a pas lieu*) as meaning not "in other words" but "on the other hand." That is, a reading of Hegel that would not fall under the decision of Hegel would have to be one that did not take place—but in a sense of not taking place different from, other than, the opposition to take place/not to take place. In other words, it would be an other not taking place that is not the negation of taking place—an other negative. It is such an other negative that the fragment introduces by taking advantage of the French idiomatic expression *avoir lieu* (to take place, to happen) to create a nonplace (*non-lieu*) that is not the negation of place—a space in which the reading of Hegel in quotation marks (neither reading nor not reading) can take place without taking place. It is necessarily impossible that there *be* such a nonplace, for its space (and time) would necessarily be other than that of any dialectical logic or ontologic. So: a nonhappening is turned into an impossible nonplace where we are supposed to read, Hegel, in quotation marks—a reading that makes necessary a rewriting of both the "we" and "death" in a different sense, in a sense different from the "finished Sense" (*Sens achevée*) of Hegel.

Small wonder, then, that reading—Hegel, for example—is dreadful, for it comes up against a Nothing that does not turn over into Being (nor does it reveal and conceal Being) but rather rereads and rewrites Nothing. (This is perhaps how we should read Hegel's "invincibility." As another fragment from "Fragmentaire" puts it: "The correct critique of the System does not consist of catching it in error [as one often delights in doing] or in interpreting it as insufficient [this happens even to Heidegger] but to render it invincible, uncritiquable, or, as one says, un-get-around-able. Thus, nothing escaping its omnipresent unity and recollection of everything, no more place remains for fragmentary writing [*il ne reste plus de place à l'écriture fragmentaire*] except to disengage as the necessary impossible [*sauf à se dégager comme le nécessaire impossible*]: that which therefore writes itself in the name of the time outside time, in a suspension that, unreservedly [*sans retenue*], breaks the seal of the unity, precisely in not breaking it, but in leaving it to the side [*de côté*] without one's being able to know it." In other words, the third, other, neuter reading of Hegel is not a dialectical trick—like, say, Hegel's critique of what he calls the bad infinity [an infinity that does not include finitude is finite, limited by the finitude it does not include] or of "absolute difference" [an absolute difference is different from everything, including itself, difference, and therefore turns over into absolute identity]—rendering the System invincible in order to demonstrate that its invincibility is limited by its not containing "vincibility" but rather a rewriting of its seal of invincibility elsewhere, otherwise, on the side.)

Such a rewriting of Hegel's negative in another place, to the side, is what takes place in Blanchot's readings of Hegel in the 1940s—in particular "Literature and the Right to Death" (La Littérature et le droit à la mort")[2]—and what accounts for their peculiar "distance" from the text of the *Phenomenology* as formulated in the essay's first footnote: "It should be understood that the remarks that follow are quite remote (*fort loin*) from the text of the *Phenomenology* and make no attempt to illuminate (*éclairer*) it." If we remember this footnote, we will not make the mistake of charging Blanchot with having taken out of context and mixed up specific moments of different dialectics in the *Phenomenology*: the attempt is not to explain Hegel but to rewrite him in an other place. But it is also no answer to dismiss this rewriting as Blanchot's flippant "tendency to allegorize philosophical texts as parables of writing," for the question remains: what does such allegorization mean for and do to the reading of the *Phenomenology*? In order to determine the other place, to the side, in which moments of the *Phenomenology* as diverse as Hegel's remarks on death in the Preface, the dialectics of work, of universal freedom and Terror, the unhappy consciousness, master and slave, etc., can all be read as though on the same level and rewritten into parables of writing, we will begin with Blanchot's rewriting of Hegel on (the) work and Hegel on death: what takes place (and where), what difference does it make, when work and death are read as writing? In regard to work, an immediate answer would be: nothing takes place, it makes no difference, for here Blanchot's essay seems to follow Hegel quite closely. Just as in the *Phenomenology* the individual (*das Individuum*) who is going to take action finds himself "in a circle in which each moment already presupposes the other"—that is, he can know the end or goal (*Zweck*) of his action only from the act, but he can act only if he already has that end or goal—so in Blanchot's essay the writer finds himself in a double bind: "He has no talent until he has written, but he needs talent in order to write (*Il n'a du talent qu'après avoir écrit, mais il lui en faut pour écrire*)."

And yet substituting "writer" for "individual" here makes all the difference to the resolution of the double bind, to how one breaks the circle and begins to take action or to write. For the individual, there is an immediate way out, indeed, immediacy *is* the way out: "The individual who is going to act seems, therefore, to find himself in a circle in which each moment already presupposes the other, and thus he seems unable to find a beginning, because he only gets to know his original nature, which must be his End (*Zweck*), *from the deed*, while, in order to act, he must have that End beforehand. But for that very reason he has to start immediately (*unmittelbar*), and, whatever the circumstances, without further scruples about beginning, means (*Mittel*), or End, proceed to action; for his essence and *intrinsic* nature (*ansichseiende Natur*) is beginning, means, and End, all in one."[3] That is, as Hegel continues, the beginning is provided by the given circumstances (*vorgefundene Umstände*) in which the individual finds himself—this is the "in itself" (*an sich*) of the individual—the end is the "interest" (*Interesse*) that the individual posits (*setzt*) for himself—this is the "for itself" (*das seinige*) of the individual—and "the union and sublation of this opposition (*die Verknüpfung und Aufhebung dieses Gegensatzes*)" is the means (*Mittel*). In short, taking immediate (*unmittelbar*) action is the means (*Mittel*) that mediate between the individual's circumstances and interest, what it finds and what it posits, in itself (*an sich*) and for itself (*für sich*), immediacy and mediation. But then what about the writer? Can he break the circle by beginning to write immediately? The writer's circumstances, his given in itself, are that he cannot write until he has written (i.e., that he is not a writer *before* he has written), but that once he has written he is no longer writing (i.e., that he is not a writer *after* he has written): he is always not yet and always no longer a writer writing. (As Blanchot's *Après coup* puts it: "From the 'not yet' to the 'no longer,' such would be the itinerary of what one calls the writer [*Du 'ne pas encore' au 'ne plus,' tel serait le parcours de ce qu'on nomme l'écrivain*].")

The writer's interest—the end or goal he posits for himself—is to *be* a writer, and this interest cannot be mediated with the circumstances of his always not yet and always no longer being a writer because the means are lacking. That is, the writer's only means are writing, but writing is not a means; it does not take place immediately, here and now, but always in a different place and a deferred time—not yet, no longer, suspended, interrupted. In short, there is no such thing as beginning to write immediately—writing neither begins nor ends—and hence the writer takes a different way out. He writes (the means) the impossibility (the circumstances) of being (the interest) a writer: a nonsynthesis, a nonaction, exterior to itself. And yet if writing "must be recognized as the highest form of work"—as Blanchot's essay puts it—its conditions would necessarily be, on the one hand, the conditions of possibility of all work and, on the other hand, the conditions of *im*possibility of all work in that the condition of writing is the unmediatability of beginnings and ends, circumstances and interest, immediacy and mediation, and so on. Hence to substitute the work of the writer for the work of the individual would mean, in the case of the *Phenomenology*, to replace the order of presentation (*Darstellung*) by the order of that which makes the presentation possible—but which needs to be excluded because it also makes it impossible. A good example of the way writing functions as an excluded condition of possibility and impossibility for the work of dialectical mediation is a skit that dramatizes the critique of the immediacy claimed by the first figure of apparent knowing in Hegel's *Phenomenology*: sense-certainty.

The "work" of sense-certainty, what it claims as its truth, is the most immediate kind of apprehension of Being as "the this" under the double aspect of the "Now" and the "Here." After asking sense-certainty "What is the Now?" and answering for example "The Now is the Night," the critique of sense-certainty tests its truth: "To test the truth of this sense-certainty, a simple experiment is sufficient. We write down this truth; a truth can't lose anything by being written down; much less can it lose anything from our preserving it. If we look again at this written down truth *now, this noon*, we shall have to say that it has become stale."[4] Now the critique of sense-certainty's truth hardly requires comment: instead of an immediate, particular now, sense-certainty, as soon as it says anything, is able to say only a mediated, universal now that is indifferent to the particularity of night and day. But more interesting for our purposes here is the work of writing that allows the critique to take place; that is, in spite of the fact that neither sense-certainty nor we can say an immediate, particular, self-identical Now (or Here), our critique of that Now depends on another self-identical Now (and Here), a self-simultaneous moment, in which we were able to read and compare "Now is the night" and "Now is the day." In other words, the very critique of sense-certainty's Now and Here requires another Now—a time of reading—and another Here—a place of writing: it requires, in short, this piece of paper on which I write this and this.[5] But, of course, this piece of paper on which I write and read this is not the particular piece of paper sewn into my copy of the *Phenomenology* and that I can see, touch, smell, and taste. It is also not the particular piece of manuscript paper preserved in the Hegel archives in Bochum on which Hegel wrote "Now is the day" and "Now is the night" and compared them. To identify it with *that* piece of paper would be to fall back into the position of sense-certainty: the Now of reading and of writing is not one we can see; it can only be written and read. This does not mean that we are talking about an ideal, universal piece of paper, as it were. No, this piece of paper on which I write "Now is the day" and "Now is the night" and read them is the material condition of possibility of the opposition between particular and universal. It is neither the particular, immediate, phenomenal piece of paper available to the senses nor the universal, mediated, intelligible piece of paper available to the mind, but other: a piece of paper that exists in the here and how of writing and reading. It is a piece of paper conditioned by the materiality (as distinguished from phenomenality) of reading and writing. And the necessary exclusion of this conditioning materiality from Hegel's construction and critique of sense-certainty's phenomenality is readable in the text's suppression of the act of reading: when we come back to sense-certainty now, this noon, with the piece of paper on which we had written "Now is the night," we do not *read* it, says the text, but rather look at it (*sehen. . . wieder an*)—when it is only *reading* the inscription that will allow us to compare night and day.

This switch from reading to looking—from the materiality of the text to the phenomenality of the book, from something that can only be written or read to something that can be the object of a consciousness's knowledge—is a necessary condition of the *Phenomenology*, what allows it to begin and end by mediating beginning and end. For in order to begin, Hegel, like the individual, has to begin immediately with the given circumstances of immediate knowing and the posited end—absolute knowing, the Absolute—a standard against which he can measure all too immediate forms of knowing. But to do so he has to forget the means—writing: the material fact that the Absolute in order to be (i.e., to become) has to have been *not* presupposed and posited (nor, as Heidegger would have it, dis-concealed) but *written*. In short, in order to begin Hegel has to forget the material fact that he has already begun in a way he should not have, in a way that makes all beginning (and all ending) impossible: with an inscription of the Absolute, here and now (i.e., somewhere and sometime else). Without such forgetting the work of the *Phenomenology* would become the impossible work of writing—always not yet and always no longer written. That is, the impossibility of *writing* the *Phenomenology* would become readable: the *presentation* (*Darstellung*) of the *Phenomenology* is possible, its writing, no; the writing of a *text* is possible, the writing of a *work* (like the *Phenomenology*), no. The writing of the text takes place elsewhere in a nonplace written by a "Hegel"—in quotation marks—who could not, did not, write the *Phenomenology of Spirit*—a Hegel more like a Nietzsche or a Blanchot. This would be one way to read the nonexistence of the text—the *Phenomenology*, for example—at bottom. (It would also be one way of justifying Blanchot's taking different moments of different dialectics out of context and rewriting them as though they were on the "same level." They *are* on the same level, for his reading takes place on the level of the *text*, the space and time not of the dialectical presentation [*Darstellung*], but the other space and time of the writing [and reading] of the text.)

If Blanchot's reading of work as writing makes work impossible (and yet is its condition of possibility), death read as writing makes death impossible (and yet is its condition of possibility). It is important to distinguish this death without death—language, literature, writing, the word, as the "life that endures death and maintains itself in it (*das Leben. . .das ihn erträgt und in ihm sich erhält*)," a phrase that is rewritten several times in "Literature and the Right to Death"—from the deaths of Hegel. In the "Introduction" to the *Phenomenology* Hegel himself distinguishes between two deaths: that of natural life and that of consciousness. What is limited to a natural life (*natürliches Leben*), he says, cannot by itself go beyond its immediate existence, but it is driven out beyond it by something else, and this something else is its death. Consciousness, however, is driven out beyond its immediate existence by a violence it suffers at its own hands: that is, because it is its own concept (*Begriff*), because it carries its own standard (of the truth of knowing: the Absolute) within itself, it is constantly dissatisfied with its immediate existence. In short, consciousness is always also self-consciousness; it carries its own death within itself. And this necessary condition of consciousness—the fact that it can and has to make its own death an object of (self-)consciousness—is what distinguishes it from mere "natural life." A cat squashed by a truck does not *die*, properly speaking; its "natural life" is, as it were, extinguished. But unlike the cat, consciousness can die because it can know its own death; it can represent its own death to itself—indeed, such self-representation is the "truth" of consciousness (i.e., self-consciousness). In other words, a condition of consciousness is its having to represent its own death to itself, but such representation is not possible without a subterfuge, as Bataille would put it: in order to be "we," we have to die while watching ourselves die. We require a spectacle, theater, sacrifice, a comedy in which we can represent our own death to ourselves and survive it.

But Blanchot recognizes that this comedy of sacrifice—identifying our own death, ourselves, in the extinguishment of a cat, say—is a linguistic operation, a matter of (impossible) *signification* rather than representation, since death is not a something (or a nothing) that can ever become an object of consciousness's knowing; just as I cannot *experience* death, I can only name it, impose a sense on it (by catachresis, say), give it a face, eyes, and a point of view (by prosopopoeia, as Hegel does when he speaks of looking into the face [*Angesicht*] of death). In order to bring death into the world, we (in order to be "we") bring death into the word. And from the point of view of what Blanchot calls everyday language, the word "death," like all words, works—by negation: "for a moment everyday language is right, in that even if the word excludes the existence of what it designates, it still refers to it through the thing's nonexistence, which has become its essence. To name the cat is, if you like, to make it into a noncat, a cat that has ceased to exist, has ceased to be a living cat, but this does not mean one is making it into a dog, or even a nondog." Death, in the word, works all right, but what Blanchot calls literary language observes that "the word cat is not only the nonexistence of the cat, but a nonexistence made *word*, that is, a completely determined and objective reality." In other words, the word "cat" gives us not only the noncat, the cat in his nonexistence, but also the *word* "cat," just as the word "death" gives us not only a nondeath, the negation *of* death that we can put to work in the world, but also an other death in its determinate and objective reality—a linguistic death, the death of the word. And this third, other death—the death without death—falls completely out of the grasp of a consciousness or a self or a subject. When I say "I die," I suffer the death of the impossibility of dying: on the one hand, saying "I die" is the condition of possibility of any "I" whatsoever; on the other hand, "I die" is not anything that can be said *by* an "I" since death can have no, *is* no, subject. At most, I can say "I dies"—in other words, I can never *say* my own death, I can only write (or read) it as the death of an other "I," a linguistic, grammatical subject, someone or something else's. In short, in order to *be* an "I," I must say "I die" while forgetting that I could never have said it—that in saying it I turn myself into *the* "I" and say "I dies"—while forgetting that I could only have *written* it and thereby had dispossessed myself of my "I" and my own death (death as negation) forever. (So: just as writing was the condition of [im]possibility of the work, so writing is the conditon of [im]possibility of death.)

Blanchot's reading of work and death in Hegel as writing is particularly helpful for a rereading of the famous passage in the Preface of the *Phenomenology* quoted repeatedly in "Literature and the Right to Death," and the master/slave dialectic—one place where work and death are explicitly conjoined—to which that passage points. "The life of Spirit," writes Hegel, "is not the life that shrinks from death and keeps itself untouched by devastation, but rather the life that endures it and maintains itself in it." In the struggle for self-recognition, it would seem to be the master who looks death in the face, who is willing to risk death for the sake of recognition, whereas the slave becomes the slave because he shrinks from death, is not willing to risk his life. But, of course, the master's "victory" is already his loss, for the death he faces is only natural death and the life he risks is only "natural life." That is, the master is willing to give up his life in its immediacy, but because he is willing to give up this immediacy *too immediately*, he falls back into an immediate relation to nature. In other words, the slave now satisfies immediately the master's merely appetitive, natural needs, and the master does not have to work to satisfy them; he does not have to exercise his freedom on nature by appropriating it. It is the slave who—precisely because he was afraid of natural death, because he was not willing to give up his natural life—looks the death of consciousness in the face: he gives his death a name and a face—master death—and thereby appropriates, masters, death by working nature, putting (natural) death to work. This is a familiar dialectic. Blanchot's supplementary insight consists in noting that the slave's very first work—giving voice to his dumb (*stumm*) absolute fear of death, naming death as his own negation—- brings into the world still another, third, neuter death, whose excess can never be re-covered by the work of (determinate) negation. It is thanks to this excess of death—death as written (and read)—that the System works like an invincible impostor.[6]

Notes

All translations are the author's unless otherwise attributed.

Reading Chiasms: An Introduction

1. Jacques Derrida, *Of Grammatology*, trans. G. C. Spivak (Baltimore: Johns Hopkins University Press, 1976), p. 200.

2. Pierre Aubenque, *Le Problème de l'être chez Aristote* (Paris: P.U.F., 1966), pp. 460-72.

3. Wolfgang Iser, *The Act of Reading* (Baltimore: Johns Hopkins University Press, 1980), pp. 130-31.

4. Philippe Lacoue-Labarthe, "The Cesura of the Speculative," *Glyph* 4 (Baltimore: Johns Hopkins University Press, 1978), p. 83.

5. Henri Morier, *Dictionnaire de poétique et de rhétorique* (Paris: P.U.F., 1961), p. 77.

6. John W. Welch, "Introduction," in *Chiasmus in Antiquity: Structures, Analyses, Exegesis*, ed. J. W. Welch (Hildesheim: Gerstenberg, 1981), p. 11.

7. John W. Welch, "Chiasmus in Ancient Greek and Latin Literatures," in *Chiasmus in Antiquity*, p. 251.

8. Ibid., p. 252.

9. Samuel E. Bassett, "Hysteron Proteron Homerikos," *Harvard Studies in Classical Philology 31 (1920):45*.

10. Quoted after Jean Greisch, *Herméneutique et grammatologie* (Paris: Ed. du CNRS, 1977) p. 216.

11. Kathleen Freeman, *Ancilla to the Pre-Socratic Philosophers* (Cambridge, Mass.: Harvard University Press, 1983), p. 25.

12. Plato, *The Collected Dialogues*, ed. E. Hamilton and H. Cairns (Princeton: Princeton University Press, 1980), p. 540 (187a-b).

13. Paul de Man, *Allegories of Reading* (New Haven: Yale University Press, 1979), p. 113.

14. Jacques Derrida, *Positions*, trans. A. Bass (Chicago: Chicago University Press, 1981), p. 70.

15. Jacques Derrida, *Dissemination*, trans. B. Johnson (Chicago: Chicago University Press, 1981), pp. 127-28.

16. "The chiasmus bends with a supplementary deflection." Jacques Derrida, *Archeology of the Frivolous*, trans. John P. Leavy (Pittsburgh: Duquesne University Press, 1980), p. 134.

17. Derrida, *Dissemination*, p. 127.

18. Jacques Derrida, "The *Retrait* of Metaphor," *Enclitic* 2, no. 2 (Fall 1978):14.

19. Jacques Derrida, "Living On: *Border Lines*," in *Deconstruction and Criticism*, ed. H. Bloom et al. (New York: Seabury, 1979), pp. 100-101.

20. Ibid., p. 97.

21. Ibid., p. 166.

22. Ibid., p. 100.

23. Ibid., p. 103.

24. Maurice Merleau-Ponty, *The Visible and the Invisible*, trans. A. Lingis (Evanston: Northwestern University Press, 1968), pp. 268, 193, and 130.

25. Ibid., pp. 139-40.

26. Ibid., p. 152.

27. Ibid., p. 147.

28. Ibid., p. 155 and 147.

29. Whereas for Merleau-Ponty, the sensible qualities of the reversing function of the chiasm limit the synthesizing power of the prereflexive opening toward the world (without, for that matter, limiting its generality), the elementary opening on the world that Bachelard calls "reverie", which also relies on chiasmic crisscrossing, gives rise to effectively integrated totalities. The prerational and prereflexive states of experiential plenitude that Bachelard thematizes are, therefore, distinguished by repose, happiness, fullness, and so on. Yet, although the synthesizing power of chiasmic reversal in reverie is not put into question by Bachelard, but forcefully emphasized instead, the unbreached totalities it engenders are, for him, always concrete, particular, and finite openings. As in Merleau-Ponty, this finitude, however, does not impinge on the generality of these openings toward the world. See Gaston Bachelard, *The Poetics of Reverie*, trans. D. Russell (Boston: Beacon Press, 1971).

30. Jacques Derrida, "The Law of the Genre," *Glyph* 7 (Baltimore: Johns Hopkins University Press, 1980), p. 219.

31. Let us also note that on several occasions Derrida has pointed to the fact that the logic that rules philosophy's desire to achieve closure and continuity resembles the "sophistry" of the borrowed kettle Freud refers to in *Interpretation of Dreams* and in *Jokes and Their Relation to the Unconscious*. Yet, does the contradictory coherence designated by the "sophistry" in question not represent a kind of perversion of chiasmatic totalization and, thus, a "symptom" of the impossibility of philosophy's ever achieving its goal? Now, since deconstruction must be understood as the attempt to account for philosophy's contradictory coherence, it may well be that its critical relation to chiasm as a device productive of philosophical continuity is much broader and more essential than we have outlined here.

32. Unfortunately this text was finished before we could consult Jean-François Mattèi's essay on the chiasm in Martin Heidegger's work. See Dominique Janicaud and Jean-François Mattèi, *La métaphysique à la limite* (Paris: P.U.F., 1983), pp. 49-162.

33. "The essence of a riddle consists in describing a fact by an impossible combination of words." (Aristotle, *Poetics*, trans. W. H. Fyfe [Cambridge, Mass.: Harvard University Press, 1927], 1458a 24-30.) Let us recall here that the riddle called either *ainigma* or *griphos* in Greek takes its name from a specific kind of fishnet of homologous designation. Indeed, the riddle is braided in the same way as a fishnet, that is, through intertwinement of opposite terms. See Konrad Ohlert, *Rätsel und Gesellschaftsspiele der alten Griechen* (Berlin: Mayer & Miller, 1886).

34. de Man, *Allegories of Reading*, p. 49.

Prefatory Postscript: Interpretation and Reading

1. Maurice Blanchot, *L'Espace littéraire* (Paris; Gallimard, 1955); modified English translation from *The Space of Literature* (Lincoln, Neb.: University of Nebraska Press, 1982).

2. For an instructive reading of deconstruction's strategy in relation to politics, see Wlad Godzich, "The Culture of Illiteracy," which appears as "Die politische Ent-stellung des Post-Strukturalismus" in *Hefte für kritische Literaturwissenschaft* 5 (Frankfurt: Suhrkamp, 1984).

3. On deconstruction and the institution, see Derrida's remarks on women's studies in "A Seminar with Jacques Derrida," entitled "Women in The Beehive," *subjects/objects* (Spring 1984): 5-19. The point for deconstruction, then, is neither to remain outside the institution (of the university, for example) or to demand a place within the institution alongside of other approaches (e.g., Marxian, psychoanalytic, New Critical, historicist, etc.)—for then it would only confirm the institution and its Law (phallogocentric, metaphysical, etc.)—but rather to institute a different, other relation to the institution. Reading "deconstruction" is already a way to begin, since the institution (departments of philosophy, literature, etc.) is constituted by nonreading, and *not* reading deconstruction is its strategy of defusing it.

4. We quote from Schlechta's edition of Nietzsche's *Werke I* (Munich: Carl Hanser, 1969) and modify Walter Kaufmann's translation of *The Birth of Tragedy* (New York; Random House, 1967).

5. Sarah Kofman, *Nietzsche et la scène philosophique* (Paris: Union Générale d'Éditions, 1979), pp. 76-77. The final phrase is an allusion to Bernard Pautrat, *Versions du soleil* (Paris: Editions du Seuil, 1971).

6. Kofman, *Nietzsche*, p. 80.

7. It is a strategy that comes out of a certain, I would say premature, reading of Derrida's "White Mythology" best exemplified in Philippe Lacoue-Labarthe's suggestive essay "Le détour," first version in *Poétique* 5 (1971):53-76, now in Lacoue-Labarthe's *Le Sujet de la philosophie* (Paris: Aubier-Flammarion, 1979). See Paul de Man's critique of this strategy in "Genesis and Genealogy," *Allegories of Reading* (New Haven: Yale University Press, 1979).

8. Kofman, *Nietzsche*, p. 80.

9. In other words, Kofman, in order to account for Nietzsche's "displacement" of the metaphysical point of view by "rhetoric," would have to think rhetoric "un-metaphysically"—read rhetoric as text—and this her interpretation cannot do.

10. Paul de Man, "Genesis and Genealogy," in *Allegories of Reading*, p. 92.

11. Paul de Man, "Shelley Disfigured," in *The Rhetoric of Romanticism* (New York: Columbia University Press, 1984), p. 118.

12. Our reading of the metaphor's nonsense can be taken as a reading of a footnote (that speaks volumes) in Paul de Man, "Reading (Proust)," in *Allegories of Reading*, pp. 60-61.

13. Nietzsche, "Über Wahrheit and Lüge im aussermoralischen Sinne," *Werke III*, ed. Schlechta, p. 313.

14. It is a figure that *does* what it *says, performs* (like a kind of little tragedy) what it *states* (its truth), and since what it states (its truth) is the statement that there is a discrepancy, a radical disjunction, between saying (truth) and doing, stating (the truth) and performing, it can never *do* exactly what it *says*, perform its statement, symmetrically, adequately; for there is always a discrepancy, disruption, disjunction, gap, break, between its saying and its doing, statement and performance, the truth it knows and the performance of this truth. It can never reflect on itself enough to render itself transparent to itself, know itself completely; nor can it ever *do* enough to dissolve the question of self-knowing. There is always too much or (and/or) too little *knowledge* for the *act*; and there is always too much or (and/or) too little *act* for the *knowledge*.

15. Paul de Man, "Genesis and Genealogy," *Allegories of Reading*, p. 102.

16. Eugen Fink, *Nietzsches Philosophie* (Stuttgart: W. Kohlhammer, 1960), p. 17.

17. Immanuel Kant, *Critique of Pure Reason*, trans. Norman Kemp Smith (New York: St.

Martin's Press, 1965), P. 211. For a reading of Kant's Second Analogy (through Kleist), see Andrzej Warminski, "A Question of an Other Order: Deflections of the Straight Man," *Diacritics* 9 (December 1979):70-78.

18. The interpreters of Nietzsche who foreground the famous statement "for it is only as an *aesthetic phenomenon* that existence and the world are eternally *justified*" always manage to forget the rest of Nietzsche's sentence: "On the contrary, we may assume that we are merely images and artistic projections for the true author, and that we have our highest dignity in our significance as works of art—for it is only as an *aesthetic phenomenon* that existence and the world are eternally *justified*—while of course our consciousness of our own significance (*Bedeutung*) hardly differs from that which the soldiers painted on canvas have of the battle represented on it."

19. Jacques Derrida, "The Double Session," in *Dissemination*, trans. Barbara Johnson (Chicago: University of Chicago Press, 1981), p. 221. French text ("une cheville syntaxique") in *La Dissémination* (Paris: Editions du Seuil, 1972), p. 250.

20. Jacques Derrida, "White Mythology," in *Margins of Philosophy*, trans. Alan Bass (Chicago: University of Chicago Press, 1982), p. 236. French text in *Marges de la philosophie* (Paris: Editions de Minuit, 1972), p. 281.

21. Derrida, "White Mythology," *Margins*, p. 233.

22. Aristotle, *On Poetry and Style*, trans. G. M. A. Grube (New York: Bobbs-Merrill, 1958), p. 45.

23. Derrida, "White Mythology," *Margins*, p. 243. Translation modified.

24. Ibid.

25. Vincent van Gogh, *Dear Theo*, ed. Irving Stone (Boston: Houghton Mifflin, 1937), p. 423.

26. Cf. Pierre Fontanier, *Les Figures du discours* (Paris: Flammarion, 1968), p. 213 on catachresis: "Elle est, par conséquent, tout Trope d'un usage forcé et nécessaire, tout Trope d'où résulte un *sens* purement *extensif*" (Hence it is every trope of a forced and necessary usage, every trope from which results a purely *extended sense*).

27. Putting the difference that reading makes in terms of the radically asymmetrical "relation" semantics/syntax was suggested by Rodolphe Gasché's essay "Joining the Text: From Heidegger to Derrida," in *The Yale Critics: Deconstruction in America* (Minneapolis: University of Minnesota Press, 1983), and Derrida's remarks on undecidability as "the irreducible excess of the syntactic over the semantic" in "The Double Session," *Dissemination*, pp. 219-22, that it points to. For another deployment of this strategy, see Andrzej Warminski, "Missed Crossing: Wordsworth's Apocalypses," *MLN* 99 (December 1984):983-1006.

Chapter 1. Endpapers: Hölderlin's Textual History

1. Martin Heidegger, "Hölderlin und das Wesen der Dichtung," in *Erläuterungen zu Hölderlins Dichtung* (Frankfurt am Main: Vittorio Klostermann, 1971), p. 34.

2. Perhaps the quickest way to orient oneself in relation to the interpretations of Hölderlin's various "turnings" is to read Wilhelm Michel, *Hölderlins abendländische Wendung* (Jena: Eugen Diederichs, 1923); Beda Allemann, *Hölderlin und Heidegger* (Zürich: Atlantis Verlag, 1954); Walter Hof, "Zur Frage einer späten 'Wendung' oder 'Umkehr' Hölderlins," *Hölderlin-Jahrbuch* 11 (1958-60):120-60; and Peter Szondi, "Überwindung des Klassizismus," in *Hölderlin-Studien* (Frankfurt am Main: Suhrkamp, 1970), pp. 95-118.

3. We quote the big Stuttgart edition by volume (mostly vol. 4) and page number: Friedrich Hölderlin, *Sämtliche Werke*, ed. Friedrich Beissner (Stuttgart: Berlag W. Kohlhammer, 1961). The modernized spelling is according to Friedrich Hölderlin, *Sämtliche Werke und Briefe*, ed. Günter Mieth (Munich: Hanser, 1970). This edition is based on Beissner's big Stuttgart edition.

4. Dieter Henrich, "Hölderlin über Urteil und Sein: Eine Studie zur Entstehungsgeschichte des Idealismus," *Hölderlin-Jahrbuch* 14 (1965-66): 73-96.

5. A later Hölderlin text in which the aporias of self-consciousness are put in very similar terms is "Über die Verfahrungsweise des poetischen Geistes." See the analysis of Michael Konrad in his *Hölderlins Philosophie im Grundriss* (Bonn: H. Bouvier, 1967), pp. 196-200.

6. For the early Hegel's use of the word *Rücksicht*, see, for example, the fragment "Glauben ist die Art. . ." ("Glauben und Sein") (1798) in Georg Wilhelm Friedrich Hegel, *Der Geist des Christentums: Schriften, 1796-1800*, ed. Werner Hamacher (Berlin: Ullstein Verlag, 1978), pp. 369-72, and the analysis by H. S. Harris, *Hegel's Development: Toward the Sunlight, 1770-1801* (London: Oxford University Press, 1972), pp. 310-22. Harris prints English translations of both this fragment and "Judgment and Being" in an appendix to the book.

7. Harris, *Hegel's Development*, p. 515.

8. Dieter Henrich in unpublished "Lectures on German Idealism" delivered at Harvard in 1973.

9. See *McGraw-Hill Dictionary of Physics and Mathematics* (1978).

10. Henrich, "Hölderlin über Urteil and Sein," p. 83.

11. This reading of the flyleaf can be taken as a footnote to Jacques Derrida, *La Carte postale* (Paris: Flammarion, 1980).

12. Henrich, "Hölderlin über Urteil und Sein," p. 83.

13. This question is a paraphrase of a question asked (?) by Paul de Man, "Semiology and Rhetoric," in *Allegories of Reading* (New Haven: Yale University Press, 1979), p. 10. For a similarly undecidable question see Maurice Blanchot's note (1970) to his introductory essay, "La Folie par excéllence," in the new edition of Karl Jaspers, *Strindberg et Van Gogh* (Paris: Minuit, 1953), pp. 30-32.

14. On the look of Orpheus, see Maurice Blanchot, "Le Regard d'Orphée," in *L'Espace littéraire* (Paris: Gallimard, 1955), pp. 227-34. On the look of Narcissus, see Blanchot, "Une Scène primitive," *Le Nouveau Commerce* 39-40 (Spring 1978):49-51.

15. Some helpful interpretations of Hölderlin's *Empedocles:* Wolfgang Schadewaldt, "Die Empedokles-Tragödie Hölderlins," *Hölderlin-Jahrbuch*" (1958-60):40-54; Max Kommerell, "Hölderlins Empedokles-Dichtungen," in *Geist und Buchstabe der Dichtung* (Frankfurt am Main: Vittorio Klostermann, 1962); pp. 318-57; Johannes Hoffmeister, *Hölderlins Empedokles* (Bonn: H. Bouvier, 1963); Emil Staiger, "Der Opfertod von Hölderlins Empedokles," *Hölderlin-Jahrbuch* 13 (1963/1964):1-20; Klaus-Rüdiger Wöhrmann, *Hölderlins Wille zur Tragödie* (Munich: Wilhelm Fink, 1967); Friedrich Beissner, "Hölderlins Trauerspiel *Der Tod des Empedokles* in seinen drei Fassungen," in *Hölderlin; Reden und Aufsätze* (Cologne: Böhlau Verlag, 1969), pp. 67-91; Leonardus Van de Velde, *Herrschaft und Knechtschaft bei Hölderlin* (Assen: Van Gorcum, 1973). Some short but suggestive discussions can be found in: Paul de Man, "Keats and Hölderlin," *Comparative Literature* 8, no. 1 (1956):28-45; Maurice Blanchot, "L'Itinéraire de Hölderlin," in *L'Espace littéraire*; Jean Laplanche, *Hölderlin et la question du père* (Paris: PUF, 1961); Michel Foucault, "Le 'Non' du père," *Critique* 18, no. 178 (1962):195-209.

16. Philippe Lacoue-Labarthe, "The Caesura of the Speculative," *Glyph 4*, ed. Samuel Weber et al. (Baltimore: Johns Hopkins University Press, 1978), p. 76.

17. We put a lot of weight on the word *fremd* ("foreign") in this context and elsewhere in Hölderlin. In other words, the poet transfers "his personality, his subjectivity," etc., not into *his own* object, not into *his own* other, but into a "foreign" subject/object relation, i.e., someone else's. Such a reading—whose validity the rest of this essay would demonstrate—disagrees with Laplanche's dialectical interpretation of the "Grund zum Empedokles" in his *Hölderlin et la question du père*, pp. 104-22.

18. A most suggestive interpretation of the Manes-scene is Maria Cornelissen, "Die Manes-

Szene in Hölderlins Trauerspiel 'Der Tod des Empedokles,'" *Hölderlin-Jahrbuch* 14 (1965-66):97-109. Her long footnote on Plato (pp. 103-4) pointed the way toward our reallegorization of Empedocles.

19. Plato, *Collected Dialogues*, ed. Edith Hamilton and Huntington Cairns (Princeton: Princeton University Press, 1973), pp. 1157-60.

20. Cf. the "Böhlendorff-Brief": "Ich habe lange daran laboriert und weiss nun, dass ausser dem, was bei den Griechen und uns das Höchste sein muss, nämlich dem lebendigen Verhältnis und Geschick, wir nicht wohl etwas *gleich* mit ihnen haben dürfen." (I have labored long on it and know now that aside from that which has to be the highest for the Greeks and for us, namely the living relation and the skill, we ought not to have anything *in common* with them).

21. Sophocles, "Oedipus the King," trans. David Grene, in *Sophocles I* (Chicago: The University of Chicago Press, 1966), p. 27.

22. The reading that follows can be taken as a response to, commentary on, or continuation of two essays by Philippe Lacoue-Labarthe: "The Caesura of the Speculative," *Glyph 4*, and "Hölderlin et les Grecs," *Poétique* 40 (November 1979):465-74.

23. The way we read the "caesura" in Hölderlin's interpretation of *Oedipus*, for example, is as follows: in Tiresias, Oedipus sees himself (i.e., a blind man whose knowledge does him no good), but the reason he cannot recognize himself is not because there is anything wrong with his eyesight, say, but because he cannot *read* himself. In order to recognize himself in Tiresias, he would have to be able to read Tiresias's physical, literal blindness as a figure for his own spiritual, figurative blindness; he would have to be able to read Tiresias's useless prophetic knowledge as a sign for his own useless objective, scientific knowledge (one that was able to solve the riddle of the Sphinx). In short, he would have to read a figure of speech: a chiasmus. In any case, the point is that representation representing itself as representation is not something one can *see*; it is "something" that has to be *read*.

24. Cf. "Der Gesichtspunkt, aus dem wir das Altertum anzusehen haben": "wir träumen von Originalität und Selbständigkeit, wir glauben lauter Neues zu sagen, und alles dies ist doch Reaktion, gleichsam eine milde Rache gegen die Knechtschaft, womit wir uns verhalten haben gegen das Altertum" (we dream of originality and independence, we believe we say nothing but what is new, and all this is still reaction, as it were a gentle revenge against the slavery of how we have related to antiquity).

25. On a slightly different "Empedocles complex" see Gaston Bachelard, "Le Complexe d'Empédocle," in *La Psychanalyse du feu* (Paris: Gallimard, 1949).

26. We owe the "identification" of Pausanias as Manes (and vice versa) to Paul de Man in his response to "The Deaths of Empedocles" at the MLA convention in San Francisco (December 1979).

27. Such an impossible identification is implicit as early as the "Thalia-Fragment" of *Hyperion*: " 'Solche Herrlichkeit zernichtet uns Arme. Freilich waren es goldne Tage, wo man die Waffen tauschte, und sich liebte bis zum Tode, wo man unsterbliche Kinder zeugte in der Begeisterung der Liebe und Schönheit, Taten fürs Vaterland, und himmlische Gesänge, und ewige Worte der Weisheit, ach! wo der ägyptische Priester dem Solon noch vorwarf: 'Ihr Griechen seid alle Zeit Jünglinge!' Wir sind nun Greise geworden, klüger, als alle die Herrlichen, die dahin sind; nur schade, dass so manche Kraft verschmachtet in diesem fremden Elemente!' " (3:169) (Such splendor destroys us poor ones. Of course those were golden days, when one exchanged arms, and loved one another until death, where one conceived immortal children in the rapture of love and beauty, deeds for the fatherland, and heavenly songs, and eternal words of wisdom, ah! where the Egyptian priest still reproached Solon: 'You Greeks are always youngsters!' We have become old men, more clever than all the magnificent ones that have passed on; only it is a shame that so much strength passes away in this foreign element).

28. The targets of this preliminary "rhetoricization" of the historical scheme suggested in Hölderlin's "Böhlendorff-Brief" are the exemplary dialectical interpretations of Peter Szondi,

"Überwindung des Klassizismus," in *Hölderlin-Studien* and Theodor W. Adorno, "Parataxis," in *Noten zur Literatur III* (Frankfurt am Main: Suhrkamp, 1965), pp. 156-209. As Timothy Bahti pointed out—in the discussion following "Endpapers: Hölderlin's Textual History" (delivered at a conference on "Writing Literary History" held at the University of Minnesota in October 1980)—of our two figures for the caesura, the "Möbius band" could be read as a *spatial* and the "chiasmus" as a *temporal* articulation. What makes possible our passage, our turning, from one figure to the other? A "Möbius band/chiasmus"—in which formulation the slash is, again, a caesura: an unreadable condition of (im)possibility of space and time, a simulacrum of the transcendental.

29. E. H. Gombrich in "Reflections on the Greek Revolution," in *Art and Illusion* (Princeton: Princeton University Press, 1972) not only says that "we must never forget that we look at Egyptian art with the mental set we have all derived from the Greeks" (p. 122) but also that "there are indications in works of art to confirm that the Greeks of the archaic period were in fact inclined to read the pictograms of Egypt as if they were representations of an imagined reality" (p. 135). In brief and in our terms: the Greeks took Egyptian allegorical signs literally.

30. Even if (or especially if), one should like to add, it allows us to solve riddles like that of the Sphinx or of modern physics.

31. Such a re-allegorization would be like Hölderlin's own "orientalizing" translations of Sophocles. See his letter to his editor, Friedrich Wilmans (28 September 1803). See also the careful interpretation of Wolfgang Schadewaldt, "Hölderlins Übersetzung des Sophokles," in *Über Hölderlin*, ed. Jochen Schmidt (Frankfurt am Main: Insel, 1970), pp. 237-93.

32. Beda Allemann's notion of an *empedokleisches Prinzip* and Hölderlin's turning away from it is both too simple and too simplistic. See Beda Allemann, *Hölderlin und Heidegger* (above, n. 27), pp. 16-27.

33. This sentence is a paraphrase of sentences in Kostas Axelos, "Planetary Interlude," in *Game, Play, Literature*, ed. Jacques Ehrmann (Boston: Beacon Press, 1971), p. 9: " 'Game' is not a slogan. After you have discovered it, it is no great exploit to find it; the difficulty will be henceforth to forget it." (Cf. Nietzsche's note to Georg Brandes [January 4, 1889].) The danger of (non)concepts like the "caesura" is, as always, twofold and requires a twofold word of caution: (1) They should not be taken "too literally" or in too positivistic a sense, lest we think that we have found a "caesura" whenever Hölderlin's text breaks off or when there is a break in his syntax. Philippe Lacoue-Labarthe's and Jean-Luc Nancy's reflections on "the fragment" are therapeutic in this regard: "L'Exigence fragmentaire," in *L'Absolu littéraire* (Paris: Editions du Seuil, 1978), pp. 57-80. (2) They should not be taken "too figuratively" or in a transcendental sense, lest we think that the caesura is an ungrounded ground or a condition of possibility.

34. Dante's characterization of allegorical reading in the "Letter to Can Grande della Scala" (in *Critical Theory since Plato,* ed. Hazard Adams [New York: Harcourt Brace Jovanovich, 1971], p. 122) is peculiarly appropriate in this context: "for it is one sense which we get through the letter, and another which we get through the thing the letter signifies; and the first is called literal, but the second allegorical or mystic. And this mode of treatment, for its better manifestation, may be considered in this verse: 'When Israel came out of Egypt, and the house of Jacob from a people of strange speech, Judea became his sanctification, Israel his power.' For if we inspect the letter alone the departure of the children of Israel from Egypt in the time of Moses is presented to us; if the allegory, our redemption wrought by Christ."

35. The "identification" of Manes as simultaneously John the Baptist and John the Apostle—"Manes, der gleichsam des Empedokles Täufer und Apostel Johannes in einem ist"—is made by Walter Hof, "Zur Frage einer späten 'Wendung' oder 'Umkehr' Hölderlins (above, n. 2), p. 139.

36. Maurice Blanchot, "Fragmentaire," in *A Bram Van Velde* (Montpellier: Fata Morgana, 1975), p. 21. On the doubly absent sense, see Blanchot, "L'Ecriture du désastre," *La Nouvelle Revue Francaise*, no. 330-31 (July-August 1980):1-33.

Chapter 2. Hölderlin in France

1. E. M. Butler, *The Tyranny of Greece over Germany* (Boston: Beacon Press, 1958), pp. 203-4.

2. *The American Heritage Dictionary of the English Language.*

3. All page references within the body of the text are to the big Stuttgart edition of Hölderlin's works published by Cotta—*Sämtliche Werke*, ed. Friedrich Beissner (Stuttgart: Cotta, 1943-61)—and are given by volume and page number. Translations from the second letter to Böhlendorff are those of Michael Hamburger, in Friedrich Hölderlin, *Poems and Fragments* (Cambridge: Cambridge University Press, 1980), pp. 12-14.

4. For a reading of the uneasy relationship of poetics and hermeneutics, see Paul de Man's "Introduction" to Hans Robert Jauss, *Toward an Aesthetic of Reception*, trans. Timothy Bahti (Minneapolis: University of Minnesota Press, 1982). The critique of the category of the "aesthetic" in de Man's recent work has helped us understand the theoretical issues of our reading-in-progress of Hölderlin: "Sign and Symbol in Hegel's *Aesthetics,*" *Critical Inquiry* 8, no. 4 (Summer 1982):761-75; "Hypogram and Inscription: Michael Riffaterre's Poetics of Reading," *Diacritics* 11, no. 4 (Winter 1981):17-35; "Hegel on the Sublime," in *Displacement*, ed. Mark Krupnick (Bloomington: Indiana University Press, 1983), pp. 139-53.

5. On Böhlendorff, see the notes to volume 6 of the big Stuttgart edition (6:1074).

6. Needless to say, a "descendant" in a most problematic sense. See chapter 3, "Heidegger Reading Hölderlin."

7. Peter Szondi, "Überwindung des Klassizismus," in *Hölderlin-Studien* (Frankfurt am Main: Suhrkamp, 1970), p. 98.

8. Ibid., pp. 109-10.

9. Ibid., p. 116.

10. Ibid., pp. 112-13. This is even more explicit in Szondi's *Poetik und Geschichtsphilosophie II* (Frankfurt am Main: Suhrkamp, 1974), p. 170: "Sowenig Homer dem naiven Kuntscharakter seiner Epen deren Ausgangspunkt (die *Bedeutung*), nämlich das heroische Gegeneinander *grosser Bestrebungen* geopfert hat, sowenig darf, so betont es der Brief an Böhlendorff, über dem Erlernen des Fremden das Eigene vergessen werden, dessen freier Gebrauch also nicht mehr das Ausgeliefertsein an ihn, sondern seine reflektierte Verwendung als eines Momentes im Kunstwerk, das Schwerste sein soll" (As little as Homer sacrificed the point of departure (the *meaning*), namely the heroic confrontation of *great strivings*, to the naive technical character of his epics, just as little, maintains the letter to Böhlendorff, should that which is one's own be forgotten for the sake of acquiring the foreign, whose [i.e., that which is one's own] free use—that is, no longer being merely exposed to it but rather its reflected use as a moment in the work of art—is supposed to be that which is most difficult).

11. Szondi, "Gattungspoetik und Geschichtsphilosophie," also in *Hölderlin-Studien*.

12. Szondi, "Überwindung," p. 100.

13. In chapter 1, "Endpapers: Hölderlin's Textual History."

14. Szondi, "Überwindung," p. 118.

15. In the somewhat later essay "Gattungspoetik und Geschichtsphilosophie," Szondi speaks of a change in the late Hölderlin's conception of the relation of Greece and Hesperia, as no longer a sublatable mirror symmetry but a qualitative jump (*zum qualitativen Sprung*). In doing so, Szondi does not give up the Greeks as the aesthetic moment in the history of the West; he only transfers it into a history of Hölderlin's poetic development—the first letter to Böhlendorff would now mark the aesthetic moment in Hölderlin's itinerary (of at least a theoretically successful dialectical mediation between Greece and Hesperia). In such a scheme the early work could then be taken as "prereflective," and the very last work as a falling apart of the oppositions mediated in the first letter to Böhlendorff—both former and latter constituted *as* "pre-" and "post-" thanks to the invention of the synthesis in the letter, thanks, as always, to the reinvention of the

Greeks. Szondi's own itinerary could also be read in terms of such a scheme—with his interpretation of the letter to Böhlendorff serving as the "Greek" moment—which is not at all surprising in the case of a reader who inscribes himself in Hölderlin's text as the addressee of the first letter to Böhlendorff.

16. Philippe Lacoue-Labarthe, "La Césure du spéculatif," in Hölderlin, *L'Antigone de Sophocle* trans. Lacoue-Labarthe (Paris: Christian Bourgoig, 1978), pp. 183-223. This essay first appeared in English translation in *Glyph 4* (Baltimore: Johns Hopkins University Press, pp. 57-84. The French text incorporates a couple of small but significant changes. "Hölderlin et les Grecs," *Poetique* 40 (November 1979):465-74.

17. Lacoue-Labarthe, "Hölderlin et les Grecs," p. 470.

18. Ibid., p. 473.

19. Lacoue-Labarthe, "La Césure," p. 206.

20. Ibid., p. 204.

21. This is quite "visible" in Lacoue-Labarthe's uncritical quotation of Hölderlin on tragedy: that is, without asking to what extent terms like *Zeichen, Metapher, Übertragung,* etc., are assimilable to a speculative conception of tragedy. For instance, tragedy defined as "the *metaphor*of an intellectual intuition" (*Es ist die Metapher einer intellektuellen Anschauung*) is not easily recovered by a speculative model.

22. Georges Bataille, "Hegel, la mort et le sacrifice," *Deucalion* 40 (October 1955):21-43. Lacoue-Labarthe alludes to this text at the beginning of "La Césure."

23. Therapeutic in this regard is, as always, Jacques Derrida, "Les Fins de l'homme," in *Marges* (Paris: Minuit, 1972), pp. 129-64.

24. Bataille, "Hegel, la mort et le sacrifice," p. 32.

25. G. W. F. Hegel, *Phänomenologie des Geistes* (Hamburg: Meiner, 1952), p. 30.

26. See Maurice Blanchot, "La Littérature et le droit à la mort," in *La Part du feu* (Paris: Gallimard, 1949), pp. 291-331.

27. E. H. Gombrich, *Art and Illusion* (Princeton: Princeton University Press, 1969), p. 129.

28. Ibid., pp. 122-23.

29. Ibid., p. 134.

30. Ibid., pp. 134-36.

Chapter 3. Heidegger Reading Hölderlin

1. Martin Heidegger, *Holzwege* (Frankfurt am Main: Vittorio Klostermann, 1972), pp. 43-44.

2. See Paul de Man's essays on Kant and Hegel and my "Introduction," in Paul de Man, *Aesthetic Ideology,* ed. Andrzej Warminski (Minneapolis: University of Minnesota Press, forthcoming).

3. See Martin Heidegger, *Hölderlins Hymne 'Der Ister'* (Frankfurt am Main: Vittorio Klostermann, 1984), p. 30: "Wir behaupten deshalb: Hölderlins Stromdichtung, ja seine Hymnendichtung im Ganzen, ist nicht sinnbildlich. Darin liegt die weitertragende Behauptung: Diese Dichtkunst ist nicht metaphysisch. Insofern es Kunst im strengen abendländischen Begriff nur als metaphysische Kunst gibt, ist Hölderlins Dichtung, wenn sie nicht mehr metaphysisch ist, auch nicht mehr 'Kunst' " (We therefore contend: Hölderlin's river-poetry, indeed the poetry of his hymns as a whole, is not symbolic. In this rests the further contention: this art of poetry is not metaphysical. Insofar as art, according to the strict Western conception, exists only as metaphysical art, Hölderlin's poetry, if it is no longer metaphysical, is also no longer "art").

4. All page references within the body of the text marked by *E* followed by a page number are to Martin Heidegger, *Erläuterungen zu Hölderlins Dichtung* (Franfurt am Main: Vittorio Klostermann, 1971). For "Hölderlin and the Essence of Poetry," I usually quote the translation of Douglas Scott in the volume edited by Werner Brock, *Existence and Being* (Chicago: Henry Regnery Company, 1949).

5. There are too many treatments of the subject even to begin listing them here, but the following two statements can serve as emblems. One by Paul de Man in "Les Exégèses de Hölderlin par Martin Heidegger," *Critique* (September-October 1955), p. 809: "c'est que Hölderlin dit exactement le contraire de ce que lui fait dire Heidegger" (it is that Hölderlin says exactly the opposite of what Heidegger makes him say). (See also n. 43.) The other by Max Kommerell in a letter to Hans Georg Gadamer (22 December 1941): "Heidegger hat mir seinen Essay geschickt. Er ist ein produktives Eisenbahn-Unglück, über das die Eisenbahnwärter der Literaturgeschichte die Hände über dem Kopf zusammenschlagen müssen (soweit sie ehrlich sind)" (Heidegger has sent me his essay. It is a productive train wreck, over which the train signalmen of literary history [to the extent that they are honest] will have to throw up their hands). Quoted in Max Kommerell, *Briefe und Aufzeichnungen, 1919-1944*, ed. Inge Jens (Olten und Freiburg im Breisgau: Walter-Verlag, 1967), p. 403.

6. Martin Heidegger, "Der Fehl heiliger Namen," *Contre toute attente* (Spring-Summer 1981):39-55.

7. Heidegger, *Holzwege*, p. 252: "Aber es wäre und ist die einzige Not, nüchtern denkend im Gesagten seiner Dichtung das Ungesprochene zu erfahren" (But there would be and there is the sole necessity in thinking soberly to experience the unspoken in that which his poetry says).

8. Kommerell, *Briefe und Aufzeichnungen, 1919-1944*, pp. 400-401.

9. Ibid., pp. 404-5. Heidegger also rejects any possibility of his *identifying* with Hölderlin: "Alles aufrichtige Denken ist zum Unterschied der Dichter in seinem unmittelbaren Wirken eine Verunglückung. Daraus ersehen Sie schon, dass ich mich nicht und nirgends mit Hölderlin identifizieren *kann*. Hier ist die Auseinandersetzung eines Denkens mit einem Dichter im Gang, wobei die Aus-einander-setzung sogar den Entgegnenden erst setzt. Ist das Willkür oder höchste Freiheit?" (In contrast to the poets, all honest thinking is in its immediate effect a failure. From this you can already see that I *may* not ever identify with Hölderlin. Here the altercation of a thinking and a poet is under way, which "altercation" first posits the interlocutors. Is this arbitrariness or highest freedom?).

10. All references marked by *HH* followed by a page number are to Martin Heidegger, *Hölderlins Hymnen 'Germanien' und 'Der Rhein'* (Frankfurt am Main: Vittorio Klostermann, 1980). This is volume 39 of the *Gesamtausgabe*.

11. I quote the big Stuttgart edition of Hölderlin's works by volume and page number: Friedrich Hölderlin, *Sämtliche Werke*, ed. Friedrich Beissner (Stuttgart: Cotta, 1943-61).

12. And their politics too: "Hiezu kam die wundergrosse That des Theseus, die freiwillige Beschränkung seiner eignen königlichen Gewalt" (3:79) (Add to this the wonderfully great act of Theseus, the voluntary limitation of his own royal power).

13. Friedrich Schiller, *An Anthology for Our Time* (New York: Frederick Ungar, 1959), p. 356.

14. See the "Übergang zur griechischen Welt" in G. W. F. Hegel, *Vorlesungen über die Philosophie der Geschichte* (Frankfurt am Main: Suhrkamp, 1970), XII, p. 271: "Ein ägyptischer Priester hat gesagt, dass die Griechen ewig nur Kinder bleiben; umgekehrt können wir sagen, die Ägypter seien die kräftigen, in sich drängenden *Knaben*, welche nichts als der Klarheit über sich, der ideellen Form nach, bedürfen, um Jünglinge zu werden." The translation can be found in G. W. F. Hegel, *The Philosophy of History*, trans. J. Sibree (New York: Dover, 1956), pp. 219-20: "An Egyptian priest is reported to have said, that the Greeks remain eternally children. We may say, on the contrary, that the Egyptians are vigorous *boys*, eager for self-comprehension, who require nothing but the clear understanding of themselves in an ideal form, in order to become *Young Men*." Cf. "Thalia-Fragment" of *Hyperion* (3:169) and our reading of the Egyptian priest's wisdom in the "third version" of Hölderlin's *Tod des Empedokles* above in chapter 1: "Endpapers: Hölderlin's Textual History."

15. Cf. Hegel's commentary on this saying in the *Vorlesungen über die Geschichte der Philosophie I* (Frankfurt am Main: Suhrkamp, 1971), XVIII, p. 327.

16. Note that although he does say "Sons of the North," Hyperion never says *South* for the Egyptians, who remain Oriental.

17. For a good example of such speaking, see Edward W. Said's remarks on Aeschylus's *The Persians* in *Orientalism* (New York: Vintage Books, 1979), p. 56. Greece makes Asia *say* her defeat by Greece; Greece makes Asia "herself" say that she is empty.

18. This includes Ernst Cassirer, "Hölderlin und der deutsche Idealismus," in *Idee und Gestalt* (Darmstadt: Wissenschaftliche Buchgesellschaft, 1975), pp. 113-56, and, especially, what one could call the "George-Kreis" interpretation of Hölderlin, whose influence extends to much in Heidegger's interpretations of Hölderlin (perhaps the tone above all). See, for example, Friedrich Gundolf, "Hölderlins Archipelagus," in *Dem lebendigen Geist* (Heidelberg-Darmstadt: Verlag Lambert Schneider, 1962), pp. 25-40. But the more dialectically minded interpreter—for example, Peter Szondi—also leaves out the Egyptians and the Orient. See "Überwindung des Klassizismus," in *Hölderlin-Studien* (Frankfurt am Main: Suhrkamp, 1967), pp. 95-118. The explicitly Hegelian interpretation of Hölderlin's historical scheme begins to waver when, appropriately enough, Szondi turns to questions of *poetics* in "Gattungspoetik und Geschichtsphilosophie," p. 161: "Denn auch die Konzeption dieser Entsprechung muss durch den Wandel in Hölderlins Verständnis der griechischen Kunst erchüttert worden sein. Wird diese nicht mehr als *Äusserung* des *heiligen Pathos*, des *Apollonsreichs*, im Medium der *Nüchternheit* gesehen, sondern als Verleugnung jener um dieser willen, treten die beiden der *Grundstimmung* und dem *Kunstkarakter* korrespondierenden Momente des Eigenen und des Fremden, statt mitcinander sich zu vermitteln, antagonistisch auseinander, so lässt sich der Unterschied zwischen Hellas und Hesperien: dass nämlich, was dort das *Reich der Kunst* stiftet, Nüchternheit und Darstellungsgabe, hier ein Nationelles ist, während, was dort der Kunst zuliebe verleugnet und versäumt wird, hier allererst Kunst konstituicrt, nicht mehr in der Konzeption von Spiegelsymmetrie als ein Unterschied formaler Natur aufheben: er wird zum qualitativen Sprung" (For the conception of this correspondance must also have been shaken by the change in Hölderlin's understanding of Greek art. If Greek art is no longer seen as the *expression* of *holy pathos*, of the *Apollonian realm*, in the medium of *sobriety*, but rather as the repression of the former for the sake of the latter, if the two moments of that which is one's own and that which is foreign (which correspond to the *grounding tone* and the *artistic character*) diverge antagonistically instead of mediating themselves with one another, then the difference of Greece and Hesperia—that, namely, what founded the *realm of art* there, sobriety and the talent for representation, is here something national, while what there was repressed and mistaken for the sake of art, here all constitutes art—no longer allows itself to be sublated in the conception of a mirror-symmetry as a difference of purely formal nature: it becomes a qualitative jump).

19. See Manfred Frank, *Der unendliche Mangel an Sein* (Frankfurt am Main: Suhrkamp, 1975).

20. Martin Heidegger, *Basic Writings*, ed. David Farrell Krell (New York: Harper and Row, 1977), p. 218. German in *Wegmarken* (Frankfurt am Main: Vittorio Klostermann, 1967), p. 169.

21. And Hölderlin may be a Ulysses who reflects the nature of our "modernity" so long and so hard—*reads* it—that he reaches East by going West, or, better, reaches a point in his reflection, in his reading, where it is impossible (and yet necessary) to decide between East and West, Egypt and Hesperia, between a religion and art of death, tombs, and monuments and a religion and art of sacrificial death and resurrection. Somewhat like the Ulysses of Homer and of Dante in one, he does not know whether he returns home or not; or, better, he returns home all right, but this home is not *his* home but someone else's, his own and an other's at once.

22. The translations here are those of Douglas Scott in Martin Heidegger, *Existence and Being*, ed. Werner Brock (Chicago: Henry Regnery Company, 1949).

23. We translate *Seiendes* in the plural as "beings" in order to distinguish it (aurally) more from Being (*Sein*).

24. Kenneth Burke, *Language as Symbolic Action* (Berkeley: University of California Press, 1966), p. 454.

25. See Rudolf Carnap's famous critique, "The Elimination of Metaphysics through Logical Analysis," in *Logical Positivism*, ed. A. J. Ayer (Glencoe: Free Press, 1960), pp. 60-81.

26. Martin Heidegger, "Was ist Metaphysik?" in *Wegmarken*, p. 13. The translation—with my capitalization of "Not" and "Nothing"—is from *Basic Writings*, p. 107.

27. This is from the last paragraph of Martin Heidegger, *Platons Lehre von der Wahrheit* (Bern: Francke Verlag, 1954), p. 51. Cf. Paul Friedländer's critique of Heidegger on *aletheia* in his *Plato: An Introduction* (New York: Harper and Row, 1964), pp. 221-29.

28. Henri Birault, *Heidegger et l'expérience de la pensée* (Paris: Gallimard, 1978), p. 553. Some other helpful discussions of Heidegger's *Nichts*: Jean Beaufret, "La Pensée du rien dans l'oeuvre de Heidegger," in *Introduction aux philosophies de l'existence* (Paris: Editions Denoël, 1971) pp. 157-66; Stanley Rosen, "Thinking about Nothing," in *Heidegger and Modern Philosophy*, ed. Michael Murray (New Haven: Yale University Press, 1978), pp. 116-37. Best of all is, as always, Maurice Blanchot.

29. Cf. Heidegger's later formulation (in "Zur Seinsfrage" *Wegmarken* [Frankfurt am Main: Klostermann, 1967], pp. 213-54) that we come too late for the gods and too early for Being.

30. Heidegger's text provides us with one pointer toward the other Not of reading in the discussion of the second danger of language, that is, its self-endangerment, the fact that "the word as word never gives any immediate guarantee as to whether it is an essential word (*ein wesentliches Wort*) or a delusion (*ein Blendwerk*)" (*E*, 37). Now as long as Heidegger stays with this opposition—or "illusory appearance" (*Schein*) and "authentic saying" (*das echte Sagen*)—which, of course, is not really an opposition but an (asymmetrical) difference determined by the ontological difference, language's self-endangerment can indeed be thought as a threat to Being from beings (and vice versa). Nevertheless, along with this system of (non)oppositions between appearance (with the optical metaphor very visible: *Blendwerk, Schein*, etc.) and authentic Being, the text introduces still another version of language's *Schein* that is not so easily mastered by the ontological difference: "And on the other hand that which is dressed up to look like the essential, is only something recited by heart or repeated (*Und was sich andererseits in seinem Aufputz den Anschein des Wesentlichen gibt, ist nur ein Her- und Nachgesagtes*)" (*E*, 37). The (non)opposition between "appearance" (*Anschein*) and the "essential" (*das Wesentliche*) seems to fit the pattern of the others, but here something more is added: "only something recited by heart or repeated (*nur ein Her- und Nachgesagtes*)."

Although one should perhaps not put too much weight on something as invisible, innocuous, "by the way," as these words "only something recited by heart or repeated (*nur ein Her- und Nachgesagtes*)"—we can say that they name something that is to the side of or asymmetrical to the (already asymmetrical) opposition illusory appearance/authentic saying. And this is not just because a merely mechanical memory and repetition introduces a metaphor different from the chain delusion (*Blendwerk*), dressing up (*Aufputz*), illusory appearance (*Schein* and *Anschein*), and so on—although the fact that this one metaphor is not a matter of *sight* is certainly a signal for the reader—but rather because it introduces a completely other danger *of* language *to* language: namely, the danger of a delusion, illusion, or inauthenticity that has nothing to do with appearance or deception—whether it be understood in a classically (subjectivist) metaphysical sense or in Heidegger's fundamentally ontological sense (i.e., as ontic, inauthentic, etc.)—and has everything to do with reading, that is, taking literally or figuratively, without or within quotation marks. In short, the phrase introduces what Derrida calls "iterability": that is, if every word *as* word (i.e., as soon as it is thought, spoken, written, etc., as soon as it is a word) can be quoted, if its "quotability" is the condition of every word whatsoever, then every word is always already divided radically (nonoppositionally) against itself as "original" and "quotation." If it is said once, it is always already said twice, and there is no way to decide whether the word we hear (or think or read or write) is within or without quotation marks without *reading* it. And this constitutive (but not in a transcendental sense) "inauthenticity" of language, any and every language whatsoever, is due not to any deceptions of the ontic, any veil of *māyā* of beings, but to the mechanical, differential marks (whether visible or invisible) that make language what it is—always already written. To summarize, iterability names a danger *of* language that is other than, different from, the threat of beings to Being. But it is still only a name. We should not think that by pointing to this phrase in Heidegger's essay—"only something recited by heart or repeated"—we have set off what some would call the text's "self-deconstruction." More labor of the "negative" of writing is necessary to read the "other Not" of Hölderlin and Heidegger.

Yet even if we were to accept provisionally the fundamental ontologist's response that "authentic speaking" (*echtes Sagen*) is (ontologically) prior to language's writing—"*Iterabilität gibt es nur innerhalb der Metaphysik*," Heidegger might say (although he would be misreading Derrida, for iterability, language's writing, is not a question of visible or invisible, bodily or spiritual, etc., marks but of differential marks that distinguish mere "noise" from articulate sounds)—we would still have to deal with Heidegger's active and resourceful (and for the most part unthematized) exploitation of precisely language's purely mechanical memory (quotation marks, italics, crossings-out, puns, mistranslations, etc.) to distinguish authentic saying from something only recited by heart or repeated, an other speaking (more like writing), an other Not—something as dead as a quotation or the gods of Greece. But that remains to be read. Is there an "other Not"—unthought and unthinkable—to be read in the (already other) double Not of Heidegger's interpretation of Hölderlin? Or, again, can one go from the essence of poetry to the essence of language and back without losing or gaining anything on the trip—without losing or gaining a nothing that is not the Not of Being but the not of language as poetry (and poetry as language)? (See Jacques Derrida, "Signature Event Context," in *Glyph 1*, ed. Samuel Weber et al. (Baltimore: The Johns Hopkins University Press, 1977), pp. 172-97 and "Limited Inc," *Glyph 2*, (1977), pp. 162-254.

31. The translations of "Germanien" are those of Michael Hamburger in Friedrich Hölderlin, *Poems and Fragments* (Cambridge: Cambridge University Press, 1966).

32. Cf.: "Wenn wir hier schon eine sogenannte 'Definition' des Menschen sehen wollen, dann ist es eine geschichtliche, auf die Zeit bezogene und nach früher Gesagtem offenbar auf die Zeit der Völker, die keiner weiss, jene Zeit, von der wir hörten, dass sie nur erst wird, wenn wir selbst 'Teilnehmende' werden, teilnehmend am Gespräch, wenn wir uns entscheiden zu dem, was wir geschichtlich sein können. Wir verstehen das Wort des Dichters erst und nur so lange, als wir selbst in diese Entscheidung treten und in ihr stehen" (*HH*, 69) (If we want already to see a so-called definition of man here, then it is a historical definition, related to time and, according to that which was said above, clearly to the time of the peoples, which no one knows, that time about which we heard that it first exists only when we ourselves become "participants," participating in the dialogue, when we decide ourselves to that which we can historically be. We understand the word of the poet only and only as long as we ourselves step into this decision and stand in it).

33. Heidegger interprets this threefoldedness on the basis of the triple (*dreifach*) *Empfindung* in Hölderlin's "Über die Verfahrungsweise des poetischen Geistes."

34. Heidegger, *Wegmarken*, p. 189.

35. See the "Vorbemerkung" to the *Hölderlins Hymnen 'Germanien' und 'Der Rhein'* lectures: "Man nimmt Hölderlin 'historisch' und verkennt jenes einzig Wesentliche, dass sein noch zeit-raum-loses Werk unser historisches Getue schon überwunden und den Anfang einer anderen Geschichte gegründet hat, jener Geschichte, die anhebt mit dem Kampf um die Entscheidung über Ankunft oder Flucht des Gottes" (*HH*, 1) (One takes Hölderlin "historiologically" and mistakes that which is solely essential, that his still time- and space-less work has already

overcome our historiological doings and has founded the beginning of an other history, that history which originates in the battle over the decision of the coming or fleeing of the god).

36. Paul de Man, *Allegories of Reading* (New Haven: Yale University Press, 1979), p. 12.

37. What we in a sense do, then, is to "rhetoricize" the dialectic—which would thus no longer be a dialectic—between Paul de Man's two remarks (and thus between Hölderlin and Heidegger) in "Les Exégèses de Hölderlin par Martin Heidegger," *Critique* (1955), p. 809: (1) "Hölderlin says exactly the opposite of what Heidegger makes him say (*Hölderlin dit exactement le contraire de ce que lui fait dire Heidegger*)" and (2) "To say the opposite is still to be talking about the same thing (*Dire le contraire, c'est encore parler de la meme chose*)." (See Wlad Godzich's reading of this dialectic in "The Domestication of Derrida," in *The Yale Critics*, ed. Jonathan Arac, Wlad Godzich, and Wallace Martin [Minneapolis: University of Minnesota Press, 1983], and Godzich's translation of the de Man essay in the new edition of Paul de Man, *Blindness and Insight* [Minneapolis: University of Minnesota Press, 1983].) Insofar as we "rhetoricize" with the help of de Man's later work (e.g., "Semiology and Rhetoric" in *Allegories of Reading*), we read only what was always already "there"—but not in a Hegelian (dialectical) sense or a Heideggerian (hermeneutic) sense—in the essay of 1955.

An additional note on the rhetorical (?) question: in the case of de Man's famous (infamous?) example of Archie Bunker's "What's the difference?" one could say that if the listener could hear Archie's tone or interpret better, say, a particular shrug of the shoulder—if she were a hermeneutician, in short—she would be able to decide the difference between Archie's asking or not asking to know the difference. That is, Archie's question could ultimately be taken as merely ambiguous (which would not affect the particular point about the relation of grammar and rhetoric de Man's example illustrates). The example of the last line of Yeats's "Among School Children"—"How can we know the dancer from the dance?"—is more radical because its question is truly *undecidable*: there is no way to decide whether the question is literal or rhetorical on the basis of "tone" or "context" because, as de Man shows, the *question* is what decides the tone or context. And if we cannot decide the question, we cannot decide the tone or context on the basis of which we had hoped to decide the question. The question of "Germanien" is undecidable—and perhaps even more clearly than the line from Yeats because Heidegger explicitly decides the "grounding mood" (*Grundstimmung*), the tone, of the poem on it. In short, what distinguishes mere ambiguity from undecidability is that the former is merely a question of a stable reading subject's coming up against a multiplicity of (perhaps contradictory) meanings that he may try to decide one way or the other. Undecidability, however, puts the subject radically into question in that at stake in it is precisely the reading subject's status: in order to read "Germanien," in order to be he or she who he or she is, the reader *has* to decide the question but *cannot* do so (and hence can neither read "Germanien" nor be himself). No subject can read or write an undecidable question.

The refusal or inability to understand the difference between ambiguity and undecidability is one of the main reasons for the misunderstanding of "deconstruction" by both its detractors and many of its would-be practitioners. For instance, here is David Hoy, "Deciding Derrida" (*London Review of Books*, 18 February-3 March 1982) on the undecidability of the *pharmakon*: "This familiar point is not strong enough, however, to support Derrida's conclusion that the failure of the translation to capture the ambiguity makes an 'understanding of the context' probably 'impossible' and the reference undecidable. Clearly the translator can understand the context well enough to choose the appropriate modern term accurately, even with some loss of ambiguity that can be corrected only with a successful paraphrase like Derrida's own. Without further arguments for the indeterminacy of translation Derrida's theory of textuality appears ungrounded, since what he takes to be a fundamental paradox is not really so difficult to understand." The trouble is that in cases where the key term (or a key structure of meaning) is truly undecidable, the translator can never "understand the context well enough" because he cannot decide what the context *is* without deciding the undecidable key term. (Another way to put it: Hoy here invokes the authority of the "hermeneutic circle" when undecidability is precisely that which disarticulates that circle and the structure of "fore-understanding.") It is not a question of faithfulness to an "original text" but rather the impossibility of there ever *having been* an "original text." Hoy's smug translator "understands" well enough because he cannot or will not *read*.

That undecidability is not just a question of the difference (or opposition) between (literal and figurative) meanings but rather the mutual interference of (for de Man) grammar and rhetoric or (for Derrida) syntax and semantics is perhaps an even clearer way of formulating its disarticulation of all hermeneutic circles. See my summary remarks at the end of this chapter.

38. See n. 30 above.

39. In short, Hölderlin would be the poet of the "Germans" only insofar as he is the poet of the "Egyptians." See Norbert von Hellingrath's 1915 lecture "Hölderlin und die Deutschen," in *Hölderlin* (Munich: Hugo Bruckmann, 1922). For Hellingrath, Hölderlin is the "most German" poet. . .why?. . .because he is the "most Greek."

In his later work, Heidegger does indeed begin to "think" the mysterious relations to the Orient that come to speech in Hölderlin's poetry. One example is a long footnote on the question of Hölderlin's "turning" in the essay on "Andenken": "Ausserdem gilt es zu sehen, dass die in der Hölderlin-Forschung viel verhandelte Frage der 'abendländischen Wendung' dieses Dichters (ob Hinwendung zum Christentum bei Abwendung vom Griechentum, ob gewandelte Zuwendung zu beiden) schon als Frage zu kurz gedacht ist und im Aussenwerk der 'historischen' Erscheinungen hängen bleibt. Denn Hölderlin hat sich zwar gewandelt, aber nicht gewendet. Er hat nur das Eigene, dem er stets zugewendet war, in der Wandlung erst gefunden. Mit seiner Wandlung wandelt sich das Wissen von der Wahrheit des Griechentums und des Christentums und *des Ostens* überhaupt. Die gewohnten Bezirke und Zeitalter der historischen Betrachtung werden hinfällig" (*E*, 90) (In addition, it needs to be seen that the question of the poet's "turn to the West" (whether as a turning toward Christianity along with a turning away from the Greeks, or as an altered turning in relation to both)—much-discussed in Hölderlin scholarship—is already as a question thought insufficiently and remains stuck in the externality of "historiological" appearances. For Hölderlin certainly did wander, but he did not turn. He found only that which is one's own, toward which he was always turned, only in wandering. Along with his wandering changes the knowledge of the truth of the Greeks and of Christianity and *of the East* as such. The usual regions and periods of historiological observation become untenable). But as his commentary on the lines from "Andenken"—"Nun aber sind zu Indiern / Die Männer gegangen" (But now to Indians / Those men have gone)—makes clear, Heidegger still thinks of Hölderlin's relation to the East as offering a possibility of self-recognition (by way of a hermeneutic journey of self-understanding): "Bei den *Indiern* ist die Ortschaft der Wende der Wanderschaft vom Fremden in das Heimische. Die Fahrt dorthin, wo es sich zu 'Germanien' wendet, bringt die Ausfahrt in die Fremde an ihren Entscheidungsort" (*E*, 140) (With the *Indians* is the turning point of the wandering from that which is foreign to that which is the at-home. The trip there, where it turns to "Germania," brings the excursion into that which is foreign to its place of decision). For us, however, the journey to Egypt, the Orient, the East, is the name of the impossibility of self-recovery or self-recognition.

Perhaps the best example of our divergence—particularly appropriate in the context of the rhetorical (or not?) question—is the following exchange in the 1966 *Spiegel* interview (published shortly after Heidegger's death) in which Heidegger is asked to read himself: "SPIEGEL: Apropos Hölderlin—wir bitten um Entschuldigung, dass wir nochmals vorlesen müssen: In Ihren 'Nietzsche'-Vorlesungen sagten Sie, dass der 'verschieden bekannte Widerstreit des Dionysischen und des Apollinischen, der heiligen Leidenschaft und der nüchternen Darstellung, ein verborgenes Stilgesetz der geschichtlichen Bestimmung der Deutschen ist und uns eines Tages bereit und vorbereitet finden muss zu seiner Gestaltung. Dieser Gegensatz ist keine Formel, mit Hilfe deren wir nur 'Kultur' beschreiben dürften. Hölderlin und Nietzsche haben mit diesem Widerstreit ein Fragezeichen vor der Augfabe der Deutschen aufgerichtet, geschichtlich ihr Wesen zu finden. Werden wir diese Zeichen verstehen? Eines ist gewiss: Die Geschichte wird sich an uns rächen, wenn wir es nicht verstehen.' Wir wissen nicht, in welchem Jahr Sie das schrieben, wir schätzen, es war 1935. HEIDEGGER: Vermutlich gehört das Zitat in die Nietzsche-Vorlesung 'Der Wille zur Macht als Kunst' 1936/37. Es kann aber auch in den folgenden Jahren gesprochen sein. SPIEGEL: Ja, möchten Sie das noch etwas erläutern? Es führt uns ja vom allgemeinen Weg auf eine konkrete Bestimmung der Deutschen. HEIDEGGER: Ich könnte das im Zitat Ausgeführte auch so sagen: Meine Überzeugung ist, dass nur von demselben Weltort aus, an dem die moderne technische Welt entstanden ist, auch eine Umkehr sich vorbereiten kann, dass sie nicht durch Übernahme von Zen-Buddhismus oder anderen östlichen Welterfahrungen geschehen kann. Es bedarf zum Umdenken der Hilfe der europäischen Überlieferung und ihrer Neuaneignung. Denken wird nur durch Denken verwandelt, das dieselbe Herkunft und Bestimmung hat. SPIEGEL: An eben dieser Stelle, wo die technische Welt entstanden ist, muss sie auch, meinen Sie. . .HEIDEGGER: . . .im Hegelschen Sinne aufgehoben werden, nicht beseitigt, sondern aufgehoben, aber nicht durch den Menschen allein. SPIEGEL: Sie messen speziell den Deutschen eine besondere Aufgabe zu? HEIDEGGER: Ja, in dem Sinne, im Gespräch mit Hölderlin" (Der Spiegel, 31 May 1976) (SPIEGEL: A propos of Hölderlin, we ask your indulgence to quote your own writings. In your Nietzsche lectures you said that the "widely known opposition between the Dionysian and the Apollonian, between the sacred passion and sober presentation, is a hidden stylistic law of the historical destiny of the Germans and we must be prepared and ready one day to be formed by it. This opposition is not a formula with whose help we describe 'culture.' With this opposition, Hölderlin and Nietzsche have put a question mark before the Germans' task to find their being historically. Will we understand this sign, this question mark? One thing is sure. History will take revenge upon us if we don't understand it." We do not know in what year you wrote that. We would guess it was in 1935. HEIDEGGER: The quote probably belongs to the Nietzsche lecture, "The Will to Power as Art," 1936-37. It could also have been written in the following years. SPIEGEL: So, would you clarify this a bit? It leads us from generalities to the concrete destiny of the Germans. HEIDEGGER: I could explain what was said in the quotation in the following way: it is my conviction that a reversal can be prepared only in the same place in the world where the modern technological world originated, and that it cannot happen because of any takeover by Zen-Buddhism or any other Eastern experiences of the world. There is need for a rethinking which is to be carried out with the help of the European tradition and of a new appropriation of that tradition. Thinking itself can be transformed only by a thinking which has the same origin and calling. SPIEGEL: It is exactly at the same place where the technological world originated, that it must, as you think. . .HEIDEGGER: . . .be transcended [aufgehoben] in the Hegelian sense, not pushed aside, but transcended, but not through man alone. SPIEGEL: You assign in particular a special task to the Germans? HEIDEGGER: Yes, in the sense of the dialogue with Hölderlin ["Only a God Can Save Us: Der Spiegel's Interview with Martin Heidegger," Philosophy Today (Winter 1976):281]).

We would make only two comments on this exchange, which in a sense contains all of the late Heidegger's thinking and could be interpreted indefinitely: (1) For Heidegger, it is a question of understanding (verstehen) the question mark (Fragezeichen) that Hölderlin and Nietzsche erected before the task of the Germans; for us, it is a question of reading that (ultimately unreadable because radically undecidable) question mark and its signs (Zeichen). (2) For Heidegger, the "returning" (Umkehr) and "rethinking" (Umdenken) of Western history and the essence of technology can take place only on the basis of the same origin (nur von demselben Weltort aus. . .Denken wird nur durch Denken verwandelt, das dieselbe Herkunft und Bestimmung hat); for us, the "sameness" of that "origin"—the East, the Orient, the Egyptians, etc.—amounts to a radical difference in sameness (like the "relation" between the literal and the figurative readings of an undecidable question, like the undecidable relation between original and quotation, or like the "two" sides of a Möbius band) and thus can never serve as an authoritative place from which to rethink the history of the West but can only be a nonplace from which to reread and misread—the other Not, the other death, death of reading, death of writing, etc.

40. All the quotations on undecidability and syntax are from Jacques Derrida, "The Double Session," in *Dissemination*, trans. Barbara Johnson (Chicago: University of Chicago Press, 1981), pp. 219-22.

41. A helpful interpretation of Heidegger on language and grammar can help us resummarize this point: "It is possible to distinguish between an ontic and an ontological aspect of language, even if such a distinction disrupts the fundamental unity of the language phenomenon. The grammar of language, Heidegger suggests, corresponds to its ontic, the words to its ontological dimension. Language can do justice to Being only if it is possible to free if from the bondage of grammar." Why so? "Grammar and logic place the word into a linguistic or logical space which threatens to obscure its meaning. There is a tendency to interpret the word entirely in terms of the context in which it appears. To learn what a word means, one should, according to this view, ask how it is used, how it operates within a given language. This brings us back to the example of the blind man, making the judgment: The sky is blue. The grammatical approach would have difficulty in finding anything wrong with this judgment. And yet, it is quite clear that the sentence when spoken by a blind man is only repetition rather than response to the call of Being. The grammatical approach fails to do justice to the problem of meaning. The demand to free language from grammar is a demand to free it for its real task of revealing meaning. The context in which a word operates should not be permitted to obscure its essential meaning." Karsten Harries, "The Search for Meaning," in George Schrader, ed., *Existentialist Philosophers: Kierkegaard to Merleau-Ponty* (New York: McGraw-Hill, 1967), pp. 197-98. What we are saying, in short, is that the grammar of language (in a broad sense) makes us all blind men, that the failure "to do justice to the problem of meaning" is a necessary, constitutive failure of language—a failure, one should add, that is almost the sole "theme" of Hölderlin's poetry (see the following chapter)—a failure that pays no attention to our "demand to free language from grammar" and that has nothing (a linguistic "nothing" here) to do with our permitting or not permitting it to "obscure essential meaning."

Chapter 4. "Patmos": The Senses of Interpretation

1. G. W. F. Hegel, *Wissenschaft der Logik I* (Frankfurt am Main: Suhrkamp Verlag, 1969), p. 114. For an interpretation of the entire remark concerning *aufheben*, see Jean-Luc Nancy, *La Remarque spéculative* (Paris: Editions Galilée, 1973).

2. G. W. F. Hegel, *Vorlesungen über die Ästhetik I* (Frankfurt am Main: Suhrkamp Verlag, 1970), p. 173. For an interpretation of the problem of *Sinn* in Hegel, see the chapter "Sens et sensible" in Jean Hyppolite, *Logique et existence* (Paris: Presses Universitaires de France, 1953), pp. 27-45.

3. See Arthur Häny, "Hölderlin: Patmos," *Schweizer Monatshefte* 24 (1945):701-24; Robert L. Beare, "Patmos, dem Landgrafen von Homburg," *The Germanic Review* 28 (1953):5-22; Alice Gladstone, "Hölderlin's 'Patmos': Voyage as Homecoming," *Quarterly Review of Literature* 10 (1959):64-76; Wolfgang Binder, "Hölderlin's Patmos-Hymne," in *Hölderlin-Aufsätze* (Frankfurt am Main: Insel Verlag, 1970), pp. 362-402.

4. P. H. Gaskill, "Hölderlin's Contact with Pietism," *The Modern Language Review* 69 (1974):805-20. Especially p. 809: "Certainly, the final verses of 'Patmos' seem close to the spirit of Bengel and Swabian biblicism"; and p. 819: "It is in 'Patmos' above all that Hölderlin in my view comes closest to the world of Bengel and the 'Schwabenväter.'"

5. The quotations are from Häny, "Hölderlin" (p. 702); Beare, "Patmos" (p. 18), and Gladstone, "Hölderlin's 'Patmos'" (p. 74), respectively.

6. See Gladstone, "Hölderlin's 'Patmos,'" pp. 74-76: "Strength still-glowing falls like lightning from the 'holy writing,' from the Revelation of the exiled John. And from all great poetry. . . the poem fulfills its own prayer, stands witness to the response of the muse. In grasping firmly 'the staff of song,' in the making of a great poem, the God is seized and held." And see Binder's interpretation of strophes 11 and 12, "Hölderlin's Patmos-Hymne," p. 389: "Die Dichtung darf von Christus erzählen, aber sie hat ihn nicht zu verkündigen; denn Dichtung ist nicht Predigt. . . Es geht, mit einem Wort, um die Hybris des Idealismus" (Poetry ought to tell of Christ but it cannot announce him; for poetry is not preaching.. . . It is a question, in a word, of the hubris of idealism); and p. 399: "Das scheint paradox gesagt, aber Hegels Geschichtsphilosophie, die wie Hölderlins Dichtung im Medium des schwäbischen Pietismus wurzelt, folgt ähnlichen Denkprinzipien" (It seems paradoxical, but Hegel's philosophy of history, which, like Hölderlin's poetry, has its roots in the medium of Swabian pietism, follows similar principles of thought). Even Adorno cannot resist making an overly neat summary of the relation between Hölderlin and Hegel in their view of Christianity. T. W. Adorno, "Parataxis, zur späten Lyrik Holderlins," in *Noten zur Literature III* (Frankfurt am Main: Suhrkamp Verlag, 1965), p. 203: "säkularisierte Hegel das Christentum zur Idee, so siedelte Hölderlin es zurück in die mythische Opferreligion" (if Hegel secularized Christianity into the Idea, Hölderlin settled it back in the mythical religion of sacrifice).

7. For discussions generally critical of Heidegger, see Adorno, "Parataxis," and Else Buddeberg, *Heidegger und die Dichtung* (Stuttgart: 1953); Paul de Man, "Les Exégèses de Hölderlin par Martin Heidegger," *Critique* 100/101 (1955):800-819; Peter Szondi, "Der andere Pfeil," in *Hölderlin-Studien* (Frankfurt am Main: Suhrkamp Verlag, 1970), pp. 37-61. Some discussions generally favorable to Heidegger are Maurice Blanchot, "La Parole sacrée de Hölderlin," in *La Part du deu* (Paris: Gallimard, 1949), pp. 115-32; Beda Allemann, *Hölderlin und Heidegger* (Zurich and Freiburg im Breisgau: Atlantis Verlag, 1954); and Karsten Harries, "Heidegger and Hölderlin: The Limits of Language," *The Personalist* 54, no. 1 (1963):5-23.

8. See Martin Heidegger, *Einführung in die Metaphysik* (Tübingen: Max Niemeyer Verlag, 1966), p. 96: "So stehen die beiden Freunde *Hegel* and *Hölderlin* in ihrer Weise im grossen und fruchtbaren Bann Heraklits, aber mit dem Unterschied, dass Hegel nach rückwärts blickt und abschliesst, Hölderlin nach vorwärts schaut und aufschliesst." A translation of this passage appears in Martin Heidegger, *An Introduction to Metaphysics*, trans. Ralph Manheim (Garden City, N.Y.: Doubleday, 1961), p. 106: "Hegel and Hölderlin were both under the great and fruitful spell of Heraclitus, but with the difference that Hegel looked backward and drew a line under the past while Hölderlin looked forward and opened up the way to the future." For what sounds like a reply to Heidegger's assertion, see Dieter Henrich, "Hegel und Hölderlin," in *Hegel im Kontext* (Frankfurt am Main: Suhrkamp Verlag, 1967), p. 34: "Auch in Hegels Denken ist das Motiv der Erinnerung wesentlich,—jedoch als die Versammlung der Gestalten aus ihrer äusserlichen Existenz in das Innere des begreifenden Geistes. Ihm ist Erinnern immer ein Verwandeln,—Er-Innerung als Überholen des An-sich-seins des Vergangenen,—eine neue Weise, es zu setzen als zugehörig dem erinnernden Ich oder dem Allgemeinen der Intelligenz. Hölderlin ist das Erinnern dagegen ein Bewahren, das unter der Forderung der Treue steht, also das Vergangene in seinem Eigenen sucht und hält. Für ihn gibt es keinen freien Ausgriff in die Zukunft, der das vergangene Leben nur von sich stösst, statt es—und die, deren Schicksal es war,—als den Gegensatz zum Eigenen erinnernd fortleben und -wirken zu lassen" (Also in Hegel's thinking the theme of memory is essential—but as the gathering of figures out of their external existence into the inwardness of the comprehending spirit. For him, remembering is always a transforming—re-membering as the taking over of the in-itself of the past—a new way to posit it as belonging to the remembering I or the universality of the intellect. For Hölderlin, on the

other hand, remembering is a preserving that stands under the claim of fidelity, and thus seeks and holds onto the past in that which is its own. For him, there is no free reach into the future, which pushes away the life that has passed, instead of letting it—and those whose fate it was—live on and have an effect in memory as the opposite to that which is one's own).

9. For a reading of Hölderlin from the Hegelian point of view, see Leonardus van de Velde, *Herrschaft und Knechtschaft bei Hölderlin* (Assen: Van Gorcum, 1973). Although his interpretations of Hölderlin's theoretical writings are most helpful, van de Velde's attempt to reduce individual poems to problems solved by dialectical mediation is less satisfying and (as van de Velde admits) cannot do away with the difficulties of the late lyrics.

10. Peter Szondi's interpretation of Hölderlin's dialectic is the best example: Peter Szondi, "Überwindung des Klassizismus," in *Hölderlin-Studien*, pp. 95-118.

11. It would entail a rigorous discussion of the relation between the literary text and the philosophical text. Most of Jacques Derrida's work is concerned with the problem, but see especially Derrida, "La Mythologie blanche," in *Marges* (Paris: Editions de Minuit, 1972), pp. 247-324. Also, see Paul de Man, "Nietzsche's Theory of Rhetoric," *Symposium* 28, no. 1 (1974):33-51.

12. What does it mean to read "in its entirety" a poem that was reworked several times and that does not exist in any "final" form? For that matter, what does it mean to read "all" of any poem?

13. All page references are to the big Stuttgart edition, Friedrich Hölderlin, *Sämtliche Werke*, ed. Friedrich Beissner (Stuttgart: Cotta, 1943-61), and are given by volume and page number. Accompanying translations are taken from Friedrich Hölderlin, *Poems and Fragments*, trans. Michael Hamburger (Cambridge: Cambridge University Press, 1980) and are followed by page number.

14. See "deuten" in Jakob Grimm and Wilhelm Grimm, *Deutsches Wörterbuch* (Leipzig: 1860), II, p. 1038: "heiszt es ursprünglich klar, hell machen, ins licht setzen, das gute hervorheben" (originally it means to make clear, bright, to put into the light, to foreground the good).

15. See "bestehen" in Grimm, (*Wörterbuch* (Leipzig: 1854), I, p. 1666: "von flüssigen dingen gebraucht, stocken, gerinnen, zu rinnen aufhören" (used of flowing things, to stand still, to stop running). Although the verb's implications depend upon its use—Grimm, p. 1670: "das intransitive setzte ruhe voraus, das transitive bewegung" (the intransitive presupposes stillness, the transitive movement)—its etymology suggests halted movement. See Keith Spalding, *An Historical Dictionary of German Figurative Usage* (Oxford: Basil Blackwell, 1956), fasc. 7, p. 283: " 'standing firm,' 'standing still,' 'coagulating, congealing,' 'stopping' with ref. to liquids, limbs, tools, mechanisms form the phys. beginnings of *bestehen*."

16. See "Buchstab" in Grimm, *Wörterbuch*, II, p. 481.

17. See "deuten" in Grimm, *Wörterbuch*, II, p. 1038.

18. See Leonardus van de Velde, *Herrschaft und Knechtschaft*, pp. 231-64.

19. See Jean Starobinski, "Le Combat avec Légion," in *Trois fureurs* (Paris: Gallimard, 1974), pp. 73-126.

20. This definition of catachresis is a paraphrase of Jacques Derrida's paraphrase of Fontanier in Derrida, "La Mythologie blanche," in *Marges*, p. 304. For a discussion of the philological (epistemological) problems involved in the question of figurative language, see Peter Szondi, "Über philologische Erkenntnis," in *Hölderlin-Studien*, pp. 9-34.

21. See "Reichtum" in Grimm, *Wörterbuch* (Leipzig: 1893), VIII, p. 616.

22. Johann Gottfried Herder, *Sprachphilosophische Schriften*, ed. Erich Heintel (Hamburg: Felix Meiner Verlag, 1964), pp. 149-50.

23. Cf. "Wink für die Darstellung und Sprache," (4:263-64).

24. Keith Spalding, *An Historical Dictionary*, fasc. 7, p. 315.

25. Cf. *Der Tod des Empedokles* (*dritte Fassung*):

> Denn viel gesündiget hab ich von Jugend auf,
> Die Menschen menschlich nie geliebt, gedient,
> Wie Wasser nur und Feuer blinder dient,
> Darum begegneten auch menschlich mir
> Sie nicht, o darum schändeten sie mir
> Mein Angesicht. . .
>
> (4:122)

> For sinned I have, and greatly, from my youth,
> Never have loved men humanly, but served
> Only as fire or water blindly serves them.
> And therefore too not humanly towards me
> They acted

26. For a strikingly similar deconstruction see Soren Kierkegaard, *Philosophical Fragments* (Princeton: Princeton University Press, 1967), pp. 55-57. Especially: "deepest down in the heart of piety lurks the mad caprice which knows that it has itself produced the God. If no specific determination of difference can be held fast, because there is no distinguishing mark, like and unlike finally become identified with one another, thus sharing the fate of all such dialectical opposites. The unlikeness clings to the Reason and confounds it, so that the Reason no longer knows itself and quite consistently confuses itself with the unlikeness. . .the God becomes the most terrible of deceivers, because the Reason has deceived itself. The Reason has brought the God as near as possible, and yet he is as far away as ever."

27. For a list and an analysis of "speculative" words in Hegel, see Jean-Luc Nancy, *La Remarque spéculative*, especially pp. 69-94.

28. For an interpretation of Kant's third *Critique*, which includes this reading of *Wohlgefallen*, see Jacques Derrida, "Le Parergon," *Digraphe*, ed. Irigaray, Ristat, et al. (Paris: Editions Galilée, 1974), pp. 21-57.

29. A similar disjunction between seeing and knowing is suggested in strophe 6, where Christ does not have words enough to say about kindness because he *sees* the wrath of the world: "denn nie genug / Hatt' er von Güte zu sagen / Der Worte, *damals*, und zu erheitern, da / Ers *sahe*, das Zürnen der Welt" (2:167) (for never / He could find words enough / To say about kindness, then, and to soothe, when / He saw it, the wrath of the world).

30. Herder, "Abhandlung über den Ursprung der Sprache," *Sprachphilosophische Schriften*, pp. 41-44.

31. In much of his *very* late poetry Hölderlin is still concerned with the problems of making sense. The closing lines of "Aussicht" read:

> Oft scheint die Innerheit der Welt umwölkt, verschlossen,
> Des Menschen Sinn von Zweifeln voll, verdroseen,
> Die prächtige Natur erheitert seine Tage
> Und ferne steht des Zweifels dunkle Frage.
>
> (2:187)

> Often the innerness of the world appears beclouded, shut up,
> Man's sense full of doubts, sullen,
> Splendid nature brightens his days
> And far away stands doubt's dark question.

The conjuring away of the doubt that clouds man's mind is accomplished unproblematically: no "aber" is needed; splendid nature simply brightens his day; and doubt's dark question is placed at a distance (until the following night, no doubt). This placing at a distance is symptomatic of all Hölderlin's very late poetry: few personal pronouns interfere, the poetry is bereft of "but's," and the subject is always "der Mensch" and "die Natur" in the abstract and in a monological relationship to one another. As if these devices were not enough to solidify and place at a distance the threatening fluidity of doubt (*Zweifel*), ambiguity (*Zweideutigkeit*), and dialogue (*Zwiegespräch*), the poem "Aussicht" is dated "the 24th of March 1671" and signed "With submission, Scardanelli" by Hölderlin, schizophrenic and monological.

Chapter 5. Pre-positional By-play

1. All page references within the body of the text are to the twenty-volume *Theorie Werkausgabe* (Frankfurt am Main: Suhrkamp, 1971-79) and are given by volume and page number.

2. Cf. Jacques Derrida, *Glas* (Paris: Editions Galilée, 1974), p. 256 (left-hand column).

3. A helpful introduction to the problem of *Vorstellung* in Hegel—especially in its relation to *Reflexion* and the logic of essence (in the big *Logic*)—is Malcolm Clark, *Logic and System* (The Hague: Nijhoff, 1971).

4. In terms of *context*, the distinction—between "System" (and the role of *Vorstellung* in it) and "text" (and the role of *Beispiel* in it)—is not an idle one, for the motive of Hegel's asking the question of the meaning of meaning is to describe the relation of the philosophy of religion to the *system* of philosophy (*Verhältnis der Religionsphilosophie zum System der Philosophie*).

5. Cf. the following page: "der Geist, der nicht erscheint, *ist* nicht" (XVI:34) (the spirit that does not appear *is* not).

6. Gerhard Wahrig, *Deutsches Wörterbuch* (Gütersloh: Bertelsmann Lexikon-Verlag, 1975).

7. See Erich Przywara, "Bild, Gleichnis, Symbol, Mythos, Misterium, Logos," *Archivio di Filosofia, Filosofia e Simbolisme*, ed. Enrico Castelli (Roma: Fratelli Bocca Editori, 1956), pp. 7-38.

8. See, for example, the *Encyclopedia* (section 20): "Die Vorstellung trifft hier mit dem *Verstande* zusammen, der sich von jener nur dadurch unterscheidet, dass er Verhältnisse von Allgemeinem und Besonderem oder von Ursache und Wirkung usf. und dadurch Beziehungen der Notwendigkeit unter den isolierten Bestimmungen der Vorstellung setzt, da diese sie in ihrem unbestimmten Raume durch das blosse *Auch* verbunden *nebeneinander* belässt" (VIII:73). See also "das Erklären" (explanation) in the *Phänomenologie des Geistes* (Hamburg: Meiner, 1952), pp. 118-21. What is here called the mere "also" is called the mere "and" in the *Jenenser Logik* (Hamburg: Meiner, 1967), p. 47.

9. The reason these "deficient forms" (*mangelhafte Formen*) (XIII:491) belong "almost exclusively" to linguistic art is this art's *additional* capacity: "Die Scheidung nun der beiden Momente des Kunstwerks führt es mit sich, dass die verschiedenen Formen, welche in diesem ganzen Kreise ihre Stellung finden, fast durchgängig nur der Kunst der Rede angehören, indem die Poesie allein solche Verselbständigung von Bedeutung und Gestalt aussprechen kann, während es die Aufgabe der bildenden Künste ist, in der äusseren Gestalt als solcher deren Inneres kundzugeben" (XIII:490) (The separation of the two moments of the work of art brings along with itself that the different forms that find their place in this circle belong almost exclusively to linguistic art, in that poetry alone can express such autonomy of meaning and form, while it is the task of the plastic arts to announce in the exterior form as such its innerness).

10. In the introduction to the *History of Philosophy* the discussion of "was Verstehen heisst" entails a similar two-sided movement (XVIII:91-92).

11. G. W. F. Hegel, *Die Vernunft in der Geschichte*, ed. Johannes Hoffmeister, (Hamburg: Meiner, 1955), p. 58. See Jacques Derrida, *Glas*, p. 38 (left-hand column): "Seule la figure du

Christ peut donc régler l'échange producteur—amortissement et bénéfice—entre la rhétorique et l'onto-logique" (Only the figure of Christ can therefore regulate the productive exchange—amortization and profit—between rhetoric and onto-logic).

12. In relation to Hegel's logic of the Holy Family, such a *Beispiel* would be an illegitimate child, a bastard. See *OED*: "Byspel, bispel. *Obs.* ?*dial.* (ME. *bispell*, OE. *bi-spell*, *bīz-spell*, f. bi, By + Spell tale, story, narration; cogn. w. MHG. *bîspel, bîspil,* 'instance,' 'example,' . . . 1. A parable. . . . 2. A proverb. . . . 3. *dial.* One whose worthlessness is proverbial, who becomes a byword. . . . 4. An illegitimate child, a bastard. Cf. By-blow."

13. A preliminary attempt to read the unreadability of Hölderlin's parable is chapter 4, " 'Patmos': The Senses of Interpretation."

14. The context is a discussion of the relation of the philosophy of religion, *this* text, to positive religion—i.e., a religion based on interpretation of a text, the Bible (*Verhältnis der Religionsphilosophie zur positiven Religion*). See n. 4.

15. Although Hegel most often calls the example *Beispiel*, he also calls it *Gleichnis*. He uses *Vergleichung* for the comparison itself (i.e., the relation between the soul and wax) and *Bild* for the side of the comparison that is the image (i.e., the wax stamped by the ring).

16. And perhaps Plato has a better claim to reading both, for, after all—or is it "first of all"?—the wax/impression example as a model for perception occurs in the *Theaetetus*—and is abandoned for reasons that would not be without interest for another reading.

17. Aristotle, *Über die Seele*, trans. Paul Gohlke (Paderborn: Ferdinand Schöningh, 1961), p. 68: "Ist nun Nahrung das, was der Körper schliesslich aufnimmt, oder das, was man zunächst isst? Das ist ein Unterschied. Wenn beides Nahrung ist, die eine in unverdautem, die andere in verdautem Zustande, dann könnte man in beiderlei Sinn von Nahrung sprechen: solange sie noch nicht verdaut ist, wird etwas durch seinen Gegensatz genährt, sobald sie verdaut ist, durch etwas Gleichartiges. Offenbar also haben beide Richtungen recht und unrecht" (Is then nourishment what the body finally takes in or that which one eats to begin with? There is a difference. If both are nourishment, the one in undigested, the other in digested form, then one could speak of nourishment in both cases: as long as it is not digested, something is nourished by its opposite, as soon as it is digested, through something of the same kind. Clearly both directions are correct and incorrect).

18. Georges Bataille, "Hegel, la mort et le sacrifice," *Deucalion* 40 (October 1955):34.

19. The introduction to the *History of Philosophy* contains an "implicit" citation as it distinguishes between *potentia* and *actus* in order to describe the movement of *Entwicklung*: "Wir sagen, der Mensch ist vernünftig, hat Vernunft von Natur; so hat er sie nur in der Anlage, im Keime." (XVIII:39-40) (We say that man is rational, has reason naturally; he has it only as a predisposition, in germ).

20. Aristotle, *Über die Seele*, p. 71: "Etwas kann nämlich entweder wissend sein, wie wir von einem Menschen sagen, er sei wissend, weil der Mensch überhaupt zu den wissenden Wesen gehört. Bisweilen nennen wir aber auch erst den wissend, der schon die Kunst des Schreibens versteht. Jeder von diesen hat die Anlage, jedoch nicht auf die gleiche Weise, der eine, weil seine Gattung und sein Körper entsprechend veranlagt ist, der andere, weil er, wenn er nur wollte und von aussen ihn nichts hindert, sein Denken betätigen könnte. Erst wer wirklich denkt, ist im eigentlichen Sinne wissend und kennt dieses bestimmte Alpha, die beiden ersten sind nur in der Anlage wissend, und zwar der eine, weil er sonst schon viel gelernt hat und schon oft aus dem Zustand der Unwissenheit herausgetreten ist, der andere, weil er die Arithmetik oder Schreibkunst schon besitzt, sie nur nicht betätigt, da er etwas anderes zu tun hat" (Namely something can be knowing, as when we say of a man that he has knowledge because man as such belongs to the knowing creatures. But also sometimes we only call him knowing who already understands the art of writing. Each of these has the capacity, but not in the same way; the one because his species and his body are appropriately equipped, the other because he can activate his

thinking when he wants and nothing external hinders him. Only he who actually thinks is knowing in the proper sense and knows this determined Alpha, the two preceding ones are only knowing potentially, the one because he has already learned much and has already often stepped out of the state of ignorance, the other because he possesses arithmetic or the art of writing, and only does not use them because he has something else to do). Cf. Aristotle, *De l'Ame*, trans. E. Barbotin (Paris: Société d'Editions Les Belles Lettres, 1966), p. 44: "En un premier sens, un être est savant à la manière dont nous dirions l'homme savant, parce que l'homme compte parmi les êtres capables de savoir et de posséder la science. En un second sens, nous appelons savant celui qui possède actuellement la science de la grammaire" (In a first sense, a being is knowing in the sense that we call a man knowing because man counts among the beings capable of knowing and possessing science. In a second sense, we call knowing him who actually possesses the science of grammar).

21. It would be a literalization of Hegel's statement (in the preface to the second edition) that the big *Logic* should be reworked not just seven but seventy-seven times.

22. See *vergleichen* in Jacob Grimm and Wilhelm Grimm, *Deutsches Wörterbuch* (Leipzig: 1956), XII, p. 456: "in neuerer zeit hat *vergleichen* vielfach eine etwas andere färbung in der bedeutung angenommen. während früher die nebeneinanderstellung und gleichstellung das zumeist betonte war, nimmt das wort später den sinn des kritischen betrachtens, abschätzens an; früher ist es mehr die gleichheit, welche bei *vergleichen* hervorgehoben wird, heute mehr das unterscheidende neben dem gleichen" (in more recent times the meaning of *vergleichen* has taken on a somewhat different coloring. While formerly putting next to and making alike was the most emphasized, later the word takes on the sense of critical observation, evaluation; earlier it is more the sameness that is stressed with *vergleichen*, today it is more that which differentiates along with that which is the same).

23. Maurice Blanchot, "Discours sur la patience," *Le Nouveau Commerce* 30-31 (1975):42. Cf. p. 24: "S'il y a rapport entre écriture et passivité, c'est que l'une et l'autre supposent l'effacement, l'exténuation du sujet: supposent un changement de temps: supposent qu'entre être et ne pas être quelque chose qui ne s'accomplit pas arrive cependant comme étant depuis toujours déjà survenu—le désoeuvrement du neutre, la rupture silencieuse du fragmentaire" (If there is a relation between writing and passivity, it is that both the one and the other suppose the effacement, the extenuation, of the subject: suppose a shift of temporality; suppose that between being and not being something that does not fulfill itself nevertheless takes place as having always already happened—the unworking of the neuter, the silent interruption of the fragmentary).

Chapter 6.   Parentheses: Hegel by Heidegger

1. Maurice Blanchot, "Fragmentaire," in *Celui qui ne peut se servir des mots, a Bram Van Velde* (Montpellier: Fata Morgana, 1975), pp. 30-31.

2. The following symbols will be used in the text to refer by page number to: *H*—Martin Heidegger, "Hegels Begriff der Erfahrung," in *Holzwege* (Frankfurt am Main: Vittorio Klostermann, 1972) pp. 105-92, *PhG*,—G. W. F. Hegel, *Phänomenologie des Geistes*, ed. Johannes Hoffmeister (Hamburg: Felix Meiner, 1952); *ID*—Martin Heidegger, *Identität und Differenz* (Pfullingen: Günther Neske, 1957). References given only by volume and page number (in parentheses) are to the twenty-volume *Theorie Werkausgabe* of G. W. F. Hegel (Frankfurt am Main: Suhrkamp, 1971-79). Translations are my own.

3. Otto Pöggeler, "Zur Deutung der Phänomenologie des Geistes," in *Hegels Idee einer Phänomenologie des Geistes* (Freiburg/Munich: Karl Alber, 1973), p. 184.

4. Ibid., p. 188.

5. Hans Friedrich Fulda and Dieter Henrich, eds., "Vorwort," *Materialien zu Hegels 'Phänomenologie des Geistes'* (Frankfurt am Main: Suhrkamp, 1973), pp. 27-29.

6. For helpful interpretations of the relation between Aristotle and Hegel, see Nicolai Hartmann, "Aristoteles und Hegel," in *Kleine Schriften II* (Berlin: Walter De Gruyter, 1957), pp. 214-52; Hans-Georg Gadamer, "Hegel und die antike Dialektik," in *Hegels Dialektik* (Tübingen: J. C. B. Mohr, 1971), pp. 7-30; Frederick Gustav Weiss, *Hegel's Critique of Aristotle's Philosophy of Mind* (The Hague: Martinus Nijhoff, 1969). For an attempt to read Hegel's reading of Aristotle's *De anima*, see chapter 5, "Pre-positional By-play."

7. It is not clear if the editors know of Jean Hyppolite, "Etude du commentaire de l'introduction à la *Phénoménologie* par Heidegger," in *Figures de la pensée philosophique* (Paris: PUF, 1971), II, pp. 625-42.

8. On the problem of the relation between the *Phenomenology* and the *Logic*, see Jean Hyppolite, *Logique et existence* (Paris: PUF, 1953) and *Genèse et structure de la Phénoménologie de l'esprit de Hegel* (Paris: Aubier Montaigne, 1946).

9. For an interesting (if inadequate) account of the *Phenomenology* as autobiography, see M. H. Abrams, *Natural Supernaturalism* (New York: Norton, 1971), pp. 225-37.

10. See the *Philosophy of Religion*, where *Vorstellung* is described as "in constant unrest (*in beständiger Unruhe*)" (XVI:141).

11. Even the more subtle interpretations of the *Phenomenology*'s "we," "for us," are subject to this forgetting: Jacob Loewenberg, "The Exoteric Approach to Hegel's 'Phenomenology,' " *Mind* 43 (1934):424-45; Jean Hyppolite, *Figures de la pensée philosophique*, I, p. 217.

12. A suggestive interpretation of Hegel's interpretation of the Fall, especially in relation to romantic poetry, is Geoffrey Hartman, "Romanticism and Anti-Self-Consciousness," in *Beyond Formalism* (New Haven and London: Yale University Press, 1970), pp. 298-310.

13. For an attempt to fix the turning point of the *Phenomenology*, see Kenley Royce Dove, "Hegel's Phenomenological Method," *The Review of Metaphysics* 23 (1970):615-41. This article provides helpful critiques of previous interpretations of the introduction to the *Phenomenology*.

14. For a helpful interpretation of "natural" in the introduction to the *Phenomenology*, see Werner Marx, *Hegels Phänomenologie des Geistes* (Frankfurt am Main: Vittorio Klostermann, 1971), translated by Peter Heath as *Hegel's Phenomenology of Spirit* (New York: Harper and Row, 1975). The fact that Hegel says "natürliches Wissen" at least once in the introduction would somewhat complicate Marx's distinctions.

15. To trace the development of *stecken* from "fix with a pointed object" to "stick in one's pocket" to "hide, conceal," see Grimm's dictionary. Loewenberg's reading of the three senses of *erscheinen* in the introduction to the *Phenomenology* bears a resemblance to this reading of *stecken*. It could also be noted that Hyppolite translates *durch ihre Natur ihr vorgesteckte Stationen* as *les stations qui lui sont prescrites par sa propre nature*.

16. This anamorphosis can be read as a rewriting of Hegel's characterization (in the chapter on "Religion" of the *Phenomenology*) of the tragic and comic heroes: in tragedy, "the hero. . .falls apart into his mask (*der Held. . .zerfällt in seine Maske*)" (*PhG*, 517); in comedy, the hero "lets the mask fall (*lässt die Maske fallen*)" (*PhG*, 518). It is precisely the possibility of such monstrous tragicomedy that is denounced (in the section "Physiognomy and Phrenology") as the "sign" of physiognomy: it "is only a sign that is indifferent to that which is signified and therefore in truth signifies nothing; it is for it [i.e., an individuality (*Individualität*)] its face as well as its mask that it can lay aside (*nur ein Zeichen ist, das gleichgültig gegen das Bezeichnete ist, und darum in Wahrheit nichts bezeichnet; es ist ihr ebensowohl ihr Gesicht als ihre Maske, die sie ablegen kann*)" (*PhG*, 233).

17. Martin Heidegger, "Zur Seinsfrage," in *Wegmarken* (Frankfurt am Main: Vittorio Klostermann, 1967), p. 234.

18. For Heidegger's making the invisible visible, turning *Nebensatz* into *Hauptsatz*, later in the essay, see "Der Satz ist unscheinbar in einen Nebensatz versteckt. Er lautet in der Form eines

Hauptsatzes: 'Das Bewusstsein prüft sich selbst' " (*H*, 159) (The statement is hidden in a subordinate clause. It reads in the form of an independent clause: "Consciousness tests itself").

19. See *Nebensatz* in Gerhard Wahrig, *Deutsches Wörterbuch* (Gutersloh: Bertelsmann Lexikon-Verlag, 1975).

20. See "substantive" in *The Random House Dictionary of the English Language* (New York: Random House, 1968).

21. This is not to say that Hegel does not use the formulation *in sich*. See, for example, the section "Physiognomy and Phrenology" in the *Phenomenology*. Reading *Hegel's* problematic *in sich* would entail the same "both. . .and"/"neither. . .nor" structure we are trying to read here.

22. For the role of *in* and *bei* in Heidegger's interpretation of *In-der-Welt-sein*, see *Sein und Zeit* (Tübingen: Max Niemeyer, 1972), pp. 54-55: "Das In-Sein meint so wenig ein räumliches 'Ineinander' Vorhandener, als 'in' ursprünglich gar nicht eine räumliche Beziehung der genannten Art bedeutet; 'in' stammt von innan-, wohnen, habitare, sich aufhalten. . . .Der Ausdruck 'bin' hängt zusammen mit 'bei'; 'ich bin' besagt wiederum: ich wohne, halte mich auf bei. . .der Welt, als dem so und so Vertrauten." A translation of the passage appears in Martin Heidegger, *Being and Time*, trans. John Macquarrie and Edward Robinson (New York: Harper and Row, 1962), pp. 79-80: "Nor does the term 'Being-in' mean a spatial 'in-one-another-ness' of things present-at-hand, any more than the word 'in' primordially signifies a spatial relationship of this kind. 'In' is derived from 'innan'—'to reside,' 'habitare,' 'to dwell.' . . .The expression 'bin' is connected with 'bei,' and so 'ich bin' ['I am'] means in its turn 'I reside' or 'dwell alongside' the world, as that which is familiar to me in such and such a way." For Heidegger's distinction between the hermeneutic and the apophantic *als*, see *Sein und Zeit*, p. 158.

23. See *Identität und Differenz*, p. 65: "Durch diese Bemerkung mag ein geringes Licht auf den Weg fallen, zu dem ein Denken unterwegs ist, das den Schritt zurück vollzieht, zurück aus der Metaphysik in das Wesen der Metaphysik, zurück aus der Vergessenheit der Differenz als solcher in das Geschick der sich entziehenden Verbergung des Austrags." Or the translation in Martin Heidegger, *Identity and Difference*, trans. Joan Stambaugh (New York: Harper and Row, 1969), p. 72: "This remark may throw a little light on the path to which thinking is on its way, that thinking which accomplishes the step back, back out of metaphysics into the active essence of metaphysics, back out of the oblivion of the difference as such into the destiny of the withdrawing concealment of perdurance."

24. See "perverse" in *The American Heritage Dictionary of the English Language* (Boston: Houghton Mifflin, 1969).

25. See *Identität und Differenz*, pp. 32-33: "Sein besagt für Hegel zunächst, aber *niemals nur*, die 'unbestimmte Unmittelbarkeit' " (For Hegel, Being means first of all but *never only* the 'undetermined immediacy').

26. Refusing to recognize the gravity of Heidegger's effort to begin a "dialogue" with Hegel, too many commentators in their critiques of Heidegger have insisted (for polemical or other ends) on charging him with this trivial, relatively harmless, perversity and have thereby kept themselves from making more fruitful insights. T. W. Adorno in "Erfahrungsgehalt," *Drei Studien zu Hegel* (Frankfurt am Main: Suhrkamp, 1970), would be one example. If Heidegger had *merely* misunderstood or distorted Hegel's thought, his reading would not be of much interest.

27. See Heidegger, "Hegel und die Griechen," in *Wegmarken*, p. 268: "Aber nicht wir setzen diese Sache als die Sache des Denkens fest. Sie ist uns längst zugesprochen und durch die ganze Geschichte der Philosophie überliefert" (But it is not we who fix this matter as the matter of thinking. It is long addressed to us and handed down by the entire history of philosophy).

28. Friedrich Nietzsche, *Götzendämmerung* (Munich: Hanser, 1969), II, p. 953.

29. See Heidegger, "Hegel und die Griechen," in *Wegmarken*, p. 263: "Um zu verstehen, wie Hegel diese Grundworte deutet, müssen wir zweierlei beachten: Einmal dasjenige, was für

Hegel bei der Auslegung der genannten Philosophen das Entscheidende ist gegenüber dem, was er nur beiläufig erwähnt'' (In order to understand how Hegel interprets these grounding words we must pay attention doubly: at once to that which is decisive for Hegel in the interpretation of the named philosophers and to its relation to that which he mentions only by the way).

30. On Heidegger's *impensé*, see the remarks of Paul de Man in the discussion following his "Ludwig Binswanger et le problème du moi poétique," in *Les Chemins actuels de la critique* (Paris: 10/18, 1968), p. 83: "Pour Heidegger, l'impensé est précisément le *cogito*" (For Heidegger, the unthought is precisely the *Cogito*). The extent to which "Descartes" in the text of Heidegger (especially *Being and Time*) plays the role of scapegoat for "Hegel" is a text that remains to be read.

31. It is worthwhile to quote this entire paragraph from "Nietzsches Wort 'Gott ist tot' '': "Jede Erläuterung muss freilich die Sache nicht nur dem Text entnehmen, sie muss auch, ohne darauf zu pochen, unvermerkt Eigenes aus ihrer Sache dazu geben. Diese Beigabe ist dasjenige, was der Laie, gemessen an dem, was er für den Inhalt des Textes hält, stets als ein Hineindeuten empfindet und mit dem Recht, das er für sich beanspruch, als Willkür bemängelt. Eine rechte Erläuterung versteht jedoch den Text nie besser als dessen Verfasser ihn verstand, wohl aber anders. Allein dieses Andere muss so sein, dass es das Selbe trifft, dem der erläuterte Text nachdenkt'' (*H*, 197). For the translation, see Martin Heidegger, "The Word of Nietzsche: 'God Is Dead','' in *The Question Concerning Technology and Other Essays* trans. William Lovitt (New York: Harper and Row, 1977), p. 58: "Every exposition must of course not only draw upon the substance of the text; it must also, without presuming, imperceptibly give to the text something out of its own substance. This part that is added is what the layman, judging on the basis of what he holds to be the content of the text, constantly perceives as a meaning read in, and with the right that he claims for himself criticizes as an arbitrary imposition. Still, while a right elucidation never understands the text better than the author understood it, it does surely understand it differently. Yet this difference must be of such a kind as to touch upon the Same toward which the elucidated text is thinking.''

32. On title and text, see Jacques Derrida in, for example, "Living On"/"Border Lines" ("Survivre"/"Journal de bord"), trans. James Hulbert, in *Deconstruction and Criticism* (New York: Seabury, 1979), pp. 75-176.

33. See Martin Heidegger, *Hegel's Concept of Experience* (New York: Harper and Row, 1970), pp. 133, 151; and *Chemins qui ne mènent nulle part* (Paris: Gallimard, 1962), pp. 160, 170.

34. See *Zwischenbemerkung* in *Cassell's German Dictionary* (New York: Funk and Wagnalls, 1965).

35. Martin Heidegger, "Identité et différence," in *Questions I*, trans. André Préau (Paris: Gallimard, 1968), p. 300.

36. See *Zwischenbemerkung* in Wahrig, *Deutsches Wörterbuch*.

37. See *Beispiel* in Wahrig, *Deutsches Wörterbuch*. The French translator remarks in a footnote Heidegger's play on the etymology of *Beispiel* (Heidegger, *Questions I*, p. 300).

38. For "attributions" of some of these words, see Heidegger, "Hegel und die Griechen," in *Wegmarken*, p. 262.

39. See Heidegger, "Zur Seinsfrage," in *Wegmarken*, p. 243. For a reading of Nietzsche's forgotten umbrella, see Jacques Derrida, *Eperons/Sporen/Spurs/Sproni* (Venezia: Corbo e Fiore Editori, 1976).

40. G. W. F. Hegel, *Enzyklopädie der philosophischen Wissenschaften im Grundrisse und andere Schriften aus der Heidelberger Zeit*, Vierte Auflage der Jubiläumsausgabe (Stuttgart: F. Fromman, 1968), VI, pp. 25-26.

41. For what we would call a "hyperbolic" (as opposed to—or supplemented by—"parabolic"?) reading of eating in the text of Hegel, see Werner Hamacher, *"pleroma—zu*

Genesis und Struktur einer dialektischen Hermeneutik bei Hegel," in his edition of Hegel's *Der Geist des Christentums* (Berlin: Ullstein, 1978). Another eating of Hegel's speculative fruit is Friedrich Engels and Karl Marx, *Die heilige Familie oder Kritik der kritischen Kritik* (Frankfurt am Main: Europäische Verlagsanstalt, 1967), pp. 62-63.

42. We should add that Heidegger's parenthesis is never really closed. The last paragraph of "The Onto-theo-logical Constitution of Metaphysics" says that the question of whether Western languages offer "other possibilities of saying and that means at the same time of saying not-saying (*andere Möglichkeiten des Sagens und d.h. zugleich des sagenden Nichtsagens*)" "has to remain open (*muss offen bleiben*)" (*ID*, 66). The last sentences would corroborate, and here we follow the American translator, Joan Stambaugh, in *Identity and Difference*, p. 74: "For what was said, was said in a seminar. A seminar, as the word implies, is a place and an opportunity to sow a seed here and there, a seed of thinking which some time or other may bloom in its own way and bring forth fruit (*Denn des Gesagte wurde in einem Seminar gesagt. Ein Seminar ist, was das Wort andeutet, ein Ort und eine Gelegenheit, hier und dort einen Samen, ein Samenkorn des Nachdenkens auszustreuen, das irgendwann einmal auf seine Weise aufgehen mag und fruchten*)" (*ID*, 67).

Chapter 7. Reading for Example: "Sense-certainty" in Hegel's *Phenomenology of Spirit*

1. All references marked as *PhG* followed by a page number are to G. W. F. Hegel, *Phänomenologie des Geistes*, ed. Johannes Hoffmeister (Hamburg: Felix Meiner, 1952). All other page references within the body of the text are to the twenty-volume *Theorie Werkausgabe* of Hegel's works (Frankfurt am Main: Suhrkamp, 1971-79) and are given by volume and page number.

2. The quotations are from Pierre-Jean Labarrière, *Structures et mouvement dialectique dans la Phénoménologie de l'esprit de Hegel* (Paris: Aubier-Montaigne, 1968), p. 76; and Jean Hyppolite, *Logique et existence* (Paris: Presses Universitaires de France, 1953), p. 17.

3. Jacques Derrida, *Glas* (Paris: Galilée, 1974), p. 7.

4. Eugenio Donato, " 'Here, Now' / 'Always Already'," *Diacritics* 6, no. 3 (Fall 1976):25.

5. See Jacob Loewenberg, "The Comedy of Immediacy in Hegel's 'Phenomenology,' " *Mind* 44, no. 173 (1935):21-38.

6. Hans-Georg Gadamer, "Hegel's 'Inverted World,' " in *Hegel's Dialectic* (New Haven and London: Yale University Press, 1976), p. 52.

7. Some of the following remarks were suggested by Jean Starobinski, "Le combat avec Légion," in *Trois fureurs* (Paris: Gallimard, 1974), pp. 73-126.

8. Cf. Gilles Deleuze, *Nietzsche et la philosophie* (Paris: Presses Universitaires de France, 1962), pp. 86-88.

9. Werner Hamacher, "Pleroma—zu Genesis und Struktur einer dialektischen Hermeneutik bei Hegel" in his edition of Hegel's *Der Geist des Christentums* (Berlin: Ullstein, 1978).

10. Jean-Luc Nancy, *La Remarque spéculative* (Paris: Galilée, 1973).

Epilogue: Dreadful Reading: Blanchot on Hegel

1. Maurice Blanchot, "Fragmentaire," in *A Bram Van Velde* (Montpellier: Fata Morgana, 1975), pp. 19-31.

2. Maurice Blancot, *La Part du feu* (Paris: Gallimard, 1949).

3. G. W. F. Hegel, *Phänomenologie des Geistes* (Hamburg: Felix Meiner, 1952), p. 288. English translation by A. V. Miller: *Phenomenology of Spirit* (Oxford: Oxford University Press, 1977), p. 240.

4. Hegel, *Phänomenologie*, p. 81; English, p. 60.

5. Our reading of "this piece of paper" crosses that of Paul de Man, "Hypogram and Inscription: Michael Riffaterre's Poetics of Reading," *Diacritics* (Winter 1981):17-35.

6. Blanchot's supplementary insight would require an extensive rereading of the master/slave dialectic. We have sketched only the barest outline of a beginning here.

Index

Andrzej Warminski received his Ph.D. in comparative literature from Yale University and has been a Yale faculty member since 1980. Born in Gdansk, Poland, Warminski graduated from Columbia College with a B.A. in English and comparative literature and also studied philosophy at the Ecole Normale Superieure and, as a Fulbright Fellow, at the University of Freiburg. He is currently an associate professor of comparative literature.

Rodolphe Gasché is a professor of comparative literature at the State University of New York at Buffalo and author of *The Tain of the Mirror: Derrida and the Philosophy of Reflection.*

6898